Praise for *Site Reliability Engineering*

Google's SREs have done our industry an enormous service by writing up the principles, practices and patterns—architectural and cultural—that enable their teams to combine continuous delivery with world-class reliability at ludicrous scale. You owe it to yourself and your organization to read this book and try out these ideas for yourself.

—*Jez Humble, coauthor of* Continuous Delivery *and* Lean Enterprise

I remember when Google first started speaking at systems administration conferences. It was like hearing a talk at a reptile show by a Gila monster expert. Sure, it was entertaining to hear about a very different world, but in the end the audience would go back to their geckos.

Now we live in a changed universe where the operational practices of Google are not so removed from those who work on a smaller scale. All of a sudden, the best practices of SRE that have been honed over the years are now of keen interest to the rest of us. For those of us facing challenges around scale, reliability and operations, this book comes none too soon.

—*David N. Blank-Edelman, Director, USENIX Board of Directors, and founding co-organizer of SREcon*

I have been waiting for this book ever since I left Google's enchanted castle. It is the gospel I am preaching to my peers at work.

—*Björn Rabenstein, Team Lead of Production Engineering at SoundCloud, Prometheus developer, and Google SRE until 2013*

A thorough discussion of Site Reliability Engineering from the company that invented the concept. Includes not only the technical details but also the thought process, goals, principles, and lessons learned over time. If you want to learn what SRE really means, start here.

—Russ Allbery, SRE and Security Engineer

With this book, Google employees have shared the processes they have taken, including the missteps, that have allowed Google services to expand to both massive scale and great reliability. I highly recommend that anyone who wants to create a set of integrated services that they hope will scale to read this book. The book provides an insider's guide to building maintainable services.

—Rik Farrow, USENIX

Writing large-scale services like Gmail is hard. Running them with high reliability is even harder, especially when you change them every day. This comprehensive "recipe book" shows how Google does it, and you'll find it much cheaper to learn from our mistakes than to make them yourself.

—Urs Hölzle, SVP Technical Infrastructure, Google

Site Reliability Engineering

How Google Runs Production Systems

*Edited by Betsy Beyer, Chris Jones, Jennifer Petoff,
and Niall Richard Murphy*

Beijing · Boston · Farnham · Sebastopol · Tokyo

Site Reliability Engineering

Edited by Betsy Beyer, Chris Jones, Jennifer Petoff, and Niall Richard Murphy

Printed in the United States of America.

Published by O'Reilly Media, Inc., 1005 Gravenstein Highway North, Sebastopol, CA 95472.

O'Reilly books may be purchased for educational, business, or sales promotional use. Online editions are also available for most titles (*http://safaribooksonline.com*). For more information, contact our corporate/institutional sales department: 800-998-9938 or *corporate@oreilly.com*.

Editor: Brian Anderson
Production Editor: Kristen Brown
Copyeditor: Kim Cofer
Proofreader: Rachel Monaghan

Indexer: Judy McConville
Interior Designer: David Futato
Cover Designer: Karen Montgomery
Illustrator: Rebecca Demarest

April 2016:   First Edition

Revision History for the First Edition
2016-03-21:   First Release

See *http://oreilly.com/catalog/errata.csp?isbn=9781491929124* for release details.

978-1-491-92912-4

[LSI]

Table of Contents

Part I.   Introduction

Part II.   Principles

Part III.   Practices

Part IV. Management

Part V.   Conclusions

Foreword

Google's story is a story of scaling up. It is one of the great success stories of the computing industry, marking a shift towards IT-centric business. Google was one of the first companies to define what business-IT alignment meant in practice, and went on to inform the concept of DevOps for a wider IT community. This book has been written by a broad cross-section of the very people who made that transition a reality.

Google grew at a time when the traditional role of the system administrator was being transformed. It questioned system administration, as if to say: we can't afford to hold tradition as an authority, we have to think anew, and we don't have time to wait for everyone else to catch up. In the introduction to *Principles of Network and System Administration* [Bur99], I claimed that system administration was a form of human-computer engineering. This was strongly rejected by some reviewers, who said "we are not yet at the stage where we can call it engineering." At the time, I felt that the field had become lost, trapped in its own wizard culture, and could not see a way forward. Then, Google drew a line in the silicon, forcing that fate into being. The revised role was called SRE, or Site Reliability Engineer. Some of my friends were among the first of this new generation of engineer; they formalized it using software and automation. Initially, they were fiercely secretive, and what happened inside and outside of Google was very different: Google's experience was unique. Over time, information and methods have flowed in both directions. This book shows a willingness to let SRE thinking come out of the shadows.

Here, we see not only how Google built its legendary infrastructure, but also how it studied, learned, and changed its mind about the tools and the technologies along the way. We, too, can face up to daunting challenges with an open spirit. The tribal nature of IT culture often entrenches practitioners in dogmatic positions that hold the industry back. If Google overcame this inertia, so can we.

This book is a collection of essays by one company, with a single common vision. The fact that the contributions are aligned around a single company's goal is what makes it special. There are common themes, and common characters (software systems) that reappear in several chapters. We see choices from different perspectives, and know that they correlate to resolve competing interests. The articles are not rigorous, academic pieces; they are personal accounts, written with pride, in a variety of personal styles, and from the perspective of individual skill sets. They are written bravely, and with an intellectual honesty that is refreshing and uncommon in industry literature. Some claim "never do this, always do that," others are more philosophical and tentative, reflecting the variety of personalities within an IT culture, and how that too plays a role in the story. We, in turn, read them with the humility of observers who were not part of the journey, and do not have all the information about the myriad conflicting challenges. Our many questions are the real legacy of the volume: Why didn't they do *X*? What if they'd done *Y*? How will we look back on this in years to come? It is by comparing our own ideas to the reasoning here that we can measure our own thoughts and experiences.

The most impressive thing of all about this book is its very existence. Today, we hear a brazen culture of "just show me the code." A culture of "ask no questions" has grown up around open source, where community rather than expertise is championed. Google is a company that dared to think about the problems from first principles, and to employ top talent with a high proportion of PhDs. Tools were only components in processes, working alongside chains of software, people, and data. Nothing here tells us how to solve problems universally, but that is the point. Stories like these are far more valuable than the code or designs they resulted in. Implementations are ephemeral, but the documented reasoning is priceless. Rarely do we have access to this kind of insight.

This, then, is the story of how one company did it. The fact that it is many overlapping stories shows us that scaling is far more than just a photographic enlargement of a textbook computer architecture. It is about scaling a business process, rather than just the machinery. This lesson alone is worth its weight in electronic paper.

We do not engage much in self-critical review in the IT world; as such, there is much reinvention and repetition. For many years, there was only the USENIX LISA conference community discussing IT infrastructure, plus a few conferences about operating systems. It is very different today, yet this book still feels like a rare offering: a detailed documentation of Google's step through a watershed epoch. The tale is not for copying—though perhaps for emulating—but it can inspire the next step for all of us. There is a unique intellectual honesty in these pages, expressing both leadership and humility. These are stories of hopes, fears, successes, and failures. I salute the courage of authors and editors in allowing such candor, so that we, who are not party to the hands-on experiences, can also benefit from the lessons learned inside the cocoon.

— Mark Burgess
author of In Search of Certainty
Oslo, March 2016

Preface

Software engineering has this in common with having children: the labor *before* the birth is painful and difficult, but the labor *after* the birth is where you actually spend most of your effort. Yet software engineering as a discipline spends much more time talking about the first period as opposed to the second, despite estimates that 40–90% of the total costs of a system are incurred after birth.[1] The popular industry model that conceives of deployed, operational software as being "stabilized" in production, and therefore needing much less attention from software engineers, is wrong. Through this lens, then, we see that if software engineering tends to focus on designing and building software systems, there must be another discipline that focuses on the *whole* lifecycle of software objects, from inception, through deployment and operation, refinement, and eventual peaceful decommissioning. This discipline uses—and needs to use—a wide range of skills, but has separate concerns from other kinds of engineers. Today, our answer is the discipline Google calls Site Reliability Engineering.

So what exactly is Site Reliability Engineering (SRE)? We admit that it's not a particularly clear name for what we do—pretty much every site reliability engineer at Google gets asked what exactly that is, and what they actually do, on a regular basis.

Unpacking the term a little, first and foremost, SREs are *engineers*. We apply the principles of computer science and engineering to the design and development of computing systems: generally, large distributed ones. Sometimes, our task is writing the software for those systems alongside our product development counterparts; sometimes, our task is building all the additional pieces those systems need, like backups or load balancing, ideally so they can be reused across systems; and sometimes, our task is figuring out how to apply existing solutions to new problems.

---

1 The very fact that there is such large variance in these estimates tells you something about software engineering as a discipline, but see, e.g., [Gla02] for more details.

Next, we focus on system *reliability*. Ben Treynor Sloss, Google's VP for 24/7 Operations, originator of the term SRE, claims that reliability is the most fundamental feature of any product: a system isn't very useful if nobody can use it! Because reliability[2] is so critical, SREs are focused on finding ways to improve the design and operation of systems to make them more scalable, more reliable, and more efficient. However, we expend effort in this direction only up to a point: when systems are "reliable enough," we instead invest our efforts in adding features or building new products.[3]

Finally, SREs are focused on operating *services* built atop our distributed computing systems, whether those services are planet-scale storage, email for hundreds of millions of users, or where Google began, web search. The "site" in our name originally referred to SRE's role in keeping the *google.com* website running, though we now run many more services, many of which aren't themselves websites—from internal infrastructure such as Bigtable to products for external developers such as the Google Cloud Platform.

Although we have represented SRE as a broad discipline, it is no surprise that it arose in the fast-moving world of web services, and perhaps in origin owes something to the peculiarities of our infrastructure. It is equally no surprise that of all the post-deployment characteristics of software that we could choose to devote special attention to, reliability is the one we regard as primary.[4] The domain of web services, both because the process of improving and changing server-side software is comparatively contained, and because managing change itself is so tightly coupled with failures of all kinds, is a natural platform from which our approach might emerge.

Despite arising at Google, and in the web community more generally, we think that this discipline has lessons applicable to other communities and other organizations. This book is an attempt to explain how we do things: both so that other organizations might make use of what we've learned, and so that we can better define the role and what the term means. To that end, we have organized the book so that general principles and more specific practices are separated where possible, and where it's appropriate to discuss a particular topic with Google-specific information, we trust that the reader will indulge us in this and will not be afraid to draw useful conclusions about their own environment.

---

2 For our purposes, reliability is "The probability that [a system] will perform a required function without failure under stated conditions for a stated period of time," following the definition in [Oco12].

3 The software systems we're concerned with are largely websites and similar services; we do not discuss the reliability concerns that face software intended for nuclear power plants, aircraft, medical equipment, or other safety-critical systems. We do, however, compare our approaches with those used in other industries in Chapter 33.

4 In this, we are distinct from the industry term DevOps, because although we definitely regard infrastructure as code, we have *reliability* as our main focus. Additionally, we are strongly oriented toward removing the necessity for operations—see Chapter 7 for more details.

We have also provided some orienting material—a description of Google's production environment and a mapping between some of our internal software and publicly available software—which should help to contextualize what we are saying and make it more directly usable.

Ultimately, of course, more reliability-oriented software and systems engineering is inherently good. However, we acknowledge that smaller organizations may be wondering how they can best use the experience represented here: much like security, the earlier you care about reliability, the better. This implies that even though a small organization has many pressing concerns and the software choices you make may differ from those Google made, it's still worth putting lightweight reliability support in place early on, because it's less costly to expand a structure later on than it is to introduce one that is not present. Part IV contains a number of best practices for training, communication, and meetings that we've found to work well for us, many of which should be immediately usable by your organization.

But for sizes between a startup and a multinational, there probably already is someone in your organization who is doing SRE work, without it necessarily being called that name, or recognized as such. Another way to get started on the path to improving reliability for your organization is to formally recognize that work, or to find these people and foster what they do—reward it. They are people who stand on the cusp between one way of looking at the world and another one: like Newton, who is sometimes called not the world's first physicist, but the world's last alchemist.

And taking the historical view, who, then, looking back, might be the first SRE?

We like to think that Margaret Hamilton, working on the Apollo program on loan from MIT, had all of the significant traits of the first SRE.[5] In her own words, "part of the culture was to learn from everyone and everything, including from that which one would least expect."

A case in point was when her young daughter Lauren came to work with her one day, while some of the team were running mission scenarios on the hybrid simulation computer. As young children do, Lauren went exploring, and she caused a "mission" to crash by selecting the DSKY keys in an unexpected way, alerting the team as to what would happen if the prelaunch program, P01, were inadvertently selected by a real astronaut during a real mission, during real midcourse. (Launching P01 inadvertently on a real mission would be a major problem, because it wipes out navigation data, and the computer was not equipped to pilot the craft with no navigation data.)

---

5 In addition to this great story, she also has a substantial claim to popularizing the term "software engineering."

With an SRE's instincts, Margaret submitted a program change request to add special error checking code in the onboard flight software in case an astronaut should, by accident, happen to select P01 during flight. But this move was considered unnecessary by the "higher-ups" at NASA: of course, that could never happen! So instead of adding error checking code, Margaret updated the mission specifications documentation to say the equivalent of "Do not select P01 during flight." (Apparently the update was amusing to many on the project, who had been told many times that astronauts would not make any mistakes—after all, they were trained to be perfect.)

Well, Margaret's suggested safeguard was only considered unnecessary until the very next mission, on Apollo 8, just days after the specifications update. During midcourse on the fourth day of flight with the astronauts Jim Lovell, William Anders, and Frank Borman on board, Jim Lovell selected P01 by mistake—as it happens, on Christmas Day—creating much havoc for all involved. This was a critical problem, because in the absence of a workaround, no navigation data meant the astronauts were never coming home. Thankfully, the documentation update had explicitly called this possibility out, and was invaluable in figuring out how to upload usable data and recover the mission, with not much time to spare.

As Margaret says, "a thorough understanding of how to operate the systems was not enough to prevent human errors," and the change request to add error detection and recovery software to the prelaunch program P01 was approved shortly afterwards.

Although the Apollo 8 incident occurred decades ago, there is much in the preceding paragraphs directly relevant to engineers' lives today, and much that will continue to be directly relevant in the future. Accordingly, for the systems you look after, for the groups you work in, or for the organizations you're building, please bear the SRE Way in mind: thoroughness and dedication, belief in the value of preparation and documentation, and an awareness of what could go wrong, coupled with a strong desire to prevent it. Welcome to our emerging profession!

How to Read This Book

This book is a series of essays written by members and alumni of Google's Site Reliability Engineering organization. It's much more like conference proceedings than it is like a standard book by an author or a small number of authors. Each chapter is intended to be read as a part of a coherent whole, but a good deal can be gained by reading on whatever subject particularly interests you. (If there are other articles that support or inform the text, we reference them so you can follow up accordingly.)

You don't need to read in any particular order, though we'd suggest at least starting with Chapters 2 and 3, which describe Google's production environment and outline how SRE approaches risk, respectively. (Risk is, in many ways, the key quality of our profession.) Reading cover-to-cover is, of course, also useful and possible; our chapters are grouped thematically, into Principles (Part II), Practices (Part III), and Management (Part IV). Each has a small introduction that highlights what the individual pieces are about, and references other articles published by Google SREs, covering specific topics in more detail. Additionally, the companion website to this book, *https://g.co/SREBook*, has a number of helpful resources.

We hope this will be at least as useful and interesting to you as putting it together was for us.

— The Editors

Conventions Used in This Book

The following typographical conventions are used in this book:

Italic
> Indicates new terms, URLs, email addresses, filenames, and file extensions.

`Constant width`
> Used for program listings, as well as within paragraphs to refer to program elements such as variable or function names, databases, data types, environment variables, statements, and keywords.

`Constant width bold`
> Shows commands or other text that should be typed literally by the user.

`Constant width italic`
> Shows text that should be replaced with user-supplied values or by values determined by context.

This element signifies a tip or suggestion.

This element signifies a general note.

 This element indicates a warning or caution.

Using Code Examples

Supplemental material is available at *https://g.co/SREBook*.

This book is here to help you get your job done. In general, if example code is offered with this book, you may use it in your programs and documentation. You do not need to contact us for permission unless you're reproducing a significant portion of the code. For example, writing a program that uses several chunks of code from this book does not require permission. Selling or distributing a CD-ROM of examples from O'Reilly books does require permission. Answering a question by citing this book and quoting example code does not require permission. Incorporating a significant amount of example code from this book into your product's documentation does require permission.

We appreciate, but do not require, attribution. An attribution usually includes the title, author, publisher, and ISBN. For example: "*Site Reliability Engineering*, edited by Betsy Beyer, Chris Jones, Jennifer Petoff, and Niall Richard Murphy (O'Reilly). Copyright 2016 Google, Inc., 978-1-491-92912-4."

If you feel your use of code examples falls outside fair use or the permission given above, feel free to contact us at *permissions@oreilly.com*.

Safari® Books Online

Safari Books Online is an on-demand digital library that delivers expert content in both book and video form from the world's leading authors in technology and business.

Technology professionals, software developers, web designers, and business and creative professionals use Safari Books Online as their primary resource for research, problem solving, learning, and certification training.

Safari Books Online offers a range of plans and pricing for enterprise, government, education, and individuals.

Members have access to thousands of books, training videos, and prepublication manuscripts in one fully searchable database from publishers like O'Reilly Media, Prentice Hall Professional, Addison-Wesley Professional, Microsoft Press, Sams, Que, Peachpit Press, Focal Press, Cisco Press, John Wiley & Sons, Syngress, Morgan Kaufmann, IBM Redbooks, Packt, Adobe Press, FT Press, Apress, Manning, New Riders, McGraw-Hill, Jones & Bartlett, Course Technology, and hundreds more. For more information about Safari Books Online, please visit us online.

How to Contact Us

Please address comments and questions concerning this book to the publisher:

O'Reilly Media, Inc.
1005 Gravenstein Highway North
Sebastopol, CA 95472
800-998-9938 (in the United States or Canada)
707-829-0515 (international or local)
707-829-0104 (fax)

We have a web page for this book, where we list errata, examples, and any additional information. You can access this page at *http://bit.ly/site-reliability-engineering*.

To comment or ask technical questions about this book, send email to *bookquestions@oreilly.com*.

For more information about our books, courses, conferences, and news, see our website at *http://www.oreilly.com*.

Find us on Facebook: *http://facebook.com/oreilly*

Follow us on Twitter: *http://twitter.com/oreillymedia*

Watch us on YouTube: *http://www.youtube.com/oreillymedia*

Acknowledgments

This book would not have been possible without the tireless efforts of our authors and technical writers. We'd also like thank the following internal reviewers for providing especially valuable feedback: Alex Matey, Dermot Duffy, JC van Winkel, John T.

Reese, Michael O'Reilly, Steve Carstensen, and Todd Underwood. Ben Lutch and Ben Treynor Sloss were this book's sponsors within Google; their belief in this project and sharing what we've learned about running large-scale services was essential to making this book happen.

We'd like to send special thanks to Rik Farrow, the editor of *;login:*, for partnering with us on a number of contributions for pre-publication via USENIX.

While the authors are specifically acknowledged in each chapter, we'd like to take time to recognize those that contributed to each chapter by providing thoughtful input, discussion, and review.

Chapter 3: Abe Rahey, Ben Treynor Sloss, Brian Stoler, Dave O'Connor, David Besbris, Jill Alvidrez, Mike Curtis, Nancy Chang, Tammy Capistrant, Tom Limoncelli

Chapter 5: Cody Smith, George Sadlier, Laurence Berland, Marc Alvidrez, Patrick Stahlberg, Peter Duff, Pim van Pelt, Ryan Anderson, Sabrina Farmer, Seth Hettich

Chapter 6: Mike Curtis, Jamie Wilkinson, Seth Hettich

Chapter 8: David Schnur, JT Goldstone, Marc Alvidrez, Marcus Lara-Reinhold, Noah Maxwell, Peter Dinges, Sumitran Raghunathan, Yutong Cho

Chapter 9: Ryan Anderson

Chapter 10: Jules Anderson, Max Luebbe, Mikel Mcdaniel, Raul Vera, Seth Hettich

Chapter 11: Andrew Stribblehill, Richard Woodbury

Chapter 12: Charles Stephen Gunn, John Hedditch, Peter Nuttall, Rob Ewaschuk, Sam Greenfield

Chapter 13: Jelena Oertel, Kripa Krishnan, Sergio Salvi, Tim Craig

Chapter 14: Amy Zhou, Carla Geisser, Grainne Sheerin, Hildo Biersma, Jelena Oertel, Perry Lorier, Rune Kristian Viken

Chapter 15: Dan Wu, Heather Sherman, Jared Brick, Mike Louer, Štěpán Davidovič, Tim Craig

Chapter 16: Andrew Stribblehill, Richard Woodbury

Chapter 17: Isaac Clerencia, Marc Alvidrez

Chapter 18: Ulric Longyear

Chapter 19: Debashish Chatterjee, Perry Lorier

Chapters 20 and 21: Adam Fletcher, Christoph Pfisterer, Lukáš Ježek, Manjot Pahwa, Micha Riser, Noah Fiedel, Pavel Herrmann, Paweł Zuzelski, Perry Lorier, Ralf Wildenhues, Tudor-Ioan Salomie, Witold Baryluk

Chapter 22: Mike Curtis, Ryan Anderson

Chapter 23: Ananth Shrinivas, Mike Burrows

Chapter 24: Ben Fried, Derek Jackson, Gabe Krabbe, Laura Nolan, Seth Hettich

Chapter 25: Abdulrahman Salem, Alex Perry, Arnar Mar Hrafnkelsson, Dieter Pearcey, Dylan Curley, Eivind Eklund, Eric Veach, Graham Poulter, Ingvar Mattsson, John Looney, Ken Grant, Michelle Duffy, Mike Hochberg, Will Robinson

Chapter 26: Corey Vickrey, Dan Ardelean, Disney Luangsisongkham, Gordon Prioreschi, Kristina Bennett, Liang Lin, Michael Kelly, Sergey Ivanyuk

Chapter 27: Vivek Rau

Chapter 28: Melissa Binde, Perry Lorier, Preston Yoshioka

Chapter 29: Ben Lutch, Carla Geisser, Dzevad Trumic, John Turek, Matt Brown

Chapter 30: Charles Stephen Gunn, Chris Heiser, Max Luebbe, Sam Greenfield

Chapter 31: Alex Kehlenbeck, Jeromy Carriere, Joel Becker, Sowmya Vijayaraghavan, Trevor Mattson-Hamilton

Chapter 32: Seth Hettich

Chapter 33: Adrian Hilton, Brad Kratochvil, Charles Ballowe, Dan Sheridan, Eddie Kennedy, Erik Gross, Gus Hartmann, Jackson Stone, Jeff Stevenson, John Li, Kevin Greer, Matt Toia, Michael Haynie, Mike Doherty, Peter Dahl, Ron Heiby

We are also grateful to the following contributors, who either provided significant material, did an excellent job of reviewing, agreed to be interviewed, supplied significant expertise or resources, or had some otherwise excellent effect on this work:

Abe Hassan, Adam Rogoyski, Alex Hidalgo, Amaya Booker, Andrew Fikes, Andrew Hurst, Ariel Goh, Ashleigh Rentz, Ayman Hourieh, Barclay Osborn, Ben Appleton, Ben Love, Ben Winslow, Bernhard Beck, Bill Duane, Bill Patry, Blair Zajac, Bob Gruber, Brian Gustafson, Bruce Murphy, Buck Clay, Cedric Cellier, Chiho Saito, Chris Carlon, Christopher Hahn, Chris Kennelly, Chris Taylor, Ciara Kamahele-Sanfratello, Colin Phipps, Colm Buckley, Craig Paterson, Daniel Eisenbud, Daniel V. Klein, Daniel Spoonhower, Dan Watson, Dave Phillips, David Hixson, Dina Betser, Doron Meyer, Dmitry Fedoruk, Eric Grosse, Eric Schrock, Filip Zyzniewski, Francis Tang, Gary Arneson, Georgina Wilcox, Gretta Bartels, Gustavo Franco, Harald Wagener, Healfdene Goguen, Hugo Santos, Hyrum Wright, Ian Gulliver, Jakub Turski, James Chivers, James O'Kane, James Youngman, Jan Monsch, Jason Parker-Burlingham, Jason Petsod, Jeffry McNeil, Jeff Dean, Jeff Peck, Jennifer Mace, Jerry Cen, Jess Frame, John Brady, John Gunderman, John Kochmar, John Tobin, Jordyn Buchanan, Joseph Bironas, Julio Merino, Julius Plenz, Kate Ward, Kathy Polizzi, Katrina Sostek, Kenn Hamm, Kirk Russell, Kripa Krishnan, Larry Greenfield, Lea Oliveira, Luca Cittadini,

Lucas Pereira, Magnus Ringman, Mahesh Palekar, Marco Paganini, Mario Bonilla, Mathew Mills, Mathew Monroe, Matt D. Brown, Matt Proud, Max Saltonstall, Michal Jaszczyk, Mihai Bivol, Misha Brukman, Olivier Oansaldi, Patrick Bernier, Pierre Palatin, Rob Shanley, Robert van Gent, Rory Ward, Rui Zhang-Shen, Salim Virji, Sanjay Ghemawat, Sarah Coty, Sean Dorward, Sean Quinlan, Sean Sechrest, Shari Trumbo-McHenry, Shawn Morrissey, Shun-Tak Leung, Stan Jedrus, Stefano Lattarini, Steven Schirripa, Tanya Reilly, Terry Bolt, Tim Chaplin, Toby Weingartner, Tom Black, Udi Meiri, Victor Terron, Vlad Grama, Wes Hertlein, and Zoltan Egyed.

We very much appreciate the thoughtful and in-depth feedback that we received from external reviewers: Andrew Fong, Björn Rabenstein, Charles Border, David Blank-Edelman, Frossie Economou, James Meickle, Josh Ryder, Mark Burgess, and Russ Allbery.

We would like to extend special thanks to Cian Synnott, original book team member and co-conspirator, who left Google before this project was completed but was deeply influential to it, and Margaret Hamilton, who so graciously allowed us to reference her story in our preface. Additionally, we would like to extend special thanks to Shylaja Nukala, who generously gave of the time of her technical writers and supported their necessary and valued efforts wholeheartedly.

The editors would also like to personally thank the following people:

Betsy Beyer: To Grandmother (my personal hero), for supplying endless amounts of phone pep talks and popcorn, and to Riba, for supplying me with the sweatpants necessary to fuel several late nights. These, of course, in addition to the cast of SRE allstars who were indeed delightful collaborators.

Chris Jones: To Michelle, for saving me from a life of crime on the high seas and for her uncanny ability to find manzanas in unexpected places, and to those who've taught me about engineering over the years.

Jennifer Petoff: To my husband Scott for being incredibly supportive during the two year process of writing this book and for keeping the editors supplied with plenty of sugar on our "Dessert Island."

Niall Murphy: To Léan, Oisín, and Fiachra, who were considerably more patient than I had any right to expect with a substantially rantier father and husband than usual, for years. To Dermot, for the transfer offer.

PART I

Introduction

This section provides some high-level guidance on what SRE is and why it is different from more conventional IT industry practices.

Ben Treynor Sloss, the senior VP overseeing technical operations at Google—and the originator of the term "Site Reliability Engineering"—provides his view on what SRE means, how it works, and how it compares to other ways of doing things in the industry, in Chapter 1.

We provide a guide to the production environment at Google in Chapter 2 as a way to help acquaint you with the wealth of new terms and systems you are about to meet in the rest of the book.

Introduction

Written by Benjamin Treynor Sloss[1]
Edited by Betsy Beyer

> *Hope is not a strategy.*
> —Traditional SRE saying

It is a truth universally acknowledged that systems do not run themselves. How, then, *should* a system—particularly a complex computing system that operates at a large scale—be run?

The Sysadmin Approach to Service Management

Historically, companies have employed systems administrators to run complex computing systems.

This systems administrator, or sysadmin, approach involves assembling existing software components and deploying them to work together to produce a service. Sysadmins are then tasked with running the service and responding to events and updates as they occur. As the system grows in complexity and traffic volume, generating a corresponding increase in events and updates, the sysadmin team grows to absorb the additional work. Because the sysadmin role requires a markedly different skill set than that required of a product's developers, developers and sysadmins are divided into discrete teams: "development" and "operations" or "ops."

The sysadmin model of service management has several advantages. For companies deciding how to run and staff a service, this approach is relatively easy to implement: as a familiar industry paradigm, there are many examples from which to learn and

---

1 Vice President, Google Engineering, founder of Google SRE

emulate. A relevant talent pool is already widely available. An array of existing tools, software components (off the shelf or otherwise), and integration companies are available to help run those assembled systems, so a novice sysadmin team doesn't have to reinvent the wheel and design a system from scratch.

The sysadmin approach and the accompanying development/ops split has a number of disadvantages and pitfalls. These fall broadly into two categories: direct costs and indirect costs.

Direct costs are neither subtle nor ambiguous. Running a service with a team that relies on manual intervention for both change management and event handling becomes expensive as the service and/or traffic to the service grows, because the size of the team necessarily scales with the load generated by the system.

The indirect costs of the development/ops split can be subtle, but are often more expensive to the organization than the direct costs. These costs arise from the fact that the two teams are quite different in background, skill set, and incentives. They use different vocabulary to describe situations; they carry different assumptions about both risk and possibilities for technical solutions; they have different assumptions about the target level of product stability. The split between the groups can easily become one of not just incentives, but also communication, goals, and eventually, trust and respect. This outcome is a pathology.

Traditional operations teams and their counterparts in product development thus often end up in conflict, most visibly over how quickly software can be released to production. At their core, the development teams want to launch new features and see them adopted by users. At *their* core, the ops teams want to make sure the service doesn't break while they are holding the pager. Because most outages are caused by some kind of change—a new configuration, a new feature launch, or a new type of user traffic—the two teams' goals are fundamentally in tension.

Both groups understand that it is unacceptable to state their interests in the baldest possible terms ("We want to launch anything, any time, without hindrance" versus "We won't want to ever change anything in the system once it works"). And because their vocabulary and risk assumptions differ, both groups often resort to a familiar form of trench warfare to advance their interests. The ops team attempts to safeguard the running system against the risk of change by introducing launch and change gates. For example, launch reviews may contain an explicit check for *every* problem that has *ever* caused an outage in the past—that could be an arbitrarily long list, with not all elements providing equal value. The dev team quickly learns how to respond. They have fewer "launches" and more "flag flips," "incremental updates," or "cherry-picks." They adopt tactics such as sharding the product so that fewer features are subject to the launch review.

Google's Approach to Service Management: Site Reliability Engineering

Conflict isn't an inevitable part of offering a software service. Google has chosen to run our systems with a different approach: our Site Reliability Engineering teams focus on hiring software engineers to run our products and to create systems to accomplish the work that would otherwise be performed, often manually, by sysadmins.

What exactly is Site Reliability Engineering, as it has come to be defined at Google? My explanation is simple: SRE is what happens when you ask a software engineer to design an operations team. When I joined Google in 2003 and was tasked with running a "Production Team" of seven engineers, my entire life up to that point had been software engineering. So I designed and managed the group the way *I* would want it to work if I worked as an SRE myself. That group has since matured to become Google's present-day SRE team, which remains true to its origins as envisioned by a lifelong software engineer.

A primary building block of Google's approach to service management is the composition of each SRE team. As a whole, SRE can be broken down two main categories.

50–60% are Google Software Engineers, or more precisely, people who have been hired via the standard procedure for Google Software Engineers. The other 40–50% are candidates who were very close to the Google Software Engineering qualifications (i.e., 85–99% of the skill set required), and who *in addition* had a set of technical skills that is useful to SRE but is rare for most software engineers. By far, UNIX system internals and networking (Layer 1 to Layer 3) expertise are the two most common types of alternate technical skills we seek.

Common to all SREs is the belief in and aptitude for developing software systems to solve complex problems. Within SRE, we track the career progress of both groups closely, and have to date found no practical difference in performance between engineers from the two tracks. In fact, the somewhat diverse background of the SRE team frequently results in clever, high-quality systems that are clearly the product of the synthesis of several skill sets.

The result of our approach to hiring for SRE is that we end up with a team of people who (a) will quickly become bored by performing tasks by hand, and (b) have the skill set necessary to write software to replace their previously manual work, even when the solution is complicated. SREs also end up sharing academic and intellectual background with the rest of the development organization. Therefore, SRE is fundamentally doing work that has historically been done by an operations team, but using engineers with software expertise, and banking on the fact that these engineers are inherently both predisposed to, and have the ability to, design and implement automation with software to replace human labor.

By design, it is crucial that SRE teams are focused on engineering. Without constant engineering, operations load increases and teams will need more people just to keep pace with the workload. Eventually, a traditional ops-focused group scales linearly with service size: if the products supported by the service succeed, the operational load will grow with traffic. That means hiring more people to do the same tasks over and over again.

To avoid this fate, the team tasked with managing a service needs to code or it will drown. Therefore, Google places *a 50% cap on the aggregate "ops" work for all SREs*—tickets, on-call, manual tasks, etc. This cap ensures that the SRE team has enough time in their schedule to make the service stable and operable. This cap is an upper bound; over time, left to their own devices, the SRE team should end up with very little operational load and almost entirely engage in development tasks, because the service basically runs and repairs itself: we want systems that are *automatic*, not just *automated*. In practice, scale and new features keep SREs on their toes.

Google's rule of thumb is that an SRE team must spend the remaining 50% of its time actually doing development. So how do we enforce that threshold? In the first place, we have to measure how SRE time is spent. With that measurement in hand, we ensure that the teams consistently spending less than 50% of their time on development work change their practices. Often this means shifting some of the operations burden back to the development team, or adding staff to the team without assigning that team additional operational responsibilities. Consciously maintaining this balance between ops and development work allows us to ensure that SREs have the bandwidth to engage in creative, autonomous engineering, while still retaining the wisdom gleaned from the operations side of running a service.

We've found that Google SRE's approach to running large-scale systems has many advantages. Because SREs are directly modifying code in their pursuit of making Google's systems run themselves, SRE teams are characterized by both rapid innovation and a large acceptance of change. Such teams are relatively inexpensive—supporting the same service with an ops-oriented team would require a significantly larger number of people. Instead, the number of SREs needed to run, maintain, and improve a system scales sublinearly with the size of the system. Finally, not only does SRE circumvent the dysfunctionality of the dev/ops split, but this structure also improves our product development teams: easy transfers between product development and SRE teams cross-train the entire group, and improve skills of developers who otherwise may have difficulty learning how to build a million-core distributed system.

Despite these net gains, the SRE model is characterized by its own distinct set of challenges. One continual challenge Google faces is hiring SREs: not only does SRE compete for the same candidates as the product development hiring pipeline, but the fact that we set the hiring bar so high in terms of both coding and system engineering skills means that our hiring pool is necessarily small. As our discipline is relatively new and unique, not much industry information exists on how to build and manage an SRE team (although hopefully this book will make strides in that direction!). And once an SRE team is in place, their potentially unorthodox approaches to service management require strong management support. For example, the decision to stop releases for the remainder of the quarter once an error budget is depleted might not be embraced by a product development team unless mandated by their management.

DevOps or SRE?

The term "DevOps" emerged in industry in late 2008 and as of this writing (early 2016) is still in a state of flux. Its core principles—involvement of the IT function in each phase of a system's design and development, heavy reliance on automation versus human effort, the application of engineering practices and tools to operations tasks—are consistent with many of SRE's principles and practices. One could view DevOps as a generalization of several core SRE principles to a wider range of organizations, management structures, and personnel. One could equivalently view SRE as a specific implementation of DevOps with some idiosyncratic extensions.

Tenets of SRE

While the nuances of workflows, priorities, and day-to-day operations vary from SRE team to SRE team, all share a set of basic responsibilities for the service(s) they support, and adhere to the same core tenets. In general, an SRE team is responsible for the *availability, latency, performance, efficiency, change management, monitoring, emergency response, and capacity planning* of their service(s). We have codified rules of engagement and principles for how SRE teams interact with their environment— not only the production environment, but also the product development teams, the testing teams, the users, and so on. Those rules and work practices help us to maintain our focus on engineering work, as opposed to operations work.

The following section discusses each of the core tenets of Google SRE.

Ensuring a Durable Focus on Engineering

As already discussed, Google caps operational work for SREs at 50% of their time. Their remaining time should be spent using their coding skills on project work. In practice, this is accomplished by monitoring the amount of operational work being done by SREs, and redirecting excess operational work to the product development teams: reassigning bugs and tickets to development managers, [re]integrating developers into on-call pager rotations, and so on. The redirection ends when the operational load drops back to 50% or lower. This also provides an effective feedback mechanism, guiding developers to build systems that don't need manual intervention. This approach works well when the entire organization—SRE and development alike —understands why the safety valve mechanism exists, and supports the goal of having no overflow events because the product doesn't generate enough operational load to require it.

When they are focused on operations work, on average, SREs should receive a maximum of two events per 8–12-hour on-call shift. This target volume gives the on-call engineer enough time to handle the event accurately and quickly, clean up and restore normal service, and then conduct a postmortem. If more than two events occur regularly per on-call shift, problems can't be investigated thoroughly and engineers are sufficiently overwhelmed to prevent them from learning from these events. A scenario of pager fatigue also won't improve with scale. Conversely, if on-call SREs consistently receive fewer than one event per shift, keeping them on point is a waste of their time.

Postmortems should be written for all significant incidents, regardless of whether or not they paged; postmortems that did not trigger a page are even more valuable, as they likely point to clear monitoring gaps. This investigation should establish what happened in detail, find all root causes of the event, and assign actions to correct the problem or improve how it is addressed next time. Google operates under a *blame-free postmortem culture*, with the goal of exposing faults and applying engineering to fix these faults, rather than avoiding or minimizing them.

Pursuing Maximum Change Velocity Without Violating a Service's SLO

Product development and SRE teams can enjoy a productive working relationship by eliminating the structural conflict in their respective goals. The structural conflict is between pace of innovation and product stability, and as described earlier, this conflict often is expressed indirectly. In SRE we bring this conflict to the fore, and then resolve it with the introduction of an *error budget*.

The error budget stems from the observation that *100% is the wrong reliability target for basically everything* (pacemakers and anti-lock brakes being notable exceptions). In general, for any software service or system, 100% is not the right reliability target because no user can tell the difference between a system being 100% available and 99.999% available. There are many other systems in the path between user and service (their laptop, their home WiFi, their ISP, the power grid...) and those systems collectively are far less than 99.999% available. Thus, the marginal difference between 99.999% and 100% gets lost in the noise of other unavailability, and the user receives no benefit from the enormous effort required to add that last 0.001% of availability.

If 100% is the wrong reliability target for a system, what, then, is the right reliability target for the system? This actually isn't a technical question at all—it's a product question, which should take the following considerations into account:

- What level of availability will the users be happy with, given how they use the product?
- What alternatives are available to users who are dissatisfied with the product's availability?
- What happens to users' usage of the product at different availability levels?

The business or the product must establish the system's availability target. Once that target is established, the error budget is one minus the availability target. A service that's 99.99% available is 0.01% unavailable. That permitted 0.01% unavailability is the service's *error budget*. We can spend the budget on anything we want, as long as we don't overspend it.

So how do we want to spend the error budget? The development team wants to launch features and attract new users. Ideally, we would spend all of our error budget taking risks with things we launch in order to launch them quickly. This basic premise describes the whole model of error budgets. As soon as SRE activities are conceptualized in this framework, freeing up the error budget through tactics such as phased rollouts and 1% experiments can optimize for quicker launches.

The use of an error budget resolves the structural conflict of incentives between development and SRE. SRE's goal is no longer "zero outages"; rather, SREs and product developers aim to spend the error budget getting maximum feature velocity. This change makes all the difference. An outage is no longer a "bad" thing—it is an expected part of the process of innovation, and an occurrence that both development and SRE teams manage rather than fear.

Monitoring

Monitoring is one of the primary means by which service owners keep track of a system's health and availability. As such, monitoring strategy should be constructed thoughtfully. A classic and common approach to monitoring is to watch for a specific value or condition, and then to trigger an email alert when that value is exceeded or that condition occurs. However, this type of email alerting is not an effective solution: a system that requires a human to read an email and decide whether or not some type of action needs to be taken in response is fundamentally flawed. Monitoring should never require a human to interpret any part of the alerting domain. Instead, software should do the interpreting, and humans should be notified only when they need to take action.

There are three kinds of valid monitoring output:

Alerts
> Signify that a human needs to take action immediately in response to something that is either happening or about to happen, in order to improve the situation.

Tickets
> Signify that a human needs to take action, but not immediately. The system cannot automatically handle the situation, but if a human takes action in a few days, no damage will result.

Logging
> No one needs to look at this information, but it is recorded for diagnostic or forensic purposes. The expectation is that no one reads logs unless something else prompts them to do so.

Emergency Response

Reliability is a function of mean time to failure (MTTF) and mean time to repair (MTTR) [Sch15]. The most relevant metric in evaluating the effectiveness of emergency response is how quickly the response team can bring the system back to health —that is, the MTTR.

Humans add latency. Even if a given system experiences more *actual* failures, a system that can avoid emergencies that require human intervention will have higher availability than a system that requires hands-on intervention. When humans are necessary, we have found that thinking through and recording the best practices ahead of time in a "playbook" produces roughly a 3x improvement in MTTR as compared to the strategy of "winging it." The hero jack-of-all-trades on-call engineer does work, but the practiced on-call engineer armed with a playbook works much better. While no playbook, no matter how comprehensive it may be, is a substitute for smart engineers able to think on the fly, clear and thorough troubleshooting steps and tips are valuable when responding to a high-stakes or time-sensitive page. Thus, Google SRE relies on on-call playbooks, in addition to exercises such as the "Wheel of Misfortune,"[2] to prepare engineers to react to on-call events.

Change Management

SRE has found that roughly 70% of outages are due to changes in a live system. Best practices in this domain use automation to accomplish the following:

---

2 See "Disaster Role Playing" on page 401.

- Implementing progressive rollouts
- Quickly and accurately detecting problems
- Rolling back changes safely when problems arise

This trio of practices effectively minimizes the aggregate number of users and operations exposed to bad changes. By removing humans from the loop, these practices avoid the normal problems of fatigue, familiarity/contempt, and inattention to highly repetitive tasks. As a result, both release velocity and safety increase.

Demand Forecasting and Capacity Planning

Demand forecasting and capacity planning can be viewed as ensuring that there is sufficient capacity and redundancy to serve projected future demand with the required availability. There's nothing particularly special about these concepts, except that a surprising number of services and teams don't take the steps necessary to ensure that the required capacity is in place by the time it is needed. Capacity planning should take both organic growth (which stems from natural product adoption and usage by customers) and inorganic growth (which results from events like feature launches, marketing campaigns, or other business-driven changes) into account.

Several steps are mandatory in capacity planning:

- An accurate organic demand forecast, which extends beyond the lead time required for acquiring capacity
- An accurate incorporation of inorganic demand sources into the demand forecast
- Regular load testing of the system to correlate raw capacity (servers, disks, and so on) to service capacity

Because capacity is critical to availability, it naturally follows that the SRE team must be in charge of capacity planning, which means they also must be in charge of provisioning.

Provisioning

Provisioning combines both change management and capacity planning. In our experience, provisioning must be conducted quickly and only when necessary, as capacity is expensive. This exercise must also be done correctly or capacity doesn't work when needed. Adding new capacity often involves spinning up a new instance or location, making significant modification to existing systems (configuration files, load balancers, networking), and validating that the new capacity performs and delivers correct results. Thus, it is a riskier operation than load shifting, which is often done multiple times per hour, and must be treated with a corresponding degree of extra caution.

Efficiency and Performance

Efficient use of resources is important any time a service cares about money. Because SRE ultimately controls provisioning, it must also be involved in any work on utilization, as utilization is a function of how a given service works and how it is provisioned. It follows that paying close attention to the provisioning strategy for a service, and therefore its utilization, provides a very, very big lever on the service's total costs.

Resource use is a function of demand (load), capacity, and software efficiency. SREs predict demand, provision capacity, and can modify the software. These three factors are a large part (though not the entirety) of a service's efficiency.

Software systems become slower as load is added to them. A slowdown in a service equates to a loss of capacity. At some point, a slowing system stops serving, which corresponds to infinite slowness. SREs provision to meet a capacity target *at a specific response speed*, and thus are keenly interested in a service's performance. SREs and product developers will (and should) monitor and modify a service to improve its performance, thus adding capacity and improving efficiency.[3]

The End of the Beginning

Site Reliability Engineering represents a significant break from existing industry best practices for managing large, complicated services. Motivated originally by familiarity —"as a software engineer, this is how I would want to invest my time to accomplish a set of repetitive tasks"—it has become much more: a set of principles, a set of practices, a set of incentives, and a field of endeavor within the larger software engineering discipline. The rest of the book explores the SRE Way in detail.

---

3 For further discussion of how this collaboration can work in practice, see "Communications: Production Meetings" on page 426.

CHAPTER 2

The Production Environment at Google, from the Viewpoint of an SRE

Written by JC van Winkel
Edited by Betsy Beyer

Google datacenters are very different from most conventional datacenters and small-scale server farms. These differences present both extra problems and opportunities. This chapter discusses the challenges and opportunities that characterize Google datacenters and introduces terminology that is used throughout the book.

Hardware

Most of Google's compute resources are in Google-designed datacenters with proprietary power distribution, cooling, networking, and compute hardware (see [Bar13]). Unlike "standard" colocation datacenters, the compute hardware in a Google-designed datacenter is the same across the board.[1] To eliminate the confusion between server hardware and server software, we use the following terminology throughout the book:

Machine
  A piece of hardware (or perhaps a VM)

Server
  A piece of software that implements a service

---

1 Well, *roughly* the same. Mostly. Except for the stuff that is different. Some datacenters end up with multiple generations of compute hardware, and sometimes we augment datacenters after they are built. But for the most part, our datacenter hardware is homogeneous.

Machines can run any server, so we don't dedicate specific machines to specific server programs. There's no specific machine that runs our mail server, for example. Instead, resource allocation is handled by our cluster operating system, *Borg*.

We realize this use of the word *server* is unusual. The common use of the word conflates "binary that accepts network connection" with *machine*, but differentiating between the two is important when talking about computing at Google. Once you get used to our usage of *server*, it becomes more apparent why it makes sense to use this specialized terminology, not just within Google but also in the rest of this book.

Figure 2-1 illustrates the topology of a Google datacenter:

- Tens of machines are placed in a *rack*.
- Racks stand in a *row*.
- One or more rows form a *cluster*.
- Usually a *datacenter* building houses multiple clusters.
- Multiple datacenter buildings that are located close together form a *campus*.

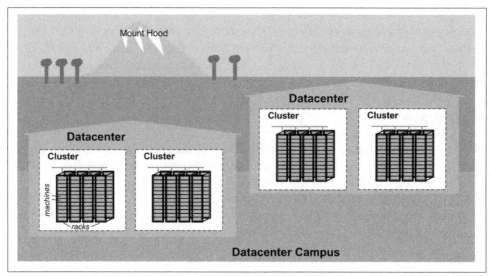

Figure 2-1. Example Google datacenter campus topology

Machines within a given datacenter need to be able to talk with each other, so we created a very fast virtual switch with tens of thousands of ports. We accomplished this by connecting hundreds of Google-built switches in a Clos network fabric [Clos53] named *Jupiter* [Sin15]. In its largest configuration, Jupiter supports 1.3 Pbps bisection bandwidth among servers.

Datacenters are connected to each other with our globe-spanning backbone network *B4* [Jai13]. B4 is a software-defined networking architecture (and uses the OpenFlow open-standard communications protocol). It supplies massive bandwidth to a modest number of sites, and uses elastic bandwidth allocation to maximize average bandwidth [Kum15].

System Software That "Organizes" the Hardware

Our hardware must be controlled and administered by software that can handle massive scale. Hardware failures are one notable problem that we manage with software. Given the large number of hardware components in a cluster, hardware failures occur quite frequently. In a single cluster in a typical year, thousands of machines fail and thousands of hard disks break; when multiplied by the number of clusters we operate globally, these numbers become somewhat breathtaking. Therefore, we want to abstract such problems away from users, and the teams running our services similarly don't want to be bothered by hardware failures. Each datacenter campus has teams dedicated to maintaining the hardware and datacenter infrastructure.

Managing Machines

Borg, illustrated in Figure 2-2, is a distributed cluster operating system [Ver15], similar to Apache Mesos.[2] Borg manages its jobs at the cluster level.

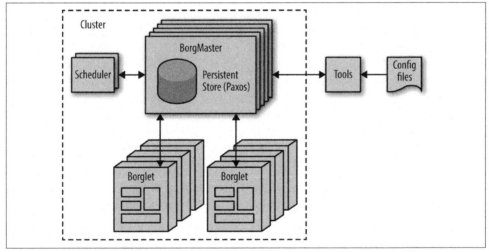

Figure 2-2. High-level Borg cluster architecture

---

2 Some readers may be more familiar with Borg's descendant, Kubernetes—an open source Container Cluster orchestration framework started by Google in 2014; see *http://kubernetes.io* and [Bur16]. For more details on the similarities between Borg and Apache Mesos, see [Ver15].

Borg is responsible for running users' *jobs*, which can either be indefinitely running servers or batch processes like a MapReduce [Dea04]. Jobs can consist of more than one (and sometimes thousands) of identical *tasks*, both for reasons of reliability and because a single process can't usually handle all cluster traffic. When Borg starts a job, it finds machines for the tasks and tells the machines to start the server program. Borg then continually monitors these tasks. If a task malfunctions, it is killed and restarted, possibly on a different machine.

Because tasks are fluidly allocated over machines, we can't simply rely on IP addresses and port numbers to refer to the tasks. We solve this problem with an extra level of indirection: when starting a job, Borg allocates a name and index number to each task using the *Borg Naming Service* (BNS). Rather than using the IP address and port number, other processes connect to Borg tasks via the BNS name, which is translated to an IP address and port number by BNS. For example, the BNS path might be a string such as `/bns/<cluster>/<user>/<job name>/<task number>`, which would resolve to `<IP address>:<port>`.

Borg is also responsible for the allocation of resources to jobs. Every job needs to specify its required resources (e.g., 3 CPU cores, 2 GiB of RAM). Using the list of requirements for all jobs, Borg can binpack the tasks over the machines in an optimal way that also accounts for failure domains (for example: Borg won't run all of a job's tasks on the same rack, as doing so means that the top of rack switch is a single point of failure for that job).

If a task tries to use more resources than it requested, Borg kills the task and restarts it (as a slowly crashlooping task is usually preferable to a task that hasn't been restarted at all).

Storage

Tasks can use the local disk on machines as a scratch pad, but we have several cluster storage options for permanent storage (and even scratch space will eventually move to the cluster storage model). These are comparable to Lustre and the Hadoop Distributed File System (HDFS), which are both open source cluster filesystems.

The storage layer is responsible for offering users easy and reliable access to the storage available for a cluster. As shown in Figure 2-3, storage has many layers:

1. The lowest layer is called *D* (for *disk*, although D uses both spinning disks and flash storage). D is a fileserver running on almost all machines in a cluster. However, users who want to access their data don't want to have to remember which machine is storing their data, which is where the next layer comes into play.

2. A layer on top of D called *Colossus* creates a cluster-wide filesystem that offers usual filesystem semantics, as well as replication and encryption. Colossus is the successor to GFS, the Google File System [Ghe03].

3. There are several database-like services built on top of Colossus:

   a. Bigtable [Cha06] is a NoSQL database system that can handle databases that are petabytes in size. A Bigtable is a sparse, distributed, persistent multidimensional sorted map that is indexed by row key, column key, and timestamp; each value in the map is an uninterpreted array of bytes. Bigtable supports eventually consistent, cross-datacenter replication.

   b. Spanner [Cor12] offers an SQL-like interface for users that require real consistency across the world.

   c. Several other database systems, such as *Blobstore*, are available. Each of these options comes with its own set of trade-offs (see Chapter 26).

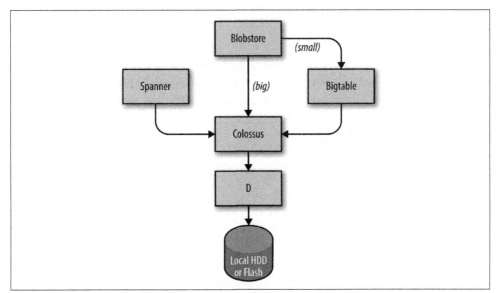

Figure 2-3. Portions of the Google storage stack

Networking

Google's network hardware is controlled in several ways. As discussed earlier, we use an OpenFlow-based software-defined network. Instead of using "smart" routing hardware, we rely on less expensive "dumb" switching components in combination with a central (duplicated) controller that precomputes best paths across the network. Therefore, we're able to move compute-expensive routing decisions away from the routers and use simple switching hardware.

Network bandwidth needs to be allocated wisely. Just as Borg limits the compute resources that a task can use, the Bandwidth Enforcer (BwE) manages the available bandwidth to maximize the average available bandwidth. Optimizing bandwidth isn't just about cost: centralized traffic engineering has been shown to solve a number of problems that are traditionally extremely difficult to solve through a combination of distributed routing and traffic engineering [Kum15].

Some services have jobs running in multiple clusters, which are distributed across the world. In order to minimize latency for globally distributed services, we want to direct users to the closest datacenter with available capacity. Our *Global Software Load Balancer* (GSLB) performs load balancing on three levels:

- Geographic load balancing for DNS requests (for example, to *www.google.com*), described in Chapter 19
- Load balancing at a user service level (for example, YouTube or Google Maps)
- Load balancing at the Remote Procedure Call (RPC) level, described in Chapter 20

Service owners specify a symbolic name for a service, a list of BNS addresses of servers, and the capacity available at each of the locations (typically measured in queries per second). GSLB then directs traffic to the BNS addresses.

Other System Software

Several other components in a datacenter are also important.

Lock Service

The *Chubby* [Bur06] lock service provides a filesystem-like API for maintaining locks. Chubby handles these locks across datacenter locations. It uses the Paxos protocol for asynchronous Consensus (see Chapter 23).

Chubby also plays an important role in master election. When a service has five replicas of a job running for reliability purposes but only one replica may perform actual work, Chubby is used to select *which* replica may proceed.

Data that must be consistent is well suited to storage in Chubby. For this reason, BNS uses Chubby to store mapping between BNS paths and IP `address:port` pairs.

Monitoring and Alerting

We want to make sure that all services are running as required. Therefore, we run many instances of our *Borgmon* monitoring program (see Chapter 10). Borgmon regularly "scrapes" metrics from monitored servers. These metrics can be used instantaneously for alerting and also stored for use in historic overviews (e.g., graphs). We can use monitoring in several ways:

- Set up alerting for acute problems.
- Compare behavior: did a software update make the server faster?
- Examine how resource consumption behavior evolves over time, which is essential for capacity planning.

Our Software Infrastructure

Our software architecture is designed to make the most efficient use of our hardware infrastructure. Our code is heavily multithreaded, so one task can easily use many cores. To facilitate dashboards, monitoring, and debugging, every server has an HTTP server that provides diagnostics and statistics for a given task.

All of Google's services communicate using a Remote Procedure Call (RPC) infrastructure named *Stubby*; an open source version, gRPC, is available.[3] Often, an RPC call is made even when a call to a subroutine in the local program needs to be performed. This makes it easier to refactor the call into a different server if more modularity is needed, or when a server's codebase grows. GSLB can load balance RPCs in the same way it load balances externally visible services.

A server receives RPC requests from its *frontend* and sends RPCs to its *backend*. In traditional terms, the frontend is called the client and the backend is called the server.

Data is transferred to and from an RPC using *protocol buffers*,[4] often abbreviated to "protobufs," which are similar to Apache's Thrift. Protocol buffers have many advantages over XML for serializing structured data: they are simpler to use, 3 to 10 times smaller, 20 to 100 times faster, and less ambiguous.

Our Development Environment

Development velocity is very important to Google, so we've built a complete development environment to make use of our infrastructure [Mor12b].

Apart from a few groups that have their own open source repositories (e.g., Android and Chrome), Google Software Engineers work from a single shared repository [Pot16]. This has a few important practical implications for our workflows:

---

3 See *http://grpc.io*.

4 Protocol buffers are a language-neutral, platform-neutral extensible mechanism for serializing structured data. For more details, see *https://developers.google.com/protocol-buffers/*.

- If engineers encounter a problem in a component outside of their project, they can fix the problem, send the proposed changes ("changelist," or *CL*) to the owner for review, and submit the CL to the mainline.

- Changes to source code in an engineer's own project require a review. All software is reviewed before being submitted.

When software is built, the build request is sent to build servers in a datacenter. Even large builds are executed quickly, as many build servers can compile in parallel. This infrastructure is also used for continuous testing. Each time a CL is submitted, tests run on all software that may depend on that CL, either directly or indirectly. If the framework determines that the change likely broke other parts in the system, it notifies the owner of the submitted change. Some projects use a push-on-green system, where a new version is automatically pushed to production after passing tests.

Shakespeare: A Sample Service

To provide a model of how a service would hypothetically be deployed in the Google production environment, let's look at an example service that interacts with multiple Google technologies. Suppose we want to offer a service that lets you determine where a given word is used throughout all of Shakespeare's works.

We can divide this system into two parts:

- A batch component that reads all of Shakespeare's texts, creates an index, and writes the index into a Bigtable. This job need only run once, or perhaps very infrequently (as you never know if a new text might be discovered!).

- An application frontend that handles end-user requests. This job is always up, as users in all time zones will want to search in Shakespeare's books.

The batch component is a MapReduce comprising three phases.

The mapping phase reads Shakespeare's texts and splits them into individual words. This is faster if performed in parallel by multiple workers.

The shuffle phase sorts the tuples by word.

In the reduce phase, a tuple of (*word, list of locations*) is created.

Each tuple is written to a row in a Bigtable, using the word as the key.

Life of a Request

Figure 2-4 shows how a user's request is serviced: first, the user points their browser to *shakespeare.google.com*. To obtain the corresponding IP address, the user's device resolves the address with its DNS server (1). This request ultimately ends up at Google's DNS server, which talks to GSLB. As GSLB keeps track of traffic load among frontend servers across regions, it picks which server IP address to send to this user.

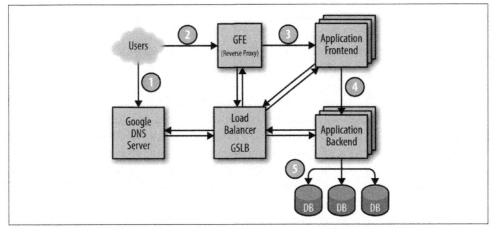

Figure 2-4. The life of a request

The browser connects to the HTTP server on this IP. This server (named the Google Frontend, or GFE) is a reverse proxy that terminates the TCP connection (2). The GFE looks up which service is required (web search, maps, or—in this case—Shakespeare). Again using GSLB, the server finds an available Shakespeare frontend server, and sends that server an RPC containing the HTML request (3).

The Shakespeare server analyzes the HTML request and constructs a protobuf containing the word to look up. The Shakespeare frontend server now needs to contact the Shakespeare backend server: the frontend server contacts GSLB to obtain the BNS address of a suitable and unloaded backend server (4). That Shakespeare backend server now contacts a Bigtable server to obtain the requested data (5).

The answer is written to the reply protobuf and returned to the Shakespeare backend server. The backend hands a protobuf containing the results to the Shakespeare frontend server, which assembles the HTML and returns the answer to the user.

This entire chain of events is executed in the blink of an eye—just a few hundred milliseconds! Because many moving parts are involved, there are many potential points of failure; in particular, a failing GSLB would wreak havoc. However, Google's policies of rigorous testing and careful rollout, in addition to our proactive error recovery methods such as graceful degradation, allow us to deliver the reliable service that our users have come to expect. After all, people regularly use *www.google.com* to check if their Internet connection is set up correctly.

Job and Data Organization

Load testing determined that our backend server can handle about 100 queries per second (QPS). Trials performed with a limited set of users lead us to expect a peak load of about 3,470 QPS, so we need at least 35 tasks. However, the following considerations mean that we need at least 37 tasks in the job, or $N + 2$:

- During updates, one task at a time will be unavailable, leaving 36 tasks.
- A machine failure might occur during a task update, leaving only 35 tasks, just enough to serve peak load.[5]

A closer examination of user traffic shows our peak usage is distributed globally: 1,430 QPS from North America, 290 from South America, 1,400 from Europe and Africa, and 350 from Asia and Australia. Instead of locating all backends at one site, we distribute them across the USA, South America, Europe, and Asia. Allowing for $N + 2$ redundancy per region means that we end up with 17 tasks in the USA, 16 in Europe, and 6 in Asia. However, we decide to use 4 tasks (instead of 5) in South America, to lower the overhead of $N + 2$ to $N + 1$. In this case, we're willing to tolerate a small risk of higher latency in exchange for lower hardware costs: if GSLB redirects traffic from one continent to another when our South American datacenter is over capacity, we can save 20% of the resources we'd spend on hardware. In the larger regions, we'll spread tasks across two or three clusters for extra resiliency.

Because the backends need to contact the Bigtable holding the data, we need to also design this storage element strategically. A backend in Asia contacting a Bigtable in the USA adds a significant amount of latency, so we replicate the Bigtable in each region. Bigtable replication helps us in two ways: it provides resilience should a Bigtable server fail, and it lowers data-access latency. While Bigtable only offers eventual consistency, it isn't a major problem because we don't need to update the contents often.

We've introduced a lot of terminology here; while you don't need to remember it all, it's useful for framing many of the other systems we'll refer to later.

---

5 We assume the probability of two simultaneous task failures in our environment is low enough to be negligible. Single points of failure, such as top-of-rack switches or power distribution, may make this assumption invalid in other environments.

PART II
Principles

This section examines the *principles* underlying how SRE teams typically work—the patterns, behaviors, and areas of concern that influence the general domain of SRE operations.

The first chapter in this section, and the most important piece to read if you want to attain the widest-angle picture of what exactly SRE does, and how we reason about it, is Chapter 3, *Embracing Risk*. It looks at SRE through the lens of risk—its assessment, management, and the use of error budgets to provide usefully neutral approaches to service management.

Service level objectives are another foundational conceptual unit for SRE. The industry commonly lumps disparate concepts under the general banner of service level agreements, a tendency that makes it harder to think about these concepts clearly. Chapter 4, *Service Level Objectives*, attempts to disentangle indicators from objectives from agreements, examines how SRE uses each of these terms, and provides some recommendations on how to find useful metrics for your own applications.

Eliminating toil is one of SRE's most important tasks, and is the subject of Chapter 5, *Eliminating Toil*. We define *toil* as mundane, repetitive operational work providing no enduring value, which scales linearly with service growth.

Whether it is at Google or elsewhere, monitoring is an absolutely essential component of doing the right thing in production. If you can't monitor a service, you don't know what's happening, and if you're blind to what's happening, you can't be reliable. Read Chapter 6, *Monitoring Distributed Systems*, for some recommendations for what and how to monitor, and some implementation-agnostic best practices.

In Chapter 7, *The Evolution of Automation at Google*, we examine SRE's approach to automation, and walk through some case studies of how SRE has implemented automation, both successfully and unsuccessfully.

Most companies treat release engineering as an afterthought. However, as you'll learn in Chapter 8, *Release Engineering*, release engineering is not just critical to overall system stability—as most outages result from pushing a change of some kind. It is also the best way to ensure that releases are consistent.

A key principle of any effective software engineering, not only reliability-oriented engineering, simplicity is a quality that, once lost, can be extraordinarily difficult to recapture. Nevertheless, as the old adage goes, a complex system that works necessarily evolved from a simple system that works. Chapter 9, *Simplicity*, goes into this topic in detail.

Further Reading from Google SRE

Increasing product velocity safely is a core principle for any organization. In "Making Push On Green a Reality" [Kle14], published in October 2014, we show that taking humans out of the release process can paradoxically reduce SREs' toil while *increasing* system reliability.

CHAPTER 3

Embracing Risk

Written by Marc Alvidrez
Edited by Kavita Guliani

You might expect Google to try to build 100% reliable services—ones that never fail. It turns out that past a certain point, however, increasing reliability is worse for a service (and its users) rather than better! Extreme reliability comes at a cost: maximizing stability limits how fast new features can be developed and how quickly products can be delivered to users, and dramatically increases their cost, which in turn reduces the numbers of features a team can afford to offer. Further, users typically don't notice the difference between high reliability and extreme reliability in a service, because the user experience is dominated by less reliable components like the cellular network or the device they are working with. Put simply, a user on a 99% reliable smartphone cannot tell the difference between 99.99% and 99.999% service reliability! With this in mind, rather than simply maximizing uptime, Site Reliability Engineering seeks to balance the risk of unavailability with the goals of rapid innovation and efficient service operations, so that users' overall happiness—with features, service, and performance—is optimized.

Managing Risk

Unreliable systems can quickly erode users' confidence, so we want to reduce the chance of system failure. However, experience shows that as we build systems, cost does not increase linearly as reliability increments—an incremental improvement in reliability may cost 100x more than the previous increment. The costliness has two dimensions:

The cost of redundant machine/compute resources
> The cost associated with redundant equipment that, for example, allows us to take systems offline for routine or unforeseen maintenance, or provides space for us to store parity code blocks that provide a minimum data durability guarantee.

The opportunity cost
> The cost borne by an organization when it allocates engineering resources to build systems or features that diminish risk instead of features that are directly visible to or usable by end users. These engineers no longer work on new features and products for end users.

In SRE, we manage service reliability largely by managing risk. We conceptualize risk as a continuum. We give equal importance to figuring out how to engineer greater reliability into Google systems and identifying the appropriate level of tolerance for the services we run. Doing so allows us to perform a cost/benefit analysis to determine, for example, where on the (nonlinear) risk continuum we should place Search, Ads, Gmail, or Photos. Our goal is to explicitly align the risk taken by a given service with the risk the business is willing to bear. We strive to make a service reliable enough, but no *more* reliable than it needs to be. That is, when we set an availability target of 99.99%,we want to exceed it, but not by much: that would waste opportunities to add features to the system, clean up technical debt, or reduce its operational costs. In a sense, we view the availability target as both a minimum and a maximum. The key advantage of this framing is that it unlocks explicit, thoughtful risktaking.

Measuring Service Risk

As standard practice at Google, we are often best served by identifying an objective metric to represent the property of a system we want to optimize. By setting a target, we can assess our current performance and track improvements or degradations over time. For service risk, it is not immediately clear how to reduce all of the potential factors into a single metric. Service failures can have many potential effects, including user dissatisfaction, harm, or loss of trust; direct or indirect revenue loss; brand or reputational impact; and undesirable press coverage. Clearly, some of these factors are very hard to measure. To make this problem tractable and consistent across many types of systems we run, we focus on *unplanned downtime*.

For most services, the most straightforward way of representing risk tolerance is in terms of the acceptable level of unplanned downtime. Unplanned downtime is captured by the desired level of *service availability*, usually expressed in terms of the number of "nines" we would like to provide: 99.9%, 99.99%, or 99.999% availability. Each additional nine corresponds to an order of magnitude improvement toward 100% availability. For serving systems, this metric is traditionally calculated based on the proportion of system uptime (see Equation 3-1).

Equation 3-1. Time-based availability

$$availability = \frac{uptime}{(uptime + downtime)}$$

Using this formula over the period of a year, we can calculate the acceptable number of minutes of downtime to reach a given number of nines of availability. For example, a system with an availability target of 99.99% can be down for up to 52.56 minutes in a year and stay within its availability target; see Appendix A for a table.

At Google, however, a time-based metric for availability is usually not meaningful because we are looking across globally distributed services. Our approach to fault isolation makes it very likely that we are serving at least a subset of traffic for a given service somewhere in the world at any given time (i.e., we are at least partially "up" at all times). Therefore, instead of using metrics around uptime, we define availability in terms of the *request success rate*. Equation 3-2 shows how this yield-based metric is calculated over a rolling window (i.e., proportion of successful requests over a one-day window).

Equation 3-2. Aggregate availability

$$availability = \frac{successful\ requests}{total\ requests}$$

For example, a system that serves 2.5M requests in a day with a daily availability target of 99.99% can serve up to 250 errors and still hit its target for that given day.

In a typical application, not all requests are equal: failing a new user sign-up request is different from failing a request polling for new email in the background. In many cases, however, availability calculated as the request success rate over all requests is a reasonable approximation of unplanned downtime, as viewed from the end-user perspective.

Quantifying unplanned downtime as a request success rate also makes this availability metric more amenable for use in systems that do not typically serve end users directly. Most nonserving systems (e.g., batch, pipeline, storage, and transactional systems) have a well-defined notion of successful and unsuccessful units of work. Indeed, while the systems discussed in this chapter are primarily consumer and infrastructure serving systems, many of the same principles also apply to nonserving systems with minimal modification.

For example, a batch process that extracts, transforms, and inserts the contents of one of our customer databases into a data warehouse to enable further analysis may be set to run periodically. Using a request success rate defined in terms of records successfully and unsuccessfully processed, we can calculate a useful availability metric despite the fact that the batch system does not run constantly.

Most often, we set quarterly availability targets for a service and track our performance against those targets on a weekly, or even daily, basis. This strategy lets us manage the service to a high-level availability objective by looking for, tracking down, and fixing meaningful deviations as they inevitably arise. See Chapter 4 for more details.

Risk Tolerance of Services

What does it mean to identify the risk tolerance of a service? In a formal environment or in the case of safety-critical systems, the risk tolerance of services is typically built directly into the basic product or service definition. At Google, services' risk tolerance tends to be less clearly defined.

To identify the risk tolerance of a service, SREs must work with the product owners to turn a set of business goals into explicit objectives to which we can engineer. In this case, the business goals we're concerned about have a direct impact on the performance and reliability of the service offered. In practice, this translation is easier said than done. While consumer services often have clear product owners, it is unusual for infrastructure services (e.g., storage systems or a general-purpose HTTP caching layer) to have a similar structure of product ownership. We'll discuss the consumer and infrastructure cases in turn.

Identifying the Risk Tolerance of Consumer Services

Our consumer services often have a product team that acts as the business owner for an application. For example, Search, Google Maps, and Google Docs each have their own product managers. These product managers are charged with understanding the users and the business, and for shaping the product for success in the marketplace. When a product team exists, that team is usually the best resource to discuss the reliability requirements for a service. In the absence of a dedicated product team, the engineers building the system often play this role either knowingly or unknowingly.

There are many factors to consider when assessing the risk tolerance of services, such as the following:

- What level of availability is required?
- Do different types of failures have different effects on the service?
- How can we use the service cost to help locate a service on the risk continuum?
- What other service metrics are important to take into account?

Target level of availability

The target level of availability for a given Google service usually depends on the function it provides and how the service is positioned in the marketplace. The following list includes issues to consider:

- What level of service will the users expect?
- Does this service tie directly to revenue (either our revenue, or our customers' revenue)?
- Is this a paid service, or is it free?
- If there are competitors in the marketplace, what level of service do those competitors provide?
- Is this service targeted at consumers, or at enterprises?

Consider the requirements of Google Apps for Work. The majority of its users are enterprise users, some large and some small. These enterprises depend on Google Apps for Work services (e.g., Gmail, Calendar, Drive, Docs) to provide tools that enable their employees to perform their daily work. Stated another way, an outage for a Google Apps for Work service is an outage not only for Google, but also for all the enterprises that critically depend on us. For a typical Google Apps for Work service, we might set an external quarterly availability target of 99.9%, and back this target with a stronger internal availability target and a contract that stipulates penalties if we fail to deliver to the external target.

YouTube provides a contrasting set of considerations. When Google acquired YouTube, we had to decide on the appropriate availability target for the website. In 2006, YouTube was focused on consumers and was in a very different phase of its business lifecycle than Google was at the time. While YouTube already had a great product, it was still changing and growing rapidly. We set a lower availability target for YouTube than for our enterprise products because rapid feature development was correspondingly more important.

Types of failures

The expected shape of failures for a given service is another important consideration. How resilient is our business to service downtime? Which is worse for the service: a constant low rate of failures, or an occasional full-site outage? Both types of failure may result in the same absolute number of errors, but may have vastly different impacts on the business.

An illustrative example of the difference between full and partial outages naturally arises in systems that serve private information. Consider a contact management application, and the difference between intermittent failures that cause profile pictures to fail to render, versus a failure case that results in a user's private contacts being shown to another user. The first case is clearly a poor user experience, and SREs would work to remediate the problem quickly. In the second case, however, the risk of exposing private data could easily undermine basic user trust in a significant way. As a result, taking down the service entirely would be appropriate during the debugging and potential clean-up phase for the second case.

At the other end of services offered by Google, it is sometimes acceptable to have regular outages during maintenance windows. A number of years ago, the Ads Frontend used to be one such service. It is used by advertisers and website publishers to set up, configure, run, and monitor their advertising campaigns. Because most of this work takes place during normal business hours, we determined that occasional, regular, scheduled outages in the form of maintenance windows would be acceptable, and we counted these scheduled outages as planned downtime, not unplanned downtime.

Cost

Cost is often the key factor in determining the appropriate availability target for a service. Ads is in a particularly good position to make this trade-off because request successes and failures can be directly translated into revenue gained or lost. In determining the availability target for each service, we ask questions such as:

- If we were to build and operate these systems at one more nine of availability, what would our incremental increase in revenue be?
- Does this additional revenue offset the cost of reaching that level of reliability?

To make this trade-off equation more concrete, consider the following cost/benefit for an example service where each request has equal value:

> Proposed improvement in availability target: 99.9% → 99.99%
> Proposed increase in availability: 0.09%
> Service revenue: $1M
> Value of improved availability: $1M * 0.0009 = $900

In this case, if the cost of improving availability by one nine is less than $900, it is worth the investment. If the cost is greater than $900, the costs will exceed the projected increase in revenue.

It may be harder to set these targets when we do not have a simple translation function between reliability and revenue. One useful strategy may be to consider the background error rate of ISPs on the Internet. If failures are being measured from the end-user perspective and it is possible to drive the error rate for the service below the background error rate, those errors will fall within the noise for a given user's Internet connection. While there are significant differences between ISPs and protocols (e.g.,

TCP versus UDP, IPv4 versus IPv6), we've measured the typical background error rate for ISPs as falling between 0.01% and 1%.

Other service metrics

Examining the risk tolerance of services in relation to metrics besides availability is often fruitful. Understanding which metrics are important and which metrics aren't important provides us with degrees of freedom when attempting to take thoughtful risks.

Service latency for our Ads systems provides an illustrative example. When Google first launched Web Search, one of the service's key distinguishing features was speed. When we introduced AdWords, which displays advertisements next to search results, a key requirement of the system was that the ads should not slow down the search experience. This requirement has driven the engineering goals in each generation of AdWords systems and is treated as an invariant.

AdSense, Google's ads system that serves contextual ads in response to requests from JavaScript code that publishers insert into their websites, has a very different latency goal. The latency goal for AdSense is to avoid slowing down the rendering of the third-party page when inserting contextual ads. The specific latency target, then, is dependent on the speed at which a given publisher's page renders. This means that AdSense ads can generally be served hundreds of milliseconds slower than AdWords ads.

This looser serving latency requirement has allowed us to make many smart trade-offs in provisioning (i.e., determining the quantity and locations of serving resources we use), which save us substantial cost over naive provisioning. In other words, given the relative insensitivity of the AdSense service to moderate changes in latency performance, we are able to consolidate serving into fewer geographical locations, reducing our operational overhead.

Identifying the Risk Tolerance of Infrastructure Services

The requirements for building and running infrastructure components differ from the requirements for consumer products in a number of ways. A fundamental difference is that, by definition, infrastructure components have multiple clients, often with varying needs.

Target level of availability

Consider Bigtable [Cha06], a massive-scale distributed storage system for structured data. Some consumer services serve data directly from Bigtable in the path of a user request. Such services need low latency and high reliability. Other teams use Bigtable as a repository for data that they use to perform offline analysis (e.g., MapReduce) on a regular basis. These teams tend to be more concerned about throughput than reliability. Risk tolerance for these two use cases is quite distinct.

One approach to meeting the needs of both use cases is to engineer all infrastructure services to be ultra-reliable. Given the fact that these infrastructure services also tend to aggregate huge amounts of resources, such an approach is usually far too expensive in practice. To understand the different needs of the different types of users, you can look at the desired state of the request queue for each type of Bigtable user.

Types of failures

The low-latency user wants Bigtable's request queues to be (almost always) empty so that the system can process each outstanding request immediately upon arrival. (Indeed, inefficient queuing is often a cause of high tail latency.) The user concerned with offline analysis is more interested in system throughput, so that user wants request queues to never be empty. To optimize for throughput, the Bigtable system should never need to idle while waiting for its next request.

As you can see, success and failure are antithetical for these sets of users. Success for the low-latency user is failure for the user concerned with offline analysis.

Cost

One way to satisfy these competing constraints in a cost-effective manner is to partition the infrastructure and offer it at multiple independent levels of service. In the Bigtable example, we can build two types of clusters: low-latency clusters and throughput clusters. The low-latency clusters are designed to be operated and used by services that need low latency and high reliability. To ensure short queue lengths and satisfy more stringent client isolation requirements, the Bigtable system can be provisioned with a substantial amount of slack capacity for reduced contention and increased redundancy. The throughput clusters, on the other hand, can be provisioned to run very hot and with less redundancy, optimizing throughput over latency. In practice, we are able to satisfy these relaxed needs at a much lower cost, perhaps as little as 10–50% of the cost of a low-latency cluster. Given Bigtable's massive scale, this cost savings becomes significant very quickly.

The key strategy with regards to infrastructure is to deliver services with explicitly delineated levels of service, thus enabling the clients to make the right risk and cost trade-offs when building their systems. With explicitly delineated levels of service, the infrastructure providers can effectively externalize the difference in the cost it takes to provide service at a given level to clients. Exposing cost in this way motivates the clients to choose the level of service with the lowest cost that still meets their needs. For example, Google+ can decide to put data critical to enforcing user privacy in a high-availability, globally consistent datastore (e.g., a globally replicated SQL-like system like Spanner [Cor12]), while putting optional data (data that isn't critical, but that enhances the user experience) in a cheaper, less reliable, less fresh, and eventually consistent datastore (e.g., a NoSQL store with best-effort replication like Bigtable).

Note that we can run multiple classes of services using identical hardware and software. We can provide vastly different service guarantees by adjusting a variety of service characteristics, such as the quantities of resources, the degree of redundancy, the geographical provisioning constraints, and, critically, the infrastructure software configuration.

Example: Frontend infrastructure

To demonstrate that these risk-tolerance assessment principles do not just apply to storage infrastructure, let's look at another large class of service: Google's frontend infrastructure. The frontend infrastructure consists of reverse proxy and load balancing systems running close to the edge of our network. These are the systems that, among other things, serve as one endpoint of the connections from end users (e.g., terminate TCP from the user's browser). Given their critical role, we engineer these systems to deliver an extremely high level of reliability. While consumer services can often limit the visibility of unreliability in backends, these infrastructure systems are not so lucky. If a request never makes it to the application service frontend server, it is lost.

We've explored the ways to identify the risk tolerance of both consumer and infrastructure services. Now, we'll discuss using that tolerance level to manage unreliability via error budgets.

Motivation for Error Budgets[1]

Written by Mark Roth
Edited by Carmela Quinito

Other chapters in this book discuss how tensions can arise between product development teams and SRE teams, given that they are generally evaluated on different metrics. Product development performance is largely evaluated on product velocity, which creates an incentive to push new code as quickly as possible. Meanwhile, SRE performance is (unsurprisingly) evaluated based upon reliability of a service, which implies an incentive to push back against a high rate of change. Information asymmetry between the two teams further amplifies this inherent tension. The product developers have more visibility into the time and effort involved in writing and releasing their code, while the SREs have more visibility into the service's reliability (and the state of production in general).

---

1 An early version of this section appeared as an article in *;login:* (August 2015, vol. 40, no. 4).

These tensions often reflect themselves in different opinions about the level of effort that should be put into engineering practices. The following list presents some typical tensions:

Software fault tolerance
How hardened do we make the software to unexpected events? Too little, and we have a brittle, unusable product. Too much, and we have a product no one wants to use (but that runs very stably).

Testing
Again, not enough testing and you have embarrassing outages, privacy data leaks, or a number of other press-worthy events. Too much testing, and you might lose your market.

Push frequency
Every push is risky. How much should we work on reducing that risk, versus doing other work?

Canary duration and size
It's a best practice to test a new release on some small subset of a typical workload, a practice often called *canarying*. How long do we wait, and how big is the canary?

Usually, preexisting teams have worked out some kind of informal balance between them as to where the risk/effort boundary lies. Unfortunately, one can rarely prove that this balance is optimal, rather than just a function of the negotiating skills of the engineers involved. Nor should such decisions be driven by politics, fear, or hope. (Indeed, Google SRE's unofficial motto is "Hope is not a strategy.") Instead, our goal is to define an objective metric, agreed upon by both sides, that can be used to guide the negotiations in a reproducible way. The more data-based the decision can be, the better.

Forming Your Error Budget

In order to base these decisions on objective data, the two teams jointly define a quarterly error budget based on the service's service level objective, or SLO (see Chapter 4). The error budget provides a clear, objective metric that determines how unreliable the service is allowed to be within a single quarter. This metric removes the politics from negotiations between the SREs and the product developers when deciding how much risk to allow.

Our practice is then as follows:

- Product Management defines an SLO, which sets an expectation of how much uptime the service should have per quarter.

- The actual uptime is measured by a neutral third party: our monitoring system.
- The difference between these two numbers is the "budget" of how much "unreliability" is remaining for the quarter.
- As long as the uptime measured is above the SLO—in other words, as long as there is error budget remaining—new releases can be pushed.

For example, imagine that a service's SLO is to successfully serve 99.999% of all queries per quarter. This means that the service's error budget is a failure rate of 0.001% for a given quarter. If a problem causes us to fail 0.0002% of the expected queries for the quarter, the problem spends 20% of the service's quarterly error budget.

Benefits

The main benefit of an error budget is that it provides a common incentive that allows both product development and SRE to focus on finding the right balance between innovation and reliability.

Many products use this control loop to manage release velocity: as long as the system's SLOs are met, releases can continue. If SLO violations occur frequently enough to expend the error budget, releases are temporarily halted while additional resources are invested in system testing and development to make the system more resilient, improve its performance, and so on. More subtle and effective approaches are available than this simple on/off technique:[2] for instance, slowing down releases or rolling them back when the SLO-violation error budget is close to being used up.

For example, if product development wants to skimp on testing or increase push velocity and SRE is resistant, the error budget guides the decision. When the budget is large, the product developers can take more risks. When the budget is nearly drained, the product developers themselves will push for more testing or slower push velocity, as they don't want to risk using up the budget and stall their launch. In effect, the product development team becomes self-policing. They know the budget and can manage their own risk. (Of course, this outcome relies on an SRE team having the authority to actually stop launches if the SLO is broken.)

What happens if a network outage or datacenter failure reduces the measured SLO? Such events also eat into the error budget. As a result, the number of new pushes may be reduced for the remainder of the quarter. The entire team supports this reduction because everyone shares the responsibility for uptime.

The budget also helps to highlight some of the costs of overly high reliability targets, in terms of both inflexibility and slow innovation. If the team is having trouble

---

2 Known as "bang/bang" control—see *https://en.wikipedia.org/wiki/Bang–bang_control*.

launching new features, they may elect to loosen the SLO (thus increasing the error budget) in order to increase innovation.

Key Insights

- Managing service reliability is largely about managing risk, and managing risk can be costly.

- 100% is probably never the right reliability target: not only is it impossible to achieve, it's typically more reliability than a service's users want or notice. Match the profile of the service to the risk the business is willing to take.

- An error budget aligns incentives and emphasizes joint ownership between SRE and product development. Error budgets make it easier to decide the rate of releases and to effectively defuse discussions about outages with stakeholders, and allows multiple teams to reach the same conclusion about production risk without rancor.

CHAPTER 4

Service Level Objectives

Written by Chris Jones, John Wilkes, and Niall Murphy
with Cody Smith
Edited by Betsy Beyer

It's impossible to manage a service correctly, let alone well, without understanding which behaviors really matter for that service and how to measure and evaluate those behaviors. To this end, we would like to define and deliver a given *level of service* to our users, whether they use an internal API or a public product.

We use intuition, experience, and an understanding of what users want to define *service level indicators* (SLIs), *objectives* (SLOs), and *agreements* (SLAs). These measurements describe basic properties of metrics that matter, what values we want those metrics to have, and how we'll react if we can't provide the expected service. Ultimately, choosing appropriate metrics helps to drive the right action if something goes wrong, and also gives an SRE team confidence that a service is healthy.

This chapter describes the framework we use to wrestle with the problems of metric modeling, metric selection, and metric analysis. Much of this explanation would be quite abstract without an example, so we'll use the Shakespeare service outlined in "Shakespeare: A Sample Service" on page 20 to illustrate our main points.

Service Level Terminology

Many readers are likely familiar with the concept of an SLA, but the terms *SLI* and *SLO* are also worth careful definition, because in common use, the term *SLA* is overloaded and has taken on a number of meanings depending on context. We prefer to separate those meanings for clarity.

Indicators

An SLI is a service level *indicator*—a carefully defined quantitative measure of some aspect of the level of service that is provided.

Most services consider *request latency*—how long it takes to return a response to a request—as a key SLI. Other common SLIs include the *error rate*, often expressed as a fraction of all requests received, and *system throughput*, typically measured in requests per second. The measurements are often aggregated: i.e., raw data is collected over a measurement window and then turned into a rate, average, or percentile.

Ideally, the SLI directly measures a service level of interest, but sometimes only a proxy is available because the desired measure may be hard to obtain or interpret. For example, client-side latency is often the more user-relevant metric, but it might only be possible to measure latency at the server.

Another kind of SLI important to SREs is *availability*, or the fraction of the time that a service is usable. It is often defined in terms of the fraction of well-formed requests that succeed, sometimes called *yield*. (*Durability*—the likelihood that data will be retained over a long period of time—is equally important for data storage systems.) Although 100% availability is impossible, near-100% availability is often readily achievable, and the industry commonly expresses high-availability values in terms of the number of "nines" in the availability percentage. For example, availabilities of 99% and 99.999% can be referred to as "2 nines" and "5 nines" availability, respectively, and the current published target for Google Compute Engine availability is "three and a half nines"—99.95% availability.

Objectives

An SLO is a *service level objective*: a target value or range of values for a service level that is measured by an SLI. A natural structure for SLOs is thus *SLI ≤ target* or *lower bound ≤ SLI ≤ upper bound*. For example, we might decide that we will return Shakespeare search results "quickly," adopting an SLO that our average search request latency should be less than 100 milliseconds.

Choosing an appropriate SLO is complex. To begin with, you don't always get to choose its value! For incoming HTTP requests from the outside world to your service, the queries per second (QPS) metric is essentially determined by the desires of your users, and you can't really set an SLO for that.

On the other hand, you *can* say that you want the average latency per request to be under 100 milliseconds, and setting such a goal could in turn motivate you to write your frontend with low-latency behaviors of various kinds or to buy certain kinds of low-latency equipment. (100 milliseconds is obviously an arbitrary value, but in general lower latency numbers are good. There are excellent reasons to believe that fast is better than slow, and that user-experienced latency above certain values actually drives people away— see "Speed Matters" [Bru09] for more details.)

Again, this is more subtle than it might at first appear, in that those two SLIs—QPS and latency—might be connected behind the scenes: higher QPS often leads to larger latencies, and it's common for services to have a performance cliff beyond some load threshold.

Choosing and publishing SLOs to users sets expectations about how a service will perform. This strategy can reduce unfounded complaints to service owners about, for example, the service being slow. Without an explicit SLO, users often develop their own beliefs about desired performance, which may be unrelated to the beliefs held by the people designing and operating the service. This dynamic can lead to both over-reliance on the service, when users incorrectly believe that a service will be more available than it actually is (as happened with Chubby: see "The Global Chubby Planned Outage"), and under-reliance, when prospective users believe a system is flakier and less reliable than it actually is.

The Global Chubby Planned Outage

Written by Marc Alvidrez

Chubby [Bur06] is Google's lock service for loosely coupled distributed systems. In the global case, we distribute Chubby instances such that each replica is in a different geographical region. Over time, we found that the failures of the global instance of Chubby consistently generated service outages, many of which were visible to end users. As it turns out, true global Chubby outages are so infrequent that service owners began to add dependencies to Chubby assuming that it would never go down. Its high reliability provided a false sense of security because the services could not function appropriately when Chubby was unavailable, however rarely that occurred.

The solution to this Chubby scenario is interesting: SRE makes sure that global Chubby meets, but does not significantly exceed, its service level objective. In any given quarter, if a true failure has not dropped availability below the target, a controlled outage will be synthesized by intentionally taking down the system. In this way, we are able to flush out unreasonable dependencies on Chubby shortly after they are added. Doing so forces service owners to reckon with the reality of distributed systems sooner rather than later.

Agreements

Finally, SLAs are service level *agreements*: an explicit or implicit contract with your users that includes consequences of meeting (or missing) the SLOs they contain. The consequences are most easily recognized when they are financial—a rebate or a penalty—but they can take other forms. An easy way to tell the difference between an SLO and an SLA is to ask "what happens if the SLOs aren't met?": if there is no explicit consequence, then you are almost certainly looking at an SLO.[1]

SRE doesn't typically get involved in constructing SLAs, because SLAs are closely tied to business and product decisions. SRE does, however, get involved in helping to avoid triggering the consequences of missed SLOs. They can also help to define the SLIs: there obviously needs to be an objective way to measure the SLOs in the agreement, or disagreements will arise.

Google Search is an example of an important service that doesn't have an SLA for the public: we want everyone to use Search as fluidly and efficiently as possible, but we haven't signed a contract with the whole world. Even so, there are still consequences if Search isn't available—unavailability results in a hit to our reputation, as well as a drop in advertising revenue. Many other Google services, such as Google for Work, do have explicit SLAs with their users. Whether or not a particular service has an SLA, it's valuable to define SLIs and SLOs and use them to manage the service.

So much for the theory—now for the experience.

Indicators in Practice

Given that we've made the case for *why* choosing appropriate metrics to measure your service is important, how do you go about identifying what metrics are meaningful to your service or system?

What Do You and Your Users Care About?

You shouldn't use every metric you can track in your monitoring system as an SLI; an understanding of what your users want from the system will inform the judicious selection of a few indicators. Choosing too many indicators makes it hard to pay the right level of attention to the indicators that matter, while choosing too few may leave significant behaviors of your system unexamined. We typically find that a handful of representative indicators are enough to evaluate and reason about a system's health.

---

[1] Most people really mean SLO when they say "SLA." One giveaway: if somebody talks about an "SLA violation," they are almost always talking about a missed SLO. A real SLA violation might trigger a court case for breach of contract.

Services tend to fall into a few broad categories in terms of the SLIs they find relevant:

- *User-facing serving systems*, such as the Shakespeare search frontends, generally care about *availability, latency,* and *throughput.* In other words: Could we respond to the request? How long did it take to respond? How many requests could be handled?

- *Storage systems* often emphasize *latency, availability,* and *durability.* In other words: How long does it take to read or write data? Can we access the data on demand? Is the data still there when we need it? See Chapter 26 for an extended discussion of these issues.

- *Big data systems*, such as data processing pipelines, tend to care about *throughput* and *end-to-end latency*. In other words: How much data is being processed? How long does it take the data to progress from ingestion to completion? (Some pipelines may also have targets for latency on individual processing stages.)

- All systems should care about *correctness*: was the right answer returned, the right data retrieved, the right analysis done? Correctness is important to track as an indicator of system health, even though it's often a property of the data in the system rather than the infrastructure *per se*, and so usually not an SRE responsibility to meet.

Collecting Indicators

Many indicator metrics are most naturally gathered on the server side, using a monitoring system such as Borgmon (see Chapter 10) or Prometheus, or with periodic log analysis—for instance, HTTP 500 responses as a fraction of all requests. However, some systems should be instrumented with *client*-side collection, because not measuring behavior at the client can miss a range of problems that affect users but don't affect server-side metrics. For example, concentrating on the response latency of the Shakespeare search backend might miss poor user latency due to problems with the page's JavaScript: in this case, measuring how long it takes for a page to become usable in the browser is a better proxy for what the user actually experiences.

Aggregation

For simplicity and usability, we often aggregate raw measurements. This needs to be done carefully.

Some metrics are seemingly straightforward, like the number of requests *per second* served, but even this apparently straightforward measurement implicitly aggregates data over the measurement window. Is the measurement obtained once a second, or by averaging requests over a minute? The latter may hide much higher instantaneous request rates in bursts that last for only a few seconds. Consider a system that serves

200 requests/s in even-numbered seconds, and 0 in the others. It has the same average load as one that serves a constant 100 requests/s, but has an *instantaneous* load that is twice as large as the *average* one. Similarly, averaging request latencies may seem attractive, but obscures an important detail: it's entirely possible for most of the requests to be fast, but for a long tail of requests to be much, much slower.

Most metrics are better thought of as *distributions* rather than averages. For example, for a latency SLI, some requests will be serviced quickly, while others will invariably take longer—sometimes much longer. A simple average can obscure these tail latencies, as well as changes in them. Figure 4-1 provides an example: although a typical request is served in about 50 ms, 5% of requests are 20 times slower! Monitoring and alerting based only on the average latency would show no change in behavior over the course of the day, when there are in fact significant changes in the tail latency (the topmost line).

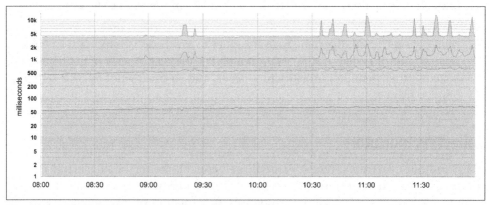

Figure 4-1. 50th, 85th, 95th, and 99th percentile latencies for a system. Note that the Y-axis has a logarithmic scale.

Using percentiles for indicators allows you to consider the shape of the distribution and its differing attributes: a high-order percentile, such as the 99th or 99.9th, shows you a plausible worst-case value, while using the 50th percentile (also known as the median) emphasizes the typical case. The higher the variance in response times, the more the typical user experience is affected by long-tail behavior, an effect exacerbated at high load by queuing effects. User studies have shown that people typically prefer a slightly slower system to one with high variance in response time, so some SRE teams focus only on high percentile values, on the grounds that if the 99.9th percentile behavior is good, then the typical experience is certainly going to be.

A Note on Statistical Fallacies

We generally prefer to work with percentiles rather than the mean (arithmetic average) of a set of values. Doing so makes it possible to consider the long tail of data points, which often have significantly different (and more interesting) characteristics than the average. Because of the artificial nature of computing systems, data points are often skewed—for instance, no request can have a response in less than 0 ms, and a timeout at 1,000 ms means that there can be no successful responses with values greater than the timeout. As a result, we cannot assume that the mean and the median are the same—or even close to each other!

We try not to assume that our data is normally distributed without verifying it first, in case some standard intuitions and approximations don't hold. For example, if the distribution is not what's expected, a process that takes action when it sees outliers (e.g., restarting a server with high request latencies) may do this too often, or not often enough.

Standardize Indicators

We recommend that you standardize on common definitions for SLIs so that you don't have to reason about them from first principles each time. Any feature that conforms to the standard definition templates can be omitted from the specification of an individual SLI, e.g.:

- Aggregation intervals: "Averaged over 1 minute"
- Aggregation regions: "All the tasks in a cluster"
- How frequently measurements are made: "Every 10 seconds"
- Which requests are included: "HTTP GETs from black-box monitoring jobs"
- How the data is acquired: "Through our monitoring, measured at the server"
- Data-access latency: "Time to last byte"

To save effort, build a set of reusable SLI templates for each common metric; these also make it simpler for everyone to understand what a specific SLI means.

Objectives in Practice

Start by thinking about (or finding out!) what your users care about, not what you can measure. Often, what your users care about is difficult or impossible to measure, so you'll end up approximating users' needs in some way. However, if you simply start with what's easy to measure, you'll end up with less useful SLOs. As a result, we've sometimes found that working from desired objectives backward to specific indicators works better than choosing indicators and then coming up with targets.

Defining Objectives

For maximum clarity, SLOs should specify how they're measured and the conditions under which they're valid. For instance, we might say the following (the second line is the same as the first, but relies on the SLI defaults of the previous section to remove redundancy):

- 99% (averaged over 1 minute) of Get RPC calls will complete in less than 100 ms (measured across all the backend servers).
- 99% of Get RPC calls will complete in less than 100 ms.

If the shape of the performance curves are important, then you can specify multiple SLO targets:

- 90% of Get RPC calls will complete in less than 1 ms.
- 99% of Get RPC calls will complete in less than 10 ms.
- 99.9% of Get RPC calls will complete in less than 100 ms.

If you have users with heterogeneous workloads such as a bulk processing pipeline that cares about throughput and an interactive client that cares about latency, it may be appropriate to define separate objectives for each class of workload:

- 95% of throughput clients' Set RPC calls will complete in < 1 s.
- 99% of latency clients' Set RPC calls with payloads < 1 kB will complete in < 10 ms.

It's both unrealistic and undesirable to insist that SLOs will be met 100% of the time: doing so can reduce the rate of innovation and deployment, require expensive, overly conservative solutions, or both. Instead, it is better to allow an error budget—a rate at which the SLOs can be missed—and track that on a daily or weekly basis. Upper management will probably want a monthly or quarterly assessment, too. (An error budget is just an SLO for meeting other SLOs!)

The rate at which SLOs are missed is a useful indicator for the user-perceived health of the service. It is helpful to track SLOs (and SLO violations) on a daily or weekly basis to see trends and get early warning of potential problems before they happen. Upper management will probably want a monthly or quarterly assessment, too.

The SLO violation rate can be compared against the error budget (see "Motivation for Error Budgets" on page 33), with the gap used as an input to the process that decides when to roll out new releases.

Choosing Targets

Choosing targets (SLOs) is not a purely technical activity because of the product and business implications, which should be reflected in both the SLIs and SLOs (and maybe SLAs) that are selected. Similarly, it may be necessary to trade off certain product attributes against others within the constraints posed by staffing, time to market, hardware availability, and funding. While SRE should be part of this conversation, and advise on the risks and viability of different options, we've learned a few lessons that can help make this a more productive discussion:

Don't pick a target based on current performance
> While understanding the merits and limits of a system is essential, adopting values without reflection may lock you into supporting a system that requires heroic efforts to meet its targets, and that cannot be improved without significant redesign.

Keep it simple
> Complicated aggregations in SLIs can obscure changes to system performance, and are also harder to reason about.

Avoid absolutes
> While it's tempting to ask for a system that can scale its load "infinitely" without any latency increase and that is "always" available, this requirement is unrealistic. Even a system that approaches such ideals will probably take a long time to design and build, and will be expensive to operate—and probably turn out to be unnecessarily better than what users would be happy (or even delighted) to have.

Have as few SLOs as possible
> Choose just enough SLOs to provide good coverage of your system's attributes. Defend the SLOs you pick: if you can't ever win a conversation about priorities by quoting a particular SLO, it's probably not worth having that SLO.[2] However, not all product attributes are amenable to SLOs: it's hard to specify "user delight" with an SLO.

Perfection can wait
> You can always refine SLO definitions and targets over time as you learn about a system's behavior. It's better to start with a loose target that you tighten than to

---

2 If you can't ever win a conversation about SLOs, it's probably not worth having an SRE team for the product.

choose an overly strict target that has to be relaxed when you discover it's unattainable.

SLOs can—and should—be a major driver in prioritizing work for SREs and product developers, because they reflect what users care about. A good SLO is a helpful, legitimate forcing function for a development team. But a poorly thought-out SLO can result in wasted work if a team uses heroic efforts to meet an overly aggressive SLO, or a bad product if the SLO is too lax. SLOs are a massive lever: use them wisely.

Control Measures

SLIs and SLOs are crucial elements in the control loops used to manage systems:

1. Monitor and measure the system's SLIs.
2. Compare the SLIs to the SLOs, and decide whether or not action is needed.
3. If action is needed, figure out *what* needs to happen in order to meet the target.
4. Take that action.

For example, if step 2 shows that request latency is increasing, and will miss the SLO in a few hours unless something is done, step 3 might include testing the hypothesis that the servers are CPU-bound, and deciding to add more of them to spread the load. Without the SLO, you wouldn't know whether (or when) to take action.

SLOs Set Expectations

Publishing SLOs sets expectations for system behavior. Users (and potential users) often want to know what they can expect from a service in order to understand whether it's appropriate for their use case. For instance, a team wanting to build a photo-sharing website might want to avoid using a service that promises very strong durability and low cost in exchange for slightly lower availability, though the same service might be a perfect fit for an archival records management system.

In order to set realistic expectations for your users, you might consider using one or both of the following tactics:

Keep a safety margin
Using a tighter internal SLO than the SLO advertised to users gives you room to respond to chronic problems before they become visible externally. An SLO buffer also makes it possible to accommodate reimplementations that trade performance for other attributes, such as cost or ease of maintenance, without having to disappoint users.

Don't overachieve

Users build on the reality of what you offer, rather than what you say you'll supply, particularly for infrastructure services. If your service's actual performance is much better than its stated SLO, users will come to rely on its current performance. You can avoid over-dependence by deliberately taking the system offline occasionally (Google's Chubby service introduced planned outages in response to being overly available),[3] throttling some requests, or designing the system so that it isn't faster under light loads.

Understanding how well a system is meeting its expectations helps decide whether to invest in making the system faster, more available, and more resilient. Alternatively, if the service is doing fine, perhaps staff time should be spent on other priorities, such as paying off technical debt, adding new features, or introducing other products.

Agreements in Practice

Crafting an SLA requires business and legal teams to pick appropriate consequences and penalties for a breach. SRE's role is to help them understand the likelihood and difficulty of meeting the SLOs contained in the SLA. Much of the advice on SLO construction is also applicable for SLAs. It is wise to be conservative in what you advertise to users, as the broader the constituency, the harder it is to change or delete SLAs that prove to be unwise or difficult to work with.

---

3 Failure injection [Ben12] serves a different purpose, but can also help set expectations.

CHAPTER 5

Eliminating Toil

Written by Vivek Rau
Edited by Betsy Beyer

If a human operator needs to touch your system during normal operations, you have a bug.
The definition of normal changes as your systems grow.
—Carla Geisser, Google SRE

In SRE, we want to spend time on long-term engineering project work instead of operational work. Because the term *operational work* may be misinterpreted, we use a specific word: *toil*.

Toil Defined

Toil is not just "work I don't like to do." It's also not simply equivalent to administrative chores or grungy work. Preferences as to what types of work are satisfying and enjoyable vary from person to person, and some people even enjoy manual, repetitive work. There are also administrative chores that have to get done, but should not be categorized as toil: this is *overhead*. Overhead is often work not directly tied to running a production service, and includes tasks like team meetings, setting and grading goals,[1] snippets,[2] and HR paperwork. Grungy work can sometimes have long-term value, and in that case, it's not toil, either. Cleaning up the entire alerting configuration for your service and removing clutter may be grungy, but it's not toil.

So what *is* toil? Toil is the kind of work tied to running a production service that tends to be manual, repetitive, automatable, tactical, devoid of enduring value, and

---

1 We use the Objectives and Key Results system, pioneered by Andy Grove at Intel; see [Kla12].

2 Googlers record short free-form summaries, or "snippets," of what we've worked on each week.

that scales linearly as a service grows. Not every task deemed toil has all these attributes, but the more closely work matches one or more of the following descriptions, the more likely it is to be toil:

Manual

> This includes work such as manually running a script that automates some task. Running a script may be quicker than manually executing each step in the script, but the *hands-on* time a human spends running that script (not the elapsed time) is still toil time.

Repetitive

> If you're performing a task for the first time ever, or even the second time, this work is not toil. Toil is work you do over and over. If you're solving a novel problem or inventing a new solution, this work is not toil.

Automatable

> If a machine could accomplish the task just as well as a human, or the need for the task could be designed away, that task is toil. If human judgment is essential for the task, there's a good chance it's not toil.[3]

Tactical

> Toil is interrupt-driven and reactive, rather than strategy-driven and proactive. Handling pager alerts is toil. We may never be able to eliminate this type of work completely, but we have to continually work toward minimizing it.

No enduring value

> If your service remains in the same state after you have finished a task, the task was probably toil. If the task produced a permanent improvement in your service, it probably wasn't toil, even if some amount of grunt work—such as digging into legacy code and configurations and straightening them out—was involved.

$O(n)$ with service growth

> If the work involved in a task scales up linearly with service size, traffic volume, or user count, that task is probably toil. An ideally managed and designed service can grow by at least one order of magnitude with zero additional work, other than some one-time efforts to add resources.

---

3 We have to be careful about saying a task is "not toil because it needs human judgment." We need to think carefully about whether the nature of the task intrinsically requires human judgment and cannot be addressed by better design. For example, one could build (and some have built) a service that alerts its SREs several times a day, where each alert requires a complex response involving plenty of human judgment. Such a service is poorly designed, with unnecessary complexity. The system needs to be simplified and rebuilt to either eliminate the underlying failure conditions or deal with these conditions automatically. Until the redesign and reimplementation are finished, and the improved service is rolled out, the work of applying human judgment to respond to each alert is definitely toil.

Why Less Toil Is Better

Our SRE organization has an advertised goal of keeping operational work (i.e., toil) below 50% of each SRE's time. At least 50% of each SRE's time should be spent on engineering project work that will either reduce future toil or add service features. Feature development typically focuses on improving reliability, performance, or utilization, which often reduces toil as a second-order effect.

We share this 50% goal because toil tends to expand if left unchecked and can quickly fill 100% of everyone's time. The work of reducing toil and scaling up services is the "Engineering" in Site Reliability Engineering. Engineering work is what enables the SRE organization to scale up sublinearly with service size and to manage services more efficiently than either a pure Dev team or a pure Ops team.

Furthermore, when we hire new SREs, we promise them that SRE is not a typical Ops organization, quoting the 50% rule just mentioned. We need to keep that promise by not allowing the SRE organization or any subteam within it to devolve into an Ops team.

Calculating Toil

If we seek to cap the time an SRE spends on toil to 50%, how is that time spent?

There's a floor on the amount of toil any SRE has to handle if they are on-call. A typical SRE has one week of primary on-call and one week of secondary on-call in each cycle (for discussion of primary versus secondary on-call shifts, see Chapter 11). It follows that in a 6-person rotation, at least 2 of every 6 weeks are dedicated to on-call shifts and interrupt handling, which means the lower bound on potential toil is 2/6 = 33% of an SRE's time. In an 8-person rotation, the lower bound is 2/8 = 25%.

Consistent with this data, SREs report that their top source of toil is interrupts (that is, non-urgent service-related messages and emails). The next leading source is on-call (urgent) response, followed by releases and pushes. Even though our release and push processes are usually handled with a fair amount of automation, there's still plenty of room for improvement in this area.

Quarterly surveys of Google's SREs show that the average time spent toiling is about 33%, so we do much better than our overall target of 50%. However, the average doesn't capture outliers: some SREs claim 0% toil (pure development projects with no on-call work) and others claim 80% toil. When individual SREs report excessive toil, it often indicates a need for managers to spread the toil load more evenly across the team and to encourage those SREs to find satisfying engineering projects.

What Qualifies as Engineering?

Engineering work is novel and intrinsically requires human judgment. It produces a permanent improvement in your service, and is guided by a strategy. It is frequently creative and innovative, taking a design-driven approach to solving a problem—the more generalized, the better. Engineering work helps your team or the SRE organization handle a larger service, or more services, with the same level of staffing.

Typical SRE activities fall into the following approximate categories:

Software engineering
> Involves writing or modifying code, in addition to any associated design and documentation work. Examples include writing automation scripts, creating tools or frameworks, adding service features for scalability and reliability, or modifying infrastructure code to make it more robust.

Systems engineering
> Involves configuring production systems, modifying configurations, or documenting systems in a way that produces lasting improvements from a one-time effort. Examples include monitoring setup and updates, load balancing configuration, server configuration, tuning of OS parameters, and load balancer setup. Systems engineering also includes consulting on architecture, design, and productionization for developer teams.

Toil
> Work directly tied to running a service that is repetitive, manual, etc.

Overhead
> Administrative work not tied directly to running a service. Examples include hiring, HR paperwork, team/company meetings, bug queue hygiene, snippets, peer reviews and self-assessments, and training courses.

Every SRE needs to spend at least 50% of their time on engineering work, when averaged over a few quarters or a year. Toil tends to be spiky, so a steady 50% of time spent on engineering may not be realistic for some SRE teams, and they may dip below that target in some quarters. But if the fraction of time spent on projects averages significantly below 50% over the long haul, the affected team needs to step back and figure out what's wrong.

Is Toil Always Bad?

Toil doesn't make everyone unhappy all the time, especially in small amounts. Predictable and repetitive tasks can be quite calming. They produce a sense of accomplishment and quick wins. They can be low-risk and low-stress activities. Some people gravitate toward tasks involving toil and may even enjoy that type of work.

Toil isn't always and invariably bad, and everyone needs to be absolutely clear that some amount of toil is unavoidable in the SRE role, and indeed in almost any engineering role. It's fine in small doses, and if you're happy with those small doses, toil is not a problem. Toil becomes toxic when experienced in large quantities. If you're burdened with too much toil, you should be very concerned and complain loudly. Among the many reasons why too much toil is bad, consider the following:

Career stagnation
> Your career progress will slow down or grind to a halt if you spend too little time on projects. Google rewards grungy work when it's inevitable and has a big positive impact, but you can't make a career out of grunge.

Low morale
> People have different limits for how much toil they can tolerate, but everyone has a limit. Too much toil leads to burnout, boredom, and discontent.

Additionally, spending too much time on toil at the expense of time spent engineering hurts an SRE organization in the following ways:

Creates confusion
> We work hard to ensure that everyone who works in or with the SRE organization understands that we are an engineering organization. Individuals or teams within SRE that engage in too much toil undermine the clarity of that communication and confuse people about our role.

Slows progress
> Excessive toil makes a team less productive. A product's feature velocity will slow if the SRE team is too busy with manual work and firefighting to roll out new features promptly.

Sets precedent
> If you're too willing to take on toil, your Dev counterparts will have incentives to load you down with even more toil, sometimes shifting operational tasks that should rightfully be performed by Devs to SRE. Other teams may also start expecting SREs to take on such work, which is bad for obvious reasons.

Promotes attrition
> Even if you're not personally unhappy with toil, your current or future teammates might like it much less. If you build too much toil into your team's procedures, you motivate the team's best engineers to start looking elsewhere for a more rewarding job.

Causes breach of faith
> New hires or transfers who joined SRE with the promise of project work will feel cheated, which is bad for morale.

Conclusion

If we all commit to eliminate a bit of toil each week with some good engineering, we'll steadily clean up our services, and we can shift our collective efforts to engineering for scale, architecting the next generation of services, and building cross-SRE toolchains. Let's invent more, and toil less.

CHAPTER 6

Monitoring Distributed Systems

Written by Rob Ewaschuk
Edited by Betsy Beyer

Google's SRE teams have some basic principles and best practices for building successful monitoring and alerting systems. This chapter offers guidelines for what issues should interrupt a human via a page, and how to deal with issues that aren't serious enough to trigger a page.

Definitions

There's no uniformly shared vocabulary for discussing all topics related to monitoring. Even within Google, usage of the following terms varies, but the most common interpretations are listed here.

Monitoring
> Collecting, processing, aggregating, and displaying real-time quantitative data about a system, such as query counts and types, error counts and types, processing times, and server lifetimes.

White-box monitoring
> Monitoring based on metrics exposed by the internals of the system, including logs, interfaces like the Java Virtual Machine Profiling Interface, or an HTTP handler that emits internal statistics.

Black-box monitoring
> Testing externally visible behavior as a user would see it.

Dashboard
> An application (usually web-based) that provides a summary view of a service's core metrics. A dashboard may have filters, selectors, and so on, but is prebuilt to

expose the metrics most important to its users. The dashboard might also display team information such as ticket queue length, a list of high-priority bugs, the current on-call engineer for a given area of responsibility, or recent pushes.

Alert
> A notification intended to be read by a human and that is pushed to a system such as a bug or ticket queue, an email alias, or a pager. Respectively, these alerts are classified as *tickets*, *email alerts*,[1] and *pages*.

Root cause
> A defect in a software or human system that, if repaired, instills confidence that this event won't happen again in the same way. A given incident might have multiple root causes: for example, perhaps it was caused by a combination of insufficient process automation, software that crashed on bogus input, *and* insufficient testing of the script used to generate the configuration. Each of these factors might stand alone as a root cause, and each should be repaired.

Node and machine
> Used interchangeably to indicate a single instance of a running kernel in either a physical server, virtual machine, or container. There might be multiple *services* worth monitoring on a single machine. The services may either be:
>
> - Related to each other: for example, a caching server and a web server
> - Unrelated services sharing hardware: for example, a code repository and a master for a configuration system like Puppet (*https://puppetlabs.com/puppet/puppet-open-source*) or Chef (*https://www.chef.io/chef/*)

Push
> Any change to a service's running software or its configuration.

Why Monitor?

There are many reasons to monitor a system, including:

Analyzing long-term trends
> How big is my database and how fast is it growing? How quickly is my daily-active user count growing?

Comparing over time or experiment groups
> Are queries faster with Acme Bucket of Bytes 2.72 versus Ajax DB 3.14? How much better is my memcache hit rate with an extra node? Is my site slower than it was last week?

---

1 Sometimes known as "alert spam," as they are rarely read or acted on.

Alerting
> Something is broken, and somebody needs to fix it right now! Or, something might break soon, so somebody should look soon.

Building dashboards
> Dashboards should answer basic questions about your service, and normally include some form of the four golden signals (discussed in "The Four Golden Signals" on page 60).

Conducting ad hoc retrospective analysis (i.e., debugging)
> Our latency just shot up; what else happened around the same time?

System monitoring is also helpful in supplying raw input into business analytics and in facilitating analysis of security breaches. Because this book focuses on the engineering domains in which SRE has particular expertise, we won't discuss these applications of monitoring here.

Monitoring and alerting enables a system to tell us when it's broken, or perhaps to tell us what's about to break. When the system isn't able to automatically fix itself, we want a human to investigate the alert, determine if there's a real problem at hand, mitigate the problem, and determine the root cause of the problem. Unless you're performing security auditing on very narrowly scoped components of a system, you should never trigger an alert simply because "something seems a bit weird."

Paging a human is a quite expensive use of an employee's time. If an employee is at work, a page interrupts their workflow. If the employee is at home, a page interrupts their personal time, and perhaps even their sleep. When pages occur too frequently, employees second-guess, skim, or even ignore incoming alerts, sometimes even ignoring a "real" page that's masked by the noise. Outages can be prolonged because other noise interferes with a rapid diagnosis and fix. Effective alerting systems have good signal and very low noise.

Setting Reasonable Expectations for Monitoring

Monitoring a complex application is a significant engineering endeavor in and of itself. Even with substantial existing infrastructure for instrumentation, collection, display, and alerting in place, a Google SRE team with 10–12 members typically has one or sometimes two members whose primary assignment is to build and maintain monitoring systems for their service. This number has decreased over time as we generalize and centralize common monitoring infrastructure, but every SRE team typically has at least one "monitoring person." (That being said, while it can be fun to have access to traffic graph dashboards and the like, SRE teams carefully avoid any situation that requires someone to "stare at a screen to watch for problems.")

In general, Google has trended toward simpler and faster monitoring systems, with better tools for *post hoc* analysis. We avoid "magic" systems that try to learn thresholds or automatically detect causality. Rules that detect unexpected changes in end-user request rates are one counterexample; while these rules are still kept as simple as possible, they give a very quick detection of a very simple, specific, severe anomaly. Other uses of monitoring data such as capacity planning and traffic prediction can tolerate more fragility, and thus, more complexity. Observational experiments conducted over a very long time horizon (months or years) with a low sampling rate (hours or days) can also often tolerate more fragility because occasional missed samples won't hide a long-running trend.

Google SRE has experienced only limited success with complex dependency hierarchies. We seldom use rules such as, "If I know the database is slow, alert for a slow database; otherwise, alert for the website being generally slow." Dependency-reliant rules usually pertain to very stable parts of our system, such as our system for draining user traffic away from a datacenter. For example, "If a datacenter is drained, then don't alert me on its latency" is one common datacenter alerting rule. Few teams at Google maintain complex dependency hierarchies because our infrastructure has a steady rate of continuous refactoring.

Some of the ideas described in this chapter are still aspirational: there is always room to move more rapidly from symptom to root cause(s), especially in ever-changing systems. So while this chapter sets out some goals for monitoring systems, and some ways to achieve these goals, it's important that monitoring systems—especially the critical path from the onset of a production problem, through a page to a human, through basic triage and deep debugging—be kept simple and comprehensible by everyone on the team.

Similarly, to keep noise low and signal high, the elements of your monitoring system that direct to a pager need to be very simple and robust. Rules that generate alerts for humans should be simple to understand and represent a clear failure.

Symptoms Versus Causes

Your monitoring system should address two questions: what's broken, and why?

The "what's broken" indicates the symptom; the "why" indicates a (possibly intermediate) cause. Table 6-1 lists some hypothetical symptoms and corresponding causes.

Table 6-1. Example symptoms and causes

Symptom	Cause
I'm serving HTTP 500s or 404s	Database servers are refusing connections
My responses are slow	CPUs are overloaded by a bogosort, or an Ethernet cable is crimped under a rack, visible as partial packet loss
Users in Antarctica aren't receiving animated cat GIFs	Your Content Distribution Network hates scientists and felines, and thus blacklisted some client IPs
Private content is world-readable	A new software push caused ACLs to be forgotten and allowed all requests

"What" versus "why" is one of the most important distinctions in writing good monitoring with maximum signal and minimum noise.

Black-Box Versus White-Box

We combine heavy use of white-box monitoring with modest but critical uses of black-box monitoring. The simplest way to think about black-box monitoring versus white-box monitoring is that black-box monitoring is symptom-oriented and represents active—not predicted—problems: "The system isn't working correctly, right now." White-box monitoring depends on the ability to inspect the innards of the system, such as logs or HTTP endpoints, with instrumentation. White-box monitoring therefore allows detection of imminent problems, failures masked by retries, and so forth.

Note that in a multilayered system, one person's symptom is another person's cause. For example, suppose that a database's performance is slow. Slow database reads are a symptom for the database SRE who detects them. However, for the frontend SRE observing a slow website, the same slow database reads are a cause. Therefore, white-box monitoring is sometimes symptom-oriented, and sometimes cause-oriented, depending on just how informative your white-box is.

When collecting telemetry for debugging, white-box monitoring is essential. If web servers seem slow on database-heavy requests, you need to know both how fast the web server perceives the database to be, and how fast the database believes itself to be. Otherwise, you can't distinguish an actually slow database server from a network problem between your web server and your database.

For paging, black-box monitoring has the key benefit of forcing discipline to only nag a human when a problem is both already ongoing and contributing to real symptoms. On the other hand, for not-yet-occurring but imminent problems, black-box monitoring is fairly useless.

The Four Golden Signals

The four golden signals of monitoring are latency, traffic, errors, and saturation. If you can only measure four metrics of your user-facing system, focus on these four.

Latency

The time it takes to service a request. It's important to distinguish between the latency of successful requests and the latency of failed requests. For example, an HTTP 500 error triggered due to loss of connection to a database or other critical backend might be served very quickly; however, as an HTTP 500 error indicates a failed request, factoring 500s into your overall latency might result in misleading calculations. On the other hand, a slow error is even worse than a fast error! Therefore, it's important to track error latency, as opposed to just filtering out errors.

Traffic

A measure of how much demand is being placed on your system, measured in a high-level system-specific metric. For a web service, this measurement is usually HTTP requests per second, perhaps broken out by the nature of the requests (e.g., static versus dynamic content). For an audio streaming system, this measurement might focus on network I/O rate or concurrent sessions. For a key-value storage system, this measurement might be transactions and retrievals per second.

Errors

The rate of requests that fail, either explicitly (e.g., HTTP 500s), implicitly (for example, an HTTP 200 success response, but coupled with the wrong content), or by policy (for example, "If you committed to one-second response times, any request over one second is an error"). Where protocol response codes are insufficient to express all failure conditions, secondary (internal) protocols may be necessary to track partial failure modes. Monitoring these cases can be drastically different: catching HTTP 500s at your load balancer can do a decent job of catching all completely failed requests, while only end-to-end system tests can detect that you're serving the wrong content.

Saturation

How "full" your service is. A measure of your system fraction, emphasizing the resources that are most constrained (e.g., in a memory-constrained system, show memory; in an I/O-constrained system, show I/O). Note that many systems degrade in performance before they achieve 100% utilization, so having a utilization target is essential.

In complex systems, saturation can be supplemented with higher-level load measurement: can your service properly handle double the traffic, handle only 10% more traffic, or handle even less traffic than it currently receives? For very simple services that have no parameters that alter the complexity of the request (e.g., "Give me a nonce" or "I need a globally unique monotonic integer") that rarely change configuration, a static value from a load test might be adequate. As discussed in the previous paragraph, however, most services need to use indirect signals like CPU utilization or network bandwidth that have a known upper bound. Latency increases are often a leading indicator of saturation. Measuring your 99th percentile response time over some small window (e.g., one minute) can give a very early signal of saturation.

Finally, saturation is also concerned with predictions of impending saturation, such as "It looks like your database will fill its hard drive in 4 hours."

If you measure all four golden signals and page a human when one signal is problematic (or, in the case of saturation, nearly problematic), your service will be at least decently covered by monitoring.

Worrying About Your Tail (or, Instrumentation and Performance)

When building a monitoring system from scratch, it's tempting to design a system based upon the mean of some quantity: the mean latency, the mean CPU usage of your nodes, or the mean fullness of your databases. The danger presented by the latter two cases is obvious: CPUs and databases can easily be utilized in a very imbalanced way. The same holds for latency. If you run a web service with an average latency of 100 ms at 1,000 requests per second, 1% of requests might easily take 5 seconds.[2] If your users depend on several such web services to render their page, the 99th percentile of one backend can easily become the median response of your frontend.

The simplest way to differentiate between a slow average and a very slow "tail" of requests is to collect request counts bucketed by latencies (suitable for rendering a histogram), rather than actual latencies: how many requests did I serve that took between 0 ms and 10 ms, between 10 ms and 30 ms, between 30 ms and 100 ms, between 100 ms and 300 ms, and so on? Distributing the histogram boundaries approximately exponentially (in this case by factors of roughly 3) is often an easy way to visualize the distribution of your requests.

---

2 If 1% of your requests are 10x the average, it means that the rest of your requests are about twice as fast as the average. But if you're not measuring your distribution, the idea that most of your requests are near the mean is just hopeful thinking.

Choosing an Appropriate Resolution for Measurements

Different aspects of a system should be measured with different levels of granularity. For example:

- Observing CPU load over the time span of a minute won't reveal even quite long-lived spikes that drive high tail latencies.
- On the other hand, for a web service targeting no more than 9 hours aggregate downtime per year (99.9% annual uptime), probing for a 200 (success) status more than once or twice a minute is probably unnecessarily frequent.
- Similarly, checking hard drive fullness for a service targeting 99.9% availability more than once every 1–2 minutes is probably unnecessary.

Take care in how you structure the granularity of your measurements. Collecting per-second measurements of CPU load might yield interesting data, but such frequent measurements may be very expensive to collect, store, and analyze. If your monitoring goal calls for high resolution but doesn't require extremely low latency, you can reduce these costs by performing internal sampling on the server, then configuring an external system to collect and aggregate that distribution over time or across servers. You might:

1. Record the current CPU utilization each second.
2. Using buckets of 5% granularity, increment the appropriate CPU utilization bucket each second.
3. Aggregate those values every minute.

This strategy allows you to observe brief CPU hotspots without incurring very high cost due to collection and retention.

As Simple as Possible, No Simpler

Piling all these requirements on top of each other can add up to a very complex monitoring system—your system might end up with the following levels of complexity:

- Alerts on different latency thresholds, at different percentiles, on all kinds of different metrics
- Extra code to detect and expose possible causes
- Associated dashboards for each of these possible causes

The sources of potential complexity are never-ending. Like all software systems, monitoring can become so complex that it's fragile, complicated to change, and a maintenance burden.

Therefore, design your monitoring system with an eye toward simplicity. In choosing what to monitor, keep the following guidelines in mind:

- The rules that catch real incidents most often should be as simple, predictable, and reliable as possible.
- Data collection, aggregation, and alerting configuration that is rarely exercised (e.g., less than once a quarter for some SRE teams) should be up for removal.
- Signals that are collected, but not exposed in any prebaked dashboard nor used by any alert, are candidates for removal.

In Google's experience, basic collection and aggregation of metrics, paired with alerting and dashboards, has worked well as a relatively standalone system. (In fact Google's monitoring system is broken up into several binaries, but typically people learn about all aspects of these binaries.) It can be tempting to combine monitoring with other aspects of inspecting complex systems, such as detailed system profiling, single-process debugging, tracking details about exceptions or crashes, load testing, log collection and analysis, or traffic inspection. While most of these subjects share commonalities with basic monitoring, blending together too many results in overly complex and fragile systems. As in many other aspects of software engineering, maintaining distinct systems with clear, simple, loosely coupled points of integration is a better strategy (for example, using web APIs for pulling summary data in a format that can remain constant over an extended period of time).

Tying These Principles Together

The principles discussed in this chapter can be tied together into a philosophy on monitoring and alerting that's widely endorsed and followed within Google SRE teams. While this monitoring philosophy is a bit aspirational, it's a good starting point for writing or reviewing a new alert, and it can help your organization ask the right questions, regardless of the size of your organization or the complexity of your service or system.

When creating rules for monitoring and alerting, asking the following questions can help you avoid false positives and pager burnout:[3]

- Does this rule detect *an otherwise undetected condition* that is urgent, actionable, and actively or imminently user-visible?[4]

---

3 See *Applying Cardiac Alarm Management Techniques to Your On-Call* [Hol14] for an example of alert fatigue in another context.

4 Zero-redundancy ($N + 0$) situations count as imminent, as do "nearly full" parts of your service! For more details about the concept of redundancy, see *https://en.wikipedia.org/wiki/N%2B1_redundancy*.

- Will I ever be able to ignore this alert, knowing it's benign? When and why will I be able to ignore this alert, and how can I avoid this scenario?

- Does this alert definitely indicate that users are being negatively affected? Are there detectable cases in which users aren't being negatively impacted, such as drained traffic or test deployments, that should be filtered out?

- Can I take action in response to this alert? Is that action urgent, or could it wait until morning? Could the action be safely automated? Will that action be a long-term fix, or just a short-term workaround?

- Are other people getting paged for this issue, therefore rendering at least one of the pages unnecessary?

These questions reflect a fundamental philosophy on pages and pagers:

- Every time the pager goes off, I should be able to react with a sense of urgency. I can only react with a sense of urgency a few times a day before I become fatigued.

- Every page should be actionable.

- Every page response should require intelligence. If a page merely merits a robotic response, it shouldn't be a page.

- Pages should be about a novel problem or an event that hasn't been seen before.

Such a perspective dissipates certain distinctions: if a page satisfies the preceding four bullets, it's irrelevant whether the page is triggered by white-box or black-box monitoring. This perspective also amplifies certain distinctions: it's better to spend much more effort on catching symptoms than causes; when it comes to causes, only worry about very definite, very imminent causes.

Monitoring for the Long Term

In modern production systems, monitoring systems track an ever-evolving system with changing software architecture, load characteristics, and performance targets. An alert that's currently exceptionally rare and hard to automate might become frequent, perhaps even meriting a hacked-together script to resolve it. At this point, someone should find and eliminate the root causes of the problem; if such resolution isn't possible, the alert response deserves to be fully automated.

It's important that decisions about monitoring be made with long-term goals in mind. Every page that happens today distracts a human from improving the system for tomorrow, so there is often a case for taking a short-term hit to availability or performance in order to improve the long-term outlook for the system. Let's take a look at two case studies that illustrate this trade-off.

Bigtable SRE: A Tale of Over-Alerting

Google's internal infrastructure is typically offered and measured against a service level objective (SLO; see Chapter 4). Many years ago, the Bigtable service's SLO was based on a synthetic well-behaved client's mean performance. Because of problems in Bigtable and lower layers of the storage stack, the mean performance was driven by a "large" tail: the worst 5% of requests were often significantly slower than the rest.

Email alerts were triggered as the SLO approached, and paging alerts were triggered when the SLO was exceeded. Both types of alerts were firing voluminously, consuming unacceptable amounts of engineering time: the team spent significant amounts of time triaging the alerts to find the few that were really actionable, and we often missed the problems that actually affected users, because so few of them did. Many of the pages were non-urgent, due to well-understood problems in the infrastructure, and had either rote responses or received no response.

To remedy the situation, the team used a three-pronged approach: while making great efforts to improve the performance of Bigtable, we also temporarily dialed back our SLO target, using the 75th percentile request latency. We also disabled email alerts, as there were so many that spending time diagnosing them was infeasible.

This strategy gave us enough breathing room to actually fix the longer-term problems in Bigtable and the lower layers of the storage stack, rather than constantly fixing tactical problems. On-call engineers could actually accomplish work when they weren't being kept up by pages at all hours. Ultimately, temporarily backing off on our alerts allowed us to make faster progress toward a better service.

Gmail: Predictable, Scriptable Responses from Humans

In the very early days of Gmail, the service was built on a retrofitted distributed process management system called Workqueue, which was originally created for batch processing of pieces of the search index. Workqueue was "adapted" to long-lived processes and subsequently applied to Gmail, but certain bugs in the relatively opaque codebase in the scheduler proved hard to beat.

At that time, the Gmail monitoring was structured such that alerts fired when individual tasks were "de-scheduled" by Workqueue. This setup was less than ideal because even at that time, Gmail had many, many thousands of tasks, each task representing a fraction of a percent of our users. We cared deeply about providing a good user experience for Gmail users, but such an alerting setup was unmaintainable.

To address this problem, Gmail SRE built a tool that helped "poke" the scheduler in just the right way to minimize impact to users. The team had several discussions about whether or not we should simply automate the entire loop from detecting the problem to nudging the rescheduler, until a better long-term solution was achieved, but some worried this kind of workaround would delay a real fix.

This kind of tension is common within a team, and often reflects an underlying mistrust of the team's self-discipline: while some team members want to implement a "hack" to allow time for a proper fix, others worry that a hack will be forgotten or that the proper fix will be deprioritized indefinitely. This concern is credible, as it's easy to build layers of unmaintainable technical debt by patching over problems instead of making real fixes. Managers and technical leaders play a key role in implementing true, long-term fixes by supporting and prioritizing potentially time-consuming long-term fixes even when the initial "pain" of paging subsides.

Pages with rote, algorithmic responses should be a red flag. Unwillingness on the part of your team to automate such pages implies that the team lacks confidence that they can clean up their technical debt. This is a major problem worth escalating.

The Long Run

A common theme connects the previous examples of Bigtable and Gmail: a tension between short-term and long-term availability. Often, sheer force of effort can help a rickety system achieve high availability, but this path is usually short-lived and fraught with burnout and dependence on a small number of heroic team members. Taking a controlled, short-term decrease in availability is often a painful, but strategic trade for the long-run stability of the system. It's important not to think of every page as an event in isolation, but to consider whether the overall *level* of paging leads toward a healthy, appropriately available system with a healthy, viable team and long-term outlook. We review statistics about page frequency (usually expressed as incidents per shift, where an incident might be composed of a few related pages) in quarterly reports with management, ensuring that decision makers are kept up to date on the pager load and overall health of their teams.

Conclusion

A healthy monitoring and alerting pipeline is simple and easy to reason about. It focuses primarily on symptoms for paging, reserving cause-oriented heuristics to serve as aids to debugging problems. Monitoring symptoms is easier the further "up" your stack you monitor, though monitoring saturation and performance of subsystems such as databases often must be performed directly on the subsystem itself. Email alerts are of very limited value and tend to easily become overrun with noise; instead, you should favor a dashboard that monitors all ongoing subcritical problems for the sort of information that typically ends up in email alerts. A dashboard might also be paired with a log, in order to analyze historical correlations.

Over the long haul, achieving a successful on-call rotation and product includes choosing to alert on symptoms or imminent real problems, adapting your targets to goals that are actually achievable, and making sure that your monitoring supports rapid diagnosis.

CHAPTER 7

The Evolution of Automation at Google

Written by Niall Murphy with John Looney and Michael Kacirek
Edited by Betsy Beyer

> *Besides black art, there is only automation and mechanization.*
> —Federico García Lorca (1898–1936), Spanish poet and playwright

For SRE, automation is a force multiplier, not a panacea. Of course, just *multiplying* force does not naturally change the accuracy of where that force is applied: doing automation thoughtlessly can create as many problems as it solves. Therefore, while we believe that software-based automation is superior to manual operation in most circumstances, better than either option is a higher-level system design requiring neither of them—an *autonomous* system. Or to put it another way, the value of automation comes from both what it does and its judicious application. We'll discuss both the value of automation and how our attitude has evolved over time.

The Value of Automation

What exactly is the value of automation?[1]

Consistency

Although scale is an obvious motivation for automation, there are many other reasons to use it. Take the example of university computing systems, where many systems engineering folks started their careers. Systems administrators of that background were generally charged with running a collection of machines or some

---

[1] For readers who already feel they precisely understand the value of automation, skip ahead to "The Value for Google SRE" on page 70. However, note that our description contains some nuances that might be useful to keep in mind while reading the rest of the chapter.

software, and were accustomed to manually performing various actions in the discharge of that duty. One common example is creating user accounts; others include purely operational duties like making sure backups happen, managing server failover, and small data manipulations like changing the upstream DNS servers' *resolv.conf*, DNS server zone data, and similar activities. Ultimately, however, this prevalence of manual tasks is unsatisfactory for both the organizations and indeed the people maintaining systems in this way. For a start, any action performed by a human or humans hundreds of times won't be performed the same way each time: even with the best will in the world, very few of us will ever be as consistent as a machine. This inevitable lack of consistency leads to mistakes, oversights, issues with data quality, and, yes, reliability problems. In this domain—the execution of well-scoped, known procedures—the value of consistency is in many ways the primary value of automation.

A Platform

Automation doesn't just provide consistency. Designed and done properly, automatic systems also provide a *platform* that can be extended, applied to more systems, or perhaps even spun out for profit.[2] (The alternative, no automation, is neither cost effective nor extensible: it is instead a tax levied on the operation of a system.)

A platform also *centralizes mistakes*. In other words, a bug fixed in the code will be fixed there once and forever, unlike a sufficiently large set of humans performing the same procedure, as discussed previously. A platform can be extended to perform additional tasks more easily than humans can be instructed to perform them (or sometimes even realize that they have to be done). Depending on the nature of the task, it can run either continuously or much more frequently than humans could appropriately accomplish the task, or at times that are inconvenient for humans. Furthermore, a platform can export metrics about its performance, or otherwise allow you to discover details about your process you didn't know previously, because these details are more easily measurable within the context of a platform.

Faster Repairs

There's an additional benefit for systems where automation is used to resolve common faults in a system (a frequent situation for SRE-created automation). If automation runs regularly and successfully enough, the result is a reduced mean time to repair (MTTR) for those common faults. You can then spend your time on other tasks instead, thereby achieving increased developer velocity because you don't have to spend time either preventing a problem or (more commonly) cleaning up after it.

---

2 The expertise acquired in building such automation is also valuable in itself; engineers both deeply understand the existing processes they have automated and can later automate novel processes more quickly.

As is well understood in the industry, the later in the product lifecycle a problem is discovered, the more expensive it is to fix; see Chapter 17. Generally, problems that occur in actual production are most expensive to fix, both in terms of time and money, which means that an automated system looking for problems as soon as they arise has a good chance of lowering the total cost of the system, given that the system is sufficiently large.

Faster Action

In the infrastructural situations where SRE automation tends to be deployed, humans don't usually react as fast as machines. In most common cases, where, for example, failover or traffic switching can be well defined for a particular application, it makes no sense to effectively require a human to intermittently press a button called "Allow system to continue to run." (Yes, it is true that sometimes automatic procedures can end up making a bad situation worse, but that is why such procedures should be scoped over well-defined domains.) Google has a large amount of automation; in many cases, the services we support could not long survive without this automation because they crossed the threshold of manageable manual operation long ago.

Time Saving

Finally, time saving is an oft-quoted rationale for automation. Although people cite this rationale for automation more than the others, in many ways the benefit is often less immediately calculable. Engineers often waver over whether a particular piece of automation or code is worth writing, in terms of effort saved in not requiring a task to be performed manually versus the effort required to write it.[3] It's easy to overlook the fact that once you have encapsulated some task in automation, anyone can execute the task. Therefore, the time savings apply across anyone who would plausibly use the automation. Decoupling operator from operation is very powerful.

Joseph Bironas, an SRE who led Google's datacenter turnup efforts for a time, forcefully argued:

"If we are engineering processes and solutions that are not automatable, we continue having to staff humans to maintain the system. If we have to staff humans to do the work, we are feeding the machines with the blood, sweat, and tears of human beings. Think *The Matrix* with less special effects and more pissed off System Administrators."

---

3 See the following XKCD cartoon: *http://xkcd.com/1205/*.

The Value for Google SRE

All of these benefits and trade-offs apply to us just as much as anyone else, and Google does have a strong bias toward automation. Part of our preference for automation springs from our particular business challenges: the products and services we look after are planet-spanning in scale, and we don't typically have time to engage in the same kind of machine or service hand-holding common in other organizations.[4] For truly large services, the factors of consistency, quickness, and reliability dominate most conversations about the trade-offs of performing automation.

Another argument in favor of automation, particularly in the case of Google, is our complicated yet surprisingly uniform production environment, described in Chapter 2. While other organizations might have an important piece of equipment without a readily accessible API, software for which no source code is available, or another impediment to complete control over production operations, Google generally avoids such scenarios. We have built APIs for systems when no API was available from the vendor. Even though purchasing software for a particular task would have been much cheaper in the short term, we chose to write our own solutions, because doing so produced APIs with the potential for much greater long-term benefits. We spent a lot of time overcoming obstacles to automatic system management, and then resolutely developed that automatic system management itself. Given how Google manages its source code [Pot16], the availability of that code for more or less any system that SRE touches also means that our mission to "own the product in production" is much easier because we control the entirety of the stack.

Of course, although Google is ideologically bent upon using machines to manage machines where possible, reality requires some modification of our approach. It isn't appropriate to automate every component of every system, and not everyone has the ability or inclination to develop automation at a particular time. Some essential systems started out as quick prototypes, not designed to last or to interface with automation. The previous paragraphs state a maximalist view of our position, but one that we have been broadly successful at putting into action within the Google context. In general, we have chosen to create platforms where we could, or to *position* ourselves so that we could create platforms over time. We view this platform-based approach as necessary for manageability and scalability.

The Use Cases for Automation

In the industry, *automation* is the term generally used for writing code to solve a wide variety of problems, although the motivations for writing this code, and the solutions

---

4 See, for example, *http://blog.engineyard.com/2014/pets-vs-cattle*.

themselves, are often quite different. More broadly, in this view, automation is "meta-software"—software to act on software.

As we implied earlier, there are a number of use cases for automation. Here is a non-exhaustive list of examples:

- User account creation
- Cluster turnup and turndown for services
- Software or hardware installation preparation and decommissioning
- Rollouts of new software versions
- Runtime configuration changes
- A special case of runtime config changes: changes to your dependencies

This list could continue essentially *ad infinitum*.

Google SRE's Use Cases for Automation

In Google, we have all of the use cases just listed, and more.

However, within Google SRE, our primary affinity has typically been for running infrastructure, as opposed to managing the quality of the data that passes over that infrastructure. This line isn't totally clear—for example, we care deeply if half of a dataset vanishes after a push, and therefore we alert on coarse-grain differences like this, but it's rare for us to write the equivalent of changing the properties of some arbitrary subset of accounts on a system. Therefore, the context for our automation is often automation to manage the lifecycle of systems, not their data: for example, deployments of a service in a new cluster.

To this extent, SRE's automation efforts are not far off what many other people and organizations do, except that we use different tools to manage it and have a different focus (as we'll discuss).

Widely available tools like Puppet, Chef, cfengine, and even Perl, which all provide ways to automate particular tasks, differ mostly in terms of the level of abstraction of the components provided to help the act of automating. A full language like Perl provides POSIX-level affordances, which in theory provide an essentially unlimited scope of automation across the APIs accessible to the system,[5] whereas Chef and Puppet provide out-of-the-box abstractions with which services or other higher-level entities can be manipulated. The trade-off here is classic: higher-level abstractions are easier to manage and reason about, but when you encounter a "leaky abstraction,"

---

5 Of course, not every system that needs to be managed actually provides callable APIs for management—forcing some tooling to use, e.g., CLI invocations or automated website clicks.

you fail systemically, repeatedly, and potentially inconsistently. For example, we often assume that pushing a new binary to a cluster is atomic; the cluster will either end up with the old version, or the new version. However, real-world behavior is more complicated: that cluster's network can fail halfway through; machines can fail; communication to the cluster management layer can fail, leaving the system in an inconsistent state; depending on the situation, new binaries could be staged but not pushed, or pushed but not restarted, or restarted but not verifiable. Very few abstractions model these kinds of outcomes successfully, and most generally end up halting themselves and calling for intervention. Truly bad automation systems don't even do that.

SRE has a number of philosophies and products in the domain of automation, some of which look more like generic rollout tools without particularly detailed modeling of higher-level entities, and some of which look more like languages for describing service deployment (and so on) at a very abstract level. Work done in the latter tends to be more reusable and be more of a common platform than the former, but the complexity of our production environment sometimes means that the former approach is the most immediately tractable option.

A Hierarchy of Automation Classes

Although all of these automation steps are valuable, and indeed an automation platform is valuable in and of itself, in an ideal world, we wouldn't need externalized automation. In fact, instead of having a system that *has* to have external glue logic, it would be even better to have a system that needs *no glue logic at all*, not just because internalization is more efficient (although such efficiency is useful), but because it has been designed to not need glue logic in the first place. Accomplishing that involves taking the use cases for glue logic—generally "first order" manipulations of a system, such as adding accounts or performing system turnup—and finding a way to handle those use cases directly within the application.

As a more detailed example, most turnup automation at Google is problematic because it ends up being maintained separately from the core system and therefore suffers from "bit rot," i.e., not changing when the underlying systems change. Despite the best of intentions, attempting to more tightly couple the two (turnup automation and the core system) often fails due to unaligned priorities, as product developers will, not unreasonably, resist a test deployment requirement for every change. Secondly, automation that is crucial but only executed at infrequent intervals and therefore difficult to test is often particularly fragile because of the extended feedback cycle. Cluster failover is one classic example of infrequently executed automation: failovers might only occur every few months, or infrequently enough that inconsistencies between instances are introduced. The evolution of automation follows a path:

1) No automation

Database master is failed over manually between locations.

2) Externally maintained system-specific automation

An SRE has a failover script in his or her home directory.

3) Externally maintained generic automation

The SRE adds database support to a "generic failover" script that everyone uses.

4) Internally maintained system-specific automation

The database ships with its own failover script.

5) Systems that don't need any automation

The database notices problems, and automatically fails over without human intervention.

SRE hates manual operations, so we obviously try to create systems that don't require them. However, sometimes manual operations are unavoidable.

There is additionally a subvariety of automation that applies changes not across the domain of specific system-related configuration, but across the domain of production as a whole. In a highly centralized proprietary production environment like Google's, there are a large number of changes that have a non–service-specific scope—e.g., changing upstream Chubby servers, a flag change to the Bigtable client library to make access more reliable, and so on—which nonetheless need to be safely managed and rolled back if necessary. Beyond a certain volume of changes, it is infeasible for production-wide changes to be accomplished manually, and at some time before that point, it's a waste to have manual oversight for a process where a large proportion of the changes are either trivial or accomplished successfully by basic relaunch-and-check strategies.

Let's use internal case studies to illustrate some of the preceding points in detail. The first case study is about how, due to some diligent, far-sighted work, we managed to achieve the self-professed nirvana of SRE: to automate ourselves out of a job.

Automate Yourself Out of a Job: Automate ALL the Things!

For a long while, the Ads products at Google stored their data in a MySQL database. Because Ads data obviously has high reliability requirements, an SRE team was charged with looking after that infrastructure. From 2005 to 2008, the Ads Database mostly ran in what we considered to be a mature and managed state. For example, we had automated away the worst, but not all, of the routine work for standard replica replacements. We believed the Ads Database was well managed and that we had harvested most of the low-hanging fruit in terms of optimization and scale. However, as daily operations became comfortable, team members began to look at the next level of system development: migrating MySQL onto Google's cluster scheduling system, Borg.

We hoped this migration would provide two main benefits:

- *Completely* eliminate machine/replica maintenance: Borg would automatically handle the setup/restart of new and broken tasks.
- Enable bin-packing of multiple MySQL instances on the same physical machine: Borg would enable more efficient use of machine resources via Containers.

In late 2008, we successfully deployed a proof of concept MySQL instance on Borg. Unfortunately, this was accompanied by a significant new difficulty. A core operating characteristic of Borg is that its tasks move around automatically. Tasks commonly move within Borg as frequently as once or twice per week. This frequency was tolerable for our database replicas, but unacceptable for our masters.

At that time, the process for master failover took 30–90 minutes per instance. Simply because we ran on shared machines and were subject to reboots for kernel upgrades, in addition to the normal rate of machine failure, we had to expect a number of otherwise unrelated failovers every week. This factor, in combination with the number of shards on which our system was hosted, meant that:

- Manual failovers would consume a substantial amount of human hours and would give us best-case availability of 99% uptime, which fell short of the actual business requirements of the product.
- In order to meet our error budgets, each failover would have to take less than 30 seconds of downtime. There was no way to optimize a human-dependent procedure to make downtime shorter than 30 seconds.

Therefore, our only choice was to automate failover. Actually, we needed to automate more than just failover.

In 2009 Ads SRE completed our automated failover daemon, which we dubbed "Decider." Decider could complete MySQL failovers for both planned and unplanned failovers in less than 30 seconds 95% of the time. With the creation of Decider, MySQL on Borg (MoB) finally became a reality. We graduated from optimizing our infrastructure for a lack of failover to embracing the idea that failure is inevitable, and therefore optimizing to recover quickly through automation.

While automation let us achieve highly available MySQL in a world that forced up to two restarts per week, it did come with its own set of costs. All of our applications had to be changed to include significantly more failure-handling logic than before. Given that the norm in the MySQL development world is to assume that the MySQL instance will be the most stable component in the stack, this switch meant customizing software like JDBC to be more tolerant of our failure-prone environment. However, the benefits of migrating to MoB with Decider were well worth these costs. Once on MoB, the time our team spent on mundane operational tasks dropped by 95%. Our failovers were automated, so an outage of a single database task no longer paged a human.

The main upshot of this new automation was that we had a lot more free time to spend on improving other parts of the infrastructure. Such improvements had a cascading effect: the more time we saved, the more time we were able to spend on optimizing and automating other tedious work. Eventually, we were able to automate schema changes, causing the cost of total operational maintenance of the Ads Database to drop by nearly 95%. Some might say that we had successfully automated ourselves out of this job. The hardware side of our domain also saw improvement. Migrating to MoB freed up considerable resources because we could schedule multiple MySQL instances on the same machines, which improved utilization of our hardware. In total, we were able to free up about 60% of our hardware. Our team was now flush with hardware and engineering resources.

This example demonstrates the wisdom of going the extra mile to deliver a platform rather than replacing existing manual procedures. The next example comes from the cluster infrastructure group, and illustrates some of the more difficult trade-offs you might encounter on your way to automating *all* the things.

Soothing the Pain: Applying Automation to Cluster Turnups

Ten years ago, the Cluster Infrastructure SRE team seemed to get a new hire every few months. As it turned out, that was approximately the same frequency at which we turned up a new cluster. Because turning up a service in a new cluster gives new hires exposure to a service's internals, this task seemed like a natural and useful training tool.

The steps taken to get a cluster ready for use were something like the following:

1. Fit out a datacenter building for power and cooling.
2. Install and configure core switches and connections to the backbone.
3. Install a few initial racks of servers.
4. Configure basic services such as DNS and installers, then configure a lock service, storage, and computing.
5. Deploy the remaining racks of machines.
6. Assign user-facing services resources, so their teams can set up the services.

Steps 4 and 6 were extremely complex. While basic services like DNS are relatively simple, the storage and compute subsystems at that time were still in heavy development, so new flags, components, and optimizations were added weekly.

Some services had more than a hundred different component subsystems, each with a complex web of dependencies. Failing to configure one subsystem, or configuring a system or component differently than other deployments, is a customer-impacting outage waiting to happen.

In one case, a multi-petabyte Bigtable cluster was configured to not use the first (logging) disk on 12-disk systems, for latency reasons. A year later, some automation assumed that if a machine's first disk wasn't being used, that machine didn't have any storage configured; therefore, it was safe to wipe the machine and set it up from scratch. All of the Bigtable data was wiped, instantly. Thankfully we had multiple real-time replicas of the dataset, but such surprises are unwelcome. Automation needs to be careful about relying on implicit "safety" signals.

Early automation focused on accelerating cluster delivery. This approach tended to rely upon creative use of SSH for tedious package distribution and service initialization problems. This strategy was an initial win, but those free-form scripts became a cholesterol of technical debt.

Detecting Inconsistencies with Prodtest

As the numbers of clusters grew, some clusters required hand-tuned flags and settings. As a result, teams wasted more and more time chasing down difficult-to-spot misconfigurations. If a flag that made GFS more responsive to log processing leaked into the default templates, cells with many files could run out of memory under load. Infuriating and time-consuming misconfigurations crept in with nearly every large configuration change.

The creative—though brittle—shell scripts we used to configure clusters were neither scaling to the number of people who wanted to make changes nor to the sheer number of cluster permutations that needed to be built. These shell scripts also failed to resolve more significant concerns before declaring that a service was good to take customer-facing traffic, such as:

- Were all of the service's dependencies available and correctly configured?
- Were all configurations and packages consistent with other deployments?
- Could the team confirm that every configuration exception was desired?

Prodtest (Production Test) was an ingenious solution to these unwelcome surprises. We extended the Python unit test framework to allow for unit testing of real-world services. These unit tests have dependencies, allowing a chain of tests, and a failure in one test would quickly abort. Take the test shown in Figure 7-1 as an example.

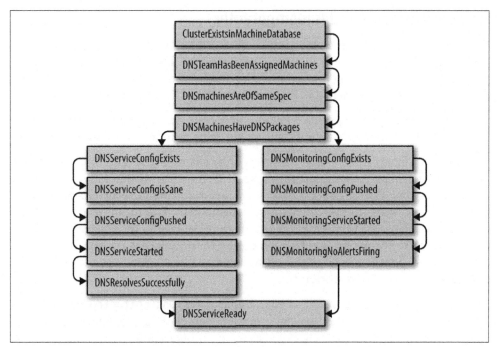

Figure 7-1. ProdTest for DNS Service, showing how one failed test aborts the subsequent chain of tests

A given team's Prodtest was given the cluster name, and it could validate that team's services in that cluster. Later additions allowed us to generate a graph of the unit tests and their states. This functionality allowed an engineer to see quickly if their service was correctly configured in all clusters, and if not, why. The graph highlighted the failed step, and the failing Python unit test output a more verbose error message.

Any time a team encountered a delay due to another team's unexpected misconfiguration, a bug could be filed to extend their Prodtest. This ensured that a similar problem would be discovered earlier in the future. SREs were proud to be able to assure their customers that all services—both newly turned up services and existing services with new configuration—would reliably serve production traffic.

For the first time, our project managers could predict when a cluster could "go live," and had a complete understanding of *why* each clusters took six or more weeks to go from "network-ready" to "serving live traffic." Out of the blue, SRE received a mission from senior management: *In three months, five new clusters will reach network-ready on the same day. Please turn them up in one week.*

Resolving Inconsistencies Idempotently

A "One Week Turnup" was a terrifying mission. We had tens of thousands of lines of shell script owned by dozens of teams. We could quickly tell how unprepared any given cluster was, but fixing it meant that the dozens of teams would have to file hundreds of bugs, and then we had to hope that these bugs would be promptly fixed.

We realized that evolving from "Python unit tests finding misconfigurations" to "Python code fixing misconfigurations" could enable us to fix these issues faster.

The unit test already knew which cluster we were examining and the specific test that was failing, so we paired each test with a fix. If each fix was written to be idempotent, and could assume that all dependencies were met, resolving the problem should have been easy—and safe—to resolve. Requiring idempotent fixes meant teams could run their "fix script" every 15 minutes without fearing damage to the cluster's configuration. If the DNS team's test was blocked on the Machine Database team's configuration of a new cluster, as soon as the cluster appeared in the database, the DNS team's tests and fixes would start working.

Take the test shown in Figure 7-2 as an example. If `TestDnsMonitoringConfigExists` fails, as shown, we can call `FixDnsMonitoringCreateConfig`, which scrapes configuration from a database, then checks a skeleton configuration file into our revision control system. Then `TestDnsMonitoringConfigExists` passes on retry, and the `TestDnsMonitoringConfigPushed` test can be attempted. If the test fails, the `FixDnsMonitoringPushConfig` step runs. If a fix fails multiple times, the automation assumes that the fix failed and stops, notifying the user.

Armed with these scripts, a small group of engineers could ensure that we could go from "The network works, and machines are listed in the database" to "Serving 1% of websearch and ads traffic" in a matter of a week or two. At the time, this seemed to be the apex of automation technology.

Looking back, this approach was deeply flawed; the latency between the test, the fix, and then a second test introduced *flaky* tests that sometimes worked and sometimes failed. Not all fixes were naturally idempotent, so a flaky test that was followed by a fix might render the system in an inconsistent state.

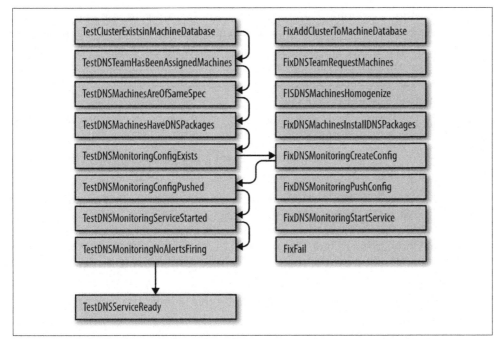

Figure 7-2. ProdTest for DNS Service, showing that one failed test resulted in only running one fix

The Inclination to Specialize

Automation processes can vary in three respects:

- *Competence*, i.e., their accuracy
- *Latency*, how quickly all steps are executed when initiated
- *Relevance*, or proportion of real-world process covered by automation

We began with a process that was highly competent (maintained and run by the service owners), high-latency (the service owners performed the process in their spare time or assigned it to new engineers), and very relevant (the service owners knew when the real world changed, and could fix the automation).

To reduce turnup latency, many service owning teams instructed a single "turnup team" what automation to run. The turnup team used tickets to start each stage in the turnup so that we could track the remaining tasks, and who those tasks were assigned to. If the human interactions regarding automation modules occurred between people in the same room, cluster turnups could happen in a much shorter time. Finally, we had our competent, accurate, and timely automation process!

But this state didn't last long. The real world is chaotic: software, configuration, data, etc. changed, resulting in over a thousand separate changes a day to affected systems. The people most affected by automation bugs were no longer domain experts, so the automation became less relevant (meaning that new steps were missed) and less competent (new flags might have caused automation to fail). However, it took a while for this drop in quality to impact velocity.

Automation code, like unit test code, dies when the maintaining team isn't obsessive about keeping the code in sync with the codebase it covers. The world changes around the code: the DNS team adds new configuration options, the storage team changes their package names, and the networking team needs to support new devices.

By relieving teams who ran services of the responsibility to maintain and run their automation code, we created ugly organizational incentives:

- A team whose primary task is to speed up the current turnup has no incentive to reduce the technical debt of the service-owning team running the service in production later.

- A team not running automation has no incentive to build systems that are easy to automate.

- A product manager whose schedule is not affected by low-quality automation will always prioritize new features over simplicity and automation.

The most functional tools are usually written by those who use them. A similar argument applies to why product development teams benefit from keeping at least some operational awareness of their systems in production.

Turnups were again high-latency, inaccurate, and incompetent—the worst of all worlds. However, an unrelated security mandate allowed us out of this trap. Much of distributed automation relied at that time on SSH. This is clumsy from a security perspective, because people must have root on many machines to run most commands. A growing awareness of advanced, persistent security threats drove us to reduce the privileges SREs enjoyed to the absolute minimum they needed to do their jobs. We had to replace our use of sshd with an authenticated, ACL-driven, RPC-based Local Admin Daemon, also known as Admin Servers, which had permissions to perform those local changes. As a result, no one could install or modify a server without an audit trail. Changes to the Local Admin Daemon and the Package Repo were gated on code reviews, making it very difficult for someone to exceed their authority; giving someone the access to install packages would not let them view colocated logs. The Admin Server logged the RPC requestor, any parameters, and the results of all RPCs to enhance debugging and security audits.

Service-Oriented Cluster-Turnup

In the next iteration, Admin Servers became part of service teams' workflows, both as related to the machine-specific Admin Servers (for installing packages and rebooting) and cluster-level Admin Servers (for actions like draining or turning up a service). SREs moved from writing shell scripts in their home directories to building peer-reviewed RPC servers with fine-grained ACLs.

Later on, after the realization that turnup processes had to be owned by the teams that owned the services fully sank in, we saw this as a way to approach cluster turnup as a Service-Oriented Architecture (SOA) problem: service owners would be responsible for creating an Admin Server to handle cluster turnup/turndown RPCs, sent by the system that knew when clusters were ready. In turn, each team would provide the contract (API) that the turnup automation needed, while still being free to change the underlying implementation. As a cluster reached "network-ready," automation sent an RPC to each Admin Server that played a part in turning up the cluster.

We now have a low-latency, competent, and accurate process; most importantly, this process has stayed strong as the rate of change, the number of teams, and the number of services seem to double each year.

As mentioned earlier, our evolution of turnup automation followed a path:

1. Operator-triggered manual action (no automation)
2. Operator-written, system-specific automation
3. Externally maintained generic automation
4. Internally maintained, system-specific automation
5. Autonomous systems that need no human intervention

While this evolution has, broadly speaking, been a success, the Borg case study illustrates another way we have come to think of the problem of automation.

Borg: Birth of the Warehouse-Scale Computer

Another way to understand the development of our attitude toward automation, and when and where that automation is best deployed, is to consider the history of the development of our cluster management systems.[6] Like MySQL on Borg, which demonstrated the success of converting manual operations to automatic ones, and the cluster turnup process, which demonstrated the downside of not thinking carefully enough about where and how automation was implemented, developing cluster man-

---

6 We have compressed and simplified this history to aid understanding.

agement also ended up demonstrating another lesson about how automation should be done. Like our previous two examples, something quite sophisticated was created as the eventual result of continuous evolution from simpler beginnings.

Google's clusters were initially deployed much like everyone else's small networks of the time: racks of machines with specific purposes and heterogeneous configurations. Engineers would log in to some well-known "master" machine to perform administrative tasks; "golden" binaries and configuration lived on these masters. As we had only one colo provider, most naming logic implicitly assumed that location. As production grew, and we began to use multiple clusters, different domains (cluster names) entered the picture. It became necessary to have a file describing what each machine did, which grouped machines under some loose naming strategy. This descriptor file, in combination with the equivalent of a parallel SSH, allowed us to reboot (for example) all the search machines in one go. Around this time, it was common to get tickets like "search is done with machine x1, crawl can have the machine now."

Automation development began. Initially automation consisted of simple Python scripts for operations such as the following:

- Service management: keeping services running (e.g., restarts after segfaults)
- Tracking what services were supposed to run on which machines
- Log message parsing: SSHing into each machine and looking for regexps

Automation eventually mutated into a proper database that tracked machine state, and also incorporated more sophisticated monitoring tools. With the union set of the automation available, we could now automatically manage much of the lifecycle of machines: noticing when machines were broken, removing the services, sending them to repair, and restoring the configuration when they came back from repair.

But to take a step back, this automation was useful yet profoundly limited, due to the fact that abstractions of the system were relentlessly tied to physical machines. We needed a new approach, hence Borg [Ver15] was born: a system that moved away from the relatively static host/port/job assignments of the previous world, toward treating a collection of machines as a managed sea of resources. Central to its success —and its conception—was the notion of turning cluster management into an entity for which API calls could be issued, to some central coordinator. This liberated extra dimensions of efficiency, flexibility, and reliability: unlike the previous model of machine "ownership," Borg could allow machines to schedule, for example, batch *and* user-facing tasks on the same machine.

This functionality ultimately resulted in continuous and automatic operating system upgrades with a very small amount of constant[7] effort—effort that does *not* scale with the total size of production deployments. Slight deviations in machine state are now automatically fixed; brokenness and lifecycle management are essentially no-ops for SRE at this point. Thousands of machines are born, die, and go into repairs daily with no SRE effort. To echo the words of Ben Treynor Sloss: by taking the approach that this was a software problem, the initial automation bought us enough time to turn cluster management into something autonomous, as opposed to automated. We achieved this goal by bringing ideas related to data distribution, APIs, hub-and-spoke architectures, and classic distributed system software development to bear upon the domain of infrastructure management.

An interesting analogy is possible here: we can make a direct mapping between the single machine case and the development of cluster management abstractions. In this view, rescheduling on another machine looks a lot like a process moving from one CPU to another: of course, those compute resources happen to be at the other end of a network link, but to what extent does that actually matter? Thinking in these terms, rescheduling looks like an intrinsic feature of the system rather than something one would "automate"—humans couldn't react fast enough anyway. Similarly in the case of cluster turnup: in this metaphor, cluster turnup is simply additional schedulable capacity, a bit like adding disk or RAM to a single computer. However, a single-node computer is not, in general, expected to continue operating when a large number of components fail. The global computer is—it *must* be self-repairing to operate once it grows past a certain size, due to the essentially statistically guaranteed large number of failures taking place every second. This implies that as we move systems up the hierarchy from manually triggered, to automatically triggered, to autonomous, some capacity for self-introspection is necessary to survive.

Reliability Is the Fundamental Feature

Of course, for effective troubleshooting, the details of internal operation that the introspection relies upon should also be exposed to the humans managing the overall system. Analogous discussions about the impact of automation in the noncomputer domain—for example, in airplane flight[8] or industrial applications—often point out the downside of highly effective automation:[9] human operators are progressively more relieved of useful direct contact with the system as the automation covers more and more daily activities over time. Inevitably, then, a situation arises in which the automation fails, and the humans are now unable to successfully operate the system.

---

7 As in a small, unchanging number.

8 See, e.g., *https://en.wikipedia.org/wiki/Air_France_Flight_447*.

9 See, e.g., [Bai83] and [Sar97].

The fluidity of their reactions has been lost due to lack of practice, and their mental models of what the system *should* be doing no longer reflect the reality of what it *is* doing.[10] This situation arises more when the system is nonautonomous—i.e., where automation replaces manual actions, and the manual actions are presumed to be always performable and available just as they were before. Sadly, over time, this ultimately becomes false: those manual actions are not always performable because the functionality to permit them no longer exists.

We, too, have experienced situations where automation has been actively harmful on a number of occasions—see "Automation: Enabling Failure at Scale" on page 85—but in Google's experience, there are more systems for which automation or autonomous behavior are no longer optional extras. As you scale, this is of course the case, but there are still strong arguments for more autonomous behavior of systems irrespective of size. Reliability is the fundamental feature, and autonomous, resilient behavior is one useful way to get that.

Recommendations

You might read the examples in this chapter and decide that you need to be Google-scale before you have anything to do with automation whatsoever. This is untrue, for two reasons: automation provides more than just time saving, so it's worth implementing in more cases than a simple time-expended versus time-saved calculation might suggest. But the approach with the highest leverage actually occurs in the design phase: shipping and iterating rapidly might allow you to implement functionality faster, yet rarely makes for a resilient system. Autonomous operation is difficult to convincingly retrofit to sufficiently large systems, but standard good practices in software engineering will help considerably: having decoupled subsystems, introducing APIs, minimizing side effects, and so on.

---

10 This is yet another good reason for regular practice drills; see "Disaster Role Playing" on page 401.

Automation: Enabling Failure at Scale

Google runs over a dozen of its own large datacenters, but we also depend on machines in many third-party colocation facilities (or "colos"). Our machines in these colos are used to terminate most incoming connections, or as a cache for our own Content Delivery Network, in order to lower end-user latency. At any point in time, a number of these racks are being installed or decommissioned; both of these processes are largely automated. One step during decommission involves overwriting the full content of the disk of all the machines in the rack, after which point an independent system verifies the successful erase. We call this process "Diskerase."

Once upon a time, the automation in charge of decommissioning a particular rack failed, but only after the Diskerase step had completed successfully. Later, the decommission process was restarted from the beginning, to debug the failure. On that iteration, when trying to send the set of machines in the rack to Diskerase, the automation determined that the set of machines that still needed to be Diskerased was (correctly) empty. Unfortunately, the empty set was used as a special value, interpreted to mean "everything." This means the automation sent almost all the machines we have in all colos to Diskerase.

Within minutes, the highly efficient Diskerase wiped the disks on all machines in our CDN, and the machines were no longer able to terminate connections from users (or do anything else useful). We were still able to serve all the users from our own datacenters, and after a few minutes the only effect visible externally was a slight increase in latency. As far as we could tell, very few users noticed the problem at all, thanks to good capacity planning (at least we got that right!). Meanwhile, we spent the better part of two days reinstalling the machines in the affected colo racks; then we spent the following weeks auditing and adding more sanity checks—including rate limiting—into our automation, and making our decommission workflow idempotent.

CHAPTER 8

Release Engineering

Written by Dinah McNutt
Edited by Betsy Beyer and Tim Harvey

Release engineering is a relatively new and fast-growing discipline of software engineering that can be concisely described as building and delivering software [McN14a]. Release engineers have a solid (if not expert) understanding of source code management, compilers, build configuration languages, automated build tools, package managers, and installers. Their skill set includes deep knowledge of multiple domains: development, configuration management, test integration, system administration, and customer support.

Running reliable services requires reliable release processes. Site Reliability Engineers (SREs) need to know that the binaries and configurations they use are built in a reproducible, automated way so that releases are repeatable and aren't "unique snowflakes." Changes to any aspect of the release process should be intentional, rather than accidental. SREs care about this process from source code to deployment.

Release engineering is a specific job function at Google. Release engineers work with software engineers (SWEs) in product development and SREs to define all the steps required to release software—from how the software is stored in the source code repository, to build rules for compilation, to how testing, packaging, and deployment are conducted.

The Role of a Release Engineer

Google is a data-driven company and release engineering follows suit. We have tools that report on a host of metrics, such as how much time it takes for a code change to be deployed into production (in other words, release velocity) and statistics on what features are being used in build configuration files [Ada15]. Most of these tools were envisioned and developed by release engineers.

Release engineers define best practices for using our tools in order to make sure projects are released using consistent and repeatable methodologies. Our best practices cover all elements of the release process. Examples include compiler flags, formats for build identification tags, and required steps during a build. Making sure that our tools behave correctly by default and are adequately documented makes it easy for teams to stay focused on features and users, rather than spending time reinventing the wheel (poorly) when it comes to releasing software.

Google has a large number of SREs who are charged with safely deploying products and keeping Google services up and running. In order to make sure our release processes meet business requirements, release engineers and SREs work together to develop strategies for canarying changes, pushing out new releases without interrupting services, and rolling back features that demonstrate problems.

Philosophy

Release engineering is guided by an engineering and service philosophy that's expressed through four major principles, detailed in the following sections.

Self-Service Model

In order to work at scale, teams must be self-sufficient. Release engineering has developed best practices and tools that allow our product development teams to control and run their own release processes. Although we have thousands of engineers and products, we can achieve a high release velocity because individual teams can decide how often and when to release new versions of their products. Release processes can be automated to the point that they require minimal involvement by the engineers, and many projects are automatically built and released using a combination of our automated build system and our deployment tools. Releases are truly automatic, and only require engineer involvement if and when problems arise.

High Velocity

User-facing software (such as many components of Google Search) is rebuilt frequently, as we aim to roll out customer-facing features as quickly as possible. We have embraced the philosophy that frequent releases result in fewer changes between versions. This approach makes testing and troubleshooting easier. Some teams perform hourly builds and then select the version to actually deploy to production from the resulting pool of builds. Selection is based upon the test results and the features contained in a given build. Other teams have adopted a "Push on Green" release model and deploy every build that passes all tests [Kle14].

Hermetic Builds

Build tools must allow us to ensure consistency and repeatability. If two people attempt to build the same product at the same revision number in the source code repository on different machines, we expect identical results.[1] Our builds are hermetic, meaning that they are insensitive to the libraries and other software installed on the build machine. Instead, builds depend on known versions of build tools, such as compilers, and dependencies, such as libraries. The build process is self-contained and must not rely on services that are external to the build environment.

Rebuilding older releases when we need to fix a bug in software that's running in production can be a challenge. We accomplish this task by rebuilding at the same revision as the original build and including specific changes that were submitted after that point in time. We call this tactic *cherry picking*. Our build tools are themselves versioned based on the revision in the source code repository for the project being built. Therefore, a project built last month won't use this month's version of the compiler if a cherry pick is required, because that version may contain incompatible or undesired features.

Enforcement of Policies and Procedures

Several layers of security and access control determine who can perform specific operations when releasing a project. Gated operations include:

- Approving source code changes—this operation is managed through configuration files scattered throughout the codebase
- Specifying the actions to be performed during the release process
- Creating a new release
- Approving the initial integration proposal (which is a request to perform a build at a specific revision number in the source code repository) and subsequent cherry picks
- Deploying a new release
- Making changes to a project's build configuration

Almost all changes to the codebase require a code review, which is a streamlined action integrated into our normal developer workflow. Our automated release system produces a report of all changes contained in a release, which is archived with other build artifacts. By allowing SREs to understand what changes are included in a new

---

1 Google uses a monolithic unified source code repository; see [Pot16].

release of a project, this report can expedite troubleshooting when there are problems with a release.

Continuous Build and Deployment

Google has developed an automated release system called *Rapid*. Rapid is a system that leverages a number of Google technologies to provide a framework that delivers scalable, hermetic, and reliable releases. The following sections describe the software lifecycle at Google and how it is managed using Rapid and other associated tools.

Building

Blaze[2] is Google's build tool of choice. It supports building binaries from a range of languages, including our standard languages of C++, Java, Python, Go, and Java-Script. Engineers use Blaze to define build targets (e.g., the output of a build, such as a JAR file), and to specify the dependencies for each target. When performing a build, Blaze automatically builds the dependency targets.

Build targets for binaries and unit tests are defined in Rapid's project configuration files. Project-specific flags, such as a unique build identifier, are passed by Rapid to Blaze. All binaries support a flag that displays the build date, the revision number, and the build identifier, which allow us to easily associate a binary to a record of how it was built.

Branching

All code is checked into the main branch of the source code tree (mainline). However, most major projects don't release directly from the mainline. Instead, we branch from the mainline at a specific revision and never merge changes from the branch back into the mainline. Bug fixes are submitted to the mainline and then cherry picked into the branch for inclusion in the release. This practice avoids inadvertently picking up unrelated changes submitted to the mainline since the original build occurred. Using this branch and cherry pick method, we know the exact contents of each release.

Testing

A continuous test system runs unit tests against the code in the mainline each time a change is submitted, allowing us to detect build and test failures quickly. Release engineering recommends that the continuous build test targets correspond to the same test targets that gate the project release. We also recommend creating releases at

---

2 Blaze has been open sourced as Bazel. See "Bazel FAQ" on the Bazel website, *http://bazel.io/faq.html*.

the revision number (version) of the last continuous test build that successfully completed all tests. These measures decrease the chance that subsequent changes made to the mainline will cause failures during the build performed at release time.

During the release process, we re-run the unit tests using the release branch and create an audit trail showing that all the tests passed. This step is important because if a release involves cherry picks, the release branch may contain a version of the code that doesn't exist anywhere on the mainline. We want to guarantee that the tests pass in the context of what's actually being released.

To complement the continuous test system, we use an independent testing environment that runs system-level tests on packaged build artifacts. These tests can be launched manually or from Rapid.

Packaging

Software is distributed to our production machines via the Midas Package Manager (MPM) [McN14c]. MPM assembles packages based on Blaze rules that list the build artifacts to include, along with their owners and permissions. Packages are named (e.g., *search/shakespeare/frontend*), versioned with a unique hash, and signed to ensure authenticity. MPM supports applying labels to a particular version of a package. Rapid applies a label containing the build ID, which guarantees that a package can be uniquely referenced using the name of the package and this label.

Labels can be applied to an MPM package to indicate a package's location in the release process (e.g., dev, canary, or production). If you apply an existing label to a new package, the label is automatically moved from the old package to the new package. For example: if a package is labeled as canary, someone subsequently installing the canary version of that package will automatically receive the newest version of the package with the label canary.

Rapid

Figure 8-1 shows the main components of the Rapid system. Rapid is configured with files called *blueprints*. Blueprints are written in an internal configuration language and are used to define build and test targets, rules for deployment, and administrative information (like project owners). Role-based access control lists determine who can perform specific actions on a Rapid project.

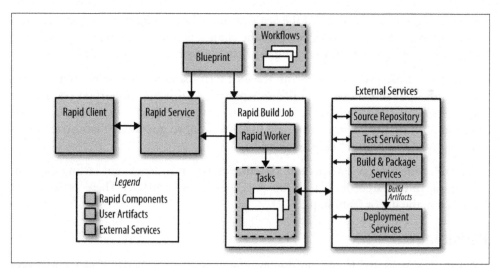

Figure 8-1. Simplified view of Rapid architecture showing the main components of the system

Each Rapid project has workflows that define the actions to perform during the release process. Workflow actions can be performed serially or in parallel, and a workflow can launch other workflows. Rapid dispatches work requests to tasks running as a Borg job on our production servers. Because Rapid uses our production infrastructure, it can handle thousands of release requests simultaneously.

A typical release process proceeds as follows:

1. Rapid uses the requested integration revision number (often obtained automatically from our continuous test system) to create a release branch.

2. Rapid uses Blaze to compile all the binaries and execute the unit tests, often performing these two steps in parallel. Compilation and testing occur in environments dedicated to those specific tasks, as opposed to taking place in the Borg job where the Rapid workflow is executing. This separation allows us to parallelize work easily.

3. Build artifacts are then available for system testing and canary deployments. A typical canary deployment involves starting a few jobs in our production environment after the completion of system tests.

4. The results of each step of the process are logged. A report of all changes since the last release is created.

Rapid allows us to manage our release branches and cherry picks; individual cherry pick requests can be approved or rejected for inclusion in a release.

Deployment

Rapid is often used to drive simple deployments directly. It updates the Borg jobs to use newly built MPM packages based on deployment definitions in the blueprint files and specialized task executors.

For more complicated deployments, we use Sisyphus, which is a general-purpose rollout automation framework developed by SRE. A rollout is a logical unit of work that is composed of one or more individual tasks. Sisyphus provides a set of Python classes that can be extended to support any deployment process. It has a dashboard that allows for finer control on how the rollout is performed and provides a way to monitor the rollout's progress.

In a typical integration, Rapid creates a rollout in a long-running Sisyphus job. Rapid knows the build label associated with the MPM package it created, and can specify that build label when creating the rollout in Sisyphus. Sisyphus uses the build label to specify which version of the MPM packages should be deployed.

With Sisyphus, the rollout process can be as simple or complicated as necessary. For example, it can update all the associated jobs immediately or it can roll out a new binary to successive clusters over a period of several hours.

Our goal is to fit the deployment process to the risk profile of a given service. In development or pre-production environments, we may build hourly and push releases automatically when all tests pass. For large user-facing services, we may push by starting in one cluster and expand exponentially until all clusters are updated. For sensitive pieces of infrastructure, we may extend the rollout over several days, interleaving them across instances in different geographic regions.

Configuration Management

Configuration management is one area of particularly close collaboration between release engineers and SREs. Although configuration management may initially seem a deceptively simple problem, configuration changes are a potential source of instability. As a result, our approach to releasing and managing system and service configurations has evolved substantially over time. Today we use several models for distributing configuration files, as described in the following paragraphs. All schemes involve storing configuration in our primary source code repository and enforcing a strict code review requirement.

Use the mainline for configuration. This was the first method used to configure services in Borg (and the systems that pre-dated Borg). Using this scheme, developers and SREs modify configuration files at the head of the main branch. The changes are reviewed and then applied to the running system. As a result, binary releases and configuration changes are decoupled. While conceptually and procedurally simple, this technique often leads to skew between the checked-in version of the configuration files and the running version of the configuration file because jobs must be updated in order to pick up the changes.

Include configuration files and binaries in the same MPM package. For projects with few configuration files or projects where the files (or a subset of files) change with each release cycle, the configuration files can be included in the MPM package with the binaries. While this strategy limits flexibility by binding the binary and configuration files tightly, it simplifies deployment, because it only requires installing one package.

Package configuration files into MPM "configuration packages." We can apply the hermetic principle to configuration management. Binary configurations tend to be tightly bound to particular versions of binaries, so we leverage the build and packaging systems to snapshot and release configuration files alongside their binaries. Similar to our treatment of binaries, we can use the build ID to reconstruct the configuration at a specific point in time.

For example, a change that implements a new feature can be released with a flag setting that configures that feature. By generating two MPM packages, one for the binary and one for the configuration, we retain the ability to change each package independently. That is, if the feature was released with a flag setting of `first_folio` but we realize it should instead be `bad_quarto`, we can cherry pick that change onto the release branch, rebuild the configuration package, and deploy it. This approach has the advantage of not requiring a new binary build.

We can leverage MPM's labeling feature to indicate which versions of MPM packages should be installed together. A label of `much_ado` can be applied to the MPM packages described in the previous paragraph, which allows us to fetch both packages using this label. When a new version of the project is built, the `much_ado` label will be applied to the new packages. Because these tags are unique within the namespace for an MPM package, only the latest package with that tag will be used.

Read configuration files from an external store. Some projects have configuration files that need to change frequently or dynamically (i.e., while the binary is running). These files can be stored in Chubby, Bigtable, or our source-based filesystem [Kem11].

In summary, project owners consider the different options for distributing and managing configuration files and decide which works best on a case-by-case basis.

Conclusions

While this chapter has specifically discussed Google's approach to release engineering and the ways in which release engineers work and collaborate with SREs, these practices can also be applied more widely.

It's Not Just for Googlers

When equipped with the right tools, proper automation, and well-defined policies, developers and SREs shouldn't have to worry about releasing software. Releases can be as painless as simply pressing a button.

Most companies deal with the same set of release engineering problems regardless of their size or the tools they use: How should you handle versioning of your packages? Should you use a continuous build and deploy model, or perform periodic builds? How often should you release? What configuration management policies should you use? What release metrics are of interest?

Google Release Engineers have developed our own tools out of necessity because open sourced or vendor-supplied tools don't work at the scale we require. Custom tools allow us to include functionality to support (and even enforce) release process policies. However, these policies must first be defined in order to add appropriate features to our tools, and all companies should take the effort to define their release processes whether or not the processes can be automated and/or enforced.

Start Release Engineering at the Beginning

Release engineering has often been an afterthought, and this way of thinking must change as platforms and services continue to grow in size and complexity.

Teams should budget for release engineering resources at the beginning of the product development cycle. It's cheaper to put good practices and process in place early, rather than have to retrofit your system later.

It is essential that the developers, SREs, and release engineers work together. The release engineer needs to understand the intention of how the code should be built and deployed. The developers shouldn't build and "throw the results over the fence" to be handled by the release engineers.

Individual project teams decide when release engineering becomes involved in a project. Because release engineering is still a relatively young discipline, managers don't always plan and budget for release engineering in the early stages of a project. Therefore, when considering how to incorporate release engineering practices, be sure that you consider its role as applied to the entire lifecycle of your product or service—particularly the early stages.

More Information

For more information on release engineering, see the following presentations, each of which has video available online:

- *How Embracing Continuous Release Reduced Change Complexity* (*http://usenix.org/conference/ures14west/summit-program/presentation/dickson*), USENIX Release Engineering Summit West 2014, [Dic14]

- *Maintaining Consistency in a Massively Parallel Environment* (*https://www.usenix.org/conference/ucms13/summit-program/presentation/mcnutt*), USENIX Configuration Management Summit 2013, [McN13]

- *The 10 Commandments of Release Engineering* (*https://www.youtube.com/watch?v=RNMjYV_UsQ8*), 2nd International Workshop on Release Engineering 2014, [McN14b]

- *Distributing Software in a Massively Parallel Environment* (*https://www.usenix.org/conference/lisa14/conference-program/presentation/mcnutt*), LISA 2014, [McN14c]

CHAPTER 9

Simplicity

Written by Max Luebbe
Edited by Tim Harvey

> *The price of reliability is the pursuit of the utmost simplicity.*
> —C.A.R. Hoare, Turing Award lecture

Software systems are inherently dynamic and unstable.[1] A software system can only be perfectly stable if it exists in a vacuum. If we stop changing the codebase, we stop introducing bugs. If the underlying hardware or libraries never change, neither of these components will introduce bugs. If we freeze the current user base, we'll never have to scale the system. In fact, a good summary of the SRE approach to managing systems is: "At the end of the day, our job is to keep agility and stability in balance in the system."[2]

System Stability Versus Agility

It sometimes makes sense to sacrifice stability for the sake of agility. I've often approached an unfamiliar problem domain by conducting what I call exploratory coding—setting an explicit shelf life for whatever code I write with the understanding that I'll need to try and fail once in order to really understand the task I need to accomplish. Code that comes with an expiration date can be much more liberal with test coverage and release management because it will never be shipped to production or be seen by users.

---

1 This is often true of complex systems in general; see [Per99] and [Coo00].

2 Coined by my former manager, Johan Anderson, around the time I became an SRE.

For the majority of production software systems, we want a balanced mix of stability and agility. SREs work to create procedures, practices, and tools that render software more reliable. At the same time, SREs ensure that this work has as little impact on developer agility as possible. In fact, SRE's experience has found that reliable processes tend to actually increase developer agility: rapid, reliable production rollouts make changes in production easier to see. As a result, once a bug surfaces, it takes less time to find and fix that bug. Building reliability into development allows developers to focus their attention on what we really do care about—the functionality and performance of their software and systems.

The Virtue of Boring

Unlike just about everything else in life, "boring" is actually a positive attribute when it comes to software! We don't want our programs to be spontaneous and interesting; we want them to stick to the script and predictably accomplish their business goals. In the words of Google engineer Robert Muth, "Unlike a detective story, the lack of excitement, suspense, and puzzles is actually a desirable property of source code." Surprises in production are the nemeses of SRE.

As Fred Brooks suggests in his "No Silver Bullet" essay [Bro95], it is very important to consider the difference between essential complexity and accidental complexity. Essential complexity is the complexity inherent in a given situation that cannot be removed from a problem definition, whereas accidental complexity is more fluid and can be resolved with engineering effort. For example, writing a web server entails dealing with the essential complexity of serving web pages quickly. However, if we write a web server in Java, we may introduce accidental complexity when trying to minimize the performance impact of garbage collection.

With an eye towards minimizing accidental complexity, SRE teams should:

- Push back when accidental complexity is introduced into the systems for which they are responsible
- Constantly strive to eliminate complexity in systems they onboard and for which they assume operational responsibility

I Won't Give Up My Code!

Because engineers are human beings who often form an emotional attachment to their creations, confrontations over large-scale purges of the source tree are not uncommon. Some might protest, "What if we need that code later?" "Why don't we just comment the code out so we can easily add it again later?" or "Why don't we gate the code with a flag instead of deleting it?" These are all terrible suggestions. Source control systems make it easy to reverse changes, whereas hundreds of lines of commented code create distractions and confusion (especially as the source files continue to evolve), and code that is never executed, gated by a flag that is always disabled, is a metaphorical time bomb waiting to explode, as painfully experienced by Knight Capital, for example (see "Order In the Matter of Knight Capital Americas LLC" [Sec13]).

At the risk of sounding extreme, when you consider a web service that's expected to be available 24/7, to some extent, every new line of code written is a liability. SRE promotes practices that make it more likely that all code has an essential purpose, such as scrutinizing code to make sure that it actually drives business goals, routinely removing dead code, and building bloat detection into all levels of testing.

The "Negative Lines of Code" Metric

The term "software bloat" was coined to describe the tendency of software to become slower and bigger over time as a result of a constant stream of additional features. While bloated software seems intuitively undesirable, its negative aspects become even more clear when considered from the SRE perspective: every line of code changed or added to a project creates the potential for introducing new defects and bugs. A smaller project is easier to understand, easier to test, and frequently has fewer defects. Bearing this perspective in mind, we should perhaps entertain reservations when we have the urge to add new features to a project. Some of the most satisfying coding I've ever done was deleting thousands of lines of code at a time when it was no longer useful.

Minimal APIs

French poet Antoine de Saint Exupery wrote, "perfection is finally attained not when there is no longer more to add, but when there is no longer anything to take away" [Sai39]. This principle is also applicable to the design and construction of software. APIs are a particularly clear expression of why this rule should be followed.

Writing clear, minimal APIs is an essential aspect of managing simplicity in a software system. The fewer methods and arguments we provide to consumers of the API, the easier that API will be to understand, and the more effort we can devote to making those methods as good as they can possibly be. Again, a recurring theme appears: the conscious decision to not take on certain problems allows us to focus on our core problem and make the solutions we explicitly set out to create substantially better. In software, less is more! A small, simple API is usually also a hallmark of a well-understood problem.

Modularity

Expanding outward from APIs and single binaries, many of the rules of thumb that apply to object-oriented programming also apply to the design of distributed systems. The ability to make changes to parts of the system in isolation is essential to creating a supportable system. Specifically, loose coupling between binaries, or between binaries and configuration, is a simplicity pattern that simultaneously promotes developer agility and system stability. If a bug is discovered in one program that is a component of a larger system, that bug can be fixed and pushed to production independent of the rest of the system.

While the modularity that APIs offer may seem straightforward, it is not so apparent that the notion of modularity also extends to how changes to APIs are introduced. Just a single change to an API can force developers to rebuild their entire system and run the risk of introducing new bugs. Versioning APIs allows developers to continue to use the version that their system depends upon while they upgrade to a newer version in a safe and considered way. The release cadence can vary throughout a system, instead of requiring a full production push of the entire system every time a feature is added or improved.

As a system grows more complex, the separation of responsibility between APIs and between binaries becomes increasingly important. This is a direct analogy to object-oriented class design: just as it is understood that it is poor practice to write a "grab bag" class that contains unrelated functions, it is also poor practice to create and put into production a "util" or "misc" binary. A well-designed distributed system consists of collaborators, each of which has a clear and well-scoped purpose.

The concept of modularity also applies to data formats. One of the central strengths and design goals of Google's protocol buffers[3] was to create a wire format that was backward and forward compatible.

Release Simplicity

Simple releases are generally better than complicated releases. It is much easier to measure and understand the impact of a single change rather than a batch of changes released simultaneously. If we release 100 unrelated changes to a system at the same time and performance gets worse, understanding which changes impacted performance, and how they did so, will take considerable effort or additional instrumentation. If the release is performed in smaller batches, we can move faster with more

---

[3] Protocol buffers, also referred to as "protobufs," are a language-neutral, platform-neutral extensible mechanism for serializing structured data. For more details, see *https://developers.google.com/protocol-buffers/docs/overview#a-bit-of-history*.

confidence because each code change can be understood in isolation in the larger system. This approach to releases can be compared to gradient descent in machine learning, in which we find an optimum solution by taking small steps at a time, and considering if each change results in an improvement or degradation.

A Simple Conclusion

This chapter has repeated one theme over and over: software simplicity is a prerequisite to reliability. We are not being lazy when we consider how we might simplify each step of a given task. Instead, we are clarifying what it is we actually want to accomplish and how we might most easily do so. Every time we say "no" to a feature, we are not restricting innovation; we are keeping the environment uncluttered of distractions so that focus remains squarely on innovation, and real engineering can proceed.

PART III

Practices

Put simply, SREs run services—a set of related systems, operated for users, who may be internal or external—and are ultimately responsible for the health of these services. Successfully operating a service entails a wide range of activities: developing monitoring systems, planning capacity, responding to incidents, ensuring the root causes of outages are addressed, and so on. This section addresses the theory and practice of an SRE's day-to-day activity: building and operating large distributed computing systems.

We can characterize the health of a service—in much the same way that Abraham Maslow categorized human needs [Mas43]—from the most basic requirements needed for a system to function as a service at all to the higher levels of function—permitting self-actualization and taking active control of the direction of the service rather than reactively fighting fires. This understanding is so fundamental to how we evaluate services at Google that it wasn't explicitly developed until a number of Google SREs, including our former colleague Mikey Dickerson,[1] temporarily joined the radically different culture of the United States government to help with the launch of *healthcare.gov* in late 2013 and early 2014: they needed a way to explain how to increase systems' reliability.

We'll use this hierarchy, illustrated in Figure III-1, to look at the elements that go into making a service reliable, from most basic to most advanced.

---

1 Mikey left Google in summer 2014 to become the first administrator of the US Digital Service (*https://www.whitehouse.gov/digital/united-states-digital-service*), an agency intended (in part) to bring SRE principles and practices to the US government's IT systems.

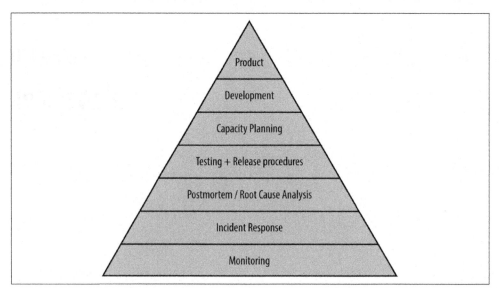

Figure III-1. Service Reliability Hierarchy

Monitoring

Without monitoring, you have no way to tell whether the service is even working; absent a thoughtfully designed monitoring infrastructure, you're flying blind. Maybe everyone who tries to use the website gets an error, maybe not—but you want to be aware of problems before your users notice them. We discuss tools and philosophy in Chapter 10, *Practical Alerting from Time-Series Data.*

Incident Response

SREs don't go on-call merely for the sake of it: rather, on-call support is a tool we use to achieve our larger mission and remain in touch with how distributed computing systems actually work (and fail!). If we could find a way to relieve ourselves of carrying a pager, we would. In Chapter 11, *Being On-Call*, we explain how we balance on-call duties with our other responsibilities.

Once you're aware that there is a problem, how do you make it go away? That doesn't necessarily mean fixing it once and for all—maybe you can stop the bleeding by reducing the system's precision or turning off some features temporarily, allowing it to gracefully degrade, or maybe you can direct traffic to another instance of the service that's working properly. The details of the solution you choose to implement are necessarily specific to your service and your organization. Responding effectively to incidents, however, is something applicable to all teams.

Figuring out what's wrong is the first step; we offer a structured approach in Chapter 12, *Effective Troubleshooting*.

During an incident, it's often tempting to give in to adrenalin and start responding ad hoc. We advise against this temptation in Chapter 13, *Emergency Response*, and counsel in Chapter 14, *Managing Incidents*, that managing incidents effectively should reduce their impact and limit outage-induced anxiety.

Postmortem and Root-Cause Analysis

We aim to be alerted on and manually solve only new and exciting problems presented by our service; it's woefully boring to "fix" the same issue over and over. In fact, this mindset is one of the key differentiators between the SRE philosophy and some more traditional operations-focused environments. This theme is explored in two chapters.

Building a blameless postmortem culture is the first step in understanding what went wrong (and what went right!), as described in Chapter 15, *Postmortem Culture: Learning from Failure*.

Related to that discussion, in Chapter 16, *Tracking Outages*, we briefly describe an internal tool, the outage tracker, that allows SRE teams to keep track of recent production incidents, their causes, and actions taken in response to them.

Testing

Once we understand what tends to go wrong, our next step is attempting to prevent it, because an ounce of prevention is worth a pound of cure. Test suites offer some assurance that our software isn't making certain classes of errors before it's released to production; we talk about how best to use these in Chapter 17, *Testing for Reliability*.

Capacity Planning

In Chapter 18, *Software Engineering in SRE*, we offer a case study of software engineering in SRE with Auxon, a tool for automating capacity planning.

Naturally following capacity planning, load balancing ensures we're properly using the capacity we've built. We discuss how requests to our services get sent to datacenters in Chapter 19, *Load Balancing at the Frontend*. Then we continue the discussion in Chapter 20, *Load Balancing in the Datacenter* and Chapter 21, *Handling Overload*, both of which are essential for ensuring service reliability.

Finally, in Chapter 22, *Addressing Cascading Failures*, we offer advice for addressing cascading failures, both in system design and should your service be caught in a cascading failure.

Development

One of the key aspects of Google's approach to Site Reliability Engineering is that we do significant large-scale system design and software engineering work within the organization.

In Chapter 23, *Managing Critical State: Distributed Consensus for Reliability*, we explain distributed consensus, which (in the guise of Paxos) is at the core of many of Google's distributed systems, including our globally distributed Cron system. In Chapter 24, *Distributed Periodic Scheduling with Cron*, we outline a system that scales to whole datacenters and beyond, which is no easy task.

Chapter 25, *Data Processing Pipelines*, discusses the various forms that data processing pipelines can take: from one-shot MapReduce jobs running periodically to systems that operate in near real-time. Different architectures can lead to surprising and counterintuitive challenges.

Making sure that the data you stored is still there when you want to read it is the heart of data integrity; in Chapter 26, *Data Integrity: What You Read Is What You Wrote*, we explain how to keep data safe.

Product

Finally, having made our way up the reliability pyramid, we find ourselves at the point of having a workable product. In Chapter 27, *Reliable Product Launches at Scale*, we write about how Google does reliable product launches at scale to try to give users the best possible experience starting from Day Zero.

Further Reading from Google SRE

As discussed previously, testing is subtle, and its improper execution can have large effects on overall stability. In an ACM article [Kri12], we explain how Google performs *company-wide* resilience testing to ensure we're capable of weathering the unexpected should a zombie apocalypse or other disaster strike.

While it's often thought of as a dark art, full of mystifying spreadsheets divining the future, capacity planning is nonetheless vital, and as [Hix15a] shows, you don't actually *need* a crystal ball to do it right.

Finally, an interesting and new approach to corporate network security is detailed in [War14], an initiative to replace privileged intranets with device and user credentials. Driven by SREs at the infrastructure level, this is definitely an approach to keep in mind when you're creating your next network.

CHAPTER 10

Practical Alerting from Time-Series Data

Written by Jamie Wilkinson
Edited by Kavita Guliani

May the queries flow, and the pager stay silent.
—Traditional SRE blessing

Monitoring, the bottom layer of the *Hierarchy of Production Needs*, is fundamental to running a stable service. Monitoring enables service owners to make rational decisions about the impact of changes to the service, apply the scientific method to incident response, and of course ensure their reason for existence: to measure the service's alignment with business goals (see Chapter 6).

Regardless of whether or not a service enjoys SRE support, it should be run in a symbiotic relationship with its monitoring. But having been tasked with ultimate responsibility for Google Production, SREs develop a particularly intimate knowledge of the monitoring infrastructure that supports their service.

Monitoring a very large system is challenging for a couple of reasons:

- The sheer number of components being analyzed
- The need to maintain a reasonably low maintenance burden on the engineers responsible for the system

Google's monitoring systems don't just measure simple metrics, such as the average response time of an unladen European web server; we also need to understand the distribution of those response times across all web servers in that region. This knowledge enables us to identify the factors contributing to the latency tail.

At the scale our systems operate, being alerted for single-machine failures is unacceptable because such data is too noisy to be actionable. Instead we try to build systems that are robust against failures in the systems they depend on. Rather than requiring management of many individual components, a large system should be designed to aggregate signals and prune outliers. We need monitoring systems that allow us to alert for high-level service objectives, but retain the granularity to inspect individual components as needed.

Google's monitoring systems evolved over the course of 10 years from the traditional model of custom scripts that check responses and alert, wholly separated from visual display of trends, to a new paradigm. This new model made the collection of time-series a first-class role of the monitoring system, and replaced those check scripts with a rich language for manipulating time-series into charts and alerts.

The Rise of Borgmon

Shortly after the job scheduling infrastructure Borg [Ver15] was created in 2003, a new monitoring system—Borgmon—was built to complement it.

Time-Series Monitoring Outside of Google

This chapter describes the architecture and programming interface of an internal monitoring tool that was foundational for the growth and reliability of Google for almost 10 years...but how does that help you, our dear reader?

In recent years, monitoring has undergone a Cambrian Explosion: Riemann, Heka, Bosun, and Prometheus have emerged as open source tools that are very similar to Borgmon's time-series–based alerting. In particular, Prometheus[1] shares many similarities with Borgmon, especially when you compare the two rule languages. The principles of variable collection and rule evaluation remain the same across all these tools and provide an environment with which you can experiment, and hopefully launch into production, the ideas inspired by this chapter.

Instead of executing custom scripts to detect system failures, Borgmon relies on a common data exposition format; this enables mass data collection with low overheads and avoids the costs of subprocess execution and network connection setup. We call this *white-box monitoring* (see Chapter 6 for a comparison of white-box and black-box monitoring).

---

1 Prometheus is an open source monitoring and time-series database system available at *http://prometheus.io*.

The data is used both for rendering charts and creating alerts, which are accomplished using simple arithmetic. Because collection is no longer in a short-lived process, the history of the collected data can be used for that alert computation as well.

These features help to meet the goal of simplicity described in Chapter 6. They allow the system overhead to be kept low so that the people running the services can remain agile and respond to continuous change in the system as it grows.

To facilitate mass collection, the metrics format had to be standardized. An older method of exporting the internal state (known as *varz*)[2] was formalized to allow the collection of all metrics from a single target in one HTTP fetch. For example, to view a page of metrics manually, you could use the following command:

```
% curl http://webserver:80/varz
http_requests 37
errors_total 12
```

A Borgmon can collect from other Borgmon,[3] so we can build hierarchies that follow the topology of the service, aggregating and summarizing information and discarding some strategically at each level. Typically, a team runs a single Borgmon per cluster, and a pair at the global level. Some very large services shard below the cluster level into many *scraper* Borgmon, which in turn feed to the cluster-level Borgmon.

Instrumentation of Applications

The /varz HTTP handler simply lists all the exported variables in plain text, as space-separated keys and values, one per line. A later extension added a mapped variable, which allows the exporter to define several labels on a variable name, and then export a table of values or a histogram. An example *map-valued* variable looks like the following, showing 25 HTTP 200 responses and 12 HTTP 500s:

```
http_responses map:code 200:25 404:0 500:12
```

Adding a metric to a program only requires a single declaration in the code where the metric is needed.

In hindsight, it's apparent that this schemaless textual interface makes the barrier to adding new instrumentation very low, which is a positive for both the software engineering and SRE teams. However, this has a trade-off against ongoing maintenance; the decoupling of the variable definition from its use in Borgmon rules requires care-

---

2 Google was born in the USA, so we pronounce this *"var-zee."*

3 The plural of Borgmon is Borgmon, like sheep.

ful change management. In practice, this trade-off has been satisfactory because tools to validate and generate rules have been written as well.[4]

Exporting Variables

Google's web roots run deep: each of the major languages used at Google has an implementation of the exported variable interface that automagically registers with the HTTP server built into every Google binary by default.[5] The instances of the variable to be exported allow the server author to perform obvious operations like adding an amount to the current value, setting a key to a specific value, and so forth. The Go expvar library[6] and its JSON output form have a variant of this API.

Collection of Exported Data

To find its targets, a Borgmon instance is configured with a list of targets using one of many name resolution methods.[7] The target list is often dynamic, so using service discovery reduces the cost of maintaining it and allows the monitoring to scale.

At predefined intervals, Borgmon fetches the /varz URI on each target, decodes the results, and stores the values in memory. Borgmon also spreads the collection from each instance in the target list over the whole interval, so that collection from each target is not in lockstep with its peers.

Borgmon also records "synthetic" variables for each target in order to identify:

- If the name was resolved to a host and port
- If the target responded to a collection
- If the target responded to a health check
- What time the collection finished

These synthetic variables make it easy to write rules to detect if the monitored tasks are unavailable.

---

4 Many non-SRE teams use a generator to stamp out the initial boilerplate and ongoing updates, and find the generator much easier to use (though less powerful) than directly editing the rules.

5 Many other applications use their service protocol to export their internal state, as well. OpenLDAP exports it through the cn=Monitor subtree; MySQL can report state with a SHOW VARIABLES query; Apache has its mod_status handler.

6 *https://golang.org/pkg/expvar/*

7 The Borg Name System (BNS) is described in Chapter 2.

It's interesting that varz is quite dissimilar to SNMP (Simple Networking Monitoring Protocol), which "is designed [...] to have minimal transport requirements and to continue working when most other network applications fail" [Mic03]. Scraping targets over HTTP seems to be at odds with this design principle; however, experience shows that this is rarely an issue.[8] The system itself is already designed to be robust against network and machine failures, and Borgmon allows engineers to write smarter alerting rules by using the collection failure itself as a signal.

Storage in the Time-Series Arena

A service is typically made up of many binaries running as many tasks, on many machines, in many clusters. Borgmon needs to keep all that data organized, while allowing flexible querying and slicing of that data.

Borgmon stores all the data in an in-memory database, regularly checkpointed to disk. The data points have the form (`timestamp`, `value`), and are stored in chronological lists called *time-series*, and each time-series is named by a unique set of *labels*, of the form `name=value`.

As presented in Figure 10-1, a time-series is conceptually a one-dimensional matrix of numbers, progressing through time. As you add permutations of labels to this time-series, the matrix becomes multidimensional.

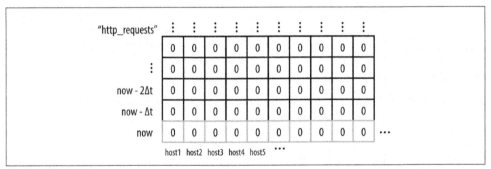

Figure 10-1. A time-series for errors labeled by the original host each was collected from

In practice, the structure is a fixed-sized block of memory, known as the *time-series arena*, with a garbage collector that expires the oldest entries once the arena is full. The time interval between the most recent and oldest entries in the arena is the *horizon*, which indicates how much queryable data is kept in RAM. Typically, datacenter

---

8 Recall in Chapter 6 the distinction between alerting on symptoms and on causes.

and global Borgmon are sized to hold about 12 hours of data[9] for rendering consoles, and much less time if they are the lowest-level collector shards. The memory requirement for a single data point is about 24 bytes, so we can fit 1 million unique time-series for 12 hours at 1-minute intervals in under 17 GB of RAM.

Periodically, the in-memory state is archived to an external system known as the Time-Series Database (TSDB). Borgmon can query TSDB for older data and, while slower, TSDB is cheaper and larger than a Borgmon's RAM.

Labels and Vectors

As shown in the example time-series in Figure 10-2, time-series are stored as sequences of numbers and timestamps, which are referred to as *vectors*. Like vectors in linear algebra, these vectors are slices and cross-sections of the multidimensional matrix of data points in the arena. Conceptually the timestamps can be ignored, because the values are inserted in the vector at regular intervals in time—for example, 1 or 10 seconds or 1 minute apart.

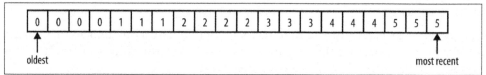

Figure 10-2. An example time-series

The name of a time-series is a *labelset*, because it's implemented as a set of labels expressed as key=value pairs. One of these labels is the variable name itself, the key that appears on the varz page.

A few label names are declared as important. For the time-series in the time-series database to be identifiable, it must at minimum have the following labels:

var
    The name of the variable

job
    The name given to the type of server being monitored

service
    A loosely defined collection of jobs that provide a service to users, either internal or external

---

9 This 12-hour horizon is a magic number that aims to have enough information for debugging an incident in RAM for fast queries without costing *too much* RAM.

---

zone

A Google convention that refers to the location (typically the datacenter) of the Borgmon that performed the collection of this variable

Together, these variables appear something like the following, called the *variable expression*:

```
{var=http_requests,job=webserver,instance=host0:80,service=web,zone=us-west}
```

A query for a time-series does not require specification of all these labels, and a search for a *labelset* returns all matching time-series in a vector. So we could return a vector of results by removing the `instance` label in the preceding query, if there were more than one instance in the cluster. For example:

```
{var=http_requests,job=webserver,service=web,zone=us-west}
```

might have a result of five rows in a vector, with the most recent value in the time-series like so:

```
{var=http_requests,job=webserver,instance=host0:80,service=web,zone=us-west} 10
{var=http_requests,job=webserver,instance=host1:80,service=web,zone=us-west} 9
{var=http_requests,job=webserver,instance=host2:80,service=web,zone=us-west} 11
{var=http_requests,job=webserver,instance=host3:80,service=web,zone=us-west} 0
{var=http_requests,job=webserver,instance=host4:80,service=web,zone=us-west} 10
```

Labels can be added to a time-series from:

- The target's name, e.g., the job and instance
- The target itself, e.g., via map-valued variables
- The Borgmon configuration, e.g., annotations about location or relabeling
- The Borgmon rules being evaluated

We can also query time-series in time, by specifying a duration to the variable expression:

```
{var=http_requests,job=webserver,service=web,zone=us-west}[10m]
```

This returns the last 10 minutes of history of the time-series that matched the expression. If we were collecting data points once per minute, we would expect to return 10 data points in a 10-minute window, like so:[10]

```
{var=http_requests,job=webserver,instance=host0:80, ...} 0 1 2 3 4 5 6 7 8 9 10
{var=http_requests,job=webserver,instance=host1:80, ...} 0 1 2 3 4 4 5 6 7 8 9
{var=http_requests,job=webserver,instance=host2:80, ...} 0 1 2 3 5 6 7 8 9 9 11
{var=http_requests,job=webserver,instance=host3:80, ...} 0 0 0 0 0 0 0 0 0 0 0
{var=http_requests,job=webserver,instance=host4:80, ...} 0 1 2 3 4 5 6 7 8 9 10
```

---

10 The `service` and `zone` labels are elided here for space, but are present in the returned expression.

Rule Evaluation

Borgmon is really just a programmable calculator, with some syntactic sugar that enables it to generate alerts. The data collection and storage components already described are just necessary evils to make that programmable calculator ultimately fit for purpose here as a monitoring system. :)

 Centralizing the rule evaluation in a monitoring system, rather than delegating it to forked subprocesses, means that computations can run in parallel against many similar targets. This practice keeps the configuration relatively small in size (for example, by removing duplication of code) yet more powerful through its expressiveness.

The Borgmon program code, also known as *Borgmon rules*, consists of simple algebraic expressions that compute time-series from other time-series. These rules can be quite powerful because they can query the history of a single time-series (i.e., the time axis), query different subsets of labels from many time-series at once (i.e., the space axis), and apply many mathematical operations.

Rules run in a parallel threadpool where possible, but are dependent on ordering when using previously defined rules as input. The size of the vectors returned by their query expressions also determines the overall runtime of a rule. Thus, it is typically the case that one can add CPU resources to a Borgmon task in response to it running slow. To assist more detailed analysis, internal metrics on the runtime of rules are exported for performance debugging and for monitoring the monitoring.

Aggregation is the cornerstone of rule evaluation in a distributed environment. Aggregation entails taking the sum of a set of time-series from the tasks in a job in order to treat the job as a whole. From those sums, overall rates can be computed. For example, the total queries-per-second rate of a job in a datacenter is the sum of all the rates of change[11] of all the query counters.[12]

---

11 Computing the sum of rates instead of the rate of sums defends the result against counter resets or missing data, perhaps due to a task restart or failed collection of data.

12 Despite being untyped, the majority of varz are simple counters. Borgmon's rate function handles all the corner cases of counter resets.

A counter is any nonmonotonically decreasing variable—which is to say, counters only increase in value. Gauges, on the other hand, may take any value they like. Counters measure increasing values, such as the total number of kilometers driven, while gauges show current state, such as the amount of fuel remaining or current speed. When collecting Borgmon-style data, it's better to use counters, because they don't lose meaning when events occur between sampling intervals. Should any activity or changes occur between sampling intervals, a gauge collection is likely to miss that activity.

For an example web server, we might want to alert when our web server cluster starts to serve more errors as a percent of requests than we think is normal—or more technically, when the sum of the rates of non-HTTP-200 return codes on all tasks in the cluster, divided by the sum of the rates of requests to all tasks in that cluster, is greater than some value.

This is accomplished by:

1. Aggregating the rates of response codes across all tasks, outputting a vector of rates at that point in time, one for each code.

2. Computing the total error rate as the sum of that vector, outputting a single value for the cluster at that point in time. This total error rate excludes the 200 code from the sum, because it is not an error.

3. Computing the cluster-wide ratio of errors to requests, dividing the total error rate by the rate of requests that arrived, and again outputting a single value for the cluster at that point in time.

Each of these outputs at a point in time gets appended to its named variable expression, which creates the new time-series. As a result, we will be able to inspect the history of error rates and error ratios some other time.

The rate of requests rules would be written in Borgmon's rule language as the following:

```
rules <<<
  # Compute the rate of requests for each task from the count of requests
  {var=task:http_requests:rate10m,job=webserver} =
    rate({var=http_requests,job=webserver}[10m]);

  # Sum the rates to get the aggregate rate of queries for the cluster;
  # 'without instance' instructs Borgmon to remove the instance label
  # from the right hand side.
  {var=dc:http_requests:rate10m,job=webserver} =
    sum without instance({var=task:http_requests:rate10m,job=webserver})
>>>
```

The rate() function takes the enclosed expression and returns the total delta divided by the total time between the earliest and latest values.

With the example time-series data from the query before, the results for the task:http_requests:rate10m rule would look like:[13]

```
{var=task:http_requests:rate10m,job=webserver,instance=host0:80, ...} 1
{var=task:http_requests:rate10m,job=webserver,instance=host2:80, ...} 0.9
{var=task:http_requests:rate10m,job=webserver,instance=host3:80, ...} 1.1
{var=task:http_requests:rate10m,job=webserver,instance=host4:80, ...} 0
{var=task:http_requests:rate10m,job=webserver,instance=host5:80, ...} 1
```

and the results for the dc:http_requests:rate10m rule would be:

```
{var=dc:http_requests:rate10m,job=webserver,service=web,zone=us-west} 4
```

because the second rule uses the first one as input.

> The instance label is missing in the output now, discarded by the aggregation rule. If it had remained in the rule, then Borgmon would not have been able to sum the five rows together.

In these examples, we use a time window because we're dealing with discrete points in the time-series, as opposed to continuous functions. Doing so makes the rate calculation easier than performing calculus, but means that to compute a rate, we need to select a sufficient number of data points. We also have to deal with the possibility that some recent collections have failed. Recall that the historical variable expression notation uses the range [10m] to avoid missing data points caused by collection errors.

The example also uses a Google convention that helps readability. Each computed variable name contains a colon-separated triplet indicating the aggregation level, the variable name, and the operation that created that name. In this example, the left-hand variables are "task HTTP requests 10-minute rate" and "datacenter HTTP requests 10-minute rate."

Now that we know how to create a rate of queries, we can build on that to also compute a rate of errors, and then we can calculate the ratio of responses to requests to understand how much useful work the service is doing. We can compare the ratio rate of errors to our service level objective (see Chapter 4) and alert if this objective is missed or in danger of being missed:

---

13 The service and zone labels are elided for space.

```
rules <<<
  # Compute a rate pertask and per 'code' label
  {var=task:http_responses:rate10m,job=webserver} =
    rate by code({var=http_responses,job=webserver}[10m]);

  # Compute a cluster level response rate per 'code' label
  {var=dc:http_responses:rate10m,job=webserver} =
    sum without instance({var=task:http_responses:rate10m,job=webserver});

  # Compute a new cluster level rate summing all non 200 codes
  {var=dc:http_errors:rate10m,job=webserver} = sum without code(
    {var=dc:http_responses:rate10m,jobwebserver,code=!/200/};

  # Compute the ratio of the rate of errors to the rate of requests
  {var=dc:http_errors:ratio_rate10m,job=webserver} =
    {var=dc:http_errors:rate10m,job=webserver}
    /
    {var=dc:http_requests:rate10m,job=webserver};
>>>
```

Again, this calculation demonstrates the convention of suffixing the new time-series variable name with the operation that created it. This result is read as "datacenter HTTP errors 10 minute ratio of rates."

The output of these rules might look like:[14]

`{var=task:http_responses:rate10m,job=webserver}`

```
{var=task:http_responses:rate10m,job=webserver,code=200,instance=host0:80, ...} 1
{var=task:http_responses:rate10m,job=webserver,code=500,instance=host0:80, ...} 0
{var=task:http_responses:rate10m,job=webserver,code=200,instance=host1:80, ...} 0.5
{var=task:http_responses:rate10m,job=webserver,code=500,instance=host1:80, ...} 0.4
{var=task:http_responses:rate10m,job=webserver,code=200,instance=host2:80, ...} 1
{var=task:http_responses:rate10m,job=webserver,code=500,instance=host2:80, ...} 0.1
{var=task:http_responses:rate10m,job=webserver,code=200,instance=host3:80, ...} 0
{var=task:http_responses:rate10m,job=webserver,code=500,instance=host3:80, ...} 0
{var=task:http_responses:rate10m,job=webserver,code=200,instance=host4:80, ...} 0.9
{var=task:http_responses:rate10m,job=webserver,code=500,instance=host4:80, ...} 0.1
```

`{var=dc:http_responses:rate10m,job=webserver}`

```
{var=dc:http_responses:rate10m,job=webserver,code=200, ...} 3.4
{var=dc:http_responses:rate10m,job=webserver,code=500, ...} 0.6
```

`{var=dc:http_responses:rate10m,jobwebserver,code=!/200/}`

```
{var=dc:http_responses:rate10m,job=webserver,code=500, ...} 0.6
```

`{var=dc:http_errors:rate10m,job=webserver}`

```
{var=dc:http_errors:rate10m,job=webserver, ...} 0.6
```

---

14 The service and zone labels are elided for space.

```
{var=dc:http_errors:ratio_rate10m,job=webserver}

  {var=dc:http_errors:ratio_rate10m,job=webserver} 0.15
```

 The preceding output shows the intermediate query in the
dc:http_errors:rate10m rule that filters the non-200 error codes.
Though the value of the expressions are the same, observe that the
code label is retained in one but removed from the other.

As mentioned previously, Borgmon rules create new time-series, so the results of the computations are kept in the time-series arena and can be inspected just as the source time-series are. The ability to do so allows for ad hoc querying, evaluation, and exploration as tables or charts. This is a useful feature for debugging while on-call, and if these ad hoc queries prove useful, they can be made permanent visualizations on a service console.

Alerting

When an alerting rule is evaluated by a Borgmon, the result is either true, in which case the alert is triggered, or false. Experience shows that alerts can "flap" (toggle their state quickly); therefore, the rules allow a minimum duration for which the alerting rule must be true before the alert is sent. Typically, this duration is set to at least two rule evaluation cycles to ensure no missed collections cause a false alert.

The following example creates an alert when the error ratio over 10 minutes exceeds 1% and the total number of errors exceeds 1:

```
rules <<<
  {var=dc:http_errors:ratio_rate10m,job=webserver} > 0.01
    and by job, error
  {var=dc:http_errors:rate10m,job=webserver} > 1
    for 2m
    => ErrorRatioTooHigh
      details "webserver error ratio at [[trigger_value]]"
      labels {severity=page};
>>>
```

Our example holds the ratio rate at 0.15, which is well over the threshold of 0.01 in the alerting rule. However, the number of errors is not greater than 1 at this moment, so the alert won't be active. Once the number of errors exceeds 1, the alert will go *pending* for two minutes to ensure it isn't a transient state, and only then will it *fire*.

The alert rule contains a small template for filling out a message containing contextual information: which job the alert is for, the name of the alert, the numerical value of the triggering rule, and so on. The contextual information is filled out by Borgmon when the alert fires and is sent in the Alert RPC.

Borgmon is connected to a centrally run service, known as the Alertmanager, which receives Alert RPCs when the rule first triggers, and then again when the alert is considered to be "firing." The Alertmanager is responsible for routing the alert notification to the correct destination. Alertmanager can be configured to do the following:

- Inhibit certain alerts when others are active
- Deduplicate alerts from multiple Borgmon that have the same labelsets
- Fan-in or fan-out alerts based on their labelsets when multiple alerts with similar labelsets fire

As described in Chapter 6, teams send their page-worthy alerts to their on-call rotation and their important but subcritical alerts to their ticket queues. All other alerts should be retained as informational data for status dashboards.

A more comprehensive guide to alert design can be found in Chapter 4.

Sharding the Monitoring Topology

A Borgmon can import time-series data from other Borgmon, as well. While one could attempt to collect from all tasks in a service globally, doing so quickly becomes a scaling bottleneck and introduces a single point of failure into the design. Instead, a streaming protocol is used to transmit time-series data between Borgmon, saving CPU time and network bytes compared to the text-based varz format. A typical such deployment uses two or more global Borgmon for top-level aggregation and one Borgmon in each datacenter to monitor all the jobs running at that location. (Google divides the production network into zones for production changes, so having two or more global replicas provides diversity in the face of maintenance and outages for this otherwise single point of failure.)

As shown in Figure 10-3, more complicated deployments shard the datacenter Borgmon further into a purely scraping-only layer (often due to RAM and CPU constraints in a single Borgmon for very large services) and a DC aggregation layer that performs mostly rule evaluation for aggregation. Sometimes the global layer is split between rule evaluation and dashboarding. Upper-tier Borgmon can filter the data they want to stream from the lower-tier Borgmon, so that the global Borgmon does not fill its arena with all the per-task time-series from the lower tiers. Thus, the aggregation hierarchy builds local caches of relevant time-series that can be drilled down into when required.

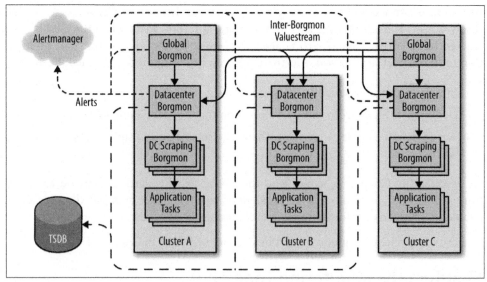

Figure 10-3. A data flow model of a hierarchy of Borgmon in three clusters

Black-Box Monitoring

Borgmon is a white-box monitoring system—it inspects the internal state of the target service, and the rules are written with knowledge of the internals in mind. The transparent nature of this model provides great power to identify quickly what components are failing, which queues are full, and where bottlenecks occur, both when responding to an incident and when testing a new feature deployment.

However, white-box monitoring does not provide a full picture of the system being monitored; relying solely upon white-box monitoring means that you aren't aware of what the users see. You only see the queries that arrive at the target; the queries that never make it due to a DNS error are invisible, while queries lost due to a server crash never make a sound. You can only alert on the failures that you expected.

Teams at Google solve this coverage issue with Prober, which runs a protocol check against a target and reports success or failure. The prober can send alerts directly to Alertmanager, or its own varz can be collected by a Borgmon. Prober can validate the response payload of the protocol (e.g., the HTML contents of an HTTP response) and validate that the contents are expected, and even extract and export values as time-series. Teams often use Prober to export histograms of response times by operation type and payload size so that they can slice and dice the user-visible performance. Prober is a hybrid of the check-and-test model with some richer variable extraction to create time-series.

Prober can be pointed at either the frontend domain or behind the load balancer. By using both targets, we can detect localized failures and suppress alerts. For example, we might monitor both the load balanced *www.google.com* and the web servers in each datacenter behind the load balancer. This setup allows us to either know that traffic is still served when a datacenter fails, or to quickly isolate an edge in the traffic flow graph where a failure has occurred.

Maintaining the Configuration

Borgmon configuration separates the definition of the rules from the targets being monitored. This means the same sets of rules can be applied to many targets at once, instead of writing nearly identical configuration over and over. This separation of concerns might seem incidental, but it greatly reduces the cost of maintaining the monitoring by avoiding lots of repetition in describing the target systems.

Borgmon also supports language templates. This macro-like system enables engineers to construct libraries of rules that can be reused. This functionality again reduces repetition, thus reducing the likelihood of bugs in the configuration.

Of course, any high-level programming environment creates the opportunity for complexity, so Borgmon provides a way to build extensive unit and regression tests by synthesizing time-series data, in order to ensure that the rules behave as the author thinks they do. The Production Monitoring team runs a continuous integration service that executes a suite of these tests, packages the configuration, and ships the configuration to all the Borgmon in production, which then validate the configuration before accepting it.

In the vast library of common templates that have been created, two classes of monitoring configuration have emerged. The first class simply codifies the emergent schema of variables exported from a given library of code, such that any user of the library can reuse the template of its varz. Such templates exist for the HTTP server library, memory allocation, the storage client library, and generic RPC services, among others. (While the varz interface declares no schema, the rule library associated with the code library ends up declaring a schema.)

The second class of library emerged as we built templates to manage the aggregation of data from a single-server task to the global service footprint. These libraries contain generic aggregation rules for exported variables that engineers can use to model the topology of their service.

For example, a service may provide a single global API, but be homed in many data-centers. Within each datacenter, the service is composed of several shards, and each shard is composed of several jobs with various numbers of tasks. An engineer can model this breakdown with Borgmon rules so that when debugging, subcomponents can be isolated from the rest of the system. These groupings typically follow the shared fate of components; e.g., individual tasks share fate due to configuration files, jobs in a shard share fate because they're homed in the same datacenter, and physical sites share fate due to networking.

Labeling conventions make such division possible: a Borgmon adds labels indicating the target's instance name and the shard and datacenter it occupies, which can be used to group and aggregate those time-series together.

Thus, we have multiple uses for labels on a time-series, though all are interchangeable:

- Labels that define breakdowns of the data itself (e.g., our HTTP response code on the http_responses variable)
- Labels that define the source of the data (e.g., the instance or job name)
- Labels that indicate the locality or aggregation of the data within the service as a whole (e.g., the zone label describing a physical location, a shard label describing a logical grouping of tasks)

The templated nature of these libraries allows flexibility in their use. The same template can be used to aggregate from each tier.

Ten Years On...

Borgmon transposed the model of check-and-alert per target into mass variable collection and a centralized rule evaluation across the time-series for alerting and diagnostics.

This decoupling allows the size of the system being monitored to scale independently of the size of alerting rules. These rules cost less to maintain because they're abstracted over a common time-series format. New applications come ready with metric exports in all components and libraries to which they link, and well-traveled aggregation and console templates, which further reduces the burden of implementation.

Ensuring that the cost of maintenance scales sublinearly with the size of the service is key to making monitoring (and all sustaining operations work) maintainable. This theme recurs in all SRE work, as SREs work to scale all aspects of their work to the global scale.

Ten years is a long time, though, and of course today the shape of the monitoring landscape within Google has evolved with experiments and changes, striving for continual improvement as the company grows.

Even though Borgmon remains internal to Google, the idea of treating time-series data as a data source for generating alerts is now accessible to everyone through those open source tools like Prometheus, Riemann, Heka, and Bosun, and probably others by the time you read this.

CHAPTER 11

Being On-Call

Written by Andrea Spadaccini[1]
Edited by Kavita Guliani

Being on-call is a critical duty that many operations and engineering teams must undertake in order to keep their services reliable and available. However, there are several pitfalls in the organization of on-call rotations and responsibilities that can lead to serious consequences for the services and for the teams if not avoided. This chapter describes the primary tenets of the approach to on-call that Google's Site Reliability Engineers (SREs) have developed over years, and explains how that approach has led to reliable services and sustainable workload over time.

Introduction

Several professions require employees to perform some sort of on-call duty, which entails being available for calls during both working and nonworking hours. In the IT context, on-call activities have historically been performed by dedicated Ops teams tasked with the primary responsibility of keeping the service(s) for which they are responsible in good health.

Many important services in Google, e.g., Search, Ads, and Gmail, have dedicated teams of SREs responsible for the performance and reliability of these services. Thus, SREs are on-call for the services they support. The SRE teams are quite different from purely operational teams in that they place heavy emphasis on the use of engineering to approach problems. These problems, which typically fall in the operational domain, exist at a scale that would be intractable without software engineering solutions.

---

1 An earlier version of this chapter appeared as an article in *;login:* (October 2015, vol. 40, no. 5).

To enforce this type of problem solving, Google hires people with a diverse background in systems and software engineering into SRE teams. We cap the amount of time SREs spend on purely operational work at 50%; at minimum, 50% of an SRE's time should be allocated to engineering projects that further scale the impact of the team through automation, in addition to improving the service.

Life of an On-Call Engineer

This section describes the typical activities of an on-call engineer and provides some background for the rest of the chapter.

As the guardians of production systems, on-call engineers take care of their assigned operations by managing outages that affect the team and performing and/or vetting production changes.

When on-call, an engineer is available to perform operations on production systems within minutes, according to the paging response times agreed to by the team and the business system owners. Typical values are 5 minutes for user-facing or otherwise highly time-critical services, and 30 minutes for less time-sensitive systems. The company provides the page-receiving device, which is typically a phone. Google has flexible alert delivery systems that can dispatch pages via multiple mechanisms (email, SMS, robot call, app) across multiple devices.

Response times are related to desired service availability, as demonstrated by the following simplistic example: if a user-facing system must obtain 4 nines of availability in a given quarter (99.99%), the allowed quarterly downtime is around 13 minutes (Appendix A). This constraint implies that the reaction time of on-call engineers has to be in the order of minutes (strictly speaking, 13 minutes). For systems with more relaxed SLOs, the reaction time can be on the order of tens of minutes.

As soon as a page is received and acknowledged, the on-call engineer is expected to triage the problem and work toward its resolution, possibly involving other team members and escalating as needed.

Nonpaging production events, such as lower priority alerts or software releases, can also be handled and/or vetted by the on-call engineer during business hours. These activities are less urgent than paging events, which take priority over almost every other task, including project work. For more insight on interrupts and other nonpaging events that contribute to operational load, see Chapter 29.

Many teams have both a primary and a secondary on-call rotation. The distribution of duties between the primary and the secondary varies from team to team. One team might employ the secondary as a fall-through for the pages the primary on-call misses. Another team might specify that the primary on-call handles only pages, while the secondary handles all other non-urgent production activities.

In teams for which a secondary rotation is not strictly required for duty distribution, it is common for two related teams to serve as secondary on-call for each other, with fall-through handling duties. This setup eliminates the need for an exclusive secondary on-call rotation.

There are many ways to organize on-call rotations; for detailed analysis, refer to the "Oncall" chapter of [Lim14].

Balanced On-Call

SRE teams have specific constraints on the quantity and quality of on-call shifts. The quantity of on-call can be calculated by the percent of time spent by engineers on on-call duties. The quality of on-call can be calculated by the number of incidents that occur during an on-call shift.

SRE managers have the responsibility of keeping the on-call workload balanced and sustainable across these two axes.

Balance in Quantity

We strongly believe that the "E" in "SRE" is a defining characteristic of our organization, so we strive to invest at least 50% of SRE time into engineering: of the remainder, no more than 25% can be spent on-call, leaving up to another 25% on other types of operational, nonproject work.

Using the 25% on-call rule, we can derive the minimum number of SREs required to sustain a 24/7 on-call rotation. Assuming that there are always two people on-call (primary and secondary, with different duties), the minimum number of engineers needed for on-call duty from a single-site team is eight: assuming week-long shifts, each engineer is on-call (primary or secondary) for one week every month. For dual-site teams, a reasonable minimum size of each team is six, both to honor the 25% rule and to ensure a substantial and critical mass of engineers for the team.

If a service entails enough work to justify growing a single-site team, we prefer to create a multi-site team. A multi-site team is advantageous for two reasons:

- Night shifts have detrimental effects on people's health [Dur05], and a multi-site "follow the sun" rotation allows teams to avoid night shifts altogether.
- Limiting the number of engineers in the on-call rotation ensures that engineers do not lose touch with the production systems (see "A Treacherous Enemy: Operational Underload" on page 132).

However, multi-site teams incur communication and coordination overhead. Therefore, the decision to go multi-site or single-site should be based upon the trade-offs each option entails, the importance of the system, and the workload each system generates.

Balance in Quality

For each on-call shift, an engineer should have sufficient time to deal with any incidents and follow-up activities such as writing postmortems [Loo10]. Let's define an incident as a sequence of events and alerts that are related to the same root cause and would be discussed as part of the same postmortem. We've found that on average, dealing with the tasks involved in an on-call incident—root-cause analysis, remediation, and follow-up activities like writing a postmortem and fixing bugs—takes 6 hours. It follows that the maximum number of incidents per day is 2 per 12-hour on-call shift. In order to stay within this upper bound, the distribution of paging events should be very flat over time, with a likely median value of 0: if a given component or issue causes pages every day (median incidents/day > 1), it is likely that something else will break at some point, thus causing more incidents than should be permitted.

If this limit is temporarily exceeded, e.g., for a quarter, corrective measures should be put in place to make sure that the operational load returns to a sustainable state (see "Operational Overload" on page 130 and Chapter 30).

Compensation

Adequate compensation needs to be considered for out-of-hours support. Different organizations handle on-call compensation in different ways; Google offers time-off-in-lieu or straight cash compensation, capped at some proportion of overall salary. The compensation cap represents, in practice, a limit on the amount of on-call work that will be taken on by any individual. This compensation structure ensures incentivization to be involved in on-call duties as required by the team, but also promotes a balanced on-call work distribution and limits potential drawbacks of excessive on-call work, such as burnout or inadequate time for project work.

Feeling Safe

As mentioned earlier, SRE teams support Google's most critical systems. Being an SRE on-call typically means assuming responsibility for user-facing, revenue-critical systems or for the infrastructure required to keep these systems up and running. SRE methodology for thinking about and tackling problems is vital for the appropriate operation of services.

Modern research identifies two distinct ways of thinking that an individual may, consciously or subconsciously, choose when faced with challenges [Kah11]:

- Intuitive, automatic, and rapid action
- Rational, focused, and deliberate cognitive functions

When one is dealing with the outages related to complex systems, the second of these options is more likely to produce better results and lead to well-planned incident handling.

To make sure that the engineers are in the appropriate frame of mind to leverage the latter mindset, it's important to reduce the stress related to being on-call. The importance and the impact of the services and the consequences of potential outages can create significant pressure on the on-call engineers, damaging the well-being of individual team members and possibly prompting SREs to make incorrect choices that can endanger the availability of the service. Stress hormones like cortisol and corticotropin-releasing hormone (CRH) are known to cause behavioral consequences —including fear—that can impair cognitive functions and cause suboptimal decision making [Chr09].

Under the influence of these stress hormones, the more deliberate cognitive approach is typically subsumed by unreflective and unconsidered (but immediate) action, leading to potential abuse of heuristics. Heuristics are very tempting behaviors when one is on-call. For example, when the same alert pages for the fourth time in the week, and the previous three pages were initiated by an external infrastructure system, it is extremely tempting to exercise confirmation bias by automatically associating this fourth occurrence of the problem with the previous cause.

While intuition and quick reactions can seem like desirable traits in the middle of incident management, they have downsides. Intuition can be wrong and is often less supportable by obvious data. Thus, following intuition can lead an engineer to waste time pursuing a line of reasoning that is incorrect from the start. Quick reactions are deep-rooted in habit, and habitual responses are unconsidered, which means they can be disastrous. The ideal methodology in incident management strikes the perfect balance of taking steps at the desired pace when enough data is available to make a reasonable decision while simultaneously critically examining your assumptions.

It's important that on-call SREs understand that they can rely on several resources that make the experience of being on-call less daunting than it may seem. The most important on-call resources are:

- Clear escalation paths
- Well-defined incident-management procedures
- A blameless postmortem culture ([Loo10], [All12])

The developer teams of SRE-supported systems usually participate in a 24/7 on-call rotation, and it is always possible to escalate to these partner teams when necessary.

The appropriate escalation of outages is generally a principled way to react to serious outages with significant unknown dimensions.

When one is handling incidents, if the issue is complex enough to involve multiple teams or if, after some investigation, it is not yet possible to estimate an upper bound for the incident's time span, it can be useful to adopt a formal incident-management protocol. Google SRE uses the protocol described in Chapter 14, which offers an easy-to-follow and well-defined set of steps that aid an on-call engineer to rationally pursue a satisfactory incident resolution with all the required help. This protocol is internally supported by a web-based tool that automates most of the incident management actions, such as handing off roles and recording and communicating status updates. This tool allows incident managers to focus on dealing with the incident, rather than spending time and cognitive effort on mundane actions such as formatting emails or updating several communication channels at once.

Finally, when an incident occurs, it's important to evaluate what went wrong, recognize what went well, and take action to prevent the same errors from recurring in the future. SRE teams must write postmortems after significant incidents and detail a full timeline of the events that occurred. By focusing on events rather than the people, these postmortems provide significant value. Rather than placing blame on individuals, they derive value from the systematic analysis of production incidents. Mistakes happen, and software should make sure that we make as few mistakes as possible. Recognizing automation opportunities is one of the best ways to prevent human errors [Loo10].

Avoiding Inappropriate Operational Load

As mentioned in "Balanced On-Call" on page 127, SREs spend at most 50% of their time on operational work. What happens if operational activities exceed this limit?

Operational Overload

The SRE team and leadership are responsible for including concrete objectives in quarterly work planning in order to make sure that the workload returns to sustainable levels. Temporarily loaning an experienced SRE to an overloaded team, discussed in Chapter 30, can provide enough breathing room so that the team can make headway in addressing issues.

Ideally, symptoms of operational overload should be measurable, so that the goals can be quantified (e.g., number of daily tickets < 5, paging events per shift < 2).

Misconfigured monitoring is a common cause of operational overload. Paging alerts should be aligned with the symptoms that threaten a service's SLOs. All paging alerts should also be actionable. Low-priority alerts that bother the on-call engineer every hour (or more frequently) disrupt productivity, and the fatigue such alerts induce can also cause serious alerts to be treated with less attention than necessary. See Chapter 29 for further discussion.

It is also important to control the number of alerts that the on-call engineers receive for a single incident. Sometimes a single abnormal condition can generate several alerts, so it's important to regulate the alert fan-out by ensuring that related alerts are grouped together by the monitoring or alerting system. If, for any reason, duplicate or uninformative alerts are generated during an incident, silencing those alerts can provide the necessary quiet for the on-call engineer to focus on the incident itself. Noisy alerts that systematically generate more than one alert per incident should be tweaked to approach a 1:1 alert/incident ratio. Doing so allows the on-call engineer to focus on the incident instead of triaging duplicate alerts.

Sometimes the changes that cause operational overload are not under the control of the SRE teams. For example, the application developers might introduce changes that cause the system to be more noisy, less reliable, or both. In this case, it is appropriate to work together with the application developers to set common goals to improve the system.

In extreme cases, SRE teams may have the option to "give back the pager"—SRE can ask the developer team to be exclusively on-call for the system until it meets the standards of the SRE team in question. Giving back the pager doesn't happen very frequently, because it's almost always possible to work with the developer team to reduce the operational load and make a given system more reliable. In some cases, though, complex or architectural changes spanning multiple quarters might be required to make a system sustainable from an operational point of view. In such cases, the SRE team should not be subject to an excessive operational load. Instead, it is appropriate to negotiate the reorganization of on-call responsibilities with the development team, possibly routing some or all paging alerts to the developer on-call. Such a solution is typically a temporary measure, during which time the SRE and developer teams work together to get the service in shape to be on-boarded by the SRE team again.

The possibility of renegotiating on-call responsibilities between SRE and product development teams attests to the balance of powers between the teams.[2] This working relationship also exemplifies how the healthy tension between these two teams and the values that they represent—reliability versus feature velocity—is typically resolved by greatly benefiting the service and, by extension, the company as a whole.

---

2 For more discussion on the natural tension between SRE and product development teams, see Chapter 1.

A Treacherous Enemy: Operational Underload

Being on-call for a quiet system is blissful, but what happens if the system is too quiet or when SREs are not on-call often enough? An operational underload is undesirable for an SRE team. Being out of touch with production for long periods of time can lead to confidence issues, both in terms of overconfidence and underconfidence, while knowledge gaps are discovered only when an incident occurs.

To counteract this eventuality, SRE teams should be sized to allow every engineer to be on-call at least once or twice a quarter, thus ensuring that each team member is sufficiently exposed to production. "Wheel of Misfortune" exercises (discussed in Chapter 28) are also useful team activities that can help to hone and improve trouble-shooting skills and knowledge of the service. Google also has a company-wide annual disaster recovery event called DiRT (Disaster Recovery Training) that combines theoretical and practical drills to perform multiday testing of infrastructure systems and individual services; see [Kri12].

Conclusions

The approach to on-call described in this chapter serves as a guideline for all SRE teams in Google and is key to fostering a sustainable and manageable work environment. Google's approach to on-call has enabled us to use engineering work as the primary means to scale production responsibilities and maintain high reliability and availability despite the increasing complexity and number of systems and services for which SREs are responsible.

While this approach might not be immediately applicable to all contexts in which engineers need to be on-call for IT services, we believe it represents a solid model that organizations can adopt in scaling to meet a growing volume of on-call work.

CHAPTER 12

Effective Troubleshooting

Written by Chris Jones

Be warned that being an expert is more than understanding how a system is supposed to work. Expertise is gained by investigating why a system doesn't work.
—Brian Redman

Ways in which things go right are special cases of the ways in which things go wrong.
—John Allspaw

Troubleshooting is a critical skill for anyone who operates distributed computing systems—especially SREs—but it's often viewed as an innate skill that some people have and others don't. One reason for this assumption is that, for those who troubleshoot often, it's an ingrained process; explaining *how* to troubleshoot is difficult, much like explaining how to ride a bike. However, we believe that troubleshooting is *both* learnable and teachable.

Novices are often tripped up when troubleshooting because the exercise ideally depends upon two factors: an understanding of how to troubleshoot generically (i.e., without any particular system knowledge) and a solid knowledge of the system. While you can investigate a problem using only the generic process and derivation from first principles,[1] we usually find this approach to be less efficient and less effective than understanding how things are supposed to work. Knowledge of the system typically limits the effectiveness of an SRE new to a system; there's little substitute to learning how the system is designed and built.

---

1 Indeed, using only first principles and troubleshooting skills is often an effective way to learn how a system works; see Chapter 28.

Let's look at a general model of the troubleshooting process. Readers with expertise in troubleshooting may quibble with our definitions and process; if your method is effective for you, there's no reason not to stick with it.

Theory

Formally, we can think of the troubleshooting process as an application of the hypothetico-deductive method:[2] given a set of observations about a system and a theoretical basis for understanding system behavior, we iteratively hypothesize potential causes for the failure and try to test those hypotheses.

In an idealized model such as that in Figure 12-1, we'd start with a problem report telling us that something is wrong with the system. Then we can look at the system's telemetry[3] and logs to understand its current state. This information, combined with our knowledge of how the system is built, how it should operate, and its failure modes, enables us to identify some possible causes.

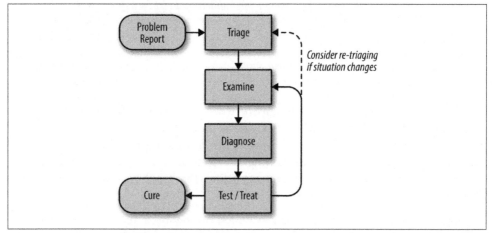

Figure 12-1. A process for troubleshooting

---

2 See *https://en.wikipedia.org/wiki/Hypothetico-deductive_model*.

3 For instance, exported variables as described in Chapter 10.

We can then test our hypotheses in one of two ways. We can compare the observed state of the system against our theories to find confirming or disconfirming evidence. Or, in some cases, we can actively "treat" the system—that is, change the system in a controlled way—and observe the results. This second approach refines our understanding of the system's state and possible cause(s) of the reported problems. Using either of these strategies, we repeatedly test until a root cause is identified, at which point we can then take corrective action to prevent a recurrence and write a postmortem. Of course, fixing the proximate cause(s) needn't always wait for root-causing or postmortem writing.

Common Pitfalls

Ineffective troubleshooting sessions are plagued by problems at the Triage, Examine, and Diagnose steps, often because of a lack of deep system understanding. The following are common pitfalls to avoid:

- Looking at symptoms that aren't relevant or misunderstanding the meaning of system metrics. Wild goose chases often result.

- Misunderstanding how to change the system, its inputs, or its environment, so as to safely and effectively test hypotheses.

- Coming up with wildly improbable theories about what's wrong, or latching on to causes of past problems, reasoning that since it happened once, it must be happening again.

- Hunting down spurious correlations that are actually coincidences or are correlated with shared causes.

Fixing the first and second common pitfalls is a matter of learning the system in question and becoming experienced with the common patterns used in distributed systems. The third trap is a set of logical fallacies that can be avoided by remembering that not all failures are equally probable—as doctors are taught, "when you hear hoofbeats, think of horses not zebras."[4] Also remember that, all things being equal, we should prefer simpler explanations.[5]

---

4 Attributed to Theodore Woodward, of the University of Maryland School of Medicine, in the 1940s. See *https://en.wikipedia.org/wiki/Zebra_(medicine)*. This works in some domains, but in some systems, entire classes of failures may be eliminable: for instance, using a well-designed cluster filesystem means that a latency problem is unlikely to be due to a single dead disk.

5 Occam's Razor; see *https://en.wikipedia.org/wiki/Occam%27s_razor*. But remember that it may still be the case that there are multiple problems; in particular, it may be more likely that a system has a number of common low-grade problems that, taken together, explain all the symptoms rather than a single rare problem that causes them all. Cf *https://en.wikipedia.org/wiki/Hickam%27s_dictum*.

Finally, we should remember that correlation is not causation:[6] some correlated events, say packet loss within a cluster and failed hard drives in the cluster, share common causes—in this case, a power outage, though network failure clearly doesn't cause the hard drive failures nor vice versa. Even worse, as systems grow in size and complexity and as more metrics are monitored, it's inevitable that there will be events that happen to correlate well with other events, purely by coincidence.[7]

Understanding failures in our reasoning process is the first step to avoiding them and becoming more effective in solving problems. A methodical approach to knowing what we do know, what we don't know, and what we need to know, makes it simpler and more straightforward to figure out what's gone wrong and how to fix it.

In Practice

In practice, of course, troubleshooting is never as clean as our idealized model suggests it should be. There are some steps that can make the process less painful and more productive for both those experiencing system problems and those responding to them.

Problem Report

Every problem starts with a problem report, which might be an automated alert or one of your colleagues saying, "The system is slow." An effective report should tell you the *expected* behavior, the *actual* behavior, and, if possible, how to reproduce the behavior.[8] Ideally, the reports should have a consistent form and be stored in a searchable location, such as a bug tracking system. Here, our teams often have customized forms or small web apps that ask for information that's relevant to diagnosing the particular systems they support, which then automatically generate and route a bug. This may also be a good point at which to provide tools for problem reporters to try self-diagnosing or self-repairing common issues on their own.

It's common practice at Google to open a bug for every issue, even those received via email or instant messaging. Doing so creates a log of investigation and remediation activities that can be referenced in the future. Many teams discourage reporting problems directly to a person for several reasons: this practice introduces an additional step of transcribing the report into a bug, produces lower-quality reports that aren't

---

6 Of course, see *https://xkcd.com/552*.

7 At least, we have no plausible theory to explain why the number of PhDs awarded in Computer Science in the US should be extremely well correlated ($r^2 = 0.9416$) with the per capita consumption of cheese, between 2000 and 2009: *http://tylervigen.com/view_correlation?id=1099*.

8 It may be useful to refer prospective bug reporters to [Tat99] to help them provide high-quality problem reports.

---

visible to other members of the team, and tends to concentrate the problem-solving load on a handful of team members that the reporters happen to know, rather than the person currently on duty (see also Chapter 29).

Shakespeare Has a Problem

You're on-call for the Shakespeare search service and receive an alert, Shakespeare-BlackboxProbe_SearchFailure: your black-box monitoring hasn't been able to find search results for "the forms of things unknown" for the past five minutes. The alerting system has filed a bug—with links to the black-box prober's recent results and to the playbook entry for this alert—and assigned it to you. Time to spring into action!

Triage

Once you receive a problem report, the next step is to figure out what to do about it. Problems can vary in severity: an issue might affect only one user under very specific circumstances (and might have a workaround), or it might entail a complete global outage for a service. Your response should be appropriate for the problem's impact: it's appropriate to declare an all-hands-on-deck emergency for the latter (see Chapter 14), but doing so for the former is overkill. Assessing an issue's severity requires an exercise of good engineering judgment and, often, a degree of calm under pressure.

Your first response in a major outage may be to start troubleshooting and try to find a root cause as quickly as possible. Ignore that instinct!

Instead, your course of action should be to *make the system work as well as it can under the circumstances.* This may entail emergency options, such as diverting traffic from a broken cluster to others that are still working, dropping traffic wholesale to prevent a cascading failure, or disabling subsystems to lighten the load. Stopping the bleeding should be your first priority; you aren't helping your users if the system dies while you're root-causing. Of course, an emphasis on rapid triage doesn't preclude taking steps to preserve evidence of what's going wrong, such as logs, to help with subsequent root-cause analysis.

Novice pilots are taught that their first responsibility in an emergency is to fly the airplane [Gaw09]; troubleshooting is secondary to getting the plane and everyone on it *safely* onto the ground. This approach is also applicable to computer systems: for example, if a bug is leading to possibly unrecoverable data corruption, freezing the system to prevent further failure may be better than letting this behavior continue.

This realization is often quite unsettling and counterintuitive for new SREs, particularly those whose prior experience was in product development organizations.

Examine

We need to be able to examine what each component in the system is doing in order to understand whether or not it's behaving correctly.

Ideally, a monitoring system is recording metrics for your system as discussed in Chapter 10. These metrics are a good place to start figuring out what's wrong. Graphing time-series and operations on time-series can be an effective way to understand the behavior of specific pieces of a system and find correlations that might suggest where problems began.[9]

Logging is another invaluable tool. Exporting information about each operation and about system state makes it possible to understand exactly what a process was doing at a given point in time. You may need to analyze system logs across one or many processes. Tracing requests through the whole stack using tools such as Dapper [Sig10] provides a very powerful way to understand how a distributed system is working, though varying use cases imply significantly different tracing designs [Sam14].

Logging

Text logs are very helpful for reactive debugging in real time, while storing logs in a structured binary format can make it possible to build tools to conduct retrospective analysis with much more information.

It's really useful to have multiple verbosity levels available, along with a way to increase these levels on the fly. This functionality enables you to examine any or all operations in incredible detail without having to restart your process, while still allowing you to dial back the verbosity levels when your service is operating normally. Depending of the volume of traffic your service receives, it might be better to use statistical sampling; for example, you might show one out of every 1,000 operations.

A next step is to include a selection language so that you can say "show me operations that match X," for a wide range of X—e.g., Set RPCs with a payload size below 1,024 bytes, or operations that took longer than 10 ms to return, or which called doSome thingInteresting() in *rpc_handler.py*. You might even want to design your logging infrastructure so that you can turn it on as needed, quickly and selectively.

Exposing current state is the third trick in our toolbox. For example, Google servers have endpoints that show a sample of RPCs recently sent or received, so it's possible to understand how any one server is communicating with others without referencing

---

9 But beware false correlations that can lead you down wrong paths!

an architecture diagram. These endpoints also show histograms of error rates and latency for each type of RPC, so that it's possible to quickly tell what's unhealthy. Some systems have endpoints that show their current configuration or allow examination of their data; for instance, Google's Borgmon servers (Chapter 10) can show the monitoring rules they're using, and even allow tracing a particular computation step-by-step to the source metrics from which a value is derived.

Finally, you may even need to instrument a client to experiment with, in order to discover what a component is returning in response to requests.

Debugging Shakespeare

Using the link to the black-box monitoring results in the bug, you discover that the prober sends an HTTP GET request to the /api/search endpoint:

```
{
    'search_text': 'the forms of things unknown'
}
```

It expects to receive a response with an HTTP 200 response code and a JSON payload exactly matching:

```
[{
        "work": "A Midsummer Night's Dream",
        "act": 5,
        "scene": 1,
        "line": 2526,
        "speaker": "Theseus"
}]
```

The system is set up to send a probe once a minute; over the past 10 minutes, about half the probes have succeeded, though with no discernible pattern. Unfortunately, the prober doesn't show you *what* was returned when it failed; you make a note to fix that for the future.

Using curl, you manually send requests to the search endpoint and get a failed response with HTTP response code 502 (Bad Gateway) and no payload. It has an HTTP header, X-Request-Trace, which lists the addresses of the backend servers responsible for responding to that request. With this information, you can now examine those backends to test whether they're responding appropriately.

Diagnose

A thorough understanding of the system's design is decidedly helpful for coming up with plausible hypotheses about what's gone wrong, but there are also some generic practices that will help even without domain knowledge.

Simplify and reduce

Ideally, components in a system have well-defined interfaces and perform known transformations from their input to their output (in our example, given an input search text, a component might return output containing possible matches). It's then possible to look at the connections *between* components—or, equivalently, at the data flowing between them—to determine whether a given component is working properly. Injecting known test data in order to check that the resulting output is expected (a form of black-box testing) at each step can be especially effective, as can injecting data intended to probe possible causes of errors. Having a solid reproducible test case makes debugging much faster, and it may be possible to use the case in a nonproduction environment where more invasive or riskier techniques are available than would be possible in production.

Dividing and conquering is a very useful general-purpose solution technique. In a multilayer system where work happens throughout a stack of components, it's often best to start systematically from one end of the stack and work toward the other end, examining each component in turn. This strategy is also well-suited for use with data processing pipelines. In exceptionally large systems, proceeding linearly may be too slow; an alternative, *bisection*, splits the system in half and examines the communication paths between components on one side and the other. After determining whether one half seems to be working properly, repeat the process until you're left with a possibly faulty component.

Ask "what," "where," and "why"

A malfunctioning system is often still trying to do *something*—just not the thing you want it to be doing. Finding out *what* it's doing, then asking *why* it's doing that and *where* its resources are being used or where its output is going can help you understand how things have gone wrong.[10]

---

10 In many respects, this is similar to the "Five Whys" technique [Ohn88] introduced by Taiichi Ohno to understand the root causes of manufacturing errors.

> ## Unpacking the Causes of a Symptom
>
> **Symptom**: A Spanner cluster has high latency and RPCs to its servers are timing out.
>
> **Why?** The Spanner server tasks are using all their CPU time and can't make progress on all the requests the clients send.
>
> **Where** in the server is the CPU time being used? Profiling the server shows it's sorting entries in logs checkpointed to disk.
>
> **Where** in the log-sorting code is it being used? When evaluating a regular expression against paths to log files.
>
> **Solutions**: Rewrite the regular expression to avoid backtracking. Look in the codebase for similar patterns. Consider using RE2, which does not backtrack and guarantees linear runtime growth with input size.[11]

What touched it last

Systems have inertia: we've found that a working computer system tends to remain in motion until acted upon by an external force, such as a configuration change or a shift in the type of load served. Recent changes to a system can be a productive place to start identifying what's going wrong.[12]

Well-designed systems should have extensive production logging to track new version deployments and configuration changes at all layers of the stack, from the server binaries handling user traffic down to the packages installed on individual nodes in the cluster. Correlating changes in a system's performance and behavior with other events in the system and environment can also be helpful in constructing monitoring dashboards; for example, you might annotate a graph showing the system's error rates with the start and end times of a deployment of a new version, as seen in Figure 12-2.

---

11 In contrast to RE2, PCRE can require exponential time to evaluate some regular expressions. RE2 is available at *https://github.com/google/re2*.

12 [All15] observes this is a frequently used heuristic in resolving outages.

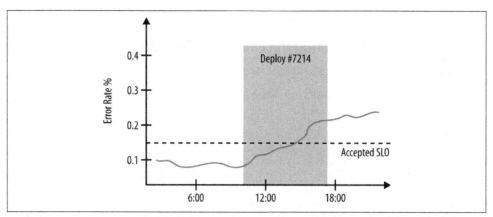

Figure 12-2. Error rates graphed against deployment start and end times

Manually sending a request to the /api/search endpoint (see "Debugging Shake-speare" on page 139) and seeing the failure listing backend servers that handled the response lets you discount the likelihood that the problem is with the API frontend server and with the load balancers: the response probably wouldn't have included that information if the request hadn't at least made it to the search backends and failed there. Now you can focus your efforts on the backends—analyzing their logs, sending test queries to see what responses they return, and examining their exported metrics.

Specific diagnoses

While the generic tools described previously are helpful across a broad range of problem domains, you will likely find it helpful to build tools and systems to help with diagnosing your particular services. Google SREs spend much of their time building such tools. While many of these tools are necessarily specific to a given system, be sure to look for commonalities between services and teams to avoid duplicating effort.

Test and Treat

Once you've come up with a short list of possible causes, it's time to try to find *which* factor is at the root of the actual problem. Using the experimental method, we can try to rule in or rule out our hypotheses. For instance, suppose we think a problem is caused by either a network failure between an application logic server and a database server, or by the database refusing connections. Trying to connect to the database with the same credentials the application logic server uses can refute the second hypothesis, while pinging the database server may be able to refute the first, depending on network topology, firewall rules, and other factors. Following the code and trying to imitate the code flow, step-by-step, may point to exactly what's going wrong.

There are a number of considerations to keep in mind when designing tests (which may be as simple as sending a ping or as complicated as removing traffic from a cluster and injecting specially formed requests to find a race condition):

- An ideal test should have mutually exclusive alternatives, so that it can rule one group of hypotheses in and rule another set out. In practice, this may be difficult to achieve.

- Consider the obvious first: perform the tests in decreasing order of likelihood, considering possible risks to the system from the test. It probably makes more sense to test for network connectivity problems between two machines before looking into whether a recent configuration change removed a user's access to the second machine.

- An experiment may provide misleading results due to confounding factors. For example, a firewall rule might permit access only from a specific IP address, which might make pinging the database from your workstation fail, even if pinging from the application logic server's machine would have succeeded.

- Active tests may have side effects that change future test results. For instance, allowing a process to use more CPUs may make operations faster, but might increase the likelihood of encountering data races. Similarly, turning on verbose logging might make a latency problem even worse and confuse your results: is the problem getting worse on its own, or because of the logging?

- Some tests may not be definitive, only suggestive. It can be very difficult to make race conditions or deadlocks happen in a timely and reproducible manner, so you may have to settle for less certain evidence that these are the causes.

Take clear notes of what ideas you had, which tests you ran, and the results you saw.[13] Particularly when you are dealing with more complicated and drawn-out cases, this documentation may be crucial in helping you remember exactly what happened and prevent having to repeat these steps.[14] If you performed active testing by changing a system—for instance by giving more resources to a process—making changes in a systematic and documented fashion will help you return the system to its pre-test setup, rather than running in an unknown hodge-podge configuration.

---

13 Using a shared document or real-time chat for notes provides a timestamp of *when* you did something, which is helpful for postmortems. It also shares that information with others, so they're up to speed with the current state of the world and don't need to interrupt your troubleshooting.

14 See also "Negative Results Are Magic" on page 144 for more on this point.

Negative Results Are Magic

Written by Randall Bosetti
Edited by Joan Wendt

A "negative" result is an experimental outcome in which the expected effect is absent —that is, any experiment that doesn't work out as planned. This includes new designs, heuristics, or human processes that fail to improve upon the systems they replace.

Negative results should not be ignored or discounted. Realizing you're wrong has much value: a clear negative result can resolve some of the hardest design questions. Often a team has two seemingly reasonable designs but progress in one direction has to address vague and speculative questions about whether the other direction might be better.

Experiments with negative results are conclusive. They tell us something certain about production, or the design space, or the performance limits of an existing system. They can help others determine whether their own experiments or designs are worthwhile. For example, a given development team might decide against using a particular web server because it can handle only ~800 connections out of the needed 8,000 connections before failing due to lock contention. When a subsequent development team decides to evaluate web servers, instead of starting from scratch, they can use this already well-documented negative result as a starting point to decide quickly whether (a) they need fewer than 800 connections or (b) the lock contention problems have been resolved.

Even when negative results do not apply directly to someone else's experiment, the supplementary data gathered can help others choose new experiments or avoid pitfalls in previous designs. Microbenchmarks, documented antipatterns, and project postmortems all fit this category. You should consider the scope of the negative result when designing an experiment, because a broad or especially robust negative result will help your peers even more.

Tools and methods can outlive the experiment and inform future work. As an example, benchmarking tools and load generators can result just as easily from a disconfirming experiment as a supporting one. Many webmasters have benefited from the difficult, detail-oriented work that produced Apache Bench, a web server loadtest, even though its first results were likely disappointing.

Building tools for repeatable experiments can have indirect benefits as well: although one application you build may not benefit from having its database on SSDs or from creating indices for dense keys, the next one just might. Writing a script that allows you to easily try out these configuration changes ensures you don't forget or miss optimizations in your next project.

Publishing negative results improves our industry's data-driven culture. Accounting for negative results and statistical insignificance reduces the bias in our metrics and provides an example to others of how to maturely accept uncertainty. By publishing everything, you encourage others to do the same, and everyone in the industry collectively learns much more quickly. SRE has already learned this lesson with high-quality postmortems, which have had a large positive effect on production stability.

Publish your results. If you are interested in an experiment's results, there's a good chance that other people are as well. When you publish the results, those people do not have to design and run a similar experiment themselves. It's tempting and common to avoid reporting negative results because it's easy to perceive that the experiment "failed." Some experiments are doomed, and they tend to be caught by review. Many more experiments are simply unreported because people mistakenly believe that negative results are not progress.

Do your part by telling everyone about the designs, algorithms, and team workflows you've ruled out. Encourage your peers by recognizing that negative results are part of thoughtful risk taking and that every well-designed experiment has merit. Be skeptical of any design document, performance review, or essay that doesn't mention failure. Such a document is potentially either too heavily filtered, or the author was not rigorous in his or her methods.

Above all, publish the results you find surprising so that others—including your future self—aren't surprised.

Cure

Ideally, you've now narrowed the set of possible causes to one. Next, we'd like to prove that it's the actual cause. Definitively proving that a given factor *caused* a problem—by reproducing it at will—can be difficult to do in production systems; often, we can only find *probable* causal factors, for the following reasons:

- *Systems are complex.* It's quite likely that there are multiple factors, each of which individually is not the cause, but which taken jointly are causes.[15] Real systems are also often path-dependent, so that they must be in a specific state before a failure occurs.

- *Reproducing the problem in a live production system may not be an option*, either because of the complexity of getting the system into a state where the failure can be triggered, or because further downtime may be unacceptable. Having a non-

---

15 See [Mea08] on how to think about systems, and also [Coo00] and [Dek14] on the limitations of finding a single root cause instead of examining the system and its environment for causative factors.

production environment can mitigate these challenges, though at the cost of having another copy of the system to run.

Once you've found the factors that caused the problem, it's time to write up notes on what went wrong with the system, how you tracked down the problem, how you fixed the problem, and how to prevent it from happening again. In other words, you need to write a postmortem (although ideally, the system is *alive* at this point!).

Case Study

App Engine,[16] part of Google's Cloud Platform, is a platform-as-a-service product that allows developers to build services atop Google's infrastructure. One of our internal customers filed a problem report indicating that they'd recently seen a dramatic increase in latency, CPU usage, and number of running processes needed to serve traffic for their app, a content-management system used to build documentation for developers.[17] The customer couldn't find any recent changes to their code that correlated with the increase in resources, and there hadn't been an increase in traffic to their app (see Figure 12-3), so they were wondering if a change in the App Engine service was responsible.

Our investigation discovered that latency had indeed increased by nearly an order of magnitude (as shown in Figure 12-4). Simultaneously, the amount of CPU time (Figure 12-5) and number of serving processes (Figure 12-6) had nearly quadrupled. Clearly something was wrong. It was time to start troubleshooting.

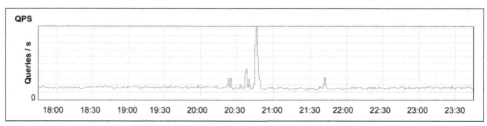

Figure 12-3. Application's requests received per second, showing a brief spike and return to normal

---

16 See *https://cloud.google.com/appengine*.

17 We have compressed and simplified this case study to aid understanding.

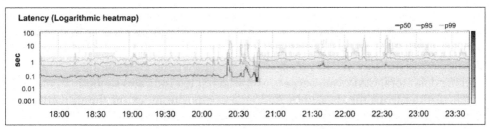

Figure 12-4. Application's latency, showing 50th, 95th, and 99th percentiles (lines) with a heatmap showing how many requests fell into a given latency bucket at any point in time (shade)

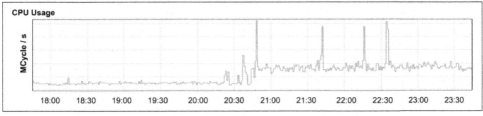

Figure 12-5. Aggregate CPU usage for the application

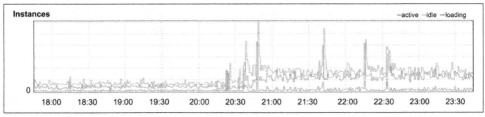

Figure 12-6. Number of instances for the application

Typically a sudden increase in latency and resource usage indicates either an increase in traffic sent to the system or a change in system configuration. However, we could easily rule out both of these possible causes: while a spike in traffic to the app around 20:45 could explain a brief surge in resource usage, we'd expect traffic to return to baseline fairly soon after request volume normalized. This spike certainly shouldn't have continued for multiple days, beginning when the app's developers filed the report and we started looking into the problem. Second, the change in performance happened on Saturday, when neither changes to the app nor the production environment were in flight. The service's most recent code pushes and configuration pushes had completed days before. Furthermore, if the problem originated with the service, we'd expect to see similar effects on other apps using the same infrastructure. However, no other apps were experiencing similar effects.

We referred the problem report to our counterparts, App Engine's developers, to investigate whether the customer was encountering any idiosyncrasies in the serving infrastructure. The developers weren't able to find any oddities, either. However, a developer did notice a correlation between the latency increase and the increase of a specific data storage API call, merge_join, which often indicates suboptimal indexing when reading from the datastore. Adding a composite index on the properties the app uses to select objects from the datastore would speed those requests, and in principle, speed the application as a whole—but we'd need to figure out *which* properties needed indexing. A quick look at the application's code didn't reveal any obvious suspects.

It was time to pull out the heavy machinery in our toolkit: using Dapper [Sig10], we traced the steps individual HTTP requests took—from their receipt by a frontend reverse proxy through to the point where the app's code returned a response—and looked at the RPCs issued by each server involved in handling that request. Doing so would allow us to see which properties were included in requests to the datastore, then create the appropriate indices.

While investigating, we discovered that requests for static content such as images, which weren't served from the datastore, were also much slower than expected. Looking at graphs with file-level granularity, we saw their responses had been much faster only a few days before. This implied that the observed correlation between merge_join and the latency increase was spurious and that our suboptimal-indexing theory was fatally flawed.

Examining the unexpectedly slow requests for static content, most of the RPCs sent from the application were to a memcache service, so the requests should have been very fast—on the order of a few milliseconds. These requests did turn out to be very fast, so the problem didn't seem to originate there. However, between the time the app started working on a request and when it made the first RPCs, there was about a 250 ms period where the app was doing...well, *something*. Because App Engine runs code provided by users, its SRE team does not profile or inspect app code, so we couldn't tell what the app was doing in that interval; similarly, Dapper couldn't help track down what was going on since it can only trace RPC calls, and none were made during that period.

Faced with what was, by this point, quite a mystery, we decided not to solve it...*yet*. The customer had a public launch scheduled for the following week, and we weren't sure how soon we'd be able to identify the problem and fix it. Instead, we recommended that the customer increase the resources allocated to their app to the most CPU-rich instance type available. Doing so reduced the app's latency to acceptable levels, though not as low as we'd prefer. We concluded that the latency mitigation was good enough that the team could conduct their launch successfully, then investigate at leisure.[18]

At this point, we suspected that the app was a victim of yet another common cause of sudden increases in latency and resource usage: a change in the type of work. We'd seen an increase in writes to the datastore from the app, just before its latency increased, but because this increase wasn't very large—nor was it sustained—we'd written it off as coincidental. However, this behavior did resemble a common pattern: an instance of the app is initialized by reading objects from the datastore, then storing them in the instance's memory. By doing so, the instance avoids reading rarely changing configuration from the datastore on each request, and instead checks the in-memory objects. Then, the time it takes to handle requests will often scale with the amount of configuration data.[19] We couldn't prove that this behavior was the root of the problem, but it's a common antipattern.

The app developers added instrumentation to understand where the app was spending its time. They identified a method that was called on every request, that checked whether a user had whitelisted access to a given path. The method used a caching layer that sought to minimize accesses to both the datastore and the memcache service, by holding whitelist objects in instances' memory. As one of the app's developers noted in the investigation, "I don't know where the fire is yet, but I'm blinded by smoke coming from this whitelist cache."

Some time later, the root cause was found: due to a long-standing bug in the app's access control system, whenever one specific path was accessed, a whitelist object would be created and stored in the datastore. In the run-up to launch, an automated security scanner had been testing the app for vulnerabilities, and as a side effect, its scan produced thousands of whitelist objects over the course of half an hour. These superfluous whitelist objects then had to be checked on every request to the app, which led to pathologically slow responses—without causing any RPC calls from the app to other services. Fixing the bug and removing those objects returned the app's performance to expected levels.

---

18 While launching with an unidentified bug isn't ideal, it's often impractical to eliminate all known bugs. Instead, sometimes we have make do with second-best measures and mitigate risk as best we can, using good engineering judgment.

19 The datastore lookup can use an index to speed the comparison, but a frequent in-memory implementation is a simple for loop comparison across all the cached objects. If there are only a few objects, it won't matter that this takes linear time—but this can cause a significant increase in latency and resource usage as the number of cached objects grows.

Making Troubleshooting Easier

There are many ways to simplify and speed troubleshooting. Perhaps the most fundamental are:

- Building observability—with both white-box metrics and structured logs—into each component from the ground up.
- Designing systems with well-understood and observable interfaces between components.

Ensuring that information is available in a consistent way throughout a system—for instance, using a unique request identifier throughout the span of RPCs generated by various components—reduces the need to figure out *which* log entry on an upstream component matches a log entry on a downstream component, speeding the time to diagnosis and recovery.

Problems in correctly representing the state of reality in a code change or an environment change often lead to a need to troubleshoot. Simplifying, controlling, and logging such changes can reduce the need for troubleshooting, and make it easier when it happens.

Conclusion

We've looked at some steps you can take to make the troubleshooting process clear and understandable to novices, so that they, too, can become effective at solving problems. Adopting a systematic approach to troubleshooting—as opposed to relying on luck or experience—can help bound your services' time to recovery, leading to a better experience for your users.

CHAPTER 13

Emergency Response

Written by Corey Adam Baye
Edited by Diane Bates

Things break; that's life.

Regardless of the stakes involved or the size of an organization, one trait that's vital to the long-term health of an organization, and that consequently sets that organization apart from others, is how the people involved respond to an emergency. Few of us naturally respond well during an emergency. A proper response takes preparation and periodic, pertinent, hands-on training. Establishing and maintaining thorough training and testing processes requires the support of the board and management, in addition to the careful attention of staff. All of these elements are essential in fostering an environment in which teams can spend money, time, energy, and possibly even uptime to ensure that systems, processes, and people respond efficiently during an emergency.

Note that the chapter on postmortem culture discusses the specifics of how to write postmortems in order to make sure that incidents that require emergency response also become a learning opportunity (see Chapter 15). This chapter provides more concrete examples of such incidents.

What to Do When Systems Break

First of all, don't panic! You aren't alone, and the sky isn't falling. You're a professional and trained to handle this sort of situation. Typically, no one is in physical danger—only those poor electrons are in peril. At the very worst, half of the Internet is down. So take a deep breath...and carry on.

If you feel overwhelmed, pull in more people. Sometimes it may even be necessary to page the entire company. If your company has an incident response process (see Chapter 14), make sure that you're familiar with it and follow that process.

Test-Induced Emergency

Google has adopted a proactive approach to disaster and emergency testing (see [Kri12]). SREs break our systems, watch how they fail, and make changes to improve reliability and prevent the failures from recurring. Most of the time, these controlled failures go as planned, and the target system and dependent systems behave in roughly the manner we expect. We identify some weaknesses or hidden dependencies and document follow-up actions to rectify the flaws we uncover. However, sometimes our assumptions and the actual results are worlds apart.

Here's one example of a test that unearthed a number of unexpected dependencies.

Details

We wanted to flush out hidden dependencies on a test database within one of our larger distributed MySQL databases. The plan was to block all access to just one database out of a hundred. No one foresaw the results that would unfold.

Response

Within minutes of commencing the test, numerous dependent services reported that both external and internal users were unable to access key systems. Some systems were intermittently or only partially accessible.

Assuming that the test was responsible, SRE immediately aborted the exercise. We attempted to roll back the permissions change, but were unsuccessful. Instead of panicking, we immediately brainstormed how to restore proper access. Using an already tested approach, we restored permissions to the replicas and failovers. In a parallel effort, we reached out to key developers to correct the flaw in the database application layer library.

Within an hour of the original decision, all access was fully restored, and all services were able to connect once again. The broad impact of this test motivated a rapid and thorough fix to the libraries and a plan for periodic retesting to prevent such a major flaw from recurring.

Findings

What went well

Dependent services that were affected by the incident immediately escalated the issues within the company. We assumed, correctly, that our controlled experiment had gotten out of hand and immediately aborted the test.

We were able to fully restore permissions within an hour of the first report, at which time systems started behaving properly. Some teams took a different approach and reconfigured their systems to avoid the test database. These parallel efforts helped to restore service as quickly as possible.

Follow-up action items were resolved quickly and thoroughly to avoid a similar outage, and we instituted periodic testing to ensure that similar flaws do not recur.

What we learned

Although this test was thoroughly reviewed and thought to be well scoped, reality revealed we had an insufficient understanding of this particular interaction among the dependent systems.

We failed to follow the incident response process, which had been put in place only a few weeks before and hadn't been thoroughly disseminated. This process would have ensured that all services and customers were aware of the outage. To avoid similar scenarios in the future, SRE continually refines and tests our incident response tools and processes, in addition to making sure that updates to our incident management procedures are clearly communicated to all relevant parties.

Because we hadn't tested our rollback procedures in a test environment, these procedures were flawed, which lengthened the outage. We now require thorough testing of rollback procedures before such large-scale tests.

Change-Induced Emergency

As you can imagine, Google has a lot of configuration—complex configuration—and we constantly make changes to that configuration. To prevent breaking our systems outright, we perform numerous tests on configuration changes to make sure they don't result in unexpected and undesired behavior. However, the scale and complexity of Google's infrastructure make it impossible to anticipate every dependency or interaction; sometimes configuration changes don't go entirely according to plan.

The following is one such example.

Details

A configuration change to the infrastructure that helps protect our services from abuse was pushed globally on a Friday. This infrastructure interacts with essentially all of our externally facing systems, and the change triggered a crash-loop bug in those systems, which caused the entire fleet to begin to crash-loop almost simultaneously. Because Google's internal infrastructure also depends upon our own services, many internal applications suddenly became unavailable as well.

Response

Within seconds, monitoring alerts started firing, indicating that certain sites were down. Some on-call engineers simultaneously experienced what they believed to be a failure of the corporate network and relocated to dedicated secure rooms (panic rooms) with backup access to the production environment. They were joined by additional engineers who were struggling with their corporate access.

Within five minutes of that first configuration push, the engineer responsible for the push, having become aware of the corporate outage but still unaware of the broader outage, pushed another configuration change to roll back the first change. At this point, services began to recover.

Within 10 minutes of the first push, on-call engineers declared an incident and proceeded to follow internal procedures for incident response. They began notifying the rest of the company about the situation. The push engineer informed the on-call engineers that the outage was likely due to the change that had been pushed and later rolled back. Nevertheless, some services experienced unrelated bugs or misconfigurations triggered by the original event and didn't fully recover for up to an hour.

Findings

What went well

There were several factors at play that prevented this incident from resulting in a longer-term outage of many of Google's internal systems.

To begin with, monitoring almost immediately detected and alerted us to the problem. However, it should be noted that in this case, our monitoring was less than ideal: alerts fired repeatedly and constantly, overwhelming the on-calls and spamming regular and emergency communication channels.

Once the problem was detected, incident management generally went well and updates were communicated often and clearly. Our out-of-band communications systems kept everyone connected even while some of the more complicated software stacks were unusable. This experience reminded us why SRE retains highly reliable, low overhead backup systems, which we use regularly.

In addition to these out-of-band communications systems, Google has command-line tools and alternative access methods that enable us to perform updates and roll back changes even when other interfaces are inaccessible. These tools and access methods worked well during the outage, with the caveat that engineers needed to be more familiar with the tools and to test them more routinely.

Google's infrastructure provided yet another layer of protection in that the affected system rate-limited how quickly it provided full updates to new clients. This behavior may have throttled the crash-loop and prevented a complete outage, allowing jobs to remain up long enough to service a few requests in between crashes.

Finally, we should not overlook the element of luck in the quick resolution of this incident: the push engineer happened to be following real-time communication channels—an additional level of diligence that's not a normal part of the release process. The push engineer noticed a large number of complaints about corporate access directly following the push and rolled back the change almost immediately. Had this swift rollback not occurred, the outage could have lasted considerably longer, becoming immensely more difficult to troubleshoot.

What we learned

An earlier push of the new feature had involved a thorough canary but didn't trigger the same bug, as it had not exercised a very rare and specific configuration keyword in combination with the new feature. The specific change that triggered this bug wasn't considered risky, and therefore followed a less stringent canary process. When the change was pushed globally, it used the untested keyword/feature combination that triggered the failure.

Ironically, improvements to canarying and automation were slated to become higher priority in the following quarter. This incident immediately raised their priority and reinforced the need for thorough canarying, regardless of the perceived risk.

As one would expect, alerting was vocal during this incident because every location was essentially offline for a few minutes. This disrupted the real work being performed by the on-call engineers and made communication among those involved in the incident more difficult.

Google relies upon our own tools. Much of the software stack that we use for trouble-shooting and communicating lies behind jobs that were crash-looping. Had this outage lasted any longer, debugging would have been severely hindered.

Process-Induced Emergency

We have poured a considerable amount of time and energy into the automation that manages our machine fleet. It's amazing how many jobs one can start, stop, or retool across the fleet with very little effort. Sometimes, the efficiency of our automation can be a bit frightening when things do not go quite according to plan.

This is one example where moving fast was not such a good thing.

Details

As part of routine automation testing, two consecutive turndown requests for the same soon-to-be-decommissioned server installation were submitted. In the case of the second turndown request, a subtle bug in the automation sent all of the machines in all of these installations globally to the Diskerase queue, where their hard drives were destined to be wiped; see "Automation: Enabling Failure at Scale" on page 85 for more details.

Response

Soon after the second turndown request was issued, the on-call engineers received a page as the first small server installation was taken offline to be decommissioned. Their investigation determined that the machines had been transferred to the Diskerase queue, so following normal procedure, the on-call engineers drained traffic from the location. Because the machines in that location had been wiped, they were unable to respond to requests. To avoid failing those requests outright, on-call engineers drained traffic away from that location. Traffic was redirected to locations that could properly respond to the requests.

Before long, pagers everywhere were firing for all such server installations around the world. In response, the on-call engineers disabled all team automation in order to prevent further damage. They stopped or froze additional automation and production maintenance shortly thereafter.

Within an hour, all traffic had been diverted to other locations. Although users may have experienced elevated latencies, their requests were fulfilled. The outage was officially over.

Now the hard part began: recovery. Some network links were reporting heavy congestion, so network engineers implemented mitigations as choke points surfaced. A server installation in one such location was chosen to be the first of many to rise from the ashes. Within three hours of the initial outage, and thanks to the tenacity of several engineers, the installation was rebuilt and brought back online, happily accepting user requests once again.

US teams handed off to their European counterparts, and SRE hatched a plan to prioritize reinstallations using a streamlined but manual process. The team was divided into three parts, with each part responsible for one step in the manual reinstall process. Within three days, the vast majority of capacity was back online, while any stragglers would be recovered over the next month or two.

Findings

What went well

Reverse proxies in large server installations are managed very differently than reverse proxies in these small installations, so large installations were not impacted. On-call engineers were able to quickly move traffic from smaller installations to large installations. By design, these large installations can handle a full load without difficulty. However, some network links became congested, and therefore required network engineers to develop workarounds. In order to reduce the impact on end users, on-call engineers targeted congested networks as their highest priority.

The turndown process for the small installations worked efficiently and well. From start to finish, it took less than an hour to successfully turn down and securely wipe a large number of these installations.

Although turndown automation quickly tore down monitoring for the small installations, on-call engineers were able to promptly revert those monitoring changes. Doing so helped them to assess the extent of the damage.

The engineers quickly followed incident response protocols, which had matured considerably in the year since the first outage described in this chapter. Communication and collaboration throughout the company and across teams was superb—a real testament to the incident management program and training. All hands within the respective teams chipped in, bringing their vast experience to bear.

What we learned

The root cause was that the turndown automation server lacked the appropriate sanity checks on the commands it sent. When the server ran again in response to the initial failed turndown, it received an empty response for the machine rack. Instead of filtering the response, it passed the empty filter to the machine database, telling the machine database to Diskerase all machines involved. Yes, sometimes zero does mean all. The machine database complied, so the turndown workflow started churning through the machines as quickly as possible.

Reinstallations of machines were slow and unreliable. This behavior was due in large part to the use of the Trivial File Transfer Protocol (TFTP) at the lowest network Quality of Service (QoS) from the distant locations. The BIOS for each machine in the system dealt poorly with the failures.[1] Depending on the network cards involved, the BIOS either halted or went into a constant reboot cycle. They were failing to transfer the boot files on each cycle and were further taxing the installers. On-call

---

1 BIOS: Basic Input/Output System. BIOS is the software built into a computer to send simple instructions to the hardware, allowing input and output before the operating system has been loaded.

engineers were able to fix these reinstall problems by reclassifying installation traffic at slightly higher priority and using automation to restart any machines that were stuck.

The machine reinstallation infrastructure was unable to handle the simultaneous setup of thousands of machines. This inability was partly due to a regression that prevented the infrastructure from running more than two setup tasks per worker machine. The regression also used improper QoS settings to transfer files and had poorly tuned timeouts. It forced kernel reinstallation, even on machines that still had the proper kernel and on which Diskerase had yet to occur. To remedy this situation, on-call engineers escalated to parties responsible for this infrastructure who were able to quickly retune it to support this unusual load.

All Problems Have Solutions

Time and experience have shown that systems will not only break, but will break in ways that one could never previously imagine. One of the greatest lessons Google has learned is that a solution exists, even if it may not be obvious, especially to the person whose pager is screaming. If you can't think of a solution, cast your net farther. Involve more of your teammates, seek help, do whatever you have to do, but do it quickly. The highest priority is to resolve the issue at hand quickly. Oftentimes, the person with the most state is the one whose actions somehow triggered the event. Utilize that person.

Very importantly, once the emergency has been mitigated, do not forget to set aside time to clean up, write up the incident, and to...

Learn from the Past. Don't Repeat It.

Keep a History of Outages

There is no better way to learn than to document what has broken in the past. History is about learning from everyone's mistakes. Be thorough, be honest, but most of all, ask hard questions. Look for specific actions that might prevent such an outage from recurring, not just tactically, but also strategically. Ensure that everyone within the company can learn what you have learned by publishing and organizing postmortems.

Hold yourself and others accountable to following up on the specific actions detailed in these postmortems. Doing so will prevent a future outage that's nearly identical to, and caused by nearly the same triggers as, an outage that has already been documented. Once you have a solid track record for learning from past outages, see what you can do to prevent future ones.

Ask the Big, Even Improbable, Questions: What If…?

There is no greater test than reality. Ask yourself some big, open-ended questions. What if the building power fails…? What if the network equipment racks are standing in two feet of water…? What if the primary datacenter suddenly goes dark…? What if someone compromises your web server…? What do you do? Who do you call? Who will write the check? Do you have a plan? Do you know how to react? Do you know how your systems will react? Could you minimize the impact if it were to happen now? Could the person sitting next to you do the same?

Encourage Proactive Testing

When it comes to failures, theory and reality are two very different realms. Until your system has actually failed, you don't truly know how that system, its dependent systems, or your users will react. Don't rely on assumptions or what you can't or haven't tested. Would you prefer that a failure happen at 2 a.m. Saturday morning when most of the company is still away on a team-building offsite in the Black Forest—or when you have your best and brightest close at hand, monitoring the test that they painstakingly reviewed in the previous weeks?

Conclusion

We've reviewed three different cases where parts of our systems broke. Although all three emergencies were triggered differently—one by a proactive test, another by a configuration change, and yet another by turndown automation—the responses shared many characteristics. The responders didn't panic. They pulled in others when they thought it necessary. The responders studied and learned from earlier outages. Subsequently, they built their systems to better respond to those types of outages. Each time new failure modes presented themselves, responders documented those failure modes. This follow-up helped other teams learn how to better troubleshoot and fortify their systems against similar outages. Responders proactively tested their systems. Such testing ensured that the changes fixed the underlying problems, and identified other weaknesses before they became outages.

And as our systems evolve the cycle continues, with each outage or test resulting in incremental improvements to both processes and systems. While the case studies in this chapter are specific to Google, this approach to emergency response can be applied over time to any organization of any size.

CHAPTER 14

Managing Incidents

Written by Andrew Stribblehill[1]
Edited by Kavita Guliani

Effective incident management is key to limiting the disruption caused by an incident and restoring normal business operations as quickly as possible. If you haven't gamed out your response to potential incidents in advance, principled incident management can go out the window in real-life situations.

This chapter walks through a portrait of an incident that spirals out of control due to ad hoc incident management practices, outlines a well-managed approach to the incident, and reviews how the same incident might have played out if handled with well-functioning incident management.

Unmanaged Incidents

Put yourself in the shoes of Mary, the on-call engineer for The Firm. It's 2 p.m. on a Friday afternoon and your pager has just exploded. Black-box monitoring tells you that your service has stopped serving *any* traffic in an entire datacenter. With a sigh, you put down your coffee and set about the job of fixing it. A few minutes into the task, another alert tells you that a second datacenter has stopped serving. Then the third out of your five datacenters fails. To exacerbate the situation, there is more traffic than the remaining datacenters can handle, so they start to overload. Before you know it, the service is overloaded and unable to serve any requests.

You stare at the logs for what seems like an eternity. Thousands of lines of logging suggest there's an error in one of the recently updated modules, so you decide to

---

revert the servers to the previous release. When you see that the rollback hasn't helped, you call Josephine, who wrote most of the code for the now-hemorrhaging service. Reminding you that it's 3:30 a.m. in her time zone, she blearily agrees to log in and take a look. Your colleagues Sabrina and Robin start poking around from their own terminals. "Just looking," they tell you.

Now one of the suits has phoned your boss and is angrily demanding to know why he wasn't informed about the "total meltdown of this business-critical service." Independently, the vice presidents are nagging you for an ETA, repeatedly asking you, "How could this possibly have happened?" You would sympathize, but doing so would require cognitive effort that you are holding in reserve for your job. The VPs call on their prior engineering experience and make irrelevant but hard-to-refute comments like, "Increase the page size!"

Time passes; the two remaining datacenters fail completely. Unbeknown to you, sleep-addled Josephine called Malcolm. He had a brainwave: something about CPU affinity. He felt certain that he could optimize the remaining server processes if he could just deploy this one simple change to the production environment, so he did so. Within seconds, the servers restarted, picking up the change. And then died.

The Anatomy of an Unmanaged Incident

Note that everybody in the preceding scenario was doing their job, as they saw it. How could things go so wrong? A few common hazards caused this incident to spiral out of control.

Sharp Focus on the Technical Problem

We tend to hire people like Mary for their technical prowess. So it's not surprising that she was busy making operational changes to the system, trying valiantly to solve the problem. She wasn't in a position to think about the bigger picture of how to mitigate the problem because the technical task at hand was overwhelming.

Poor Communication

For the same reason, Mary was far too busy to communicate clearly. Nobody knew what actions their coworkers were taking. Business leaders were angry, customers were frustrated, and other engineers who could have lent a hand in debugging or fixing the issue weren't used effectively.

Freelancing

Malcolm was making changes to the system with the best of intentions. However, he didn't coordinate with his coworkers—not even Mary, who was technically in charge of troubleshooting. His changes made a bad situation far worse.

Elements of Incident Management Process

Incident management skills and practices exist to channel the energies of enthusiastic individuals. Google's incident management system is based on the Incident Command System,[2] which is known for its clarity and scalability.

A well-designed incident management process has the following features.

Recursive Separation of Responsibilities

It's important to make sure that everybody involved in the incident knows their role and doesn't stray onto someone else's turf. Somewhat counterintuitively, a clear separation of responsibilities allows individuals more autonomy than they might otherwise have, since they need not second-guess their colleagues.

If the load on a given member becomes excessive, that person needs to ask the planning lead for more staff. They should then delegate work to others, a task that might entail creating subincidents. Alternatively, a role leader might delegate system components to colleagues, who report high-level information back up to the leaders.

Several distinct roles should be delegated to particular individuals:

Incident Command
> The incident commander holds the high-level state about the incident. They structure the incident response task force, assigning responsibilities according to need and priority. *De facto*, the commander holds all positions that they have not delegated. If appropriate, they can remove roadblocks that prevent Ops from working most effectively.

Operational Work
> The Ops lead works with the incident commander to respond to the incident by applying operational tools to the task at hand. The operations team should be the only group modifying the system during an incident.

Communication
> This person is the public face of the incident response task force. Their duties most definitely include issuing periodic updates to the incident response team and stakeholders (usually via email), and may extend to tasks such as keeping the incident document accurate and up to date.

---

2 See *http://www.fema.gov/national-incident-management-system* for further details.

Planning

The planning role supports Ops by dealing with longer-term issues, such as filing bugs, ordering dinner, arranging handoffs, and tracking how the system has diverged from the norm so it can be reverted once the incident is resolved.

A Recognized Command Post

Interested parties need to understand where they can interact with the incident commander. In many situations, locating the incident task force members into a central designated "War Room" is appropriate. Others teams may prefer to work at their desks, keeping alert to incident updates via email and IRC.

Google has found IRC to be a huge boon in incident response. IRC is very reliable and can be used as a log of communications about this event, and such a record is invaluable in keeping detailed state changes in mind. We've also written bots that log incident-related traffic (which is helpful for postmortem analysis), and other bots that log events such as alerts to the channel. IRC is also a convenient medium over which geographically distributed teams can coordinate.

Live Incident State Document

The incident commander's most important responsibility is to keep a living incident document. This can live in a wiki, but should ideally be editable by several people concurrently. Most of our teams use Google Docs, though Google Docs SRE use Google Sites: after all, depending on the software you are trying to fix as part of your incident management system is unlikely to end well.

See Appendix C for a sample incident document. This living doc can be messy, but must be functional. Using a template makes generating this documentation easier, and keeping the most important information at the top makes it more usable.Retain this documentation for postmortem analysis and, if necessary, meta analysis.

Clear, Live Handoff

It's essential that the post of incident commander be clearly handed off at the end of the working day. If you're handing off command to someone at another location, you can simply and safely update the new incident commander over the phone or a video call. Once the new incident commander is fully apprised, the outgoing commander should be explicit in their handoff, specifically stating, "You're now the incident commander, okay?", and should not leave the call until receiving firm acknowledgment of handoff. The handoff should be communicated to others working on the incident so that it's clear who is leading the incident management efforts at all times.

A Managed Incident

Now let's examine how this incident might have played out if it were handled using principles of incident management.

It's 2 p.m., and Mary is into her third coffee of the day. The pager's harsh tone surprises her, and she gulps the drink down. Problem: a datacenter has stopped serving traffic. She starts to investigate. Shortly another alert fires, and the second datacenter out of five is out of order. Because this is a rapidly growing issue, she knows that she'll benefit from the structure of her incident management framework.

Mary snags Sabrina. "Can you take command?" Nodding her agreement, Sabrina quickly gets a rundown of what's occurred thus far from Mary. She captures these details in an email that she sends to a prearranged mailing list. Sabrina recognizes that she can't yet scope the impact of the incident, so she asks for Mary's assessment. Mary responds, "Users have yet to be impacted; let's just hope we don't lose a third datacenter." Sabrina records Mary's response in a live incident document.

When the third alert fires, Sabrina sees the alert among the debugging chatter on IRC and quickly follows up to the email thread with an update. The thread keeps VPs abreast of the high-level status without bogging them down in minutiae. Sabrina asks an external communications representative to start drafting user messaging. She then follows up with Mary to see if they should contact the developer on-call (currently Josephine). Receiving Mary's approval, Sabrina loops in Josephine.

By the time Josephine logs in, Robin has already volunteered to help out. Sabrina reminds both Robin and Josephine that they are to prioritize any tasks delegated to them by Mary, and that they must keep Mary informed of any additional actions they take. Robin and Josephine quickly familiarize themselves with the current situation by reading the incident document.

By now, Mary has tried the old binary release and found it wanting: she mutters this to Robin, who updates IRC to say that this attempted fix didn't work. Sabrina pastes this update into the live incident management document.

At 5 p.m., Sabrina starts finding replacement staff to take on the incident, as she and her colleagues are about to go home. She updates the incident document. A brief phone conference takes place at 5:45 so everyone is aware of the current situation. At 6 p.m., they hand off their responsibilities to their colleagues in the sister office.

Mary returns to work the following morning to find that her transatlantic colleagues have assumed responsibility for the bug, mitigated the problem, closed the incident, and started work on the postmortem. Problem solved, she brews some fresh coffee and settles down to plan structural improvements so problems of this category don't afflict the team again.

When to Declare an Incident

It is better to declare an incident early and then find a simple fix and close out the incident than to have to spin up the incident management framework hours into a burgeoning problem. Set clear conditions for declaring an incident. My team follows these broad guidelines—if any of the following is true, the event is an incident:

- Do you need to involve a second team in fixing the problem?
- Is the outage visible to customers?
- Is the issue unsolved even after an hour's concentrated analysis?

Incident management proficiency atrophies quickly when it's not in constant use. So how can engineers keep their incident management skills up to date—handle more incidents? Fortunately, the incident management framework can apply to other operational changes that need to span time zones and/or teams. If you use the framework frequently as a regular part of your change management procedures, you can easily follow this framework when an actual incident occurs. If your organization performs disaster-recovery testing (you should, it's *fun*: see [Kri12]), incident management should be part of that testing process. We often role-play the response to an on-call issue that has already been solved, perhaps by colleagues in another location, to further familiarize ourselves with incident management.

In Summary

We've found that by formulating an incident management strategy in advance, structuring this plan to scale smoothly, and regularly putting the plan to use, we were able to reduce our mean time to recovery and provide staff a less stressful way to work on emergent problems. Any organization concerned with reliability would benefit from pursuing a similar strategy.

Best Practices for Incident Management

Prioritize. Stop the bleeding, restore service, and preserve the evidence for root-causing.

Prepare. Develop and document your incident management procedures in advance, in consultation with incident participants.

Trust. Give full autonomy within the assigned role to all incident participants.

Introspect. Pay attention to your emotional state while responding to an incident. If you start to feel panicky or overwhelmed, solicit more support.

Consider alternatives. Periodically consider your options and re-evaluate whether it still makes sense to continue what you're doing or whether you should be taking another tack in incident response.

Practice. Use the process routinely so it becomes second nature.

Change it around. Were you incident commander last time? Take on a different role this time. Encourage every team member to acquire familiarity with each role.

CHAPTER 15

Postmortem Culture: Learning from Failure

Written by John Lunney and Sue Lueder
Edited by Gary O' Connor

> *The cost of failure is education.*
> —Devin Carraway

As SREs, we work with large-scale, complex, distributed systems. We constantly enhance our services with new features and add new systems. Incidents and outages are inevitable given our scale and velocity of change. When an incident occurs, we fix the underlying issue, and services return to their normal operating conditions. Unless we have some formalized process of learning from these incidents in place, they may recur ad infinitum. Left unchecked, incidents can multiply in complexity or even cascade, overwhelming a system and its operators and ultimately impacting our users. Therefore, postmortems are an essential tool for SRE.

The postmortem concept is well known in the technology industry [All12]. A postmortem is a written record of an incident, its impact, the actions taken to mitigate or resolve it, the root cause(s), and the follow-up actions to prevent the incident from recurring. This chapter describes criteria for deciding when to conduct postmortems, some best practices around postmortems, and advice on how to cultivate a postmortem culture based on the experience we've gained over the years.

Google's Postmortem Philosophy

The primary goals of writing a postmortem are to ensure that the incident is documented, that all contributing root cause(s) are well understood, and, especially, that effective preventive actions are put in place to reduce the likelihood and/or impact of recurrence. A detailed survey of root-cause analysis techniques is beyond the scope of this chapter (instead, see [Roo04]); however, articles, best practices, and tools abound in the system quality domain. Our teams use a variety of techniques for root-cause analysis and choose the technique best suited to their services. Postmortems are expected after any significant undesirable event. Writing a postmortem is not punishment—it is a learning opportunity for the entire company. The postmortem process does present an inherent cost in terms of time or effort, so we are deliberate in choosing when to write one. Teams have some internal flexibility, but common postmortem triggers include:

- User-visible downtime or degradation beyond a certain threshold
- Data loss of any kind
- On-call engineer intervention (release rollback, rerouting of traffic, etc.)
- A resolution time above some threshold
- A monitoring failure (which usually implies manual incident discovery)

It is important to define postmortem criteria before an incident occurs so that everyone knows when a postmortem is necessary. In addition to these objective triggers, any stakeholder may request a postmortem for an event.

Blameless postmortems are a tenet of SRE culture. For a postmortem to be truly blameless, it must focus on identifying the contributing causes of the incident without indicting any individual or team for bad or inappropriate behavior. A blamelessly written postmortem assumes that everyone involved in an incident had good intentions and did the right thing with the information they had. If a culture of finger pointing and shaming individuals or teams for doing the "wrong" thing prevails, people will not bring issues to light for fear of punishment.

Blameless culture originated in the healthcare and avionics industries where mistakes can be fatal. These industries nurture an environment where every "mistake" is seen as an opportunity to strengthen the system. When postmortems shift from allocating blame to investigating the systematic reasons why an individual or team had incomplete or incorrect information, effective prevention plans can be put in place. You can't "fix" people, but you can fix systems and processes to better support people making the right choices when designing and maintaining complex systems.

When an outage does occur, a postmortem is not written as a formality to be forgotten. Instead the postmortem is seen by engineers as an opportunity not only to fix a weakness, but to make Google more resilient as a whole. While a blameless postmortem doesn't simply vent frustration by pointing fingers, it *should* call out where and how services can be improved. Here are two examples:

Pointing fingers

"We need to rewrite the entire complicated backend system! It's been breaking weekly for the last three quarters and I'm sure we're all tired of fixing things onesy-twosy. Seriously, if I get paged one more time I'll rewrite it myself..."

Blameless

"An action item to rewrite the entire backend system might actually prevent these annoying pages from continuing to happen, and the maintenance manual for this version is quite long and really difficult to be fully trained up on. I'm sure our future on-callers will thank us!"

Best Practice: Avoid Blame and Keep It Constructive

Blameless postmortems can be challenging to write, because the postmortem format clearly identifies the actions that led to the incident. Removing blame from a postmortem gives people the confidence to escalate issues without fear. It is also important not to stigmatize frequent production of postmortems by a person or team. An atmosphere of blame risks creating a culture in which incidents and issues are swept under the rug, leading to greater risk for the organization [Boy13].

Collaborate and Share Knowledge

We value collaboration, and the postmortem process is no exception. The postmortem workflow includes collaboration and knowledge-sharing at every stage.

Our postmortem documents are Google Docs, with an in-house template (see Appendix D). Regardless of the specific tool you use, look for the following key features:

Real-time collaboration

Enables the rapid collection of data and ideas. Essential during the early creation of a postmortem.

An open commenting/annotation system

Makes crowdsourcing solutions easy and improves coverage.

Email notifications

Can be directed at collaborators within the document or used to loop in others to provide input.

Writing a postmortem also involves formal review and publication. In practice, teams share the first postmortem draft internally and solicit a group of senior engineers to assess the draft for completeness. Review criteria might include:

- Was key incident data collected for posterity?
- Are the impact assessments complete?
- Was the root cause sufficiently deep?
- Is the action plan appropriate and are resulting bug fixes at appropriate priority?
- Did we share the outcome with relevant stakeholders?

Once the initial review is complete, the postmortem is shared more broadly, typically with the larger engineering team or on an internal mailing list. Our goal is to share postmortems to the widest possible audience that would benefit from the knowledge or lessons imparted. Google has stringent rules around access to any piece of information that might identify a user,[1] and even internal documents like postmortems never include such information.

Best Practice: No Postmortem Left Unreviewed

An unreviewed postmortem might as well never have existed. To ensure that each completed draft is reviewed, we encourage regular review sessions for postmortems. In these meetings, it is important to close out any ongoing discussions and comments, to capture ideas, and to finalize the state.

Once those involved are satisfied with the document and its action items, the postmortem is added to a team or organization repository of past incidents.[2] Transparent sharing makes it easier for others to find and learn from the postmortem.

Introducing a Postmortem Culture

Introducing a postmortem culture to your organization is easier said than done; such an effort requires continuous cultivation and reinforcement. We reinforce a collaborative postmortem culture through senior management's active participation in the review and collaboration process. Management can encourage this culture, but blameless postmortems are ideally the product of engineer self-motivation. In the spirit of nurturing the postmortem culture, SREs proactively create activities that disseminate what we learn about system infrastructure. Some example activities include:

---

1 See *http://www.google.com/policies/privacy/*.

2 If you'd like to start your own repository, Etsy has released *Morgue* (*https://github.com/etsy/morgue*), a tool for managing postmortems.

Postmortem of the month

In a monthly newsletter, an interesting and well-written postmortem is shared with the entire organization.

Google+ postmortem group

This group shares and discusses internal and external postmortems, best practices, and commentary about postmortems.

Postmortem reading clubs

Teams host regular postmortem reading clubs, in which an interesting or impactful postmortem is brought to the table (along with some tasty refreshments) for an open dialogue with participants, nonparticipants, and new Googlers about what happened, what lessons the incident imparted, and the aftermath of the incident. Often, the postmortem being reviewed is months or years old!

Wheel of Misfortune

New SREs are often treated to the Wheel of Misfortune exercise (see "Disaster Role Playing" on page 401), in which a previous postmortem is reenacted with a cast of engineers playing roles as laid out in the postmortem. The original incident commander attends to help make the experience as "real" as possible.

One of the biggest challenges of introducing postmortems to an organization is that some may question their value given the cost of their preparation. The following strategies can help in facing this challenge:

- Ease postmortems into the workflow. A trial period with several complete and successful postmortems may help prove their value, in addition to helping to identify what criteria should initiate a postmortem.

- Make sure that writing effective postmortems is a rewarded and celebrated practice, both publicly through the social methods mentioned earlier, and through individual and team performance management.

- Encourage senior leadership's acknowledgment and participation. Even Larry Page talks about the high value of postmortems!

Best Practice: Visibly Reward People for Doing the Right Thing

Google's founders Larry Page and Sergey Brin host TGIF, a weekly all-hands held live at our headquarters in Mountain View, California, and broadcast to Google offices around the world. A 2014 TGIF focused on "The Art of the Postmortem," which featured SRE discussion of high-impact incidents. One SRE discussed a release he had recently pushed; despite thorough testing, an unexpected interaction inadvertently took down a critical service for four minutes. The incident only lasted four minutes because the SRE had the presence of mind to roll back the change immediately, averting a much longer and larger-scale outage. Not only did this engineer receive two peer bonuses[3] immediately afterward in recognition of his quick and level-headed handling of the incident, but he also received a huge round of applause from the TGIF audience, which included the company's founders and an audience of Googlers numbering in the thousands. In addition to such a visible forum, Google has an array of internal social networks that drive peer praise toward well-written postmortems and exceptional incident handling. This is one example of many where recognition of these contributions comes from peers, CEOs, and everyone in between.[4]

Best Practice: Ask for Feedback on Postmortem Effectiveness

At Google, we strive to address problems as they arise and share innovations internally. We regularly survey our teams on how the postmortem process is supporting their goals and how the process might be improved. We ask questions such as: Is the culture supporting your work? Does writing a postmortem entail too much toil (see Chapter 5)? What best practices does your team recommend for other teams? What kinds of tools would you like to see developed? The survey results give the SREs in the trenches the opportunity to ask for improvements that will increase the effectiveness of the postmortem culture.

Beyond the operational aspects of incident management and follow-up, postmortem practice has been woven into the culture at Google: it's now a cultural norm that any significant incident is followed by a comprehensive postmortem.

---

3 Google's Peer Bonus program is a way for fellow Googlers to recognize colleagues for exceptional efforts and involves a token cash reward.

4 For further discussion of this particular incident, see Chapter 13.

Conclusion and Ongoing Improvements

We can say with confidence that thanks to our continuous investment in cultivating a postmortem culture, Google weathers fewer outages and fosters a better user experience. Our "Postmortems at Google" working group is one example of our commitment to the culture of blameless postmortems. This group coordinates postmortem efforts across the company: pulling together postmortem templates, automating postmortem creation with data from tools used during an incident, and helping automate data extraction from postmortems so we can perform trend analysis. We've been able to collaborate on best practices from products as disparate as YouTube, Google Fiber, Gmail, Google Cloud, AdWords, and Google Maps. While these products are quite diverse, they all conduct postmortems with the universal goal of learning from our darkest hours.

With a large number of postmortems produced each month across Google, tools to aggregate postmortems are becoming more and more useful. These tools help us identify common themes and areas for improvement across product boundaries. To facilitate comprehension and automated analysis, we have recently enhanced our postmortem template (see Appendix D) with additional metadata fields. Future work in this domain includes machine learning to help predict our weaknesses, facilitate real-time incident investigation, and reduce duplicate incidents.

CHAPTER 16

Tracking Outages

Written by Gabe Krabbe
Edited by Lisa Carey

Improving reliability over time is only possible if you start from a known baseline and can track progress. "Outalator," our outage tracker, is one of the tools we use to do just that. Outalator is a system that passively receives all alerts sent by our monitoring systems and allows us to annotate, group, and analyze this data.

Systematically learning from past problems is essential to effective service management. Postmortems (see Chapter 15) provide detailed information for individual outages, but they are only part of the answer. They are only written for incidents with a large impact, so issues that have individually small impact but are frequent and widespread don't fall within their scope. Similarly, postmortems tend to provide useful insights for improving a single service or set of services, but may miss opportunities that would have a small effect in individual cases, or opportunities that have a poor cost/benefit ratio, but that would have large horizontal impact.[1]

We can also get useful information from questions such as, "How many alerts per oncall shift does this team get?", "What's the ratio of actionable/nonactionable alerts over the last quarter?", or even simply "Which of the services this team manages creates the most toil?"

---

[1] For example, it might take significant engineering effort to make a particular change to Bigtable that only has a small mitigating effect for one outage. However, if that same mitigation were available across many events, the engineering effort may well be worthwhile.

Escalator

At Google, all alert notifications for SRE share a central replicated system that tracks whether a human has acknowledged receipt of the notification. If no acknowledgment is received after a configured interval, the system escalates to the next configured destination(s)—e.g., from primary on-call to secondary. This system, called "The Escalator," was initially designed as a largely transparent tool that received copies of emails sent to on-call aliases. This functionality allowed Escalator to easily integrate with existing workflows without requiring any change in user behavior (or, at the time, monitoring system behavior).

Outalator

Following Escalator's example, where we added useful features to existing infrastructure, we created a system that would deal not just with the individual escalating notifications, but with the next layer of abstraction: outages.

Outalator lets users view a time-interleaved list of notifications for multiple queues at once, instead of requiring a user to switch between queues manually. Figure 16-1 shows multiple queues as they appear in Outalator's queue view. This functionality is handy because frequently a single SRE team is the primary point of contact for services with distinct secondary escalation targets, usually the developer teams.

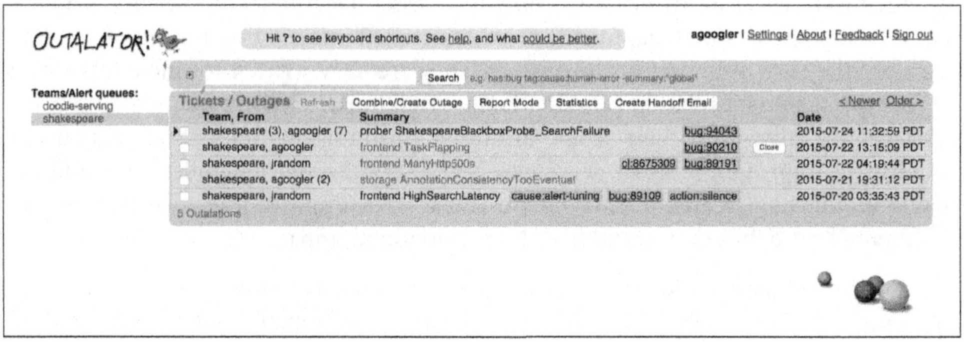

Figure 16-1. Outalator queue view

Outalator stores a copy of the original notification and allows annotating incidents. For convenience, it silently receives and saves a copy of any email replies as well. Because some follow-ups are less helpful than others (for example, a reply-all sent with the sole purpose of adding more recipients to the cc list), annotations can be marked as "important." If an annotation is important, other parts of the message are collapsed into the interface to cut down on clutter. Together, this provides more context when referring to an incident than a possibly fragmented email thread.

Multiple escalating notifications ("alerts") can be combined into a single entity ("incident") in the Outalator. These notifications may be related to the same single incident, may be otherwise unrelated and uninteresting auditable events such as privileged database access, or may be spurious monitoring failures. This grouping functionality, shown in Figure 16-2, unclutters the overview displays and allows for separate analysis of "incidents per day" versus "alerts per day."

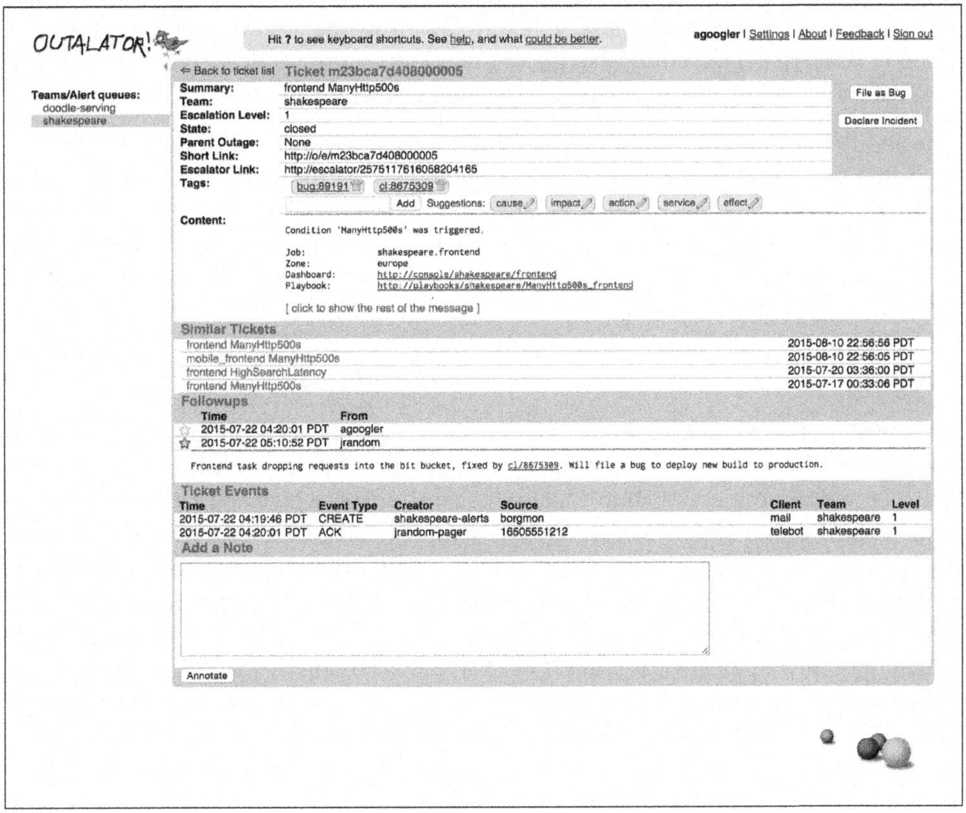

Figure 16-2. Outalator view of an incident

Building Your Own Outalator

Many organizations use messaging systems like Slack, Hipchat, or even IRC for internal communication and/or updating status dashboards. These systems are great places to hook into with a system like Outalator.

Aggregation

A single event may, and often will, trigger multiple alerts. For example, network failures cause timeouts and unreachable backend services for everyone, so all affected teams receive their own alerts, including the owners of backend services; meanwhile, the network operations center will have its own klaxons ringing. However, even smaller issues affecting a single service may trigger multiple alerts due to multiple error conditions being diagnosed. While it is worthwhile to attempt to minimize the number of alerts triggered by a single event, triggering multiple alerts is unavoidable in most trade-off calculations between false positives and false negatives.

The ability to group multiple alerts together into a single *incident* is critical in dealing with this duplication. Sending an email saying "this is the same thing as that other thing; they are symptoms of the same incident" works for a given alert: it can prevent duplication of debugging or panic. But sending an email for each alert is not a practical or scalable solution for handling duplicate alerts within a team, let alone between teams or over longer periods of time.

Tagging

Of course, not every alerting event is an incident. False-positive alerts occur, as well as test events or mistargeted emails from humans. The Outalator itself does not distinguish between these events, but it allows general-purpose *tagging* to add metadata to notifications, at any level. Tags are mostly free-form, single "words." Colons, however, are interpreted as semantic separators, which subtly promotes the use of hierarchical namespaces and allows some automatic treatment. This namespacing is supported by suggested tag prefixes, primarily "cause" and "action," but the list is team-specific and generated based on historical usage. For example, "cause:network" might be sufficient information for some teams, whereas another team might opt for more specific tags, such as "cause:network:switch" versus "cause:network:cable." Some teams may frequently use "customer:132456"-style tags, so "customer" would be suggested for those teams, but not for others.

Tags can be parsed and turned into a convenient link ("bug:76543" links to the bug tracking system). Other tags are just a single word ("bogus" is widely used for false positives). Of course, some tags are typos ("cause:netwrok") and some tags aren't particularly helpful ("problem-went-away"), but avoiding a predetermined list and allowing teams to find their own preferences and standards will result in a more useful tool and better data. Overall, tags have been a remarkably powerful tool for teams to obtain and provide an overview of a given service's pain points, even without much, or even any, formal analysis. As trivial as tagging appears, it is probably one of the Outalator's most useful unique features.

Analysis

Of course, SRE does much more than just react to incidents. Historical data is useful when one is responding to an incident—the question "what did we do last time?" is always a good starting point. But historical information is far more useful when it concerns systemic, periodic, or other wider problems that may exist. Enabling such analysis is one of the most important functions of an outage tracking tool.

The bottom layer of analysis encompasses counting and basic aggregate statistics for reporting. The details depend on the team, but include information such as incidents per week/month/quarter and alerts per incident. The next layer is more important, and easy to provide: comparison between teams/services and over time to identify first patterns and trends. This layer allows teams to determine whether a given alert load is "normal" relative to their own track record and that of other services. "That's the third time this week" can be good or bad, but knowing whether "it" used to happen five times per day or five times per month allows interpretation.

The next step in data analysis is finding wider issues, which are not just raw counts but require some semantic analysis. For example, identifying the infrastructure component causing most incidents, and therefore the potential benefit from increasing the stability or performance of this component,[2] assumes that there is a straightforward way to provide this information alongside the incident records. As a simple example: different teams have service-specific alert conditions such as "stale data" or "high latency." Both conditions may be caused by network congestion leading to database replication delays and need intervention. Or, they could be within the nominal service level objective, but are failing to meet the higher expectations of users. Examining this information across multiple teams allows us to identify systemic problems and choose the correct solution, especially if the solution may be the introduction of more artificial failures to stop over-performing.

Reporting and communication

Of more immediate use to frontline SREs is the ability to select zero or more outalations and include their subjects, tags, and "important" annotations in an email to the next on-call engineer (and an arbitrary cc list) in order to pass on recent state between shifts. For periodic reviews of the production services (which occur weekly for most teams), the Outalator also supports a "report mode," in which the important

---

2 On the one hand, "most incidents caused" is a good starting point for reducing the number of alerts triggered and improving the overall system. On the other hand, this metric may simply be an artifact of over-sensitive monitoring or a small set of client systems misbehaving or themselves running outside the agreed service level. And on the gripping hand, the number of incidents alone gives no indication as to the difficulty to fix or severity of impact.

annotations are expanded inline with the main list in order to provide a quick overview of lowlights.

Unexpected Benefits

Being able to identify that an alert, or a flood of alerts, coincides with a given other outage has obvious benefits: it increases the speed of diagnosis and reduces load on other teams by acknowledging that there is indeed an incident. There are additional nonobvious benefits. To use Bigtable as an example, if a service has a disruption due to an apparent Bigtable incident, but you can see that the Bigtable SRE team has not been alerted, manually alerting the team is probably a good idea. Improved cross-team visibility can and does make a big difference in incident resolution, or at least in incident mitigation.

Some teams across the company have gone so far as to set up dummy escalator configurations: no human receives the notifications sent there, but the notifications appear in the Outalator and can be tagged, annotated, and reviewed. One example for this "system of record" use is to log and audit the use of privileged or role accounts (though it must be noted that this functionality is basic, and used for technical, rather than legal, audits). Another use is to record and automatically annotate runs of periodic jobs that may not be idempotent—for example, automatic application of schema changes from version control to database systems.

CHAPTER 17

Testing for Reliability

Written by Alex Perry and Max Luebbe
Edited by Diane Bates

> *If you haven't tried it, assume it's broken.*
> —Unknown

One key responsibility of Site Reliability Engineers is to quantify confidence in the systems they maintain. SREs perform this task by adapting classical software testing techniques to systems at scale.[1] Confidence can be measured both by past reliability and future reliability. The former is captured by analyzing data provided by monitoring historic system behavior, while the latter is quantified by making predictions from data about past system behavior. In order for these predictions to be strong enough to be useful, one of the following conditions must hold:

- The site remains completely unchanged over time with no software releases or changes in the server fleet, which means that future behavior will be similar to past behavior.

- You can confidently describe all changes to the site, in order for analysis to allow for the uncertainty incurred by each of these changes.

---

1 This chapter explains how to maximize the value derived from investing engineering effort into testing. Once an engineer defines suitable tests (for a given system) in a generalized way, the remaining work is common across all SRE teams and thus may be considered shared infrastructure. That infrastructure consists of a scheduler (to share budgeted resources across otherwise unrelated projects) and executors (that sandbox test binaries to prevent them from being considered trusted). These two infrastructure components can each be considered an ordinary SRE-supported service (much like cluster scale storage), and therefore won't be discussed further here.

Testing is the mechanism you use to demonstrate specific areas of equivalence when changes occur.[2] Each test that passes both before and after a change reduces the uncertainty for which the analysis needs to allow. Thorough testing helps us predict the future reliability of a given site with enough detail to be practically useful.

The amount of testing you need to conduct depends on the reliability requirements for your system. As the percentage of your codebase covered by tests increases, you reduce uncertainty and the potential decrease in reliability from each change. Adequate testing coverage means that you can make more changes before reliability falls below an acceptable level. If you make too many changes too quickly, the predicted reliability approaches the acceptability limit. At this point, you may want to stop making changes while new monitoring data accumulates. The accumulating data supplements the tested coverage, which validates the reliability being asserted for revised execution paths. Assuming the served clients are randomly distributed [Woo96], sampling statistics can extrapolate from monitored metrics whether the aggregate behavior is making use of new paths. These statistics identify the areas that need better testing or other retrofitting.

Relationships Between Testing and Mean Time to Repair

Passing a test or a series of tests doesn't necessarily prove reliability. However, tests that are failing generally prove the absence of reliability.

A monitoring system can uncover bugs, but only as quickly as the reporting pipeline can react. The *Mean Time to Repair* (MTTR) measures how long it takes the operations team to fix the bug, either through a rollback or another action.

It's possible for a testing system to identify a bug with zero MTTR. Zero MTTR occurs when a system-level test is applied to a subsystem, and that test detects the exact same problem that monitoring would detect. Such a test enables the push to be blocked so the bug never reaches production (though it still needs to be repaired in the source code). Repairing zero MTTR bugs by blocking a push is both quick and convenient. The more bugs you can find with zero MTTR, the higher the *Mean Time Between Failures* (MTBF) experienced by your users.

As MTBF increases in response to better testing, developers are encouraged to release features faster. Some of these features will, of course, have bugs. New bugs result in an opposite adjustment to release velocity as these bugs are found and fixed.

---

2 For further reading on equivalence, see *http://stackoverflow.com/questions/1909280/equivalence-class-testing-vs-boundary-value-testing*.

Authors writing about software testing largely agree on what coverage is needed. Most conflicts of opinion stem from conflicting terminology, differing emphasis on the impact of testing in each of the software lifecycle phases, or the particularities of the systems on which they've conducted testing. For a discussion about testing at Google in general, see [Whi12]. The following sections specify how software testing–related terminology is used in this chapter.

Types of Software Testing

Software tests broadly fall into two categories: traditional and production. Traditional tests are more common in software development to evaluate the correctness of software offline, during development. Production tests are performed on a live web service to evaluate whether a deployed software system is working correctly.

Traditional Tests

As shown in Figure 17-1, traditional software testing begins with unit tests. Testing of more complex functionality is layered atop unit tests.

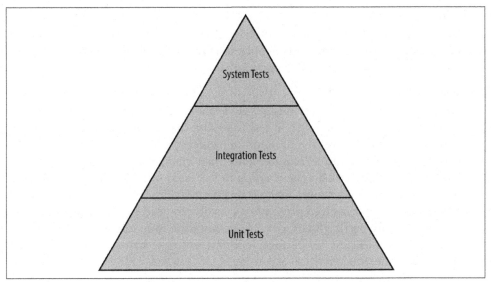

Figure 17-1. The hierarchy of traditional tests

Unit tests

A *unit test* is the smallest and simplest form of software testing. These tests are employed to assess a separable unit of software, such as a class or function, for correctness independent of the larger software system that contains the unit. Unit tests are also employed as a form of specification to ensure that a function or module exactly performs the behavior required by the system. Unit tests are commonly used to introduce test-driven development concepts.

Integration tests

Software components that pass individual unit tests are assembled into larger components. Engineers then run an *integration test* on an assembled component to verify that it functions correctly. Dependency injection, which is performed with tools such as Dagger,[3] is an extremely powerful technique for creating mocks of complex dependencies so that an engineer can cleanly test a component. A common example of a dependency injection is to replace a stateful database with a lightweight mock that has precisely specified behavior.

System tests

A *system test* is the largest scale test that engineers run for an undeployed system. All modules belonging to a specific component, such as a server that passed integration tests, are assembled into the system. Then the engineer tests the end-to-end functionality of the system. System tests come in many different flavors:

Smoke tests
> *Smoke tests*, in which engineers test very simple but critical behavior, are among the simplest type of system tests. Smoke tests are also known as *sanity testing*, and serve to short-circuit additional and more expensive testing.

Performance tests
> Once basic correctness is established via a smoke test, a common next step is to write another variant of a system test to ensure that the performance of the system stays acceptable over the duration of its lifecycle. Because response times for dependencies or resource requirements may change dramatically during the course of development, a system needs to be tested to make sure that it doesn't become incrementally slower without anyone noticing (before it gets released to users). For example, a given program may evolve to need 32 GB of memory when it formerly only needed 8 GB, or a 10 ms response time might turn into 50 ms, and then into 100 ms. A performance test ensures that over time, a system doesn't degrade or become too expensive.

Regression tests
> Another type of system test involves preventing bugs from sneaking back into the codebase. Regression tests can be analogized to a gallery of rogue bugs that historically caused the system to fail or produce incorrect results. By documenting these bugs as tests at the system or integration level, engineers refactoring the

---

3 See *https://google.github.io/dagger/*.

codebase can be sure that they don't accidentally introduce bugs that they've already invested time and effort to eliminate.

It's important to note that tests have a cost, both in terms of time and computational resources. At one extreme, unit tests are very cheap in both dimensions, as they can usually be completed in milliseconds on the resources available on a laptop. At the other end of the spectrum, bringing up a complete server with required dependencies (or mock equivalents) to run related tests can take significantly more time—from several minutes to multiple hours—and possibly require dedicated computing resources. Mindfulness of these costs is essential to developer productivity, and also encourages more efficient use of testing resources.

Production Tests

Production tests interact with a live production system, as opposed to a system in a hermetic testing environment. These tests are in many ways similar to black-box monitoring (see Chapter 6), and are therefore sometimes called *black-box testing*. Production tests are essential to running a reliable production service.

Rollouts Entangle Tests

It's often said that testing is (or should be) performed in a hermetic environment [Nar12]. This statement implies that production is not hermetic. Of course, production usually isn't hermetic, because rollout cadences make live changes to the production environment in small and well-understood chunks.

To manage uncertainty and hide risk from users, changes might not be pushed live in the same order that they were added to source control. Rollouts often happen in stages, using mechanisms that gradually shuffle users around, in addition to monitoring at each stage to ensure that the new environment isn't hitting anticipated yet unexpected problems. As a result, the entire production environment is intentionally not representative of any given version of a binary that's checked into source control.

It's possible for source control to have more than one version of a binary and its associated configuration file waiting to be made live. This scenario can cause problems when tests are conducted against the live environment. For example, the test might use the latest version of a configuration file located in source control along with an older version of the binary that's live. Or it might test an older version of the configuration file and find a bug that's been fixed in a newer version of the file.

Similarly, a system test can use the configuration files to assemble its modules before running the test. If the test passes, but its version is one in which the configuration test (discussed in the following section) fails, the result of the test is valid hermetically, but not operationally. Such an outcome is inconvenient.

Configuration test

At Google, web service configurations are described in files that are stored in our version control system. For each configuration file, a separate *configuration test* examines production to see how a particular binary is actually configured and reports discrepancies against that file. Such tests are inherently not hermetic, as they operate outside the test infrastructure sandbox.

Configuration tests are built and tested for a specific version of the checked-in configuration file. Comparing which version of the test is passing in relation to the goal version for automation implicitly indicates how far actual production currently lags behind ongoing engineering work.

These nonhermetic configuration tests tend to be especially valuable as part of a distributed monitoring solution since the pattern of passes/fails across production can identify paths through the service stack that don't have sensible combinations of the local configurations. The monitoring solution's rules try to match paths of actual user requests (from the trace logs) against that set of undesirable paths. Any matches found by the rules become alerts that ongoing releases and/or pushes are not proceeding safely and remedial action is needed.

Configuration tests can be very simple when the production deployment uses the actual file content and offers a real-time query to retrieve a copy of the content. In this case, the test code simply issues that query and diffs the response against the file. The tests become more complex when the configuration does one of the following:

- Implicitly incorporates defaults that are built into the binary (meaning that the tests are separately versioned as a result)
- Passes through a preprocessor such as bash into command-line flags (rendering the tests subject to expansion rules)
- Specifies behavioral context for a shared runtime (making the tests depend on that runtime's release schedule)

Stress test

In order to safely operate a system, SREs need to understand the limits of both the system and its components. In many cases, individual components don't gracefully degrade beyond a certain point—instead, they catastrophically fail. Engineers use *stress tests* to find the limits on a web service. Stress tests answer questions such as:

- How full can a database get before writes start to fail?
- How many queries a second can be sent to an application server before it becomes overloaded, causing requests to fail?

Canary test

The *canary test* is conspicuously absent from this list of production tests. The term *canary* comes from the phrase "canary in a coal mine," and refers to the practice of using a live bird to detect toxic gases before humans were poisoned.

To conduct a canary test, a subset of servers is upgraded to a new version or configuration and then left in an incubation period. Should no unexpected variances occur, the release continues and the rest of the servers are upgraded in a progressive fashion.[4] Should anything go awry, the single modified server can be quickly reverted to a known good state. We commonly refer to the incubation period for the upgraded server as "baking the binary."

A canary test isn't really a test; rather, it's structured user acceptance. Whereas configuration and stress tests confirm the existence of a specific condition over deterministic software, a canary test is more ad hoc. It only exposes the code under test to less predictable live production traffic, and thus, it isn't perfect and doesn't always catch newly introduced faults.

To provide a concrete example of how a canary might proceed: consider a given underlying fault that relatively rarely impacts user traffic and is being deployed with an upgrade rollout that is exponential. We expect a growing cumulative number of reported variances $CU = RK$ where R is the rate of those reports, U is the order of the fault (defined later), and K is the period over which the traffic grows by a factor of e, or 172%.[5]

In order to avoid user impact, a rollout that triggers undesirable variances needs to be quickly rolled back to the prior configuration. In the short time it takes automation to observe the variances and respond, it is likely that several additional reports will be generated. Once the dust has settled, these reports can estimate both the cumulative number C and rate R.

Dividing and correcting for K gives an estimate of U, the order of the underlying fault.[6] Some examples:

- U=1: The user's request encountered code that is simply broken.

---

4 A standard rule of thumb is to start by having the release impact 0.1% of user traffic, and then scaling by orders of magnitude every 24 hours while varying the geographic location of servers being upgraded (then on day 2: 1%, day 3: 10%, day 4: 100%).

5 For instance, assuming a 24 hour interval of continuous exponential growth between 1% and 10%,

$$K = \frac{86400}{ln\frac{0.1}{0.01}} = 37523 \text{ seconds, or about 10 hours and 25 minutes.}$$

6 We're using order here in the sense of "big O notation" order of complexity. For more context, see *https://en.wikipedia.org/wiki/Big_O_notation*.

- U=2: This user's request randomly damages data that a future user's request may see.

- U=3: The randomly damaged data is also a valid identifier to a previous request.

Most bugs are of order one: they scale linearly with the amount of user traffic [Per07]. You can generally track down these bugs by converting logs of all requests with unusual responses into new regression tests. This strategy doesn't work for higher-order bugs; a request that repeatedly fails if all the preceding requests are attempted in order will suddenly pass if some requests are omitted. It is important to catch these higher-order bugs during release, because otherwise, operational workload can increase very quickly.

Keeping the dynamics of higher- versus lower-order bugs in mind, when you are using an exponential rollout strategy, it isn't necessary to attempt to achieve fairness among fractions of user traffic. As long as each method for establishing a fraction uses the same K interval, the estimate of U will be valid even though you can't yet determine which method was instrumental in illuminating the fault. Using many methods sequentially while permitting some overlap keeps the value of K small. This strategy minimizes the total number of user-visible variances C while still allowing an early estimate of U (hoping for 1, of course).

Creating a Test and Build Environment

While it's wonderful to think about these types of tests and failure scenarios on day one of a project, frequently SREs join a developer team when a project is already well underway—once the team's project validates its research model, its library proves that the project's underlying algorithm is scalable, or perhaps when all of the user interface mocks are finally acceptable. The team's codebase is still a prototype and comprehensive testing hasn't yet been designed or deployed. In such situations, where should your testing efforts begin? Conducting unit tests for every key function and class is a completely overwhelming prospect if the current test coverage is low or nonexistent. Instead, start with testing that delivers the most impact with the least effort.

You can start your approach by asking the following questions:

- Can you prioritize the codebase in any way? To borrow a technique from feature development and project management, if every task is high priority, none of the tasks are high priority. Can you stack-rank the components of the system you're testing by any measure of importance?

- Are there particular functions or classes that are absolutely mission-critical or business-critical? For example, code that involves billing is a commonly business-critical. Billing code is also frequently cleanly separable from other parts of the system.

- Which APIs are other teams integrating against? Even the kind of breakage that never makes it past release testing to a user can be extremely harmful if it confuses another developer team, causing them to write wrong (or even just suboptimal) clients for your API.

Shipping software that is obviously broken is among the most cardinal sins of a developer. It takes little effort to create a series of smoke tests to run for every release. This type of low-effort, high-impact first step can lead to highly tested, reliable software.

One way to establish a strong testing culture[7] is to start documenting all reported bugs as test cases. If every bug is converted into a test, each test is supposed to initially fail because the bug hasn't yet been fixed. As engineers fix the bugs, the software passes testing and you're on the road to developing a comprehensive regression test suite.

Another key task for creating well-tested software is to set up a testing infrastructure. The foundation for a strong testing infrastructure is a versioned source control system that tracks every change to the codebase.

Once source control is in place, you can add a continuous build system that builds the software and runs tests every time code is submitted. We've found it optimal if the build system notifies engineers the moment a change breaks a software project. At the risk of sounding obvious, it's essential that the latest version of a software project in source control is working completely. When the build system notifies engineers about broken code, they should drop all of their other tasks and prioritize fixing the problem. It is appropriate to treat defects this seriously for a few reasons:

- It's usually harder to fix what's broken if there are changes to the codebase after the defect is introduced.
- Broken software slows down the team because they must work around the breakage.
- Release cadences, such as nightly and weekly builds, lose their value.
- The ability of the team to respond to a request for an emergency release (for example, in response to a security vulnerability disclosure) becomes much more complex and difficult.

The concepts of stability and agility are traditionally in tension in the world of SRE. The last bullet point provides an interesting case where stability actually drives agility. When the build is predictably solid and reliable, developers can iterate faster!

---

7 For more on this topic, we highly recommend [Bla14] by our former coworker and ex-Googler, Mike Bland.

Some build systems like Bazel[8] have valuable features that afford more precise control over testing. For example, Bazel creates dependency graphs for software projects. When a change is made to a file, Bazel only rebuilds the part of the software that depends on that file. Such systems provide reproducible builds. Instead of running all tests at every submit, tests only run for changed code. As a result, tests execute cheaper and faster.

There are a variety of tools to help you quantify and visualize the level of test coverage you need [Cra10]. Use these tools to shape the focus of your testing: approach the prospect of creating highly tested code as an engineering project rather than a philosophical mental exercise. Instead of repeating the ambiguous refrain "We need more tests," set explicit goals and deadlines.

Remember that not all software is created equal. Life-critical or revenue-critical systems demand substantially higher levels of test quality and coverage than a non-production script with a short shelf life.

Testing at Scale

Now that we've covered the fundamentals of testing, let's examine how SRE takes a systems perspective to testing in order to drive reliability at scale.

A small unit test might have a short list of dependencies: one source file, the testing library, the runtime libraries, the compiler, and the local hardware running the tests. A robust testing environment dictates that those dependencies each have their own test coverage, with tests that specifically address use cases that other parts of the environment expect. If the implementation of that unit test depends on a code path inside a runtime library that doesn't have test coverage, an unrelated change in the environment[9] can lead the unit test to consistently pass testing, regardless of faults in the code under test.

In contrast, a release test might depend on so many parts that it has a transitive dependency on every object in the code repository. If the test depends on a clean copy of the production environment, in principle, every small patch requires performing a full disaster recovery iteration. Practical testing environments try to select branch points among the versions and merges. Doing so resolves the maximum amount of dependent uncertainty for the minimum number of iterations. Of course,

---

8 See https://github.com/google/bazel.

9 For example, code under test that wraps a nontrivial API to provide a simpler and backward-compatible abstraction. The API that used to be synchronous instead returns a future. Calling argument errors still deliver an exception, but not until the future is evaluated. The code under test passes the API result directly back to the caller. Many cases of argument misuse may not be caught.

---

when an area of uncertainty resolves into a fault, you need to select additional branch points.

Testing Scalable Tools

As pieces of software, SRE tools also need testing.[10] SRE-developed tools might perform tasks such as the following:

- Retrieving and propagating database performance metrics
- Predicting usage metrics to plan for capacity risks
- Refactoring data within a service replica that isn't user accessible
- Changing files on a server

SRE tools share two characteristics:

- Their side effects remain within the tested mainstream API
- They're isolated from user-facing production by an existing validation and release barrier

---

Barrier Defenses Against Risky Software

Software that bypasses the usual heavily tested API (even if it does so for a good cause) could wreak havoc on a live service. For example, a database engine implementation might allow administrators to temporarily turn off transactions in order to shorten maintenance windows. If the implementation is used by batch update software, user-facing isolation may be lost if that utility is ever accidentally launched against a user-facing replica. Avoid this risk of havoc with design:

1. Use a separate tool to place a barrier in the replication configuration so that the replica cannot pass its health check. As a result, the replica isn't released to users.

2. Configure the risky software to check for the barrier upon startup. Allow the risky software to only access unhealthy replicas.

3. Use the replica health validating tool you use for black-box monitoring to remove the barrier.

---

10 This section talks specifically about tools used by SRE that need to be scalable. However, SRE also develops and uses tools that don't necessarily need to be scalable. The tools that don't need to be scalable also need to be tested, but these tools are out of scope for this section, and therefore won't be discussed here. Because their risk footprint is similar to user-facing applications, similar testing strategies are applicable on such SRE-developed tools.

Automation tools are also software. Because their risk footprint appears out-of-band for a different layer of the service, their testing needs are more subtle. Automation tools perform tasks like the following:

- Database index selection
- Load balancing between datacenters
- Shuffling relay logs for fast remastering

Automation tools share two characteristics:

- The actual operation performed is against a robust, predictable, and well-tested API
- The purpose of the operation is the side effect that is an invisible discontinuity to another API client

Testing can demonstrate the desired behavior of the other service layer, both before and after the change. It's often possible to test whether internal state, as seen through the API, is constant across the operation. For example, databases pursue correct answers, even if a suitable index isn't available for the query. On the other hand, some documented API invariants (such as a DNS cache holding until the TTL) may not hold across the operation. For example, if a runlevel change replaces a local name-server with a caching proxy, both choices can promise to retain completed lookups for many seconds. It's unlikely that the cache state is handed over from one to the other.

Given that automation tools imply additional release tests for other binaries to handle environmental transients, how do you define the environment in which those auto-mation tools run? After all, the automation for shuffling containers to improve usage is likely to try to shuffle itself at some point if it also runs in a container. It would be embarrassing if a new release of its internal algorithm yielded dirty memory pages so quickly that the network bandwidth of the associated mirroring ended up preventing the code from finalizing the live migration. Even if there's an integration test for which the binary intentionally shuffles itself around, the test likely doesn't use a production-sized model of the container fleet. It almost certainly isn't allowed to use scarce high-latency intercontinental bandwidth for testing such races.

Even more amusingly, one automation tool might be changing the environment in which another automation tool runs. Or both tools might be changing the environment of the other automation tool simultaneously! For example, a fleet upgrading tool likely consumes the most resources when it's pushing upgrades. As a result, the container rebalancing would be tempted to move the tool. In turn, the container rebalancing tool occasionally needs upgrading. This circular dependency is fine if the associated APIs have restart semantics, someone remembered to implement test coverage for those semantics, and checkpoint health is assured independently.

Testing Disaster

Many disaster recovery tools can be carefully designed to operate *offline*. Such tools do the following:

- Compute a *checkpoint* state that is equivalent to cleanly stopping the service
- Push the checkpoint state to be *loadable* by existing nondisaster validation tools
- Support the usual release *barrier* tools, which trigger the *clean start* procedure

In many cases, you can implement these phases so that the associated tests are easy to write and offer excellent coverage. If any of the constraints (offline, checkpoint, loadable, barrier, or clean start) must be broken, it's much harder to show confidence that the associated tool implementation will work at any time on short notice.

Online repair tools inherently operate outside the mainstream API and therefore become more interesting to test. One challenge you face in a distributed system is determining if normal behavior, which may be eventually consistent by nature, will interact badly with the repair. For example, consider a race condition that you can attempt to analyze using the offline tools. An offline tool is generally written to expect instant consistency, as opposed to eventual consistency, because instant consistency is less challenging to test. This situation becomes complicated because the repair binary is generally built separately from the serving production binary that it's racing against. Consequently, you might need to build a unified instrumented binary to run within these tests so that the tools can observe transactions.

Using Statistical Tests

Statistical techniques, such as Lemon [Ana07] for fuzzing, and Chaos Monkey[11] and Jepsen[12] for distributed state, aren't necessarily repeatable tests. Simply rerunning such tests after a code change doesn't definitively prove that the observed fault is fixed.[13] However, these techniques can be useful:

- They can provide a log of all the randomly selected actions that are taken in a given run—sometimes simply by logging the random number generator seed.

- If this log is immediately refactored as a release test, running it a few times before starting on the bug report is often helpful. The rate of nonfailure on replay tells you how hard it will be to later assert that the fault is fixed.

- Variations in how the fault is expressed help you pinpoint suspicious areas in the code.

- Some of those later runs may demonstrate failure situations that are more severe than those in the original run. In response, you may want to escalate the bug's severity and impact.

The Need for Speed

For every version (patch) in the code repository, every defined test provides a pass or fail indication. That indication may change for repeated and seemingly identical runs. You can estimate the actual likelihood of a test passing or failing by averaging over those many runs and computing the statistical uncertainty of that likelihood. However, performing this calculation for every test at every version point is computationally infeasible.

Instead, you must form hypotheses about the many scenarios of interest and run the appropriate number of repeats of each test and version to allow a reasonable inference. Some of these scenarios are benign (in a code quality sense), while others are actionable. These scenarios affect all the test attempts to varying extents and, because they are coupled, reliably and quickly obtaining a list of actionable hypotheses (i.e., components that are actually broken) means estimating all scenarios at the same time.

---

11 See *https://github.com/Netflix/SimianArmy/wiki/Chaos-Monkey*.

12 See *https://github.com/aphyr/jepsen*.

13 Even if the test run is repeated with the same random seed so that the task kills are in the same order, there is no serialization between the kills and the fake user traffic. Therefore, there's no guarantee that the actual previously observed code path will now be exercised again.

Engineers who use the testing infrastructure want to know if their code—usually a tiny fraction of all the source behind a given test run—is broken. Often, not being broken implies that any observed failures can be blamed on someone else's code. In other words, the engineer wants to know if their code has an unanticipated race condition that makes the test flaky (or more flaky than the test already was due to other factors).

> ## Testing Deadlines
>
> Most tests are simple, in the sense that they run as a self-contained hermetic binary that fits in a small compute container for a few seconds. These tests give engineers interactive feedback about mistakes before the engineer switches context to the next bug or task.
>
> Tests that require orchestration across many binaries and/or across a fleet that has many containers tend to have startup times measured in seconds. Such tests are usually unable to offer interactive feedback, so they can be classified as batch tests. Instead of saying "don't close the editor tab" to the engineer, these test failures are saying "this code is not ready for review" to the code reviewer.
>
> The informal deadline for the test is the point at which the engineer makes the next context switch. Test results are best given to the engineer before he or she switches context, because otherwise the next context may involve XKCD compiling.[14]

Suppose an engineer is working on a service with over 21,000 simple tests and occasionally proposes a patch against the service's codebase. To test the patch, you want to compare the vector of pass/fail results from the codebase before the patch with the vector of results from the codebase after the patch. A favorable comparison of those two vectors provisionally qualifies the codebase as releasable. This qualification creates an incentive to run the many release and integration tests, as well as other distributed binary tests that examine scaling of the system (in case the patch uses significantly more local compute resources) and complexity (in case the patch creates a superlinear workload elsewhere).

At what rate can you incorrectly flag a user's patch as damaging by miscalculating environmental flakiness? It seems likely that users would vehemently complain if 1 in 10 patches is rejected. But a rejection of 1 patch among 100 perfect patches might go without comment.

---

14 See *http://xkcd.com/303/*.

This means you're interested in the 42,000th root (one for each defined test before the patch, and one for each defined test after the patch) of 0.99 (the fraction of patches that can be rejected). This calculation:

$$0.99^{\frac{1}{2 \times 21000}}$$

suggests that those individual tests must run correctly over 99.9999% of the time. Hmm.

Pushing to Production

While production configuration management is commonly kept in a source control repository, configuration is often separate from the developer source code. Similarly, the software testing infrastructure often can't see production configuration. Even if the two are located in the same repository, changes for configuration management are made in branches and/or a segregated directory tree that test automation has historically ignored.

In a legacy corporate environment where software engineers develop binaries and throw them over the wall to the administrators who update the servers, segregation of testing infrastructure and production configuration is at best annoying, and at worst can damage reliability and agility. Such segregation might also lead to tool duplication. In a nominally integrated Ops environment, this segregation degrades resiliency because it creates subtle inconsistencies between the behavior for the two sets of tools. This segregation also limits project velocity because of commit races between the versioning systems.

In the SRE model, the impact of segregating testing infrastructure from production configuration is appreciably worse, as it prevents relating the model describing production to the model describing the application behavior. This discrepancy impacts engineers who want to find statistical inconsistencies in expectations at development time. However, this segregation doesn't slow down development so much as prevent the system architecture from changing, because there is no way to eliminate migration risk.

Consider a scenario of unified versioning and unified testing, so that the SRE methodology is applicable. What impact would the failure of a distributed architecture migration have? A fair amount of testing will probably occur. So far, it's assumed that a software engineer would likely accept the test system giving the wrong answer 1 time in 10 or so. What risk are you willing to take with the migration if you know that testing may return a false negative and the situation could become really exciting, really quickly? Clearly, some areas of test coverage need a higher level of paranoia than others. This distinction can be generalized: some test failures are indicative of a larger impact risk than other test failures.

Expect Testing Fail

Not too long ago, a software product might have released once per year. Its binaries were generated by a compiler toolchain over many hours or days, and most of the testing was performed by humans against manually written instructions. This release process was inefficient, but there was little need to automate it. The release effort was dominated by documentation, data migration, user retraining, and other factors. Mean Time Between Failure (MTBF) for those releases was one year, no matter how much testing took place. So many changes happened per release that some user-visible breakage was bound to be hiding in the software. Effectively, the reliability data from the previous release was irrelevant for the next release.

Effective API/ABI management tools and interpreted languages that scale to large amounts of code now support building and executing a new software version every few minutes. In principle, a sufficiently large army of humans[15] could complete testing on each new version using the methods described earlier and achieve the same quality bar for each incremental version. Even though ultimately only the same tests are applied to the same code, that final software version has higher quality in the resulting release that ships annually. This is because in addition to the annual versions, the intermediate versions of the code are also being tested. Using intermediates, you can unambiguously map problems found during testing back to their underlying causes and be confident that the whole issue, and not just the limited symptom that was exposed, is fixed. This principle of a shorter feedback cycle is equally effective when applied to automated test coverage.

If you let users try more versions of the software during the year, the MTBF suffers because there are more opportunities for user-visible breakage. However, you can also discover areas that would benefit from additional test coverage. If these tests are implemented, each improvement protects against some future failure. Careful reliability management combines the limits on uncertainty due to test coverage with the limits on user-visible faults in order to adjust the release cadence. This combination maximizes the knowledge that you gain from operations and end users. These gains drive test coverage and, in turn, product release velocity.

If an SRE modifies a configuration file or adjusts an automation tool's strategy (as opposed to implementing a user feature), the engineering work matches the same conceptual model. When you are defining a release cadence based on reliability, it often makes sense to segment the reliability budget by functionality, or (more con-

---

15 Perhaps acquired through *Mechanical Turk* or similar services.

veniently) by team. In such a scenario, the feature engineering team aims to achieve a given uncertainty limit that affects their goal release cadence. The SRE team has a separate budget with its own associated uncertainty, and thus an upper limit on their release rate.

In order to remain reliable and to avoid scaling the number of SREs supporting a service linearly, the production environment has to run mostly unattended. To remain unattended, the environment must be resilient against minor faults. When a major event that demands manual SRE intervention occurs, the tools used by SRE must be suitably tested. Otherwise, that intervention decreases confidence that historical data is applicable to the near future. The reduction in confidence requires waiting for an analysis of monitoring data in order to eliminate the uncertainty incurred. Whereas the previous discussion in "Testing Scalable Tools" on page 193 focused on how to meet the opportunity of test coverage for an SRE tool, here you see that testing determines how often it is appropriate to use that tool against production.

Configuration files generally exist because changing the configuration is faster than rebuilding a tool. This low latency is often a factor in keeping MTTR low. However, these same files are also changed frequently for reasons that don't need that reduced latency. When viewed from the point of view of reliability:

- A configuration file that exists to keep MTTR low, and is only modified when there's a failure, has a release cadence slower than the MTBF. There can be a fair amount of uncertainty as to whether a given manual edit is actually truly optimal without the edit impacting the overall site reliability.

- A configuration file that changes more than once per user-facing application release (for example, because it holds release state) can be a major risk if these changes are not treated the same as application releases. If testing and monitoring coverage of that configuration file is not considerably better than that of the user application, that file will dominate site reliability in a negative way.

One method of handling configuration files is to make sure that every configuration file is categorized under only one of the options in the preceding bulleted list, and to somehow enforce that rule. Should you take the latter strategy, make sure of the following:

- Each configuration file has enough test coverage to support regular routine editing.

- Before releases, file edits are somewhat delayed while waiting for release testing.

- Provide a break-glass mechanism to push the file live before completing the testing. Since breaking the glass impairs reliability, it's generally a good idea to make the break noisy by (for example) filing a bug requesting a more robust resolution for next time.

Integration

In addition to unit testing a configuration file to mitigate its risk to reliability, it's also important to consider integration testing configuration files. The contents of the configuration file are (for testing purposes) potentially hostile content to the interpreter reading the configuration. Interpreted languages such as Python are commonly used for configuration files because their interpreters can be embedded, and some simple sandboxing is available to protect against nonmalicious coding errors.

Writing your configuration files in an interpreted language is risky, as this approach is fraught with latent failures that are hard to definitively address. Because loading content actually consists of executing a program, there's no inherent upper limit on how inefficient loading can be. In addition to any other testing, you should pair this type of integration testing with careful deadline checking on all integration test methods in order to label tests that do not run to completion in a reasonable amount of time as failed.

If the configuration is instead written as text in a custom syntax, every category of test needs separate coverage from scratch. Using an existing syntax such as YAML in combination with a heavily tested parser like Python's `safe_load` removes some of the toil incurred by the configuration file. Careful choice of syntax and parser can ensure there's a hard upper limit on how long the loading operation can take. However, the implementer needs to address schema faults, and most simple strategies for doing so don't have an upper bound on runtime. Even worse, these strategies tend not to be robustly unit tested.

The benefit of using protocol buffers[16] is that the schema is defined in advance and automatically checked at load time, removing even more of the toil, yet still offering the bounded runtime.

The role of SRE generally includes writing systems engineering tools[17] (if no one else is already writing them) and adding robust validation with test coverage. All tools can behave unexpectedly due to bugs not caught by testing, so defense in depth is advisable. When one tool behaves unexpectedly, engineers need to be as confident as possible that most of their other tools are working correctly and can therefore mitigate or resolve the side effects of that misbehavior. A key element of delivering site reliability is finding each anticipated form of misbehavior and making sure that some test (or another tool's tested input validator) reports that misbehavior. The tool that finds the problem might not be able to fix or even stop it, but should at least report the problem before a catastrophic outage occurs.

For example, consider the configured list of all users (such as */etc/passwd* on a nonnetworked Unix-style machine) and imagine an edit that unintentionally causes the parser to stop after parsing only half of the file. Because recently created users haven't loaded, the machine will most likely continue to run without problem, and many users may not notice the fault. The tool that maintains home directories can easily notice the mismatch between the actual directories present and those implied by the (partial) user list and urgently report the discrepancy. This tool's value lies in reporting the problem, and it should avoid attempting to remediate on its own (by deleting lots of user data).

Production Probes

Given that testing specifies acceptable behavior in the face of known data, while monitoring confirms acceptable behavior in the face of unknown user data, it would seem that major sources of risk—both the known and the unknown—are covered by the combination of testing and monitoring. Unfortunately, actual risk is more complicated.

Known good requests should work, while known bad requests should error. Implementing both kinds of coverage as an integration test is generally a good idea. You can replay the same bank of test requests as a release test. Splitting the known good requests into those that can be replayed against production and those that can't yields three sets of requests:

---

16 See *https://github.com/google/protobuf*.

17 Not because software engineers shouldn't write them. Tools that cross between technology verticals and span abstraction layers tend to have weak associations with many software teams and a slightly stronger association with systems teams.

- Known bad requests
- Known good requests that can be replayed against production
- Known good requests that can't be replayed against production

You can use each set as both integration and release tests. Most of these tests can also be used as monitoring probes.

It would seem to be superfluous and, in principle, pointless to deploy such monitoring because these exact same requests have already been tried two other ways. However, those two ways were different for a few reasons:

- The release test probably wrapped the integrated server with a frontend and a fake backend.
- The probe test probably wrapped the release binary with a load balancing frontend and a separate scalable persistent backend.
- Frontends and backends probably have independent release cycles. It's likely that the schedules for those cycles occur at different rates (due to their adaptive release cadences).

Therefore, the monitoring probe running in production is a configuration that wasn't previously tested.

Those probes should never fail, but what does it mean if they do fail? Either the frontend API (from the load balancer) or the backend API (to the persistent store) is not equivalent between the production and release environments. Unless you already know why the production and release environments aren't equivalent, the site is likely broken.

The same production updater that gradually replaces the application also gradually replaces the probes so that all four combinations of old-or-new probes sending requests to old-or-new applications are being continuously generated. That updater can detect when one of the four combinations is generating errors and roll back to the last known good state. Usually, the updater expects each newly started application instance to be unhealthy for a short time as it prepares to start receiving lots of user traffic. If the probes are already inspected as part of the readiness check, the update safely fails indefinitely, and no user traffic is ever routed to the new version. The update remains paused until engineers have time and inclination to diagnose the fault condition and then encourage the production updater to cleanly roll back.

This production test by probe does indeed offer protection to the site, plus clear feedback to the engineers. The earlier that feedback is given to engineers, the more useful it is. It's also preferable that the test is automated so that the delivery of warnings to engineers is scalable.

Assume that each component has the older software version that's being replaced and the newer version that's rolling out (now or very soon). The newer version might be talking to the old version's peer, which forces it to use the deprecated API. Or the older version might be talking to a peer's newer version, using the API which (at the time the older version was released) didn't work properly yet. But it works now, honest! You'd better hope those tests for future compatibility (which are running as monitoring probes) had good API coverage.

Fake Backend Versions

When implementing release tests, the fake backend is often maintained by the peer service's engineering team and merely referenced as a build dependency. The hermetic test that is executed by the testing infrastructure always combines the fake backend and the test frontend at the same build point in the revision control history.

That build dependency may be providing a runnable hermetic binary and, ideally, the engineering team maintaining it cuts a release of that fake backend binary at the same time they cut their main backend application and their probes. If that backend release is available, it might be worthwhile to include hermetic frontend release tests (without the fake backend binary) in the frontend release package.

Your monitoring should be aware of all release versions on both sides of a given service interface between two peers. This setup ensures that retrieving every combination of the two releases and determining whether the test still passes doesn't take much extra configuration. This monitoring doesn't have to happen continuously— you only need to run new combinations that are the result of either team cutting a new release. Such problems don't have to block that new release itself.

On the other hand, rollout automation should ideally block the associated production rollout until the problematic combinations are no longer possible. Similarly, the peer team's automation may consider draining (and upgrading) the replicas that haven't yet moved from a problematic combination.

Conclusion

Testing is one of the most profitable investments engineers can make to improve the reliability of their product. Testing isn't an activity that happens once or twice in the lifecycle of a project; it's continuous. The amount of effort required to write good tests is substantial, as is the effort to build and maintain infrastructure that promotes a strong testing culture. You can't fix a problem until you understand it, and in engineering, you can only understand a problem by measuring it. The methodologies and techniques in this chapter provide a solid foundation for measuring faults and uncertainty in a software system, and help engineers reason about the reliability of software as it's written and released to users.

CHAPTER 18

Software Engineering in SRE

Written by Dave Helstroom and Trisha Weir
with Evan Leonard and Kurt Delimon
Edited by Kavita Guliani

Ask someone to name a Google software engineering effort and they'll likely list a consumer-facing product like Gmail or Maps; some might even mention underlying infrastructure such as Bigtable or Colossus. But in truth, there is a massive amount of behind-the-scenes software engineering that consumers never see. A number of those products are developed within SRE.

Google's production environment is—by some measures—one of the most complex machines humanity has ever built. SREs have firsthand experience with the intricacies of production, making them uniquely well suited to develop the appropriate tools to solve internal problems and use cases related to keeping production running. The majority of these tools are related to the overall directive of maintaining uptime and keeping latency low, but take many forms: examples include binary rollout mechanisms, monitoring, or a development environment built on dynamic server composition. Overall, these SRE-developed tools are full-fledged software engineering projects, distinct from one-off solutions and quick hacks, and the SREs who develop them have adopted a product-based mindset that takes both internal customers and a roadmap for future plans into account.

Why Is Software Engineering Within SRE Important?

In many ways, the vast scale of Google production has necessitated internal software development, because few third-party tools are designed at sufficient scale for Google's needs. The company's history of successful software projects has led us to appreciate the benefits of developing directly within SRE.

SREs are in a unique position to effectively develop internal software for a number of reasons:

- The breadth and depth of Google-specific production knowledge within the SRE organization allows its engineers to design and create software with the appropriate considerations for dimensions such as scalability, graceful degradation during failure, and the ability to easily interface with other infrastructure or tools.

- Because SREs are embedded in the subject matter, they easily understand the needs and requirements of the tool being developed.

- A direct relationship with the intended user—fellow SREs—results in frank and high-signal user feedback. Releasing a tool to an internal audience with high familiarity with the problem space means that a development team can launch and iterate more quickly. Internal users are typically more understanding when it comes to minimal UI and other alpha product issues.

From a purely pragmatic standpoint, Google clearly benefits from having engineers with SRE experience developing software. By deliberate design, the growth rate of SRE-supported services exceeds the growth rate of the SRE organization; one of SRE's guiding principles is that "team size should not scale directly with service growth." Achieving linear team growth in the face of exponential service growth requires perpetual automation work and efforts to streamline tools, processes, and other aspects of a service that introduce inefficiency into the day-to-day operation of production. Having the people with direct experience running production systems developing the tools that will ultimately contribute to uptime and latency goals makes a lot of sense.

On the flip side, individual SREs, as well as the broader SRE organization, also benefit from SRE-driven software development.

Fully fledged software development projects within SRE provide career development opportunities for SREs, as well as an outlet for engineers who don't want their coding skills to get rusty. Long-term project work provides much-needed balance to interrupts and on-call work, and can provide job satisfaction for engineers who want their careers to maintain a balance between software engineering and systems engineering.

Beyond the design of automation tools and other efforts to reduce the workload for engineers in SRE, software development projects can further benefit the SRE organization by attracting and helping to retain engineers with a broad variety of skills. The desirability of team diversity is doubly true for SRE, where a variety of backgrounds and problem-solving approaches can help prevent blind spots. To this end, Google always strives to staff its SRE teams with a mix of engineers with traditional software development experience and engineers with systems engineering experience.

Auxon Case Study: Project Background and Problem Space

This case study examines Auxon, a powerful tool developed within SRE to automate capacity planning for services running in Google production. To best understand how Auxon was conceived and the problems it addresses, we'll first examine the problem space associated with capacity planning, and the difficulties that traditional approaches to this task present for services at Google and across the industry as a whole. For more context on how Google uses the terms *service* and *cluster*, see Chapter 2.

Traditional Capacity Planning

There are myriad tactics for capacity planning of compute resources (see [Hix15a]), but the majority of these approaches boil down to a *cycle* that can be approximated as follows:

1) Collect demand forecasts.
How many resources are needed? When and where are these resources needed?

- Uses the best data we have available today to plan into the future

- Typically covers anywhere from several quarters to years

2) Devise build and allocation plans.
Given this forecasted outlook, what's the best way to meet this demand with additional supply of resources? How much supply, and in what locations?

3) Review and sign off on plan.
Is the forecast reasonable? Does the plan line up with budgetary, product-level, and technical considerations?

4) Deploy and configure resources.
Once resources eventually arrive (potentially in phases over the course of some defined period of time), which services get to use the resources? How do I make typically lower-level resources (CPU, disk, etc.) useful for services?

It bears stressing that capacity planning is a neverending *cycle*: assumptions change, deployments slip, and budgets are cut, resulting in revision upon revision of The Plan. And each revision has trickle-down effects that must propagate throughout the plans of all subsequent quarters. For example, a shortfall this quarter must be made up in future quarters. Traditional capacity planning uses demand as a key driver, and manually shapes supply to fit demand in response to each change.

Brittle by nature

Traditional capacity planning produces a resource allocation plan that can be disrupted by any seemingly minor change. For example:

- A service undergoes a decrease in efficiency, and needs more resources than expected to serve the same demand.
- Customer adoption rates increase, resulting in an increase in projected demand.
- The delivery date for a new cluster of compute resources slips.
- A product decision about a performance goal changes the shape of the required service deployment (the service's footprint) and the amount of required resources.

Minor changes require cross-checking the entire allocation plan to make sure that the plan is still feasible; larger changes (such as delayed resource delivery or product strategy changes) potentially require re-creating the plan from scratch. A delivery slippage in a single cluster might impact the redundancy or latency requirements of multiple services: resource allocations in other clusters must be increased to make up for the slippage, and these and any other changes would have to propagate throughout the plan.

Also, consider that the capacity plan for any given quarter (or other time frame) is based on the expected outcome of the capacity plans of previous quarters, meaning that a change in any one quarter results in work to update subsequent quarters.

Laborious and imprecise

For many teams, the process of collecting the data necessary to generate demand forecasts is slow and error-prone. And when it is time to find capacity to meet this future demand, not all resources are equally suitable. For example, if latency requirements mean that a service must commit to serve user demand on the same continent as the user, obtaining additional resources in North America won't alleviate a capacity shortfall in Asia. Every forecast has *constraints*, or parameters around how it can be fulfilled; constraints are fundamentally related to intent, which is discussed in the next section.

Mapping constrained resource requests into allocations of actual resources from the available capacity is equally slow: it's both complex and tedious to bin pack requests into limited space by hand, or to find solutions that fit a limited budget.

This process may already paint a grim picture, but to make matters worse, the tools it requires are typically unreliable or cumbersome. Spreadsheets suffer severely from scalability problems and have limited error-checking abilities. Data becomes stale, and tracking changes becomes difficult. Teams often are forced to make simplifying assumptions and reduce the complexity of their requirements, simply to render maintaining adequate capacity a tractable problem.

When service owners face the challenges of fitting a series of requests for capacity from various services into the resources available to them, in a manner that meets the various constraints a service may have, additional imprecision ensues. Bin packing is an NP-hard problem that is difficult for human beings to compute by hand. Furthermore, the capacity request from a service is generally an inflexible set of demand requirements: X cores in cluster Y. The reasons why X cores or Y cluster are needed, and any degrees of freedom around those parameters, are long lost by the time the request reaches a human trying to fit a list of demands into available supply.

The net result is a massive expenditure of human effort to come up with a bin packing that is approximate, at best. The process is brittle to change, and there are no known bounds on an optimal solution.

Our Solution: Intent-Based Capacity Planning

Specify the requirements, not the implementation.

At Google, many teams have moved to an approach we call *Intent-based Capacity Planning*. The basic premise of this approach is to programmatically encode the dependencies and parameters (*intent*) of a service's needs, and use that encoding to autogenerate an allocation plan that details which resources go to which service, in which cluster. If demand, supply, or service requirements change, we can simply autogenerate a new plan in response to the changed parameters, which is now the new best distribution of resources.

With a service's true requirements and flexibility captured, the capacity plan is now dramatically more nimble in the face of change, and we can reach an optimal solution that meets as many parameters as possible. With bin packing delegated to computers, human toil is drastically reduced, and service owners can focus on high-order priorities like SLOs, production dependencies, and service infrastructure requirements, as opposed to low-level scrounging for resources.

As an added benefit, using computational optimization to map from intent to implementation achieves much greater precision, ultimately resulting in cost savings to the organization. Bin packing is still far from a solved problem, because certain types are still considered NP-hard; however, today's algorithms can solve to a known optimal solution.

Intent-Based Capacity Planning

Intent is the rationale for how a service owner wants to run their service. Moving from concrete resource demands to motivating reasons in order to arrive at the true capacity planning intent often requires several layers of abstraction. Consider the following chain of abstraction:

1) *"I want 50 cores in clusters X, Y, and Z for service Foo."*
This is an explicit resource request. But...*why do we need this many resources specifically in these particular clusters?*

2) *"I want a 50-core footprint in any 3 clusters in geographic region YYY for service Foo."*
This request introduces more degrees of freedom and is potentially easier to fulfill, although it doesn't explain the reasoning behind its requirements. But...*why do we need this quantity of resources, and why 3 footprints?*

3) *"I want to meet service Foo's demand in each geographic region, and have N + 2 redundancy."*
Suddenly greater flexibility is introduced and we can understand at a more "human" level what happens if service Foo does not receive these resources. But...*why do we need N + 2 for service Foo?*

4) *"I want to run service Foo at 5 nines of reliability."*
This is a more abstract requirement, and the ramification if the requirement isn't met becomes clear: reliability will suffer. And we have even greater flexibility here: perhaps running at $N + 2$ is not actually sufficient or optimal for this service, and some other deployment plan would be more suitable.

So what level of intent should be used by intent-driven capacity planning? Ideally, all levels of intent should be supported together, with services benefiting the more they shift to specifying intent versus implementation. In Google's experience, services tend to achieve the best wins as they cross to step 3: good degrees of flexibility are available, and the ramifications of this request are in higher-level and understandable terms. Particularly sophisticated services may aim for step 4.

Precursors to Intent

What information do we need in order to capture a service's intent? Enter dependencies, performance metrics, and prioritization.

Dependencies

Services at Google depend on many other infrastructure and user-facing services, and these dependencies heavily influence where a service can be placed. For example, imagine user-facing service Foo, which depends upon Bar, an infrastructure storage service. Foo expresses a requirement that Bar must be located within 30 milliseconds of network latency of Foo. This requirement has important repercussions for where we place both Foo *and* Bar, and intent-driven capacity planning must take these constraints into account.

Furthermore, production dependencies are nested: to build upon the preceding example, imagine service Bar has its own dependencies on Baz, a lower-level distributed storage service, and Qux, an application management service. Therefore, where we can now place Foo depends on where we can place Bar, Baz, and Qux. A given set of production dependencies can be shared, possibly with different stipulations around intent.

Performance metrics

Demand for one service trickles down to result in demand for one or more other services. Understanding the chain of dependencies helps formulate the general scope of the bin packing problem, but we still need more information about expected resource usage. How many compute resources does service Foo need to serve N user queries? For every N queries of service Foo, how many Mbps of data do we expect for service Bar?

Performance metrics are the glue between dependencies. They convert from one or more higher-level resource type(s) to one or more lower-level resource type(s). Deriving appropriate performance metrics for a service can involve load testing and resource usage monitoring.

Prioritization

Inevitably, resource constraints result in trade-offs and hard decisions: of the many requirements that all services have, which requirements should be sacrificed in the face of insufficient capacity?

Perhaps $N + 2$ redundancy for service Foo is more important than $N + 1$ redundancy for service Bar. Or perhaps the feature launch of X is less important than $N + 0$ redundancy for service Baz.

Intent-driven planning forces these decisions to be made transparently, openly, and consistently. Resource constraints entail the same trade-offs, but all too often, the prioritization can be ad hoc and opaque to service owners. Intent-based planning allows prioritization to be as granular or coarse as needed.

Introduction to Auxon

Auxon is Google's implementation of an intent-based capacity planning and resource allocation solution, and a prime example of an SRE-designed and developed software engineering product: it was built by a small group of software engineers and a technical program manager within SRE over the course of two years. Auxon is a perfect case study to demonstrate how software development can be fostered within SRE.

Auxon is actively used to plan the use of many millions of dollars of machine resources at Google. It has become a critical component of capacity planning for several major divisions within Google.

As a product, Auxon provides the means to collect intent-based descriptions of a service's resource requirements and dependencies. These user intents are expressed as requirements for how the owner would like the service to be provisioned. Requirements might be specified as a request like, "My service must be $N + 2$ per continent" or "The frontend servers must be no more than 50 ms away from the backend servers." Auxon collects this information either via a user configuration language or via a programmatic API, thus translating human intent into machine-parseable constraints. Requirements can be prioritized, a feature that's useful if resources are insufficient to meet all requirements, and therefore trade-offs must be made. These requirements—the intent—are ultimately represented internally as a giant mixed-integer or linear program. Auxon solves the linear program, and uses the resultant bin packing solution to formulate an allocation plan for resources.

Figure 18-1 and the explanations that follow it outline Auxon's major components.

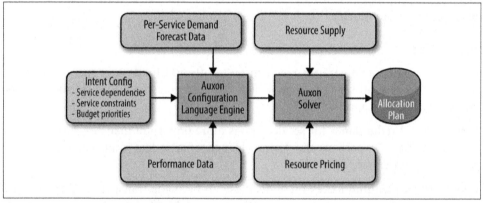

Figure 18-1. The major components of Auxon

Performance Data describes how a service scales: for every unit of demand X in cluster Y, how many units of dependency Z are used? This scaling data may be derived in a number of ways depending on the maturity of the service in question. Some services are load tested, while others infer their scaling based upon past performance.

Per-Service Demand Forecast Data describes the usage trend for forecasted demand signals. Some services derive their future usage from demand forecasts—a forecast of queries per second broken down by continent. Not all services have a demand forecast: some services (e.g., a storage service like Colossus) derive their demand purely from services that depend upon them.

Resource Supply provides data about the availability of base-level, fundamental resources: for example, the number of machines expected to be available for use at a particular point in the future. In linear program terminology, the resource supply acts as an *upper bound* that limits how services can grow and where services can be placed. Ultimately, we want to make the best use of this resource supply as the intent-based description of the combined group of services allows.

Resource Pricing provides data about how much base-level, fundamental resources cost. For instance, the cost of machines may vary globally based upon the space/power charges of a given facility. In linear program terminology, the prices inform the overall calculated costs, which act as the *objective* that we want to minimize.

Intent Config is the key to how intent-based information is fed to Auxon. It defines what constitutes a service, and how services relate to one another. The config ultimately acts as a configuration layer that allows all the other components to be wired together. It's designed to be human-readable and configurable.

Auxon Configuration Language Engine acts based upon the information it receives from the Intent Config. This component formulates a machine-readable request (a protocol buffer that can be understood by the Auxon Solver. It applies light sanity checking to the configuration, and is designed to act as the gateway between the human-configurable intent definition and the machine-parseable optimization request.

Auxon Solver is the brain of the tool. It formulates the giant mixed-integer or linear program based upon the optimization request received from the Configuration Language Engine. It is designed to be very scalable, which allows the solver to run in parallel upon hundreds or even thousands of machines running within Google's clusters. In addition to mixed-integer linear programming toolkits, there are also components within the Auxon Solver that handle tasks such as scheduling, managing a pool of workers, and descending decision trees.

Allocation Plan is the output of the Auxon Solver. It prescribes which resources should be allocated to which services in what locations. It is the computed implementation details of the intent-based definition of the capacity planning problem's requirements. The Allocation Plan also includes information about any requirements that could not be satisfied—for example, if a requirement couldn't be met due to a lack of resources, or competing requirements that were otherwise too strict.

Requirements and Implementation: Successes and Lessons Learned

Auxon was first imagined by an SRE and a technical program manager who had separately been tasked by their respective teams with capacity planning large portions of Google's infrastructure. Having performed manual capacity planning in spreadsheets, they were well positioned to understand the inefficiencies and opportunities for improvement through automation, and the features such a tool might require.

Throughout Auxon's development, the SRE team behind the product continued to be deeply involved in the production world. The team maintained a role in on-call rotations for several of Google's services, and participated in design discussions and technical leadership of these services. Through these ongoing interactions, the team was able to stay grounded in the production world: they acted as both the consumer and developer of their own product. When the product failed, the team was directly impacted. Feature requests were informed through the team's own firsthand experiences. Not only did firsthand experience of the problem space buy a huge sense of ownership in the product's success, but it also helped give the product credibility and legitimacy within SRE.

Approximation

Don't focus on perfection and purity of solution, especially if the bounds of the problem aren't well known. Launch and iterate.

Any sufficiently complex software engineering effort is bound to encounter uncertainty as to how a component should be designed or how a problem should be tackled. Auxon met with such uncertainty early in its development because the linear programming world was uncharted territory for the team members. The limitations of linear programming, which seemed to be a central part of how the product would likely function, were not well understood. To address the team's consternation over this insufficiently understood dependency, we opted to initially build a simplified solver engine (the so-called "Stupid Solver") that applied some simple heuristics as to how services should be arranged based upon the user's specified requirements. While the Stupid Solver would never yield a truly optimal solution, it gave the team a sense that our vision for Auxon was achievable even if we didn't build something perfect from day one.

When deploying approximation to help speed development, it's important to undertake the work in a way that allows the team to make future enhancements and revisit approximation. In the case of the Stupid Solver, the entire solver interface was abstracted away within Auxon such that the solver internals could be swapped out at a later date. Eventually, as we built confidence in a unified linear programming model, it was a simple operation to switch out the Stupid Solver for something, well, smarter.

Auxon's product requirements also had some unknowns. Building software with fuzzy requirements can be a frustrating challenge, but some degree of uncertainty need not be a showstopper. Use this fuzziness as an incentive to ensure that the software is designed to be both general and modular. For instance, one of the aims of the Auxon project was to integrate with automation systems within Google to allow an

Allocation Plan to be directly enacted on production (assigning resources and turning up/turning down/resizing services as appropriate). However, at the time, the world of automation systems was in a great deal of flux, as a huge variety of approaches were in use. Rather than try to design unique solutions to allow Auxon to work with each individual tool, we instead shaped the Allocation Plan to be universally useful such that these automation systems could work on their own integration points. This "agnostic" approach became key to Auxon's process for onboarding new customers, because it allowed customers to begin using Auxon without switching to a particular turnup automation tool, forecasting tool, or performance data tool.

We also leveraged modular designs to deal with fuzzy requirements when building a model of machine performance within Auxon. Data on future machine platform performance (e.g., CPU) was scarce, but our users wanted a way to model various scenarios of machine power. We abstracted away the machine data behind a single interface, allowing the user to swap in different models of future machine performance. We later extended this modularity further, based on increasingly defined requirements, to provide a simple machine performance modeling library that worked within this interface.

If there's one theme to draw from our Auxon case study, it's that the old motto of "launch and iterate" is particularly relevant in SRE software development projects. Don't wait for the perfect design; rather, keep the overall vision in mind while moving ahead with design and development. When you encounter areas of uncertainty, design the software to be flexible enough so that if process or strategy changes at a higher level, you don't incur a huge rework cost. But at the same time, stay grounded by making sure that general solutions have a real-world–specific implementation that demonstrates the utility of the design.

Raising Awareness and Driving Adoption

As with any product, SRE-developed software must be designed with knowledge of its users and requirements. It needs to drive adoption through utility, performance, and demonstrated ability to both benefit Google's production reliability goals and to better the lives of SREs. The process of socializing a product and achieving buy-in across an organization is key to the project's success.

Don't underestimate the effort required to raise awareness and interest in your software product—a single presentation or email announcement isn't enough. Socializing internal software tools to a large audience demands all of the following:

- A consistent and coherent approach
- User advocacy

- The sponsorship of senior engineers and management, to whom you will have to demonstrate the utility of your product

It's important to consider the perspective of the customer in making your product usable. An engineer might not have the time or the inclination to dig into the source code to figure out how to use a tool. Although internal customers are generally more tolerant of rough edges and early alphas than external customers, it's still necessary to provide documentation. SREs are busy, and if your solution is too difficult or confusing, they will write their own solution.

Set expectations

When an engineer with years of familiarity in a problem space begins designing a product, it's easy to imagine a utopian end-state for the work. However, it's important to differentiate aspirational goals of the product from minimum success criteria (or Minimum Viable Product). Projects can lose credibility and fail by promising too much, too soon; at the same time, if a product doesn't promise a sufficiently rewarding outcome, it can be difficult to overcome the necessary activation energy to convince internal teams to try something new. Demonstrating steady, incremental progress via small releases raises user confidence in your team's ability to deliver useful software.

In the case of Auxon, we struck a balance by planning a long-term roadmap alongside short-term fixes. Teams were promised that:

- Any onboarding and configuration efforts would provide the immediate benefit of alleviating the pain of manually bin packing short-term resource requests.
- As additional features were developed for Auxon, the same configuration files would carry over and provide new, and much broader, long-term cost savings and other benefits. The project road map enabled services to quickly determine if their use cases or required features weren't implemented in the early versions. Meanwhile, Auxon's iterative development approach fed into development priorities and new milestones for the road map.

Identify appropriate customers

The team developing Auxon realized that a one-size solution might not fit all; many larger teams already had home-grown solutions for capacity planning that worked passably well. While their custom tools weren't perfect, these teams didn't experience sufficient pain in the capacity planning process to try a new tool, especially an alpha release with rough edges.

The initial versions of Auxon intentionally targeted teams that had no existing capacity planning processes in place. Because these teams would have to invest configuration effort whether they adopted an existing tool or our new approach, they were interested in adopting the newest tool. The early successes Auxon achieved with these teams demonstrated the utility of the project, and turned the customers themselves into advocates for the tool. Quantifying the usefulness of the product proved further beneficial; when we onboarded one of Google's Business Areas, the team authored a case study detailing the process and comparing the before and after results. The time savings and reduction of human toil alone presented a huge incentive for other teams to give Auxon a try.

Customer service

Even though software developed within SRE targets an audience of TPMs and engineers with high technical proficiency, any sufficiently innovative software still presents a learning curve to new users. Don't be afraid to provide white glove customer support for early adopters to help them through the onboarding process. Sometimes automation also entails a host of emotional concerns, such as fear that someone's job will be replaced by a shell script. By working one-on-one with early users, you can address those fears personally, and demonstrate that rather than owning the toil of performing a tedious task manually, the team instead owns the configurations, processes, and ultimate results of their technical work. Later adopters are convinced by the happy examples of early adopters.

Furthermore, because Google's SRE teams are distributed across the globe, early-adopter advocates for a project are particularly beneficial, because they can serve as local experts for other teams interested in trying out the project.

Designing at the right level

An idea that we've termed *agnosticism*—writing the software to be generalized to allow myriad data sources as input—was a key principle of Auxon's design. Agnosticism meant that customers weren't required to commit to any one tool in order to use the Auxon framework. This approach allowed Auxon to remain of sufficient general utility even as teams with divergent use cases began to use it. We approached potential users with the message, "come as you are; we'll work with what you've got." By avoiding over-customizing for one or two big users, we achieved broader adoption across the organization and lowered the barrier to entry for new services.

We've also consciously endeavored to avoid the pitfall of defining success as 100% adoption across the organization. In many cases, there are diminishing returns on closing the last mile to enable a feature set that is sufficient for every service in the long tail at Google.

Team Dynamics

In selecting engineers to work on an SRE software development product, we've found great benefit from creating a seed team that combines generalists who are able to get up to speed quickly on a new topic with engineers possessing a breadth of knowledge and experience. A diversity of experiences covers blind spots as well as the pitfalls of assuming that every team's use case is the same as yours.

It's essential for your team to establish a working relationship with necessary specialists, and for your engineers to be comfortable working in a new problem space. For SRE teams at most companies, venturing into this new problem space requires outsourcing tasks or working with consultants, but SRE teams at larger organizations may be able to partner with in-house experts. During the initial phases of conceptualizing and designing Auxon, we presented our design document to Google's in-house teams that specialize in Operations Research and Quantitative Analysis in order to draw upon their expertise in the field and to bootstrap the Auxon team's knowledge about capacity planning.

As project development continued and Auxon's feature set grew more broad and complex, the team acquired members with backgrounds in statistics and mathematical optimization, which at a smaller company might be akin to bringing an outside consultant in-house. These new team members were able to identify areas for improvement when the project's basic functionality was complete and adding finesse had become our top priority.

The right time to engage specialists will, of course, vary from project to project. As a rough guideline, the project should be successfully off the ground and demonstrably successful, such that the skills of the current team would be significantly bolstered by the additional expertise.

Fostering Software Engineering in SRE

What makes a project a good candidate to take the leap from one-off tool to fully fledged software engineering effort? Strong positive signals include engineers with firsthand experience in the relative domain who are interested in working on the project, and a target user base that is highly technical (and therefore able to provide high-signal bug reports during the early phases of development). The project should provide noticeable benefits, such as reducing toil for SREs, improving an existing piece of infrastructure, or streamlining a complex process.

It's important for the project to fit into the overall set of objectives for the organization, so that engineering leaders can weigh its potential impact and subsequently advocate for your project, both with their reporting teams and with other teams that might interface with their teams. Cross-organizational socialization and review help prevent disjoint or overlapping efforts, and a product that can easily be established as furthering a department-wide objective is easier to staff and support.

What makes a poor candidate project? Many of the same red flags you might instinctively identify in any software project, such as software that touches many moving parts at once, or software design that requires an all-or-nothing approach that prevents iterative development. Because Google SRE teams are currently organized around the services they run, SRE-developed projects are particularly at risk of being overly specific work that only benefits a small percentage of the organization. Because team incentives are aligned primarily to provide a great experience for the users of one particular service, projects often fail to generalize to a broader use case as standardization across SRE teams comes in second place. At the opposite end of the spectrum, overly generic frameworks can be equally problematic; if a tool strives to be too flexible and too universal, it runs the risk of not quite fitting any use case, and therefore having insufficient value in and of itself. Projects with grand scope and abstract goals often require significant development effort, but lack the concrete use cases required to deliver end-user benefit on a reasonable time frame.

As an example of a broad use case: a layer-3 load balancer developed by Google SREs proved so successful over the years that it was repurposed as a customer-facing product offering via Google Cloud Load Balancer [Eis16].

Successfully Building a Software Engineering Culture in SRE: Staffing and Development Time

SREs are often generalists, as the desire to learn breadth-first instead of depth-first lends itself well to understanding the bigger picture (and there are few pictures bigger than the intricate inner workings of modern technical infrastructure). These engineers often have strong coding and software development skills, but may not have the traditional SWE experience of being part of a product team or having to think about customer feature requests. A quote from an engineer on an early SRE software development project sums up the conventional SRE approach to software: "I have a design doc; why do we need requirements?" Partnering with engineers, TPMs, or PMs who are familiar with user-facing software development can help build a team software development culture that brings together the best of both software product development and hands-on production experience.

Dedicated, noninterrupted, project work time is essential to any software development effort. Dedicated project time is necessary to enable progress on a project, because it's nearly impossible to write code—much less to concentrate on larger, more impactful projects—when you're thrashing between several tasks in the course of an hour. Therefore, the ability to work on a software project without interrupts is often an attractive reason for engineers to begin working on a development project. Such time must be aggressively defended.

The majority of software products developed within SRE begin as side projects whose utility leads them to grow and become formalized. At this point, a product may branch off into one of several possible directions:

- Remain a grassroots effort developed in engineers' spare time
- Become established as a formal project through structured processes (see "Getting There")
- Gain executive sponsorship from within SRE leadership to expand into a fully staffed software development effort

However, in any of these scenarios—and this is a point worth stressing—it's essential that the SREs involved in any development effort continue working as SREs instead of becoming full-time developers embedded in the SRE organization. Immersion in the world of production gives SREs performing development work an invaluable perspective, as they are both the creator and the customer for any product.

Getting There

If you like the idea of organized software development in SRE, you're probably wondering how to introduce a software development model to an SRE organization focused on production support.

First, recognize that this goal is as much an organizational change as it is a technical challenge. SREs are used to working closely with their teammates, quickly analyzing and reacting to problems. Therefore, you're working against the natural instinct of an SRE to quickly write some code to meet their immediate needs. If your SRE team is small, this approach may not be problematic. However, as your organization grows, this ad hoc approach won't scale, instead resulting in largely functional, yet narrow or single-purpose, software solutions that can't be shared, which inevitably lead to duplicated efforts and wasted time.

Next, think about what you want to achieve by developing software in SRE. Do you just want to foster better software development practices within your team, or are you interested in software development that produces results that can be used across teams, possibly as a standard for the organization? In larger established organizations, the latter change will take time, possibly spanning multiple years. Such a change needs to be tackled on multiple fronts, but has a higher payback. The following are some guidelines from Google's experience:

Create and communicate a clear message
It's important to define and communicate your strategy, plans, and—most importantly—the benefits SRE gains from this effort. SREs are a skeptical lot (in fact, skepticism is a trait for which we specifically hire); an SRE's initial response to such an effort will likely be, "that sounds like too much overhead" or "it will

never work." Start by making a compelling case of how this strategy will help SRE; for example:

- Consistent and supported software solutions speed ramp-up for new SREs.
- Reducing the number of ways to perform the same task allows the entire department to benefit from the skills any single team has developed, thus making knowledge and effort portable across teams.

When SREs start to ask questions about *how* your strategy will work, rather than *if* the strategy should be pursued, you know you've passed the first hurdle.

Evaluate your organization's capabilities

SREs have many skills, but it's relatively common for an SRE to lack experience as part of a team that built and shipped a product to a set of users. In order to develop useful software, you're effectively creating a product team. That team includes required roles and skills that your SRE organization may not have formerly demanded. Will someone play the role of product manager, acting as the customer advocate? Does your tech lead or project manager have the skills and/or experience to run an agile development process?

Begin filling these gaps by taking advantage of the skills already present in your company. Ask your product development team to help you establish agile practices via training or coaching. Solicit consulting time from a product manager to help you define product requirements and prioritize feature work. Given a large enough software-development opportunity, there may be a case to hire dedicated people for these roles. Making the case to hire for these roles is easier once you have some positive experiment results.

Launch and iterate

As you initiate an SRE software development program, your efforts will be followed by many watchful eyes. It's important to establish credibility by delivering some product of value in a reasonable amount of time. Your first round of products should aim for relatively straightforward and achievable targets—ones without controversy or existing solutions. We also found success in pairing this approach with a six-month rhythm of product update releases that provided additional useful features. This release cycle allowed teams to focus on identifying the right set of features to build, and then building those features while simultaneously learning how to be a productive software development team. After the initial launch, some Google teams moved to a push-on-green model for even faster delivery and feedback.

Don't lower your standards

As you start to develop software, you may be tempted to cut corners. Resist this urge by holding yourself to the same standards to which your product development teams are held. For example:

- Ask yourself: if this product were created by a separate dev team, would you onboard the product?

- If your solution enjoys broad adoption, it may become critical to SREs in order to successfully perform their jobs. Therefore, reliability is of utmost importance. Do you have proper code review practices in place? Do you have end-to-end or integration testing? Have another SRE team review the product for production readiness as they would if onboarding any other service.

It takes a long time to build credibility for your software development efforts, but only a short time to lose credibility due to a misstep.

Conclusions

Software engineering projects within Google SRE have flourished as the organization has grown, and in many cases the lessons learned from and successful execution of earlier software development projects have paved the way for subsequent endeavors. The unique hands-on production experience that SREs bring to developing tools can lead to innovative approaches to age-old problems, as seen with the development of Auxon to address the complex problem of capacity planning. SRE-driven software projects are also noticeably beneficial to the company in developing a sustainable model for supporting services at scale. Because SREs often develop software to streamline inefficient processes or automate common tasks, these projects mean that the SRE team doesn't have to scale linearly with the size of the services they support. Ultimately, the benefits of having SREs devoting some of their time to software development are reaped by the company, the SRE organization, and the SREs themselves.

CHAPTER 19

Load Balancing at the Frontend

Written by Piotr Lewandowski
Edited by Sarah Chavis

We serve many millions of requests every second and, as you may have already guessed, we use more than a single computer to handle this demand. But even if we *did* have a supercomputer that was somehow able to handle all these requests (imagine the network connectivity such a configuration would require!), we still wouldn't employ a strategy that relied upon a single point of failure; when you're dealing with large-scale systems, putting all your eggs in one basket is a recipe for disaster.

This chapter focuses on high-level load balancing—how we balance user traffic *between* datacenters. The following chapter zooms in to explore how we implement load balancing *inside* a datacenter.

Power Isn't the Answer

For the sake of argument, let's assume we have an unbelievably powerful machine and a network that never fails. Would *that* configuration be sufficient to meet Google's needs? No. Even this configuration would still be limited by the physical constraints associated with our networking infrastructure. For example, the speed of light is a limiting factor on the communication speeds for fiber optic cable, which creates an upper bound on how quickly we can serve data based upon the distance it has to travel. Even in an ideal world, relying on an infrastructure with a single point of failure is a bad idea.

In reality, Google has thousands of machines and even more users, many of whom issue multiple requests at a time. *Traffic load balancing* is how we decide which of the many, many machines in our datacenters will serve a particular request. Ideally, traffic is distributed across multiple network links, datacenters, and machines in an "optimal" fashion. But what does "optimal" mean in this context? There's actually no single answer, because the optimal solution depends heavily on a variety of factors:

- The hierarchical level at which we evaluate the problem (global versus local)
- The technical level at which we evaluate the problem (hardware versus software)
- The nature of the traffic we're dealing with

Let's start by reviewing two common traffic scenarios: a basic search request and a video upload request. Users want to get their query results quickly, so the most important variable for the search request is latency. On the other hand, users expect video uploads to take a non-negligible amount of time, but also want such requests to succeed the first time, so the most important variable for the video upload is throughput. The differing needs of the two requests play a role in how we determine the optimal distribution for each request at the *global* level:

- The search request is sent to the nearest available datacenter—as measured in round-trip time (RTT)—because we want to minimize the latency on the request.
- The video upload stream is routed via a different path—perhaps to a link that is currently underutilized—to maximize the throughput at the expense of latency.

But on the *local* level, inside a given datacenter, we often assume that all machines within the building are equally distant to the user and connected to the same network. Therefore, optimal distribution of load focuses on optimal resource utilization and protecting a single server from overloading.

Of course, this example presents a vastly simplified picture. In reality, many more considerations factor into optimal load distribution: some requests may be directed to a datacenter that is slightly farther away in order to keep caches warm, or non-interactive traffic may be routed to a completely different region to avoid network congestion. Load balancing, especially for large systems, is anything but straightforward and static. At Google, we've approached the problem by load balancing at multiple levels, two of which are described in the following sections. For the sake of presenting a concrete discussion, we'll consider HTTP requests sent over TCP. Load balancing of stateless services (like DNS over UDP) differs slightly, but most of the mechanisms described here should be applicable to stateless services as well.

Load Balancing Using DNS

Before a client can even send an HTTP request, it often has to look up an IP address using DNS. This provides the perfect opportunity to introduce our first layer of load balancing: *DNS load balancing*. The simplest solution is to return multiple A or AAAA records in the DNS reply and let the client pick an IP address arbitrarily. While conceptually simple and trivial to implement, this solution poses multiple challenges.

The first problem is that it provides very little control over the client behavior: records are selected randomly, and each will attract a roughly equal amount of traffic. Can we mitigate this problem? In theory, we could use SRV records to specify record weights and priorities, but SRV records have not yet been adopted for HTTP.

Another potential problem stems from the fact that usually the client cannot determine the closest address. We *can* mitigate this scenario by using an anycast address for authoritative nameservers and leverage the fact that DNS queries will flow to the closest address. In its reply, the server can return addresses routed to the closest datacenter. A further improvement builds a map of all networks and their approximate physical locations, and serves DNS replies based on that mapping. However, this solution comes at the cost of having a much more complex DNS server implementation and maintaining a pipeline that will keep the location mapping up to date.

Of course, none of these solutions are trivial, due to a fundamental characteristic of DNS: end users rarely talk to authoritative nameservers directly. Instead, a recursive DNS server usually lies somewhere between end users and nameservers. This server proxies queries between a user and a server and often provides a caching layer. The DNS middleman has three very important implications on traffic management:

- Recursive resolution of IP addresses
- Nondeterministic reply paths
- Additional caching complications

Recursive resolution of IP addresses is problematic, as the IP address seen by the authoritative nameserver does not belong to a user; instead, it's the recursive resolver's. This is a serious limitation, because it only allows reply optimization for the shortest distance between resolver and the nameserver. A possible solution is to use the EDNS0 extension proposed in [Con15], which includes information about the client's subnet in the DNS query sent by a recursive resolver. This way, an authoritative nameserver returns a response that is optimal from the user's perspective, rather than the resolver's perspective. While this is not yet the official standard, its obvious advantages have led the biggest DNS resolvers (such as OpenDNS and Google[1]) to support it already.

Not only is it difficult to find the optimal IP address to return to the nameserver for a given user's request, but that nameserver may be responsible for serving thousands or millions of users, across regions varying from a single office to an entire continent. For instance, a large national ISP might run nameservers for its entire network from one datacenter, yet have network interconnects in each metropolitan area. The ISP's

---

1 See *https://groups.google.com/forum/#!topic/public-dns-announce/67oxFjSLeUM*.

nameservers would then return a response with the IP address best suited for their datacenter, despite there being better network paths for all users!

Finally, recursive resolvers typically cache responses and forward those responses within limits indicated by the time-to-live (TTL) field in the DNS record. The end result is that estimating the impact of a given reply is difficult: a single authoritative reply may reach a single user or multiple thousands of users. We solve this problem in two ways:

- We analyze traffic changes and continuously update our list of known DNS resolvers with the approximate size of the user base behind a given resolver, which allows us to track the potential impact of any given resolver.
- We estimate the geographical distribution of the users behind each tracked resolver to increase the chance that we direct those users to the best location.

Estimating geographic distribution is particularly tricky if the user base is distributed across large regions. In such cases, we make trade-offs to select the best location and optimize the experience for the majority of users.

But what does "best location" really mean in the context of DNS load balancing? The most obvious answer is the location closest to the user. However (as if determining users' locations isn't difficult in and of itself), there are additional criteria. The DNS load balancer needs to make sure that the datacenter it selects has enough capacity to serve requests from users that are likely to receive its reply. It also needs to know that the selected datacenter and its network connectivity are in good shape, because directing user requests to a datacenter that's experiencing power or networking problems isn't ideal. Fortunately, we can integrate the authoritative DNS server with our global control systems that track traffic, capacity, and the state of our infrastructure.

The third implication of the DNS middleman is related to caching. Given that authoritative nameservers cannot flush resolvers' caches, DNS records need a relatively low TTL. This effectively sets a lower bound on how quickly DNS changes can be propagated to users.[2] Unfortunately, there is little we can do other than to keep this in mind as we make load balancing decisions.

Despite all of these problems, DNS is still the simplest and most effective way to balance load before the user's connection even starts. On the other hand, it should be clear that load balancing with DNS on its own is not sufficient. Keep in mind that all DNS replies served should fit within the 512-byte limit[3] set by RFC 1035 [Moc87].

---

2 Sadly, not all DNS resolvers respect the TTL value set by authoritative nameservers.

3 Otherwise, users must establish a TCP connection just to get a list of IP addresses.

This limit sets an upper bound on the number of addresses we can squeeze into a single DNS reply, and that number is almost certainly less than our number of servers.

To *really* solve the problem of frontend load balancing, this initial level of DNS load balancing should be followed by a level that takes advantage of virtual IP addresses.

Load Balancing at the Virtual IP Address

Virtual IP addresses (VIPs) are not assigned to any particular network interface. Instead, they are usually shared across many devices. However, from the user's perspective, the VIP remains a single, regular IP address. In theory, this practice allows us to hide implementation details (such as the number of machines behind a particular VIP) and facilitates maintenance, because we can schedule upgrades or add more machines to the pool without the user knowing.

In practice, the most important part of VIP implementation is a device called the *network load balancer*. The balancer receives packets and forwards them to one of the machines behind the VIP. These backends can then further process the request.

There are several possible approaches the balancer can take in deciding which backend should receive the request. The first (and perhaps most intuitive) approach is to always prefer the least loaded backend. In theory, this approach should result in the best end-user experience because requests are always routed to the least busy machine. Unfortunately, this logic breaks down quickly in the case of stateful protocols, which must use the same backend for the duration of a request. This requirement means that the balancer must keep track of all connections sent through it in order to make sure that all subsequent packets are sent to the correct backend. The alternative is to use some parts of a packet to create a connection ID (possibly using a hash function and some information from the packet), and to use the connection ID to select a backend. For example, the connection ID could be expressed as:

```
id(packet) mod N
```

where `id` is a function that takes `packet` as an input and produces a connection ID, and `N` is the number of configured backends.

This avoids storing state, and all packets belonging to a single connection are always forwarded to the same backend. Success? Not quite yet. What happens if one backend fails and needs to be removed from the backend list? Suddenly `N` becomes `N-1` and then, `id(packet) mod N` becomes `id(packet) mod N-1`. Almost every packet suddenly maps to a different backend! If backends don't share any state between themselves, this remapping forces a reset of almost all of the existing connections. This scenario is definitely *not* the best user experience, even if such events are infrequent.

Fortunately, there *is* an alternate solution that doesn't require keeping the state of every connection in memory, but won't force all connections to reset when a single machine goes down: *consistent hashing*. Proposed in 1997, consistent hashing [Kar97] describes a way to provide a mapping algorithm that remains relatively stable even when new backends are added to or removed from the list. This approach minimizes the disruption to existing connections when the pool of backends changes. As a result, we can usually use simple connection tracking, but fall back to consistent hashing when the system is under pressure (e.g., during an ongoing denial of service attack).

Returning to the larger question: how exactly should a network load balancer forward packets to a selected VIP backend? One solution is to perform a Network Address Translation. However, this requires keeping an entry of every single connection in the tracking table, which precludes having a completely stateless fallback mechanism.

Another solution is to modify information on the data link layer (layer 2 of the OSI networking model). By changing the destination MAC address of a forwarded packet, the balancer can leave all the information in upper layers intact, so the backend receives the original source and destination IP addresses. The backend can then send a reply directly to the original sender—a technique known as *Direct Server Response* (DSR). If user requests are small and replies are large (e.g., most HTTP requests), DSR provides tremendous savings, because only a small fraction of traffic need traverse the load balancer. Even better, DSR does not require us to keep state on the load balancer device. Unfortunately, using layer 2 for internal load balancing *does* incur serious disadvantages when deployed at scale: all machines (i.e., all load balancers and all their backends) must be able to reach each other at the data link layer. This isn't an issue if this connectivity can be supported by the network and the number of machines doesn't grow excessively, because all the machines need to reside in a single broadcast domain. As you may imagine, Google outgrew this solution quite some time ago, and had to find an alternate approach.

Our current VIP load balancing solution [Eis16] uses packet encapsulation. A network load balancer puts the forwarded packet into another IP packet with Generic Routing Encapsulation (GRE) [Han94], and uses a backend's address as the destination. A backend receiving the packet strips off the outer IP+GRE layer and processes the inner IP packet as if it were delivered directly to its network interface. The network load balancer and the backend no longer need to exist in the same broadcast domain; they can even be on separate continents as long as a route between the two exists.

Packet encapsulation is a powerful mechanism that provides great flexibility in the way our networks are designed and evolve. Unfortunately, encapsulation also comes with a price: inflated packet size. Encapsulation introduces overhead (24 bytes in the case of IPv4+GRE, to be precise), which can cause the packet to exceed the available Maximum Transmission Unit (MTU) size and require fragmentation.

Once the packet reaches the datacenter, fragmentation can be avoided by using a larger MTU within the datacenter; however, this approach requires a network that supports large Protocol Data Units. As with many things at scale, load balancing sounds simple on the surface—load balance early and load balance often—but the difficulty is in the details, both for frontend load balancing and for handling packets once they reach the datacenter.

CHAPTER 20

Load Balancing in the Datacenter

Written by Alejandro Forero Cuervo
Edited by Sarah Chavis

This chapter focuses on load balancing within the datacenter. Specifically, it discusses algorithms for distributing work within a given datacenter for a stream of queries. We cover application-level policies for routing requests to individual servers that can process them. Lower-level networking principles (e.g., switches, packet routing) and datacenter selection are outside of the scope of this chapter.

Assume there is a stream of queries arriving to the datacenter—these could be coming from the datacenter itself, remote datacenters, or a mix of both—at a rate that doesn't exceed the resources that the datacenter has to process them (or only exceeds it for very short amounts of time). Also assume that there are *services* within the datacenter, against which these queries operate. These services are implemented as many homogeneous, interchangeable server processes mostly running on different machines. The smallest services typically have at least three such processes (using fewer processes means losing 50% or more of your capacity if you lose a single machine) and the largest may have more than 10,000 processes (depending on datacenter size). In the typical case, services are composed of between 100 and 1,000 processes. We call these processes *backend tasks* (or just *backends*). Other tasks, known as *client tasks*, hold connections to the backend tasks. For each incoming query, a client task must decide which backend task should handle the query. Clients communicate with backends using a protocol implemented on top of a combination of TCP and UDP.

We should note that Google datacenters house a vastly diverse set of services that implement different combinations of the policies discussed in this chapter. Our working example, as just described, doesn't fit any one service directly. It's a generalized scenario that allows us to discuss the various techniques we've found useful for various services. Some of these techniques may be more (or less) applicable to specific use cases, but these techniques were designed and implemented by several Google engineers over a span of many years.

These techniques are applied at many parts of our stack. For example, most external HTTP requests reach the GFE (Google Frontend), our HTTP reverse proxying system. The GFE uses these algorithms, along with the algorithms described in Chapter 19, to route the request payloads and metadata to the individual processes running the applications that can process this information. This is based on a configuration that maps various URL patterns to individual applications under the control of different teams. In order to produce the response payloads (which they return to the GFE, to be returned back to browsers), these applications often use these same algorithms in turn, to communicate with the infrastructure or complementary services they depend on. Sometimes the stack of dependencies can get relatively deep, where a single incoming HTTP request can trigger a long transitive chain of dependent requests to several systems, potentially with high fan-out at various points.

The Ideal Case

In an ideal case, the load for a given service is spread perfectly over all its backend tasks and, at any given point in time, the least and most loaded backend tasks consume exactly the same amount of CPU.

We can only send traffic to a datacenter until the point at which the most loaded task reaches its capacity limit; this is depicted in Figure 20-1 for two scenarios over the same time interval. During that time, the cross-datacenter load balancing algorithm must avoid sending any additional traffic to the datacenter, because doing so risks overloading some tasks.

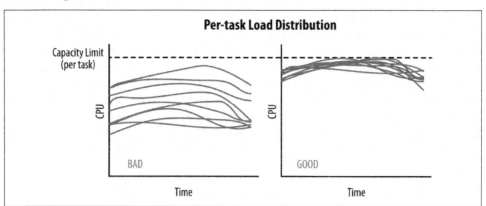

Figure 20-1. Two scenarios of per-task load distribution over time

As shown in the lefthand graph in Figure 20-2, a significant amount of capacity is wasted: the idle capacity of every task except the most loaded task.

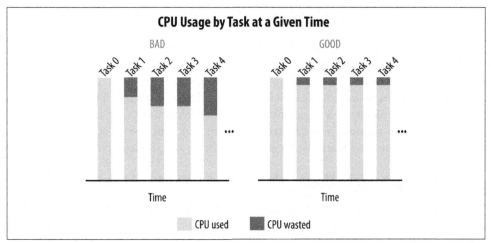

Figure 20-2. Histogram of CPU used and wasted in two scenarios

More formally, let *CPU[i]* be the CPU rate consumed by task *i* at a given point of time, and suppose that task 0 is the most loaded task. Then, in the case of a large spread, we are wasting the sum of the differences in the CPU from any task to *CPU[0]*: that is, the sum over all tasks *i* of *(CPU[0] – CPU[i])* will be wasted. In this case "wasted" means reserved, but unused.

This example illustrates how poor in-datacenter load balancing practices artificially limit resource availability: you may be reserving 1,000 CPUs for your service in a given datacenter, but be unable to actually use more than, say, 700 CPUs.

Identifying Bad Tasks: Flow Control and Lame Ducks

Before we can decide which backend task should receive a client request, we need to identify—and avoid—unhealthy tasks in our pool of backends.

A Simple Approach to Unhealthy Tasks: Flow Control

Assume our client tasks track the number of active requests they have sent on each connection to a backend task. When this active-request count reaches a configured limit, the client treats the backend as unhealthy and no longer sends it requests. For most backends, 100 is a reasonable limit; in the average case, requests tend to finish fast enough that it is very rare for the number of active requests from a given client to reach this limit under normal operating conditions. This (very basic!) form of flow control also serves as a simplistic form of load balancing: if a given backend task becomes overloaded and requests start piling up, clients will avoid that backend, and the workload spreads organically among the other backend tasks.

Unfortunately, this very simplistic approach only protects backend tasks against very extreme forms of overload and it's very easy for backends to become overloaded well before this limit is ever reached. The converse is also true: in some cases, clients may reach this limit when their backends still have plenty of spare resources. For example, some backends may have very long-lived requests that prohibit quick responses. We've seen cases in which this default limit has backfired, causing all backend tasks to become unreachable, with requests blocked in the clients until they time out and fail. Raising the active-request limit can avoid this situation, but doesn't solve the underlying problem of knowing if a task is truly unhealthy or simply slow to respond.

A Robust Approach to Unhealthy Tasks: Lame Duck State

From a client perspective, a given backend task can be in any of the following states:

Healthy
The backend task has initialized correctly and is processing requests.

Refusing connections
The backend task is unresponsive. This can happen because the task is starting up or shutting down, or because the backend is in an abnormal state (though it would be rare for a backend to stop listening on its port if it is not shutting down).

Lame duck
The backend task is listening on its port and can serve, but is explicitly asking clients to stop sending requests.

When a task enters lame duck state, it broadcasts that fact to all its active clients. But what about inactive clients? With Google's RPC implementation, inactive clients (i.e., clients with no active TCP connections) still send periodic UDP health checks. The result is that lame duck information is propagated quickly to all clients—typically in 1 or 2 RTT—regardless of their current state.

The main advantage of allowing a task to exist in a quasi-operational lame duck state is that it simplifies clean shutdown, which avoids serving errors to all the unlucky requests that happened to be active on backend tasks that are shutting down. Bringing down a backend task that has active requests without serving any errors facilitates code pushes, maintenance activities, or machine failures that may require restarting all related tasks. Such a shutdown would follow these general steps:

1. The job scheduler sends a SIGTERM signal to the backend task.

2. The backend task enters lame duck state and asks its clients to send new requests to other backend tasks. This is done through an API call in the RPC implementation that is explicitly called in the SIGTERM handler.

3. Any ongoing request started before the backend task entered lame duck state (or after it entered lame duck state but before a client detected it) executes normally.

4. As responses flow back to the clients, the number of active requests against the backend gradually decreases to zero.

5. After a configured interval, the backend task either exits cleanly or the job scheduler kills it. The interval should be set to a large enough value that all typical requests have sufficient time to finish. This value is service dependent, but a good rule of thumb is between 10s and 150s depending on client complexity.

This strategy also allows a client to establish connections to backend tasks while performing potentially long-lived initialization procedures (and thus are not yet ready to start serving). The backend tasks could otherwise start listening for connections only when they're ready to serve, but doing so would delay the negotiation of the connections unnecessarily. As soon as the backend task is ready to start serving, it signals this explicitly to the clients.

Limiting the Connections Pool with Subsetting

In addition to health management, another consideration for load balancing is *subsetting*: limiting the pool of potential backend tasks with which a client task interacts.

Each client in our RPC system maintains a pool of long-lived connections to its backends that it uses to send new requests. These connections are typically established early on as the client is starting and usually remain open, with requests flowing through them, until the client's death. An alternative model would be to establish and tear down a connection for each request, but this model has significant resource and latency costs. In the corner case of a connection that remains idle for a long time, our RPC implementation has an optimization that switches the connection to a cheap "inactive" mode where, for example, the frequency of health checks is reduced and the underlying TCP connection is dropped in favor of UDP.

Every connection requires some memory and CPU (due to periodic health checking) at both ends. While this overhead is small in theory, it can quickly become significant when it occurs across many machines. Subsetting avoids the situation in which a single client connects to a very large number of backend tasks or a single backend task receives connections from a very large number of client tasks. In both cases, you potentially waste a very large amount of resources for very little gain.

Picking the Right Subset

Picking the right subset comes down to choosing how many backend tasks each client connects to—the subset size—and the selection algorithm. We typically use a subset size of 20 to 100 backend tasks, but the "right" subset size for a system depends heavily on the typical behavior of your service. For example, you may want to use a larger subset size if:

- The number of clients is significantly smaller than the number of backends. In this case, you want the number of backends per client to be large enough that you don't end up with backend tasks that will never receive any traffic.

- There are frequent load imbalances within the client jobs (i.e., one client task sends more requests than others). This scenario is typical in situations where clients occasionally send bursts of requests. In this case, the clients themselves receive requests from other clients that occasionally have a large fan-out (e.g., "read all the information of all the followers of a given user"). Because a burst of requests will be concentrated in the client's assigned subset, you need a larger subset size to ensure the load is spread evenly across the larger set of available backend tasks.

Once the subset size is determined, we need an algorithm to define the subset of backend tasks each client task will use. This may seem like a simple task, but it becomes complex quickly when working with large-scale systems where efficient provisioning is crucial and system restarts are guaranteed.

The selection algorithm for clients should assign backends uniformly to optimize resource provisioning. For example, if subsetting overloads one backend by 10%, the whole set of backends needs to be overprovisioned by 10%. The algorithm should also handle restarts and failures gracefully and robustly by continuing to load backends as uniformly as possible while minimizing churn. In this case, "churn" relates to backend replacement selection. For example, when a backend task becomes unavailable, its clients may need to temporarily pick a replacement backend. When a replacement backend is selected, clients must create new TCP connections (and likely perform application-level negotiation), which creates additional overhead. Similarly, when a client task restarts, it needs to reopen the connections to all its backends.

The algorithm should also handle resizes in the number of clients and/or number of backends, with minimal connection churn and without knowing these numbers in advance. This functionality is particularly important (and tricky) when the entire set of client or backend tasks are restarted one at a time (e.g., to push a new version). As backends are pushed, we want clients to continue serving, transparently, with as little connection churn as possible.

A Subset Selection Algorithm: Random Subsetting

A naive implementation of a subset selection algorithm might have each client randomly shuffle the list of backends once and fill its subset by selecting resolvable/healthy backends from the list. Shuffling once and then picking backends from the start of the list handles restarts and failures robustly (e.g., with relatively little churn) because it explicitly limits them from consideration. However, we've found that this strategy actually works very poorly in most practical scenarios because it spreads load very unevenly.

During initial work on load balancing, we implemented random subsetting and calculated the expected load for various cases. As an example, consider:

- 300 clients
- 300 backends
- A subset size of 30% (each client connects to 90 backends)

As Figure 20-3 shows, the least loaded backend has just 63% of the average load (57 connections, where the average is 90 connections) and the most loaded has 121% (109 connections). In most cases, a subset size of 30% is already larger than we would want to use in practice. The calculated load distribution changes every time we run the simulation while the general pattern remains.

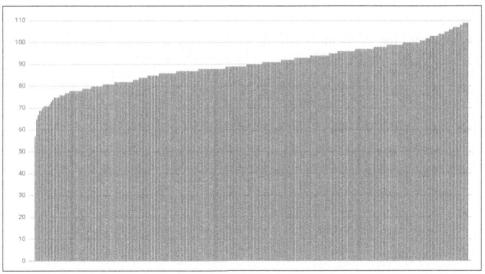

Figure 20-3. Connection distribution with 300 clients, 300 backends, and a subset size of 30%

Unfortunately, smaller subset sizes lead to even worse imbalances. For example, Figure 20-4 depicts the results if the subset size is reduced to 10% (30 backends per client). In this case, the least loaded backend receives 50% of the average load (15 connections) and the most loaded receives 150% (45 connections).

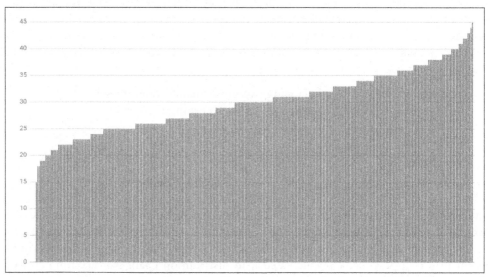

Figure 20-4. Connection distribution with 300 clients, 300 backends, and a subset size of 10%

We concluded that for random subsetting to spread the load relatively evenly across all available tasks, we would need subset sizes as large as 75%. A subset that large is simply impractical; the variance in the number of clients connecting to a task is just too large to consider random subsetting a good subset selection policy at scale.

A Subset Selection Algorithm: Deterministic Subsetting

Google's solution to the limitations of random subsetting is *deterministic* subsetting. The following code implements this algorithm, described in detail next:

```
def Subset(backends, client_id, subset_size):
  subset_count = len(backends) / subset_size

  # Group clients into rounds; each round uses the same shuffled list:
  round = client_id / subset_count
  random.seed(round)
  random.shuffle(backends)

  # The subset id corresponding to the current client:
  subset_id = client_id % subset_count

  start = subset_id * subset_size
  return backends[start:start + subset_size]
```

We divide *client* tasks into "rounds," where round i consists of subset_count consecutive client tasks, starting at task subset_count × i, and subset_count is the number of subsets (i.e., the number of backend tasks divided by the desired subset size). Within each round, each backend is assigned to exactly one client (except possibly the last round, which may not contain enough clients, so some backends may not be assigned).

For example, if we have 12 backend tasks [0, 11] and a desired subset size of 3, we will have rounds containing 4 clients each (subset_count = 12/3). If we had 10 clients, the preceding algorithm could yield the following rounds:

- Round 0: [0, 6, 3, 5, 1, 7, 11, 9, 2, 4, 8, 10]
- Round 1: [8, 11, 4, 0, 5, 6, 10, 3, 2, 7, 9, 1]
- Round 2: [8, 3, 7, 2, 1, 4, 9, 10, 6, 5, 0, 11]

The key point to notice is that each round only assigns each backend in the entire list to one client (except the last, where we run out of clients). In this example, every backend gets assigned to exactly two or three clients.

The list should be shuffled; otherwise, clients are assigned a group of consecutive backend tasks that may all become temporarily unavailable (for example, because the backend job is being updated gradually in order, from the first task to the last). Different rounds use a different seed for shuffling. If they don't, when a backend fails, the load it was receiving is only spread among the remaining backends *in its subset*. If additional backends in the subset fail, the effect compounds and the situation can quickly worsen significantly: if N backends in a subset are down, their corresponding load is spread over the remaining (subset_size - N) backends. A much better approach is to spread this load over all remaining backends by using a different shuffle for each round.

When we use a different shuffle for each round, clients in the same round will start with the same shuffled list, but clients across rounds will have different shuffled lists. From here, the algorithm builds subset *definitions* based upon the shuffled list of backends and the desired subset size. For example:

- Subset[0] = shuffled_backends[0] through shuffled_backends[2]
- Subset[1] = shuffled_backends[3] through shuffled_backends[5]
- Subset[2] = shuffled_backends[6] through shuffled_backends[8]
- Subset[3] = shuffled_backends[9] through shuffled_backends[11]

where shuffled_backend is the shuffled list created by each client. To assign a subset to a client task, we just take the subset that corresponds to its position within its round (e.g., (i % 4) for client[i] with four subsets):

- client[0], client[4], client[8] will use subset[0]
- client[1], client[5], client[9] will use subset[1]
- client[2], client[6], client[10] will use subset[2]
- client[3], client[7], client[11] will use subset[3]

Because clients across rounds will use a different value for shuffled_backends (and thus for subset) and clients within rounds use different subsets, the connection load is spread uniformly. In cases where the total number of backends is not divisible by the desired subset size, we allow a few subsets to be slightly larger than others, but in most cases the number of clients assigned to a backend will differ by at most 1.

As Figure 20-5 shows, the distribution for the former example of 300 clients each connecting to 10 of 300 backends yields very good results: each backend receives exactly the same number of connections.

Figure 20-5. Connection distribution with 300 clients and deterministic subsetting to 10 of 300 backends

Load Balancing Policies

Now that we've established the groundwork for how a given client task maintains a set of connections that are known to be healthy, let's examine *load balancing policies*. These are the mechanisms used by client tasks to select which backend task in its subset receives a client request. Many of the complexities in load balancing policies stem from the distributed nature of the decision-making process in which clients need to decide, in real time (and with only partial and/or stale backend state information), which backend should be used for each request.

Load balancing policies can be very simple and not take into account any information about the state of the backends (e.g., *Round Robin*) or can act with more information about the backends (e.g., *Least-Loaded Round Robin* or *Weighted Round Robin*).

Simple Round Robin

One very simple approach to load balancing has each client send requests in round-robin fashion to each backend task in its subset to which it can successfully connect and which isn't in lame duck state. For many years, this was our most common approach, and it's still used by many services.

Unfortunately, while Round Robin has the advantage of being very simple and performing significantly better than just selecting backend tasks randomly, the results of this policy can be very poor. While actual numbers depend on many factors, such as varying query cost and machine diversity, we've found that Round Robin can result in a spread of up to $2x$ in CPU consumption from the least to the most loaded task. Such a spread is extremely wasteful and occurs for a number of reasons, including:

- Small subsetting
- Varying query costs
- Machine diversity
- Unpredictable performance factors

Small subsetting

One of the simplest reasons Round Robin distributes load poorly is that all of its clients may not issue requests at the same rate. Different rates of requests among clients are especially likely when vastly different processes share the same backends. In this case, and especially if you're using relatively small subset sizes, backends in the subsets of the clients generating the most traffic will naturally tend to be more loaded.

Varying query costs

Many services handle requests that require vastly different amounts of resources for processing. In practice, we've found that the semantics of many services in Google are such that the most expensive requests consume $1000x$ (or more) CPU than the cheapest requests. Load balancing using Round Robin is even more difficult when query cost can't be predicted in advance. For example, a query such as "return all emails received by user XYZ in the last day" could be very cheap (if the user has received little email over the course of the day) or extremely expensive.

Load balancing in a system with large discrepancies in potential query cost is very problematic. It can become necessary to adjust the service interfaces to functionally cap the amount of work done per request. For example, in the case of the email query described previously, you could introduce a pagination interface and change the semantics of the request to "return the most recent 100 emails (or fewer) received by user XYZ in the last day." Unfortunately, it's often difficult to introduce such semantic changes. Not only does this require changes in all the client code, but it also entails additional consistency considerations. For example, the user may be receiving new emails or deleting emails as the client fetches emails page-by-page. For this use case, a client that naively iterates through the results and concatenates the responses (rather than paginating based on a fixed view of the data) will likely produce an inconsistent view, repeating some messages and/or skipping others.

To keep interfaces (and their implementations) simple, services are often defined to allow the most expensive requests to consume 100, 1,000, or even 10,000 times more resources than the cheapest requests. However, varying resource requirements per-request naturally mean that some backend tasks will be unlucky and occasionally receive more expensive requests than others. The extent to which this situation affects load balancing depends on how expensive the most expensive requests are. For example, for one of our Java backends, queries consume around 15 ms of CPU on average but some queries can easily require up to 10 seconds. Each task in this backend reserves multiple CPU cores, which reduces latency by allowing some of the computations to happen in parallel. But despite these reserved cores, when a backend receives one of these large queries, its load increases significantly for a few seconds. A poorly behaved task may run out of memory or even stop responding entirely (e.g., due to memory thrashing), but even in the normal case (i.e., the backend has sufficient resources and its load normalizes once the large query completes), the latency of other requests suffers due to resource competition with the expensive request.

Machine diversity

Another challenge to Simple Round Robin is the fact that not all machines in the same datacenter are necessarily the same. A given datacenter may have machines with CPUs of varying performance, and therefore, the same request may represent a significantly different amount of work for different machines.

Dealing with machine diversity—*without* requiring strict homogeneity—was a challenge for many years at Google. In theory, the solution to working with heterogeneous resource capacity in a fleet is simple: scale the CPU reservations depending on the processor/machine type. However, in practice, rolling out this solution required significant effort because it required our job scheduler to account for resource equivalencies based on average machine performance across a sampling of services. For example, 2 CPU units in machine X (a "slow" machine) is equivalent to 0.8 CPU units in machine Y (a "fast" machine). With this information, the job scheduler is then required to adjust CPU reservations for a process based upon the equivalence factor and the type of machine on which the process was scheduled. In an attempt to mitigate this complexity, we created a virtual unit for CPU rate called "GCU" (Google Compute Units). GCUs became the standard for modeling CPU rates, and were used to maintain a mapping from each CPU architecture in our datacenters to its corresponding GCU based upon its performance.

Unpredictable performance factors

Perhaps the largest complicating factor for Simple Round Robin is that machines—or, more accurately, the performance of backend tasks—may differ vastly due to several *unpredictable* aspects that cannot be accounted for statically.

Two of the many unpredictable factors that contribute to performance include:

Antagonistic neighbors
> Other processes (often completely unrelated and run by different teams) can have a significant impact on the performance of your processes. We've seen differences in performance of this nature of up to 20%. This difference mostly stems from competition for shared resources, such as space in memory caches or bandwidth, in ways that may not be directly obvious. For example, if the latency of outgoing requests from a backend task grows (because of competition for network resources with an antagonistic neighbor), the number of active requests will also grow, which may trigger increased garbage collection.

Task restarts
> When a task gets restarted, it often requires significantly more resources for a few minutes. As just one example, we've seen this condition affect platforms such as Java that optimize code dynamically more than others. In response, we've actually added to the logic of some server code—we keep servers in lame duck state and prewarm them (triggering these optimizations) for a period of time after they start, until their performance is nominal. The effect of task restarts can become a sizable problem when you consider we update many servers (e.g., push new builds, which requires restarting these tasks) every day.

If your load balancing policy can't adapt to unforeseen performance limitations, you will inherently end up with a suboptimal load distribution when working at scale.

Least-Loaded Round Robin

An alternative approach to Simple Round Robin is to have each client task keep track of the number of active requests it has to each backend task in its subset and use Round Robin *among the set of tasks with a minimal number of active requests*.

For example, suppose a client uses a subset of backend tasks *t0* to *t9*, and currently has the following number of active requests against each backend:

t0	t1	t2	t3	t4	t5	t6	t7	t8	t9
2	1	0	0	1	0	2	0	0	1

For a new request, the client would filter the list of potential backend tasks to just those tasks with the least number of connections (*t2*, *t3*, *t5*, *t7*, and *t8*) and choose a backend from that list. Let's assume it picks *t2*. The client's connection state table would now look like the following:

t0	t1	t2	t3	t4	t5	t6	t7	t8	t9
2	1	1	0	1	0	2	0	0	1

Assuming none of the current requests have completed, on the next request, the backend candidate pool becomes *t3*, *t5*, *t7*, and *t8*.

Let's fast-forward until we've issued four new requests. Still assuming that no request finishes in the meantime, the connection state table would look like the following:

t0	t1	t2	t3	t4	t5	t6	t7	t8	t9
2	1	1	1	1	1	2	1	1	1

At this point the set of backend candidates is all tasks except *t0* and *t6*. However, if the request against task *t4* finishes, its current state becomes "0 active requests" and a new request will be assigned to *t4*.

This implementation actually uses Round Robin, but it's applied across the set of tasks with minimal active requests. Without such filtering, the policy might not be able to spread the requests well enough to avoid a situation in which some portion of the available backend tasks goes unused. The idea behind the least-loaded policy is that loaded tasks will tend to have higher latency than those with spare capacity, and this strategy will naturally take load away from these loaded tasks.

All that said, we've learned (the hard way!) about one very dangerous pitfall of the Least-Loaded Round Robin approach: if a task is seriously unhealthy, it might start serving 100% errors. Depending on the nature of those errors, they may have very low latency; it's frequently significantly faster to just return an "I'm unhealthy!" error than to actually process a request. As a result, clients might start sending a very large amount of traffic to the unhealthy task, erroneously thinking that the task is available, as opposed to fast-failing them! We say that the unhealthy task is now *sinkholing* traffic. Fortunately, this pitfall can be solved relatively easily by modifying the policy to count recent errors as if they were active requests. This way, if a backend task becomes unhealthy, the load balancing policy begins to divert load from it the same way it would divert load from an overburdened task.

Least-Loaded Round Robin has two important limitations:

The count of active requests may not be a very good proxy for the capability of a given backend
> Many requests spend a significant portion of their life just waiting for a response from the network (i.e., waiting for responses to requests they initiate to other backends) and very little time on actual processing. For example, one backend task may be able to process twice as many requests as another (e.g., because it's running in a machine with a CPU that's twice as fast as the rest), but the latency of its requests may still be roughly the same as the latency of requests in the other task (because requests spend most of their life just waiting for the network to respond). In this case, because blocking on I/O often consumes zero CPU, very little RAM, and no bandwidth, we'd still want to send twice as many requests to the faster backend. However, Least-Loaded Round Robin will consider both backend tasks equally loaded.

The count of active requests in each client doesn't include requests from other clients to the same backends
> That is, each client task has only a very limited view into the state of its backend tasks: the view of its own requests.

In practice, we've found that large services using Least-Loaded Round Robin will see their most loaded backend task using twice as much CPU as the least loaded, performing about as poorly as Round Robin.

Weighted Round Robin

Weighted Round Robin is an important load balancing policy that improves on Simple and Least-Loaded Round Robin by incorporating backend-provided information into the decision process.

Weighted Round Robin is fairly simple in principle: each client task keeps a "capability" score for each backend in its subset. Requests are distributed in Round-Robin fashion, but clients weigh the distributions of requests to backends proportionally. In each response (including responses to health checks), backends include the current observed rates of queries and errors per second, in addition to the utilization (typically, CPU usage). Clients adjust the capability scores periodically to pick backend tasks based upon their current number of successful requests handled and at what utilization cost; failed requests result in a penalty that affects future decisions.

In practice, Weighted Round Robin has worked very well and significantly reduced the difference between the most and the least utilized tasks. Figure 20-6 shows the CPU rates for a random subset of backend tasks around the time its clients switched from Least-Loaded to Weighted Round Robin. The spread from the least to the most loaded tasks decreased drastically.

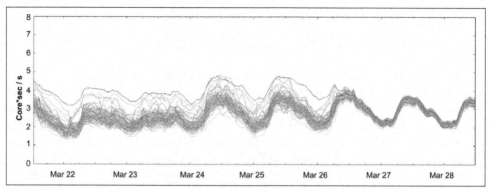

Figure 20-6. CPU distribution before and after enabling Weighted Round Robin

CHAPTER 21

Handling Overload

Written by Alejandro Forero Cuervo
Edited by Sarah Chavis

Avoiding overload is a goal of load balancing policies. But no matter how efficient your load balancing policy, *eventually* some part of your system will become overloaded. Gracefully handling overload conditions is fundamental to running a reliable serving system.

One option for handling overload is to serve degraded responses: responses that are not as accurate as or that contain less data than normal responses, but that are easier to compute. For example:

- Instead of searching an entire corpus to provide the best available results to a search query, search only a small percentage of the candidate set.

- Rely on a local copy of results that may not be fully up to date but that will be cheaper to use than going against the canonical storage.

However, under extreme overload, the service might not even be able to compute and serve degraded responses. At this point it may have no immediate option but to serve errors. One way to mitigate this scenario is to balance traffic across datacenters such that no datacenter receives more traffic than it has the capacity to process. For example, if a datacenter runs 100 backend tasks and each task can process up to 500 requests per second, the load balancing algorithm will not allow more than 50,000 queries per second to be sent to that datacenter. However, even this constraint can prove insufficient to avoid overload when you're operating at scale. At the end of the day, it's best to build clients and backends to handle resource restrictions gracefully: redirect when possible, serve degraded results when necessary, and handle resource errors transparently when all else fails.

The Pitfalls of "Queries per Second"

Different queries can have vastly different resource requirements. A query's cost can vary based on arbitrary factors such as the code in the client that issues them (for services that have many different clients) or even the time of the day (e.g., home users versus work users; or interactive end-user traffic versus batch traffic).

We learned this lesson the hard way: modeling capacity as "queries per second" or using static features of the requests that are believed to be a proxy for the resources they consume (e.g., "how many keys are the requests reading") often makes for a poor metric. Even if these metrics perform adequately at one point in time, the ratios can change. Sometimes the change is gradual, but sometimes the change is drastic (e.g., a new version of the software suddenly made some features of some requests require significantly fewer resources). A moving target makes a poor metric for designing and implementing load balancing.

A better solution is to measure capacity directly in available resources. For example, you may have a total of 500 CPU cores and 1 TB of memory reserved for a given service in a given datacenter. Naturally, it works much better to use those numbers directly to model a datacenter's capacity. We often speak about the *cost* of a request to refer to a normalized measure of how much CPU time it has consumed (over different CPU architectures, with consideration of performance differences).

In a majority of cases (although certainly not in all), we've found that simply using CPU consumption as the signal for provisioning works well, for the following reasons:

- In platforms with garbage collection, memory pressure naturally translates into increased CPU consumption.
- In other platforms, it's possible to provision the remaining resources in such a way that they're very unlikely to run out before CPU runs out.

In cases where over-provisioning the non-CPU resources is prohibitively expensive, we take each system resource into account separately when considering resource consumption.

Per-Customer Limits

One component of dealing with overload is deciding what to do in the case of *global* overload. In a perfect world, where teams coordinate their launches carefully with the owners of their backend dependencies, global overload never happens and backend services always have enough capacity to serve their customers. Unfortunately, we don't live in a perfect world. Here in reality, global overload occurs quite frequently (especially for internal services that tend to have many clients run by many teams).

When global overload *does* occur, it's vital that the service only delivers error responses to misbehaving customers, while other customers remain unaffected. To achieve this outcome, service owners provision their capacity based on the negotiated usage with their customers and define per-customer quotas according to these agreements.

For example, if a backend service has 10,000 CPUs allocated worldwide (over various datacenters), their per-customer limits might look something like the following:

- Gmail is allowed to consume up to 4,000 CPU seconds per second.
- Calendar is allowed to consume up to 4,000 CPU seconds per second.
- Android is allowed to consume up to 3,000 CPU seconds per second.
- Google+ is allowed to consume up to 2,000 CPU seconds per second.
- Every other user is allowed to consume up to 500 CPU seconds per second.

Note that these numbers may add up to more than the 10,000 CPUs allocated to the backend service. The service owner is relying on the fact that it's unlikely for *all* of their customers to hit their resource limits simultaneously.

We aggregate global usage information in real time from all backend tasks, and use that data to push effective limits to individual backend tasks. A closer look at the system that implements this logic is outside of the scope of this discussion, but we've written significant code to implement this in our backend tasks. An interesting part of the puzzle is computing in real time the amount of resources—specifically CPU—consumed by each individual request. This computation is particularly tricky for servers that don't implement a thread-per-request model, where a pool of threads just executes different parts of all requests as they come in, using nonblocking APIs.

Client-Side Throttling

When a customer is out of quota, a backend task should reject requests quickly with the expectation that returning a "customer is out of quota" error consumes significantly fewer resources than actually processing the request and serving back a correct response. However, this logic doesn't hold true for all services. For example, it's almost equally expensive to reject a request that requires a simple RAM lookup (where the overhead of the request/response protocol handling is significantly larger than the overhead of producing the response) as it is to accept and run that request. And even in the case where rejecting requests saves significant resources, those requests *still* consume some resources. If the amount of rejected requests is significant, these numbers add up quickly. In such cases, the backend can become overloaded even though the vast majority of its CPU is spent just rejecting requests!

Client-side throttling addresses this problem.[1] When a client detects that a significant portion of its recent requests have been rejected due to "out of quota" errors, it starts self-regulating and caps the amount of outgoing traffic it generates. Requests above the cap fail locally without even reaching the network.

We implemented client-side throttling through a technique we call *adaptive throttling*. Specifically, each client task keeps the following information for the last two minutes of its history:

requests
: The number of requests attempted by the application layer (at the client, on top of the adaptive throttling system)

accepts
: The number of requests accepted by the backend

Under normal conditions, the two values are equal. As the backend starts rejecting traffic, the number of accepts becomes smaller than the number of requests. Clients can continue to issue requests to the backend until requests is K times as large as accepts. Once that cutoff is reached, the client begins to self-regulate and new requests are rejected locally (i.e., at the client) with the probability calculated in Equation 21-1.

Equation 21-1. Client request rejection probability

$$\max\left(0, \frac{\text{requests} - K \times \text{accepts}}{\text{requests} + 1}\right)$$

As the client itself starts rejecting requests, requests will continue to exceed accepts. While it may seem counterintuitive, given that locally rejected requests aren't actually propagated to the backend, this is the preferred behavior. As the rate at which the application attempts requests to the client grows (relative to the rate at which the backend accepts them), we want to increase the probability of dropping new requests.

We've found adaptive throttling to work well in practice, leading to stable rates of requests overall. Even in large overload situations, backends end up rejecting one request for each request they actually process. One large advantage of this approach is that the decision is made by the client task based entirely on local information and using a relatively simple implementation: there are no additional dependencies or latency penalties.

---

1 For example, see Doorman (*https://github.com/youtube/doorman*), which provides a cooperative distributed client-side throttling system.

For services where the cost of processing a request is very close to the cost of rejecting that request, allowing roughly half of the backend resources to be consumed by rejected requests can be unacceptable. In this case, the solution is simple: modify the accepts multiplier K (e.g., 2) in the client request rejection probability (Equation 21-1). In this way:

- Reducing the multiplier will make adaptive throttling behave more aggressively
- Increasing the multiplier will make adaptive throttling behave less aggressively

For example, instead of having the client self-regulate when `requests = 2 * accepts`, have it self-regulate when `requests = 1.1 * accepts`. Reducing the modifier to 1.1 means only one request will be rejected by the backend for every 10 requests accepted.

We generally prefer the 2x multiplier. By allowing more requests to reach the backend than are expected to actually be allowed, we waste more resources at the backend, but we also speed up the propagation of state from the backend to the clients. For example, if the backend decides to stop rejecting traffic from the client tasks, the delay until all client tasks have detected this change in state is shorter.

One additional consideration is that client-side throttling may not work well with clients that only very sporadically send requests to their backends. In this case, the view that each client has of the state of the backend is reduced drastically, and approaches to increment this visibility tend to be expensive.

Criticality

Criticality is another notion that we've found very useful in the context of global quotas and throttling. A request made to a backend is associated with one of four possible criticality values, depending on how critical we consider that request:

CRITICAL_PLUS
> Reserved for the most critical requests, those that will result in serious user-visible impact if they fail.

CRITICAL
> The default value for requests sent from production jobs. These requests will result in user-visible impact, but the impact may be less severe than those of CRIT ICAL_PLUS. Services are expected to provision enough capacity for all expected CRITICAL and CRITICAL_PLUS traffic.

SHEDDABLE_PLUS
> Traffic for which partial unavailability is expected. This is the default for batch jobs, which can retry requests minutes or even hours later.

SHEDDABLE

Traffic for which frequent partial unavailability and occasional full unavailability is expected.

We found that four values were sufficiently robust to model almost every service. We've had various discussions on proposals to add more values, because doing so would allow us to classify requests more finely. However, defining additional values would require more resources to operate various criticality-aware systems.

We've made criticality a first-class notion of our RPC system and we've worked hard to integrate it into many of our control mechanisms so it can be taken into account when reacting to overload situations. For example:

- When a customer runs out of global quota, a backend task will only reject requests of a given criticality if it's already rejecting all requests of all lower criticalities (in fact, the per-customer limits that our system supports, described earlier, can be set per criticality).
- When a task is itself overloaded, it will reject requests of lower criticalities sooner.
- The adaptive throttling system also keeps separate stats for each criticality.

The criticality of a request is orthogonal to its latency requirements and thus to the underlying network quality of service (QoS) used. For example, when a system displays search results or suggestions while the user is typing a search query, the underlying requests are highly sheddable (if the system is overloaded, it's acceptable to not display these results), but tend to have stringent latency requirements.

We've also significantly extended our RPC system to propagate criticality automatically. If a backend receives request A and, as part of executing that request, issues outgoing request B and request C to other backends, request B and request C will use the same criticality as request A by default.

In the past, many systems at Google had evolved their own ad hoc notions of criticality that were often incompatible across services. By standardizing and propagating criticality as a part of our RPC system, we are now able to consistently set the criticality at specific points. This means we can be confident that overloaded dependencies will abide by the desired high-level criticality as they reject traffic, regardless of how deep down the RPC stack they are. Our practice is thus to set the criticality as close as possible to the browsers or mobile clients—typically in the HTTP frontends that produce the HTML to be returned—and only override the criticality in specific cases where it makes sense at specific points in the stack.

Utilization Signals

Our implementation of task-level overload protection is based on the notion of *utilization*. In many cases, the utilization is just a measurement of the CPU rate (i.e., the current CPU rate divided by the total CPUs reserved for the task), but in some cases we also factor in measurements such as the portion of the memory reserved that is currently being used. As utilization approaches configured thresholds, we start rejecting requests based on their criticality (higher thresholds for higher criticalities).

The utilization signals we use are based on the state local to the task (since the goal of the signals is to protect the task) and we have implementations for various signals. The most generally useful signal is based on the "load" in the process, which is determined using a system we call *executor load average*.

To find the executor load average, we count the number of active threads in the process. In this case, "active" refers to threads that are currently running or ready to run and waiting for a free processor. We smooth this value with exponential decay and begin rejecting requests as the number of active threads grows beyond the number of processors available to the task. That means that an incoming request that has a very large fan-out (i.e., one that schedules a burst of a very large number of short-lived operations) will cause the load to spike very briefly, but the smoothing will mostly swallow that spike. However, if the operations are not short-lived (i.e., the load increases and remains high for a significant amount of time), the task will start rejecting requests.

While the executor load average has proven to be a very useful signal, our system can plug in any utilization signal that a particular backend may need. For example, we might use memory pressure—which indicates whether the memory usage in a backend task has grown beyond normal operational parameters—as another possible utilization signal. The system can also be configured to combine multiple signals and reject requests that would surpass the combined (or individual) target utilization thresholds.

Handling Overload Errors

In addition to handling load gracefully, we've put a significant amount of thought into how clients should react when they receive a load-related error response. In the case of overload errors, we distinguish between two possible situations.

A large subset of backend tasks in the datacenter are overloaded.
> If the cross-datacenter load balancing system is working perfectly (i.e., it can propagate state and react instantaneously to shifts in traffic), this condition will not occur.

A small subset of backend tasks in the datacenter are overloaded.

This situation is typically caused by imperfections in the load balancing inside the datacenter. For example, a task may have very recently received a very expensive request. In this case, it is very likely that the datacenter has remaining capacity in other tasks to handle the request.

If a large subset of backend tasks in the datacenter are overloaded, requests should not be retried and errors should bubble up all the way to the caller (e.g., returning an error to the end user). It's much more typical that only a small portion of tasks become overloaded, in which case the preferred response is to retry the request immediately. In general, our cross-datacenter load balancing system tries to direct traffic from clients to their nearest available backend datacenters. In a few cases, the nearest datacenter is far away (e.g., a client may have its nearest available backend in a different continent), but we usually manage to situate clients close to their backends. That way, the additional latency of retrying a request—just a few network round trips —tends to be negligible.

From the point of view of our load balancing policies, retries of requests are indistinguishable from new requests. That is, we don't use any explicit logic to ensure that a retry actually goes to a different backend task; we just rely on the likely probability that the retry will land on a different backend task simply by virtue of the number of participating backends in the subset. Ensuring that all retries actually go to a different task would incur more complexity in our APIs than is worthwhile.

Even if a backend is only slightly overloaded, a client request is often better served if the backend rejects retry and new requests equally and quickly. These requests can then be retried immediately on a different backend task that may have spare resources. The consequence of treating retries and new requests identically at the backend is that retrying requests in different tasks becomes a form of organic load balancing: it redirects load to tasks that may be better suited for those requests.

Deciding to Retry

When a client receives a "task overloaded" error response, it needs to decide whether to retry the request. We have a few mechanisms in place to avoid retries when a significant portion of the tasks in a cluster are overloaded.

First, we implement a *per-request retry budget* of up to three attempts. If a request has already failed three times, we let the failure bubble up to the caller. The rationale is that if a request has already landed on overloaded tasks three times, it's relatively unlikely that attempting it again will help because the whole datacenter is likely overloaded.

Secondly, we implement a *per-client retry budget*. Each client keeps track of the ratio of requests that correspond to retries. A request will only be retried as long as this ratio is below 10%. The rationale is that if only a small subset of tasks are overloaded, there will be relatively little need to retry.

As a concrete example (of the worst-case scenario), let's assume a datacenter is accepting a small amount of requests and rejecting a large portion of requests. Let X be the total rate of requests attempted against the datacenter according to the client-side logic. Due to the number of retries that will occur, the number of requests will grow significantly, to somewhere just below $3X$. Although we've effectively capped the growth caused by retries, a threefold increase in requests is significant, especially if the cost of rejecting versus processing a request is considerable. However, layering on the per-client retry budget (a 10% retry ratio) reduces the growth to just 1.1x in the general case—a significant improvement.

A third approach has clients include a counter of how many times the request has already been tried in the request metadata. For instance, the counter starts at 0 in the first attempt and is incremented on every retry until it reaches 2, at which point the per-request budget causes it to stop being retried. Backends keep histograms of these values in recent history. When a backend needs to reject a request, it consults these histograms to determine the likelihood that other backend tasks are also overloaded. If these histograms reveal a significant amount of retries (indicating that other backend tasks are likely also overloaded), they return an "overloaded; don't retry" error response instead of the standard "task overloaded" error that triggers retries.

Figure 21-1 shows the number of attempts in each request received by a given backend task in various example situations, over a sliding window (corresponding to 1,000 initial requests, not counting retries). For simplicity, the per-client retry budget is ignored (i.e., these numbers assume that the only limit to retries is the retry budget of three attempts per request), and subsetting could alter these numbers somewhat.

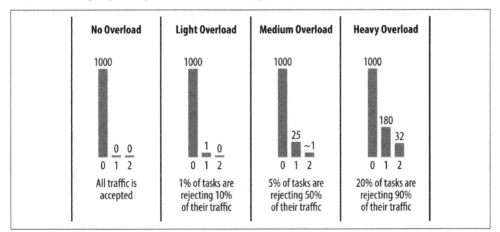

Figure 21-1. Histograms of attempts in various conditions

Our larger services tend to be deep stacks of systems, which may in turn have dependencies on each other. In this architecture, requests should only be retried at the layer immediately above the layer that is rejecting them. When we decide that a given request can't be served and shouldn't be retried, we use an "overloaded; don't retry" error and thus avoid a combinatorial retry explosion.

Consider the example from Figure 21-2 (in practice, our stacks are often significantly more complex). Imagine that the DB Frontend is currently overloaded and rejects a request. In that case:

- Backend B will then retry the request according to the preceding guidelines.

- However, once Backend B determines that the request to the DB Frontend can't be served (for example, because the request has already been attempted and rejected three times), Backend B has to return to Backend A either an "overloaded; don't retry" error or a degraded response (assuming that it can produce some moderately useful response even when its request to the DB Frontend failed).

- Backend A has exactly the same options for the request it received from the Frontend, and proceeds accordingly.

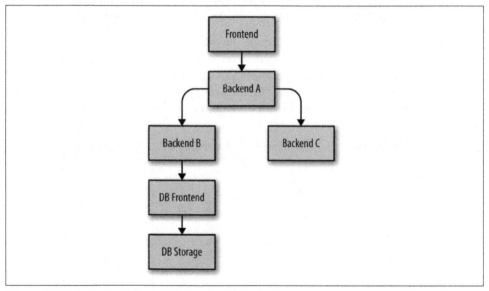

Figure 21-2. A stack of dependencies

The key point is that a failed request from the DB Frontend should only be retried by Backend B, the layer immediately above it. If multiple layers retried, we'd have a combinatorial explosion.

Load from Connections

The load associated with connections is one last factor worth mentioning. We some-times only take into account load at the backends that is caused directly by the requests they receive (which is one of the problems with approaches that model load based upon queries per second). However, doing so overlooks the CPU and memory costs of maintaining a large pool of connections or the cost of a fast rate of churn of connections. Such issues are negligible in small systems, but quickly become prob-lematic when running very large-scale RPC systems.

As mentioned previously, our RPC protocol requires inactive clients to perform peri-odic health checks. After a connection has been idle for a configurable amount of time, the client drops its TCP connection and switches to UDP for health checking. Unfortunately, this behavior is problematic when you have a very large number of cli-ent tasks that issue a very low rate of requests: health checking on the connections can require more resources than actually serving the requests. Approaches such as carefully tuning the connection parameters (e.g., significantly decreasing the fre-quency of health checks) or even creating and destroying the connections dynami-cally can significantly improve this situation.

Handling bursts of new connection requests is a second (but related) problem. We've seen bursts of this type happen in the case of very large batch jobs that create a very large number of worker client tasks all at once. The need to negotiate and maintain an excessive number of new connections simultaneously can easily overload a group of backends. In our experience, there are a couple strategies that can help mitigate this load:

- Expose the load to the cross-datacenter load balancing algorithm (e.g., base load balancing on the utilization of the cluster, rather than just on the number of requests). In this case, load from requests is effectively rebalanced away to other datacenters that have spare capacity.

- Mandate that batch client jobs use a separate set of *batch proxy* backend tasks that do nothing but forward requests to the underlying backends and hand their responses back to the clients in a controlled way. Therefore, instead of "batch cli-ent → backend," you have "batch client → batch proxy → backend." In this case, when the very large job starts, only the batch proxy job suffers, shielding the actual backends (and higher-priority clients). Effectively, the batch proxy acts like a fuse. Another advantage of using the proxy is that it typically reduces the num-ber of connections against the backend, which can improve the load balancing against the backend (e.g., the proxy tasks can use bigger subsets and probably have a better view of the state of the backend tasks).

Conclusions

This chapter and Chapter 20 have discussed how various techniques (deterministic subsetting, Weighted Round Robin, client-side throttling, customer quotas, etc.) can help to spread load over tasks in a datacenter relatively evenly. However, these mechanisms depend on the propagation of state over a distributed system. While they perform reasonably well in the general case, real-world application has resulted in a small number of situations where they work imperfectly.

As a result, we consider it critical to ensure that individual tasks are protected against overload. To state this simply: a backend task provisioned to serve a certain traffic rate should continue to serve traffic at that rate without any significant impact on latency, regardless of how much excess traffic is thrown at the task. As a corollary, the backend task should not fall over and crash under the load. These statements should hold true up to a certain rate of traffic—somewhere above $2x$ or even $10x$ what the task is provisioned to process. We accept that there might be a certain point at which a system begins to break down, and raising the threshold at which this breakdown occurs becomes relatively difficult to achieve.

The key is to take these degradation conditions seriously. When these degradation conditions are ignored, many systems will exhibit terrible behavior. And as work piles up and tasks eventually run out of memory and crash (or end up burning almost all their CPU in memory thrashing), latency suffers as traffic is dropped and tasks compete for resources. Left unchecked, the failure in a subset of a system (such as an individual backend task) might trigger the failure of other system components, potentially causing the entire system (or a considerable subset) to fail. The impact from this kind of cascading failure can be so severe that it's critical for any system operating at scale to protect against it; see Chapter 22.

It's a common mistake to assume that an overloaded backend should turn down and stop accepting all traffic. However, this assumption actually goes counter to the goal of robust load balancing. We actually want the backend to continue accepting as much traffic as possible, but to only accept that load as capacity frees up. A well-behaved backend, supported by robust load balancing policies, should accept only the requests that it can process and reject the rest gracefully.

While we have a vast array of tools to implement good load balancing and overload protections, there is no magic bullet: load balancing often requires deep understanding of a system and the semantics of its requests. The techniques described in this chapter have evolved along with the needs of many systems at Google, and will likely continue to evolve as the nature of our systems continues to change.

CHAPTER 22

Addressing Cascading Failures

Written by Mike Ulrich

> *If at first you don't succeed, back off exponentially.*
> —Dan Sandler, Google Software Engineer

> *Why do people always forget that you need to add a little jitter?*
> —Ade Oshineye, Google Developer Advocate

A cascading failure is a failure that grows over time as a result of positive feedback.[1] It can occur when a portion of an overall system fails, increasing the probability that other portions of the system fail. For example, a single replica for a service can fail due to overload, increasing load on remaining replicas and increasing their probability of failing, causing a domino effect that takes down all the replicas for a service.

We'll use the Shakespeare search service discussed in "Shakespeare: A Sample Service" on page 20 as an example throughout this chapter. Its production configuration might look something like Figure 22-1.

---

1 See Wikipedia, "Positive feedback," *https://en.wikipedia.org/wiki/Positive_feedback*.

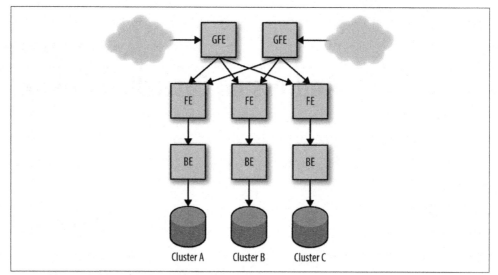

Figure 22-1. Example production configuration for the Shakespeare search service

Causes of Cascading Failures and Designing to Avoid Them

Well-thought-out system design should take into account a few typical scenarios that account for the majority of cascading failures.

Server Overload

The most common cause of cascading failures is overload. Most cascading failures described here are either directly due to server overload, or due to extensions or variations of this scenario.

Suppose the frontend in cluster A is handling 1,000 requests per second (QPS), as in Figure 22-2.

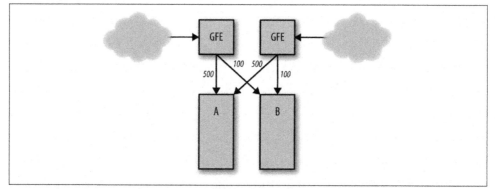

Figure 22-2. Normal server load distribution between clusters A and B

If cluster B fails (Figure 22-3), requests to cluster A increase to 1,200 QPS. The frontends in A are not able to handle requests at 1,200 QPS, and therefore start running out of resources, which causes them to crash, miss deadlines, or otherwise misbehave. As a result, the rate of successfully handled requests in A dips well below 1,000 QPS.

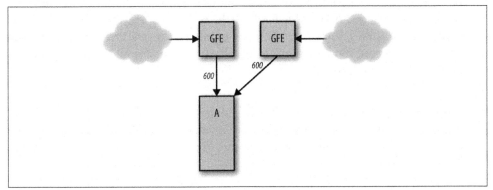

Figure 22-3. Cluster B fails, sending all traffic to cluster A

This reduction in the rate of useful work being done can spread into other failure domains, potentially spreading globally. For example, local overload in one cluster may lead to its servers crashing; in response, the load balancing controller sends requests to other clusters, overloading their servers, leading to a service-wide overload failure. It may not take long for these events to transpire (e.g., on the order of a couple minutes), because the load balancer and task scheduling systems involved may act very quickly.

Resource Exhaustion

Running out of a resource can result in higher latency, elevated error rates, or the substitution of lower-quality results. These are in fact desired effects of running out of resources: something eventually needs to give as the load increases beyond what a server can handle.

Depending on what resource becomes exhausted in a server and how the server is built, resource exhaustion can render the server less efficient or cause the server to crash, prompting the load balancer to distribute the resource problems to other servers. When this happens, the rate of successfully handled requests can drop and possibly send the cluster or an entire service into a cascade failure.

Different types of resources can be exhausted, resulting in varying effects on servers.

CPU

If there is insufficient CPU to handle the request load, typically all requests become slower. This scenario can result in various secondary effects, including the following:

Increased number of in-flight requests
Because requests take longer to handle, more requests are handled concurrently (up to a possible maximum capacity at which queuing may occur). This affects almost all resources, including memory, number of active threads (in a thread-per-request server model), number of file descriptors, and backend resources (which in turn can have other effects).

Excessively long queue lengths
If there is insufficient capacity to handle all the requests at steady state, the server will saturate its queues. This means that latency increases (the requests are queued for longer amounts of time) and the queue uses more memory. See "Queue Management" on page 266 for a discussion of mitigation strategies.

Thread starvation
When a thread can't make progress because it's waiting for a lock, health checks may fail if the health check endpoint can't be served in time.

CPU or request starvation
Internal watchdogs[2] in the server detect that the server isn't making progress, causing the servers to crash due to CPU starvation, or due to request starvation if watchdog events are triggered remotely and processed as part of the request queue.

Missed RPC deadlines
As a server becomes overloaded, its responses to RPCs from its clients arrive later, which may exceed any deadlines those clients set. The work the server did to respond is then wasted, and clients may retry the RPCs, leading to even more overload.

Reduced CPU caching benefits
As more CPU is used, the chance of spilling on to more cores increases, resulting in decreased usage of local caches and decreased CPU efficiency.

---

2 A watchdog is often implemented as a thread that wakes up periodically to see whether work has been done since the last time it checked. If not, it assumes that the server is stuck and kills it. For instance, requests of a known type can be sent to the server at regular intervals; if one hasn't been received or processed when expected, this may indicate failure—of the server, the system sending requests, or the intermediate network.

Memory

If nothing else, more in-flight requests consume more RAM from allocating the request, response, and RPC objects. Memory exhaustion can cause the following effects:

Dying tasks
> For example, a task might be evicted by the container manager (VM or otherwise) for exceeding available resource limits, or application-specific crashes may cause tasks to die.

Increased rate of garbage collection (GC) in Java, resulting in increased CPU usage
> A vicious cycle can occur in this scenario: less CPU is available, resulting in slower requests, resulting in increased RAM usage, resulting in more GC, resulting in even lower availability of CPU. This is known colloquially as the "GC death spiral."

Reduction in cache hit rates
> Reduction in available RAM can reduce application-level cache hit rates, resulting in more RPCs to the backends, which can possibly cause the backends to become overloaded.

Threads

Thread starvation can directly cause errors or lead to health check failures. If the server adds threads as needed, thread overhead can use too much RAM. In extreme cases, thread starvation can also cause you to run out of process IDs.

File descriptors

Running out of file descriptors can lead to the inability to initialize network connections, which in turn can cause health checks to fail.

Dependencies among resources

Note that many of these resource exhaustion scenarios feed from one another—a service experiencing overload often has a host of secondary symptoms that can look like the root cause, making debugging difficult.

For example, imagine the following scenario:

1. A Java frontend has poorly tuned garbage collection (GC) parameters.
2. Under high (but expected) load, the frontend runs out of CPU due to GC.
3. CPU exhaustion slows down completion of requests.
4. The increased number of in-progress requests causes more RAM to be used to process the requests.

5. Memory pressure due to requests, in combination with a fixed memory allocation for the frontend process as a whole, leaves less RAM available for caching.

6. The reduced cache size means fewer entries in the cache, in addition to a lower hit rate.

7. The increase in cache misses means that more requests fall through to the backend for servicing.

8. The backend, in turn, runs out of CPU or threads.

9. Finally, the lack of CPU causes basic health checks to fail, starting a cascading failure.

In situations as complex as the preceding scenario, it's unlikely that the causal chain will be fully diagnosed during an outage. It might be very hard to determine that the backend crash was caused by a decrease in the cache rate in the frontend, particularly if the frontend and backend components have different owners.

Service Unavailability

Resource exhaustion can lead to servers crashing; for example, servers might crash when too much RAM is allocated to a container. Once a couple of servers crash on overload, the load on the remaining servers can increase, causing them to crash as well. The problem tends to snowball and soon all servers begin to crash-loop. It's often difficult to escape this scenario because as soon as servers come back online they're bombarded with an extremely high rate of requests and fail almost immediately.

For example, if a service was healthy at 10,000 QPS, but started a cascading failure due to crashes at 11,000 QPS, dropping the load to 9,000 QPS will almost certainly not stop the crashes. This is because the service will be handling increased demand with reduced capacity; only a small fraction of servers will usually be healthy enough to handle requests. The fraction of servers that will be healthy depends on a few factors: how quickly the system is able to start the tasks, how quickly the binary can start serving at full capacity, and how long a freshly started task is able to survive the load. In this example, if 10% of the servers are healthy enough to handle requests, the request rate would need to drop to about 1,000 QPS in order for the system to stabilize and recover.

Similarly, servers can appear unhealthy to the load balancing layer, resulting in reduced load balancing capacity: servers may go into "lame duck" state (see "A Robust Approach to Unhealthy Tasks: Lame Duck State" on page 234) or fail health checks without crashing. The effect can be very similar to crashing: more servers appear unhealthy, the healthy servers tend to accept requests for a very brief period of time before becoming unhealthy, and fewer servers participate in handling requests.

Load balancing policies that avoid servers that have served errors can exacerbate problems further—a few backends serve some errors, so they don't contribute to the available capacity for the service. This increases the load on the remaining servers, starting the snowball effect.

Preventing Server Overload

The following list presents strategies for avoiding server overload in rough priority order:

Load test the server's capacity limits, and test the failure mode for overload
This is the most important important exercise you should conduct in order to prevent server overload. Unless you test in a realistic environment, it's very hard to predict exactly which resource will be exhausted and how that resource exhaustion will manifest. For details, see "Testing for Cascading Failures" on page 278.

Serve degraded results
Serve lower-quality, cheaper-to-compute results to the user. Your strategy here will be service-specific. See "Load Shedding and Graceful Degradation" on page 267.

Instrument the server to reject requests when overloaded
Servers should protect themselves from becoming overloaded and crashing. When overloaded at either the frontend or backend layers, fail early and cheaply. For details, see "Load Shedding and Graceful Degradation" on page 267.

Instrument higher-level systems to reject requests, rather than overloading servers
Note that because rate limiting often doesn't take overall service health into account, it may not be able to stop a failure that has already begun. Simple rate-limiting implementations are also likely to leave capacity unused. Rate limiting can be implemented in a number of places:

- *At the reverse proxies*, by limiting the volume of requests by criteria such as IP address to mitigate attempted denial-of-service attacks and abusive clients.

- *At the load balancers*, by dropping requests when the service enters global overload. Depending on the nature and complexity of the service, this rate limiting can be indiscriminate ("drop all traffic above X requests per second") or more selective ("drop requests that aren't from users who have recently interacted with the service" or "drop requests for low-priority operations like background synchronization, but keep serving interactive user sessions").

- *At individual tasks*, to prevent random fluctuations in load balancing from overwhelming the server.

Perform capacity planning

Good capacity planning can reduce the probability that a cascading failure will occur. Capacity planning should be coupled with performance testing to determine the load at which the service will fail. For instance, if every cluster's breaking point is 5,000 QPS, the load is evenly spread across clusters,[3] and the service's peak load is 19,000 QPS, then approximately six clusters are needed to run the service at $N + 2$.

Capacity planning reduces the probability of triggering a cascading failure, but it is not sufficient to protect the service from cascading failures. When you lose major parts of your infrastructure during a planned or unplanned event, no amount of capacity planning may be sufficient to prevent cascading failures. Load balancing problems, network partitions, or unexpected traffic increases can create pockets of high load beyond what was planned. Some systems can grow the number of tasks for your service on demand, which may prevent overload; however, proper capacity planning is still needed.

Queue Management

Most thread-per-request servers use a queue in front of a thread pool to handle requests. Requests come in, they sit on a queue, and then threads pick requests off the queue and perform the actual work (whatever actions are required by the server). Usually, if the queue is full, the server will reject new requests.

If the request rate and latency of a given task is constant, there is no reason to queue requests: a constant number of threads should be occupied. Under this idealized scenario, requests will only be queued if the steady state rate of incoming requests exceeds the rate at which the server can process requests, which results in saturation of both the thread pool and the queue.

Queued requests consume memory and increase latency. For example, if the queue size is 10x the number of threads, the time to handle the request on a thread is 100 milliseconds. If the queue is full, then a request will take 1.1 seconds to handle, most of which time is spent on the queue.

For a system with fairly steady traffic over time, it is usually better to have small queue lengths relative to the thread pool size (e.g., 50% or less), which results in the server rejecting requests early when it can't sustain the rate of incoming requests. For example, Gmail often uses queueless servers, relying instead on failover to other

---

3 This is often not a good assumption due to geography; see also "Job and Data Organization" on page 22.

server tasks when the threads are full. On the other end of the spectrum, systems with "bursty" load for which traffic patterns fluctuate drastically may do better with a queue size based on the current number of threads in use, processing time for each request, and the size and frequency of bursts.

Load Shedding and Graceful Degradation

Load shedding drops some proportion of load by dropping traffic as the server approaches overload conditions. The goal is to keep the server from running out of RAM, failing health checks, serving with extremely high latency, or any of the other symptoms associated with overload, while still doing as much useful work as it can.

One straightforward way to shed load is to do per-task throttling based on CPU, memory, or queue length; limiting queue length as discussed in "Queue Management" on page 266 is a form of this strategy. For example, one effective approach is to return an HTTP 503 (service unavailable) to any incoming request when there are more than a given number of client requests in flight.

Changing the queuing method from the standard *first-in, first-out* (FIFO) to *last-in, first-out* (LIFO) or using the *controlled delay* (CoDel) algorithm [Nic12] or similar approaches can reduce load by removing requests that are unlikely to be worth processing [Mau15]. If a user's web search is slow because an RPC has been queued for 10 seconds, there's a good chance the user has given up and refreshed their browser, issuing another request: there's no point in responding to the first one, since it will be ignored! This strategy works well when combined with propagating RPC deadlines throughout the stack, described in "Latency and Deadlines" on page 271.

More sophisticated approaches include identifying clients to be more selective about what work is dropped, or picking requests that are more important and prioritizing. Such strategies are more likely to be needed for shared services.

Graceful degradation takes the concept of load shedding one step further by reducing the amount of work that needs to be performed. In some applications, it's possible to significantly decrease the amount of work or time needed by decreasing the quality of responses. For instance, a search application might only search a subset of data stored in an in-memory cache rather than the full on-disk database or use a less-accurate (but faster) ranking algorithm when overloaded.

When evaluating load shedding or graceful degradation options for your service, consider the following:

- Which metrics should you use to determine when load shedding or graceful degradation should kick in (e.g,. CPU usage, latency, queue length, number of threads used, whether your service enters degraded mode automatically or if manual intervention is necessary)?

- What actions should be taken when the server is in degraded mode?
- At what layer should load shedding and graceful degradation be implemented? Does it make sense to implement these strategies at every layer in the stack, or is it sufficient to have a high-level choke-point?

As you evaluate options and deploy, keep the following in mind:

- Graceful degradation shouldn't trigger very often—usually in cases of a capacity planning failure or unexpected load shift. Keep the system simple and understandable, particularly if it isn't used often.
- Remember that the code path you never use is the code path that (often) doesn't work. In steady-state operation, graceful degradation mode won't be used, implying that you'll have much less operational experience with this mode and any of its quirks, which *increases* the level of risk. You can make sure that graceful degradation stays working by regularly running a small subset of servers near overload in order to exercise this code path.
- Monitor and alert when too many servers enter these modes.
- Complex load shedding and graceful degradation can cause problems themselves —excessive complexity may cause the server to trip into a degraded mode when it is not desired, or enter feedback cycles at undesired times. Design a way to quickly turn off complex graceful degradation or tune parameters if needed. Storing this configuration in a consistent system that each server can watch for changes, such as Chubby, can increase deployment speed, but also introduces its own risks of synchronized failure.

Retries

Suppose the code in the frontend that talks to the backend implements retries naively. It retries after encountering a failure and caps the number of backend RPCs per logical request to 10. Consider this code in the frontend, using gRPC in Go:

```go
func exampleRpcCall(client pb.ExampleClient, request pb.Request) *pb.Response {

    // Set RPC timeout to 5 seconds.
    opts := grpc.WithTimeout(5 * time.Second)

    // Try up to 20 times to make the RPC call.
    attempts := 20
    for attempts > 0 {
        conn, err := grpc.Dial(*serverAddr, opts...)
        if err != nil {
            // Something went wrong in setting up the connection.  Try again.
            attempts--
            continue
```

```
    }
    defer conn.Close()

    // Create a client stub and make the RPC call.
    client := pb.NewBackendClient(conn)
    response, err := client.MakeRequest(context.Background, request)
    if err != nil {
        // Something went wrong in making the call. Try again.
        attempts--
        continue
    }

    return response
}

grpclog.Fatalf("ran out of attempts")
}
```

This system can cascade in the following way:

1. Assume our backend has a known limit of 10,000 QPS per task, after which point all further requests are rejected in an attempt at graceful degradation.

2. The frontend calls MakeRequest at a constant rate of 10,100 QPS and overloads the backend by 100 QPS, which the backend rejects.

3. Those 100 failed QPS are retried in MakeRequest every 1,000 ms, and probably succeed. But the retries are themselves adding to the requests sent to the backend, which now receives 10,200 QPS—200 QPS of which are failing due to overload.

4. The volume of retries grows: 100 QPS of retries in the first second leads to 200 QPS, then to 300 QPS, and so on. Fewer and fewer requests are able to succeed on their first attempt, so less useful work is being performed as a fraction of requests to the backend.

5. If the backend task is unable to handle the increase in load—which is consuming file descriptors, memory, and CPU time on the backend—it can melt down and crash under the sheer load of requests and retries. This crash then redistributes the requests it was receiving across the remaining backend tasks, in turn further overloading those tasks.

Some simplifying assumptions were made here to illustrate this scenario,[4] but the point remains that retries can destabilize a system. Note that both temporary load spikes and slow increases in usage can cause this effect.

---

4 An instructive exercise, left for the reader: write a simple simulator and see how the amount of useful work the backend can do varies with how much it's overloaded and how many retries are permitted.

Even if the rate of calls to MakeRequest decreases to pre-meltdown levels (9,000 QPS, for example), depending on how much returning a failure costs the backend, the problem might not go away. Two factors are at play here:

- If the backend spends a significant amount of resources processing requests that will ultimately fail due to overload, then the retries themselves may be keeping the backend in an overloaded mode.

- The backend servers themselves may not be stable. Retries can amplify the effects seen in "Server Overload" on page 260.

If either of these conditions is true, in order to dig out of this outage, you must dramatically reduce or eliminate the load on the frontends until the retries stop and the backends stabilize.

This pattern has contributed to several cascading failures, whether the frontends and backends communicate via RPC messages, the "frontend" is client JavaScript code issuing XmlHttpRequest calls to an endpoint and retries on failure, or the retries originate from an offline sync protocol that retries aggressively when it encounters a failure.

When issuing automatic retries, keep in mind the following considerations:

- Most of the backend protection strategies described in "Preventing Server Overload" on page 265 apply. In particular, testing the system can highlight problems, and graceful degradation can reduce the effect of the retries on the backend.

- Always use randomized exponential backoff when scheduling retries. See also "Exponential Backoff and Jitter" (*http://www.awsarchitectureblog.com/2015/03/backoff.html*) in the AWS Architecture Blog [Bro15]. If retries aren't randomly distributed over the retry window, a small perturbation (e.g., a network blip) can cause retry ripples to schedule at the same time, which can then amplify themselves [Flo94].

- Limit retries per request. Don't retry a given request indefinitely.

- Consider having a server-wide retry budget. For example, only allow 60 retries per minute in a process, and if the retry budget is exceeded, don't retry; just fail the request. This strategy can contain the retry effect and be the difference between a capacity planning failure that leads to some dropped queries and a global cascading failure.

- Think about the service holistically and decide if you really need to perform retries at a given level. In particular, avoid amplifying retries by issuing retries at multiple levels: a single request at the highest layer may produce a number of attempts as large as the *product* of the number of attempts at each layer to the lowest layer. If the database can't service requests because it's overloaded, and the backend, frontend, and JavaScript layers all issue 3 retries (4 attempts), then a single user action may create 64 attempts (4^3) on the database. This behavior is undesirable when the database is returning those errors because it's overloaded.

- Use clear response codes and consider how different failure modes should be handled. For example, separate retriable and nonretriable error conditions. Don't retry permanent errors or malformed requests in a client, because neither will ever succeed. Return a specific status when overloaded so that clients and other layers back off and do not retry.

In an emergency, it may not be obvious that an outage is due to bad retry behavior. Graphs of retry rates can be an indication of bad retry behavior, but may be confused as a symptom instead of a compounding cause. In terms of mitigation, this is a special case of the insufficient capacity problem, with the additional caveat that you must either fix the retry behavior (usually requiring a code push), reduce load significantly, or cut requests off entirely.

Latency and Deadlines

When a frontend sends an RPC to a backend server, the frontend consumes resources waiting for a reply. RPC deadlines define how long a request can wait before the frontend gives up, limiting the time that the backend may consume the frontend's resources.

Picking a deadline

It's usually wise to set a deadline. Setting either no deadline or an extremely high deadline may cause short-term problems that have long since passed to continue to consume server resources until the server restarts.

High deadlines can result in resource consumption in higher levels of the stack when lower levels of the stack are having problems. Short deadlines can cause some more expensive requests to fail consistently. Balancing these constraints to pick a good deadline can be something of an art.

Missing deadlines

A common theme in many cascading outages is that servers spend resources handling requests that will exceed their deadlines on the client. As a result, resources are spent while no progress is made: you don't get credit for late assignments with RPCs.

Suppose an RPC has a 10-second deadline, as set by the client. The server is very overloaded, and as a result, it takes 11 seconds to move from a queue to a thread pool. At this point, the client has already given up on the request. Under most circumstances, it would be unwise for the server to attempt to handle this request, because it would be doing work for which no credit will be granted—the client doesn't care what work the server does after the deadline has passed, because it's given up on the request already.

If handling a request is performed over multiple stages (e.g., there are a few callbacks and RPC calls), the server should check the deadline left at each stage before attempting to perform any more work on the request. For example, if a request is split into parsing, backend request, and processing stages, it may make sense to check that there is enough time left to handle the request before each stage.

Deadline propagation

Rather than inventing a deadline when sending RPCs to backends, servers should employ deadline propagation and cancellation propagation.

With deadline propagation, a deadline is set high in the stack (e.g., in the frontend). The tree of RPCs emanating from an initial request will all have the same absolute deadline. For example, if server A selects a 30-second deadline, and processes the request for 7 seconds before sending an RPC to server B, the RPC from A to B will have a 23-second deadline. If server B takes 4 seconds to handle the request and sends an RPC to server C, the RPC from B to C will have a 19-second deadline, and so on. Ideally, each server in the request tree implements deadline propagation.

Without deadline propagation, the following scenario may occur:

1. Server A sends an RPC to server B with a 10-second deadline.
2. Server B takes 8 seconds to start processing the request and then sends an RPC to server C.
3. If server B uses deadline propagation, it should set a 2-second deadline, but suppose it instead uses a hardcoded 20-second deadline for the RPC to server C.
4. Server C pulls the request off its queue after 5 seconds.

Had server B used deadline propagation, server C could immediately give up on the request because the 2-second deadline was exceeded. However, in this scenario, server C processes the request thinking it has 15 seconds to spare, but is not doing useful work, since the request from server A to server B has already exceeded its deadline.

You may want to reduce the outgoing deadline a bit (e.g., a few hundred milliseconds) to account for network transit times and post-processing in the client.

Also consider setting an upper bound for outgoing deadlines. You may want to limit how long the server waits for outgoing RPCs to noncritical backends, or for RPCs to backends that typically complete in a short duration. However, be sure to understand your traffic mix, because you might otherwise inadvertently make particular types of requests fail all the time (e.g., requests with large payloads, or requests that require responding to a lot of computation).

There are some exceptions for which servers may wish to continue processing a request after the deadline has elapsed. For example, if a server receives a request that involves performing some expensive catchup operation and periodically checkpoints the progress of the catchup, it would be a good idea to check the deadline only after writing the checkpoint, instead of after the expensive operation.

Propagating cancellations avoids the potential RPC leakage that occurs if an initial RPC has a long deadline, but RPCs between deeper layers of the stack have short deadlines and time out. Using simple deadline propagation, the initial RPC continues to use server resources until it eventually times out, despite being unable to make progress.

Bimodal latency

Suppose that the frontend from the preceding example consists of 10 servers, each with 100 worker threads. This means that the frontend has a total of 1,000 threads of capacity. During usual operation, the frontends perform 1,000 QPS and requests complete in 100 ms. This means that the frontends usually have 100 worker threads occupied out of the 1,000 configured worker threads (1,000 QPS * 0.1 seconds).

Suppose an event causes 5% of the requests to never complete. This could be the result of the unavailability of some Bigtable row ranges, which renders the requests corresponding to that Bigtable keyspace unservable. As a result, 5% of the requests hit the deadline, while the remaining 95% of the requests take the usual 100 ms.

With a 100-second deadline, 5% of requests would consume 5,000 threads (50 QPS * 100 seconds), but the frontend doesn't have that many threads available. Assuming no other secondary effects, the frontend will only be able to handle 19.6% of the requests (1,000 threads available / (5,000 + 95) threads' worth of work), resulting in an 80.4% error rate.

Therefore, instead of only 5% of requests receiving an error (those that didn't complete due to keyspace unavailability), most requests receive an error.

The following guidelines can help address this class of problems:

- Detecting this problem can be very hard. In particular, it may not be clear that bimodal latency is the cause of an outage when you are looking at *mean* latency. When you see a latency increase, try to look at the *distribution* of latencies in addition to the averages.

- This problem can be avoided if the requests that don't complete return with an error early, rather than waiting the full deadline. For example, if a backend is unavailable, it's usually best to immediately return an error for that backend, rather than consuming resources until it the backend available. If your RPC layer supports a fail-fast option, use it.

- Having deadlines several orders of magnitude longer than the mean request latency is usually bad. In the preceding example, a small number of requests initially hit the deadline, but the deadline was three orders of magnitude larger than the normal mean latency, leading to thread exhaustion.

- When using shared resources that can be exhausted by some keyspace, consider either limiting in-flight requests by that keyspace or using other kinds of abuse tracking. Suppose your backend processes requests for different clients that have wildly different performance and request characteristics. You might consider only allowing 25% of your threads to be occupied by any one client in order to provide fairness in the face of heavy load by any single client misbehaving.

Slow Startup and Cold Caching

Processes are often slower at responding to requests immediately after starting than they will be in steady state. This slowness can be caused by either or both of the following:

Required initialization
Setting up connections upon receiving the first request that needs a given backend

Runtime performance improvements in some languages, particularly Java
Just-In-Time compilation, hotspot optimization, and deferred class loading

Similarly, some binaries are less efficient when caches aren't filled. For example, in the case of some of Google's services, most requests are served out of caches, so requests that miss the cache are significantly more expensive. In steady-state operation with a warm cache, only a few cache misses occur, but when the cache is completely empty, 100% of requests are costly. Other services might employ caches to keep a user's state in RAM. This might be accomplished through hard or soft stickiness between reverse proxies and service frontends.

If the service is not provisioned to handle requests under a cold cache, it's at greater risk of outages and should take steps to avoid them.

The following scenarios can lead to a cold cache:

Turning up a new cluster
A recently added cluster will have an empty cache.

Returning a cluster to service after maintenance
The cache may be stale.

Restarts

If a task with a cache has recently restarted, filling its cache will take some time. It may be worthwhile to move caching from a server to a separate binary like memcache, which also allows cache sharing between many servers, albeit at the cost of introducing another RPC and slight additional latency.

If caching has a significant effect on the service,[5] you may want to use one or some of the following strategies:

- Overprovision the service. It's important to note the distinction between a latency cache versus a capacity cache: when a latency cache is employed, the service can sustain its expected load with an empty cache, but a service using a capacity cache cannot sustain its expected load under an empty cache. Service owners should be vigilant about adding caches to their service, and make sure that any new caches are either latency caches or are sufficiently well engineered to safely function as capacity caches. Sometimes caches are added to a service to improve performance, but actually wind up being hard dependencies.

- Employ general cascading failure prevention techniques. In particular, servers should reject requests when they're overloaded or enter degraded modes, and testing should be performed to see how the service behaves after events such as a large restart.

- When adding load to a cluster, slowly increase the load. The initially small request rate warms up the cache; once the cache is warm, more traffic can be added. It's a good idea to ensure that all clusters carry nominal load and that the caches are kept warm.

Always Go Downward in the Stack

In the example Shakespeare service, the frontend talks to a backend, which in turn talks to the storage layer. A problem that manifests in the storage layer can cause problems for servers that talk to it, but fixing the storage layer will usually repair both the backend and frontend layers.

However, suppose the backends cross-communicate amongst each other. For example, the backends might proxy requests to one another to change who owns a user when the storage layer can't service a request. This intra-layer communication can be problematic for several reasons:

---

5 Sometimes you find that a meaningful proportion of your actual serving capacity is as a function of serving from a cache, and if you lost access to that cache, you wouldn't actually be able to serve that many queries. A similar observation holds for latency: a cache can help you achieve latency goals (by lowering the average response time when the query is servable from cache) that you possibly couldn't meet without that cache.

- The communication is susceptible to a distributed deadlock. Backends may use the same thread pool to wait on RPCs sent to remote backends that are simultaneously receiving requests from remote backends. Suppose backend *A*'s thread pool is full. Backend *B* sends a request to backend *A* and uses a thread in backend *B* until backend *A*'s thread pool clears. This behavior can cause the thread pool saturation to spread.

- If intra-layer communication increases in response to some kind of failure or heavy load condition (e.g., load rebalancing that is more active under high load), intra-layer communication can quickly switch from a low to high intra-layer request mode when the load increases enough.

  For example, suppose a user has a primary backend and a predetermined hot standby secondary backend in a different cluster that can take over the user. The primary backend proxies requests to the secondary backend as a result of errors from the lower layer or in response to heavy load on the master. If the entire system is overloaded, primary to secondary proxying will likely increase and add even more load to the system, due to the additional cost of parsing and waiting on the request to the secondary in the primary.

- Depending on the criticality of the cross-layer communication, bootstrapping the system may become more complex.

  It's usually better to avoid intra-layer communication—i.e., possible cycles in the communication path—in the user request path. Instead, have the client do the communication. For example, if a frontend talks to a backend but guesses the wrong backend, the backend should not proxy to the correct backend. Instead, the backend should tell the frontend to retry its request on the correct backend.

Triggering Conditions for Cascading Failures

When a service is susceptible to cascading failures, there are several possible disturbances that can initiate the domino effect. This section identifies some of the factors that trigger cascading failures.

Process Death

Some server tasks may die, reducing the amount of available capacity. Tasks might die because of a Query of Death (an RPC whose contents trigger a failure in the process), cluster issues, assertion failures, or a number of other reasons. A very small event (e.g., a couple of crashes or tasks rescheduled to other machines) may cause a service on the brink of falling to break.

Process Updates

Pushing a new version of the binary or updating its configuration may initiate a cascading failure if a large number of tasks are affected simultaneously. To prevent this scenario, either account for necessary capacity overhead when setting up the service's update infrastructure, or push off-peak. Dynamically adjusting the number of in-flight task updates based on the volume of requests and available capacity may be a workable approach.

New Rollouts

A new binary, configuration changes, or a change to the underlying infrastructure stack can result in changes to request profiles, resource usage and limits, backends, or a number of other system components that can trigger a cascading failure.

During a cascading failure, it's usually wise to check for recent changes and consider reverting them, particularly if those changes affected capacity or altered the request profile.

Your service should implement some type of change logging, which can help quickly identify recent changes.

Organic Growth

In many cases, a cascading failure isn't triggered by a specific service change, but because a growth in usage wasn't accompanied by an adjustment to capacity.

Planned Changes, Drains, or Turndowns

If your service is multihomed, some of your capacity may be unavailable because of maintenance or outages in a cluster. Similarly, one of the service's critical dependencies may be drained, resulting in a reduction in capacity for the upstream service due to drain dependencies, or an increase in latency due to having to send the requests to a more distant cluster.

Request profile changes

A backend service may receive requests from different clusters because a frontend service shifted its traffic due to load balancing configuration changes, changes in the traffic mix, or cluster fullness. Also, the average cost to handle an individual payload may have changed due to frontend code or configuration changes. Similarly, the data handled by the service may have changed organically due to increased or differing usage by existing users: for instance, both the number and size of images, *per user*, for a photo storage service tend to increase over time.

Resource limits

Some cluster operating systems allow resource overcommitment. CPU is a fungible resource; often, some machines have some amount of slack CPU available, which provides a bit of a safety net against CPU spikes. The availability of this slack CPU differs between cells, and also between machines within the cell.

Depending upon this slack CPU as your safety net is dangerous. Its availability is entirely dependent on the behavior of the other jobs in the cluster, so it might suddenly drop out at any time. For example, if a team starts a MapReduce that consumes a lot of CPU and schedules on many machines, the aggregate amount of slack CPU can suddenly decrease and trigger CPU starvation conditions for unrelated jobs. When performing load tests, make sure that you remain within your committed resource limits.

Testing for Cascading Failures

The specific ways in which a service will fail can be very hard to predict from first principles. This section discusses testing strategies that can detect if services are susceptible to cascading failures.

You should test your service to determine how it behaves under heavy load in order to gain confidence that it won't enter a cascading failure under various circumstances.

Test Until Failure and Beyond

Understanding the behavior of the service under heavy load is perhaps the most important first step in avoiding cascading failures. Knowing how your system behaves when it is overloaded helps to identify what engineering tasks are the most important for long-term fixes; at the very least, this knowledge may help bootstrap the debugging process for on-call engineers when an emergency arises.

Load test components until they break. As load increases, a component typically handles requests successfully until it reaches a point at which it can't handle more requests. At this point, the component should ideally start serving errors or degraded results in response to additional load, but not significantly reduce the rate at which it successfully handles requests. A component that is highly susceptible to a cascading failure will start crashing or serving a very high rate of errors when it becomes overloaded; a better designed component will instead be able to reject a few requests and survive.

Load testing also reveals where the breaking point is, knowledge that's fundamental to the capacity planning process. It enables you to test for regressions, provision for worst-case thresholds, and to trade off utilization versus safety margins.

Because of caching effects, gradually ramping up load may yield different results than immediately increasing to expected load levels. Therefore, consider testing both gradual and impulse load patterns.

You should also test and understand how the component behaves as it returns to nominal load after having been pushed well beyond that load. Such testing may answer questions such as:

- If a component enters a degraded mode on heavy load, is it capable of exiting the degraded mode without human intervention?
- If a couple of servers crash under heavy load, how much does the load need to drop in order for the system to stabilize?

If you're load testing a stateful service or a service that employs caching, your load test should track state between multiple interactions and check correctness at high load, which is often where subtle concurrency bugs hit.

Keep in mind that individual components may have different breaking points, so load test each component separately. You won't know in advance which component may hit the wall first, and you want to know how your system behaves when it does.

If you believe your system has proper protections against being overloaded, consider performing failure tests in a small slice of production to find the point at which the components in your system fail under real traffic. These limits may not be adequately reflected by synthetic load test traffic, so real traffic tests may provide more realistic results than load tests, at the risk of causing user-visible pain. Be careful when testing on real traffic: make sure that you have extra capacity available in case your automatic protections don't work and you need to manually fail over. You might consider some of the following production tests:

- Reducing task counts quickly or slowly over time, beyond expected traffic patterns
- Rapidly losing a cluster's worth of capacity
- Blackholing various backends

Test Popular Clients

Understand how large clients use your service. For example, you want to know if clients:

- Can queue work while the service is down
- Use randomized exponential backoff on errors

- Are vulnerable to external triggers that can create large amounts of load (e.g., an externally triggered software update might clear an offline client's cache)

Depending on your service, you may or may not be in control of all the client code that talks to your service. However, it's still a good idea to have an understanding of how large clients that interact with your service will behave.

The same principles apply to large internal clients. Stage system failures with the largest clients to see how they react. Ask internal clients how they access your service and what mechanisms they use to handle backend failure.

Test Noncritical Backends

Test your noncritical backends, and make sure their unavailability does not interfere with the critical components of your service.

For example, suppose your frontend has critical and noncritical backends. Often, a given request includes both critical components (e.g., query results) and noncritical components (e.g., spelling suggestions). Your requests may significantly slow down and consume resources waiting for noncritical backends to finish.

In addition to testing behavior when the noncritical backend is unavailable, test how the frontend behaves if the noncritical backend never responds (for example, if it is blackholing requests). Backends advertised as noncritical can still cause problems on frontends when requests have long deadlines. The frontend should not start rejecting lots of requests, running out of resources, or serving with very high latency when a noncritical backend blackholes.

Immediate Steps to Address Cascading Failures

Once you have identified that your service is experiencing a cascading failure, you can use a few different strategies to remedy the situation—and of course, a cascading failure is a good opportunity to use your incident management protocol (Chapter 14).

Increase Resources

If your system is running at degraded capacity and you have idle resources, adding tasks can be the most expedient way to recover from the outage. However, if the service has entered a death spiral of some sort, adding more resources may not be sufficient to recover.

Stop Health Check Failures/Deaths

Some cluster scheduling systems, such as Borg, check the health of tasks in a job and restart tasks that are unhealthy. This practice may create a failure mode in which health-checking itself makes the service unhealthy. For example, if half the tasks aren't able to accomplish any work because they're starting up and the other half will soon be killed because they're overloaded and failing health checks, temporarily disabling health checks may permit the system to stabilize until all the tasks are running.

Process health checking ("is this binary responding *at all*?") and service health checking ("is this binary able to respond to *this class of requests* right now?") are two conceptually distinct operations. Process health checking is relevant to the cluster scheduler, whereas service health checking is relevant to the load balancer. Clearly distinguishing between the two types of health checks can help avoid this scenario.

Restart Servers

If servers are somehow wedged and not making progress, restarting them may help. Try restarting servers when:

- Java servers are in a GC death spiral
- Some in-flight requests have no deadlines but are consuming resources, leading them to block threads, for example
- The servers are deadlocked

Make sure that you identify the source of the cascading failure before you restart your servers. Make sure that taking this action won't simply shift around load. Canary this change, and make it slowly. Your actions may amplify an existing cascading failure if the outage is actually due to an issue like a cold cache.

Drop Traffic

Dropping load is a big hammer, usually reserved for situations in which you have a true cascading failure on your hands and you cannot fix it by other means. For example, if heavy load causes most servers to crash as soon as they become healthy, you can get the service up and running again by:

1. Addressing the initial triggering condition (by adding capacity, for example).
2. Reducing load enough so that the crashing stops. Consider being aggressive here —if the entire service is crash-looping, only allow, say, 1% of the traffic through.
3. Allowing the majority of the servers to become healthy.
4. Gradually ramping up the load.

This strategy allows caches to warm up, connections to be established, etc., before load returns to normal levels.

Obviously, this tactic will cause a lot of user-visible harm. Whether or not you're able to (or if you even *should*) drop traffic indiscriminately depends on how the service is configured. If you have some mechanism to drop less important traffic (e.g., prefetching), use that mechanism first.

It is important to keep in mind that this strategy enables you to recover from a cascading outage once the underlying problem is fixed. If the issue that started the cascading failure is not fixed (e.g., insufficient global capacity), then the cascading failure may trigger shortly after all traffic returns. Therefore, before using this strategy, consider fixing (or at least papering over) the root cause or triggering condition. For example, if the service ran out of memory and is now in a death spiral, adding more memory or tasks should be your first step.

Enter Degraded Modes

Serve degraded results by doing less work or dropping unimportant traffic. This strategy must be engineered into your service, and can be implemented only if you know which traffic can be degraded and you have the ability to differentiate between the various payloads.

Eliminate Batch Load

Some services have load that is important, but not critical. Consider turning off those sources of load. For example, if index updates, data copies, or statistics gathering consume resources of the serving path, consider turning off those sources of load during an outage.

Eliminate Bad Traffic

If some queries are creating heavy load or crashes (e.g., queries of death), consider blocking them or eliminating them via other means.

Cascading Failure and Shakespeare

A documentary about Shakespeare's works airs in Japan, and explicitly points to our Shakespeare service as an excellent place to conduct further research. Following the broadcast, traffic to our Asian datacenter surges beyond the service's capacity. This capacity problem is further compounded by a major update to the Shakespeare service that simultaneously occurs in that datacenter.

Fortunately, a number of safeguards are in place that help mitigate the potential for failure. The Production Readiness Review process identified some issues that the team already addressed. For example, the developers built graceful degradation into the service. As capacity becomes scarce, the service no longer returns pictures alongside text or small maps illustrating where a story takes place. And depending on its purpose, an RPC that times out is either not retried (for example, in the case of the aforementioned pictures), or is retried with a randomized exponential backoff. Despite these safeguards, the tasks fail one by one and are then restarted by Borg, which drives the number of working tasks down even more.

As a result, some graphs on the service dashboard turn an alarming shade of red and SRE is paged. In response, SREs temporarily add capacity to the Asian datacenter by increasing the number of tasks available for the Shakespeare job. By doing so, they're able to restore the Shakespeare service in the Asian cluster.

Afterward, the SRE team writes a postmortem detailing the chain of events, what went well, what could have gone better, and a number of action items to prevent this scenario from occurring again. For example, in the case of a service overload, the GSLB load balancer will redirect some traffic to neighboring datacenters. Also, the SRE team turns on autoscaling, so that the number of tasks automatically increases with traffic, so they don't have to worry about this type of issue again.

Closing Remarks

When systems are overloaded, something needs to give in order to remedy the situation. Once a service passes its breaking point, it is better to allow some user-visible errors or lower-quality results to slip through than try to fully serve every request. Understanding where those breaking points are and how the system behaves beyond them is critical for service owners who want to avoid cascading failures.

Without proper care, some system changes meant to reduce background errors or otherwise improve the steady state can expose the service to greater risk of a full outage. Retrying on failures, shifting load around from unhealthy servers, killing unhealthy servers, adding caches to improve performance or reduce latency: all of these might be implemented to improve the normal case, but can improve the chance of causing a large-scale failure. Be careful when evaluating changes to ensure that one outage is not being traded for another.

CHAPTER 23

Managing Critical State: Distributed Consensus for Reliability

Written by Laura Nolan
Edited by Tim Harvey

Processes crash or may need to be restarted. Hard drives fail. Natural disasters can take out several datacenters in a region. Site Reliability Engineers need to anticipate these sorts of failures and develop strategies to keep systems running in spite of them. These strategies usually entail running such systems across multiple sites. Geographically distributing a system is relatively straightforward, but also introduces the need to maintain a consistent view of system state, which is a more nuanced and difficult undertaking.

Groups of processes may want to reliably agree on questions such as:

- Which process is the leader of a group of processes?
- What is the set of processes in a group?
- Has a message been successfully committed to a distributed queue?
- Does a process hold a lease or not?
- What is a value in a datastore for a given key?

We've found distributed consensus to be effective in building reliable and highly available systems that require a consistent view of some system state. The distributed consensus problem deals with reaching agreement among a group of processes connected by an unreliable communications network. For instance, several processes in a distributed system may need to be able to form a consistent view of a critical piece of configuration, whether or not a distributed lock is held, or if a message on a queue has been processed. It is one of the most fundamental concepts in distributed computing and one we rely on for virtually every service we offer. Figure 23-1 illustrates a simple model of how a group of processes can achieve a consistent view of system state through distributed consensus.

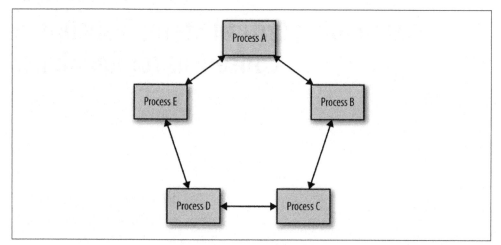

Figure 23-1. Distributed consensus: agreement among a group of processes

Whenever you see leader election, critical shared state, or distributed locking, we recommend using *distributed consensus systems that have been formally proven and tested thoroughly*. Informal approaches to solving this problem can lead to outages, and more insidiously, to subtle and hard-to-fix data consistency problems that may prolong outages in your system unnecessarily.

CAP Theorem

The CAP theorem ([Fox99], [Bre12]) holds that a distributed system cannot simultaneously have all three of the following properties:

- Consistent views of the data at each node
- Availability of the data at each node
- Tolerance to network partitions [Gil02]

The logic is intuitive: if two nodes can't communicate (because the network is partitioned), then the system as a whole can either stop serving some or all requests at some or all nodes (thus reducing availability), or it can serve requests as usual, which results in inconsistent views of the data at each node.

Because network partitions are inevitable (cables get cut, packets get lost or delayed due to congestion, hardware breaks, networking components become misconfigured, etc.), understanding distributed consensus really amounts to understanding how consistency and availability work for your particular application. Commercial pressures often demand high levels of availability, and many applications require consistent views on their data.

Systems and software engineers are usually familiar with the traditional ACID datastore semantics (Atomicity, Consistency, Isolation, and Durability), but a growing number of distributed datastore technologies provide a different set of semantics known as BASE (Basically Available, Soft state, and Eventual consistency). Datastores that support BASE semantics have useful applications for certain kinds of data and can handle large volumes of data and transactions that would be much more costly, and perhaps altogether infeasible, with datastores that support ACID semantics.

Most of these systems that support BASE semantics rely on multimaster replication, where writes can be committed to different processes concurrently, and there is some mechanism to resolve conflicts (often as simple as "latest timestamp wins"). This approach is usually known as *eventual consistency*. However, eventual consistency can lead to surprising results [Lu15], particularly in the event of *clock drift* (which is inevitable in distributed systems) or network partitioning [Kin15].[1]

It is also difficult for developers to design systems that work well with datastores that support only BASE semantics. Jeff Shute [Shu13], for example, has stated, "we find developers spend a significant fraction of their time building extremely complex and error-prone mechanisms to cope with eventual consistency and handle data that may be out of date. We think this is an unacceptable burden to place on developers and that consistency problems should be solved at the database level."

System designers cannot sacrifice correctness in order to achieve reliability or performance, particularly around critical state. For example, consider a system that handles financial transactions: reliability or performance requirements don't provide much value if the financial data is not correct. Systems need to be able to reliably synchronize critical state across multiple processes. Distributed consensus algorithms provide this functionality.

---

1 Kyle Kingsbury has written an extensive series of articles on distributed systems correctness, which contain many examples of unexpected and incorrect behavior in these kinds of datastores. See *https://aphyr.com/tags/jepsen*.

Motivating the Use of Consensus: Distributed Systems Coordination Failure

Distributed systems are complex and subtle to understand, monitor, and trouble-shoot. Engineers running such systems are often surprised by behavior in the presence of failures. Failures are relatively rare events, and it is not a usual practice to test systems under these conditions. It is very difficult to reason about system behavior during failures. Network partitions are particularly challenging—a problem that appears to be caused by a full partition may instead be the result of:

- A very slow network
- Some, but not all, messages being dropped
- Throttle occurring in one direction, but not the other direction

The following sections provide examples of problems that occurred in real-world distributed systems and discuss how leader election and distributed consensus algorithms could be used to prevent such issues.

Case Study 1: The Split-Brain Problem

A service is a content repository that allows collaboration between multiple users. It uses sets of two replicated file servers in different racks for reliability. The service needs to avoid writing data simultaneously to both file servers in a set, because doing so could result in data corruption (and possibly unrecoverable data).

Each pair of file servers has one leader and one follower. The servers monitor each other via heartbeats. If one file server cannot contact its partner, it issues a STONITH (Shoot The Other Node in the Head) command to its partner node to shut the node down, and then takes mastership of its files. This practice is an industry standard method of reducing split-brain instances, although as we shall see, it is conceptually unsound.

What happens if the network becomes slow, or starts dropping packets? In this scenario, file servers exceed their heartbeat timeouts and, as designed, send STONITH commands to their partner nodes and take mastership. However, some commands may not be delivered due to the compromised network. File server pairs may now be in a state in which both nodes are expected to be active for the same resource, or where both are down because both issued and received STONITH commands. This results in either corruption or unavailability of data.

The problem here is that the system is trying to solve a leader election problem using simple timeouts. Leader election is a reformulation of the distributed asynchronous consensus problem, which cannot be solved correctly by using heartbeats.

Case Study 2: Failover Requires Human Intervention

A highly sharded database system has a primary for each shard, which replicates synchronously to a secondary in another datacenter. An external system checks the health of the primaries, and, if they are no longer healthy, promotes the secondary to primary. If the primary can't determine the health of its secondary, it makes itself unavailable and escalates to a human in order to avoid the split-brain scenario seen in Case Study 1.

This solution doesn't risk data loss, but it does negatively impact availability of data. It also unnecessarily increases operational load on the engineers who run the system, and human intervention scales poorly. This sort of event, where a primary and secondary have problems communicating, is highly likely to occur in the case of a larger infrastructure problem, when the responding engineers may already be overloaded with other tasks. If the network is so badly affected that a distributed consensus system cannot elect a master, a human is likely not better positioned to do so.

Case Study 3: Faulty Group-Membership Algorithms

A system has a component that performs indexing and searching services. When starting, nodes use a gossip protocol to discover each other and join the cluster. The cluster elects a leader, which performs coordination. In the case of a network partition that splits the cluster, each side (incorrectly) elects a master and accepts writes and deletions, leading to a split-brain scenario and data corruption.

The problem of determining a consistent view of group membership across a group of processes is another instance of the distributed consensus problem.

In fact, many distributed systems problems turn out to be different versions of distributed consensus, including master election, group membership, all kinds of distributed locking and leasing, reliable distributed queuing and messaging, and maintenance of any kind of critical shared state that must be viewed consistently across a group of processes. All of these problems should be solved only using distributed consensus algorithms that have been proven formally correct, and whose implementations have been tested extensively. Ad hoc means of solving these sorts of problems (such as heartbeats and gossip protocols) will always have reliability problems in practice.

How Distributed Consensus Works

The consensus problem has multiple variants. When dealing with distributed software systems, we are interested in *asynchronous distributed consensus*, which applies to environments with potentially unbounded delays in message passing. (*Synchronous consensus* applies to real-time systems, in which dedicated hardware means that messages will always be passed with specific timing guarantees.)

Distributed consensus algorithms may be *crash-fail* (which assumes that crashed nodes never return to the system) or *crash-recover*. Crash-recover algorithms are much more useful, because most problems in real systems are transient in nature due to a slow network, restarts, and so on.

Algorithms may deal with Byzantine or non-Byzantine failures. *Byzantine failure* occurs when a process passes incorrect messages due to a bug or malicious activity, and are comparatively costly to handle, and less often encountered.

Technically, solving the asynchronous distributed consensus problem in bounded time is impossible. As proven by the Dijkstra Prize–winning *FLP impossibility result* [Fis85], no asynchronous distributed consensus algorithm can guarantee progress in the presence of an unreliable network.

In practice, we approach the distributed consensus problem in bounded time by ensuring that the system will have sufficient healthy replicas and network connectivity to make progress reliably most of the time. In addition, the system should have backoffs with randomized delays. This setup both prevents retries from causing cascade effects and avoids the dueling proposers problem described later in this chapter. The protocols guarantee safety, and adequate redundancy in the system encourages liveness.

The original solution to the distributed consensus problem was Lamport's Paxos protocol [Lam98], but other protocols exist that solve the problem, including Raft [Ong14], Zab [Jun11], and Mencius [Mao08]. Paxos itself has many variations intended to increase performance [Zoo14]. These usually vary only in a single detail, such as giving a special leader role to one process to streamline the protocol.

Paxos Overview: An Example Protocol

Paxos operates as a sequence of proposals, which may or may not be accepted by a majority of the processes in the system. If a proposal isn't accepted, it fails. Each proposal has a sequence number, which imposes a strict ordering on all of the operations in the system.

In the first phase of the protocol, the proposer sends a sequence number to the acceptors. Each acceptor will agree to accept the proposal only if it has not yet seen a proposal with a higher sequence number. Proposers can try again with a higher sequence number if necessary. Proposers must use unique sequence numbers (drawing from disjoint sets, or incorporating their hostname into the sequence number, for instance).

If a proposer receives agreement from a majority of the acceptors, it can commit the proposal by sending a commit message with a value.

The strict sequencing of proposals solves any problems relating to ordering of messages in the system. The requirement for a majority to commit means that two different values cannot be committed for the same proposal, because any two majorities will overlap in at least one node. Acceptors must write a journal on persistent storage whenever they agree to accept a proposal, because the acceptors need to honor these guarantees after restarting.

Paxos on its own isn't that useful: all it lets you do is to agree on a value and proposal number once. Because only a quorum of nodes need to agree on a value, any given node may not have a complete view of the set of values that have been agreed to. This limitation is true for most distributed consensus algorithms.

System Architecture Patterns for Distributed Consensus

Distributed consensus algorithms are low-level and primitive: they simply allow a set of nodes to agree on a value, once. They don't map well to real design tasks. What makes distributed consensus useful is the addition of higher-level system components such as datastores, configuration stores, queues, locking, and leader election services to provide the practical system functionality that distributed consensus algorithms don't address. Using higher-level components reduces complexity for system designers. It also allows underlying distributed consensus algorithms to be changed if necessary in response to changes in the environment in which the system runs or changes in nonfunctional requirements.

Many systems that successfully use consensus algorithms actually do so as clients of some service that implements those algorithms, such as Zookeeper, Consul, and etcd. Zookeeper [Hun10] was the first open source consensus system to gain traction in the industry because it was easy to use, even with applications that weren't designed to use distributed consensus. The Chubby service fills a similar niche at Google. Its authors point out [Bur06] that providing consensus primitives as a service rather than as libraries that engineers build into their applications frees application maintainers of having to deploy their systems in a way compatible with a highly available consensus service (running the right number of replicas, dealing with group membership, dealing with performance, etc.).

Reliable Replicated State Machines

A *replicated state machine* (RSM) is a system that executes the same set of operations, in the same order, on several processes. RSMs are the fundamental building block of useful distributed systems components and services such as data or configuration storage, locking, and leader election (described in more detail later).

The operations on an RSM are ordered globally through a consensus algorithm. This is a powerful concept: several papers ([Agu10], [Kir08], [Sch90]) show that any deterministic program can be implemented as a highly available replicated service by being implemented as an RSM.

As shown in Figure 23-2, replicated state machines are a system implemented at a logical layer above the consensus algorithm. The consensus algorithm deals with agreement on the sequence of operations, and the RSM executes the operations in that order. Because not every member of the consensus group is necessarily a member of each consensus quorum, RSMs may need to synchronize state from peers. As described by Kirsch and Amir [Kir08], you can use a *sliding-window protocol* to reconcile state between peer processes in an RSM.

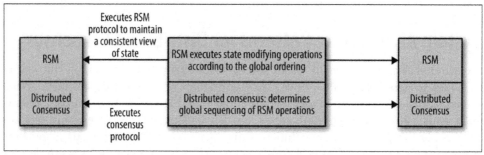

Figure 23-2. The relationship between consensus algorithms and replicated state machines

Reliable Replicated Datastores and Configuration Stores

Reliable replicated datastores are an application of replicated state machines. Replicated datastores use consensus algorithms in the critical path of their work. Thus, performance, throughput, and the ability to scale are very important in this type of design. As with datastores built with other underlying technologies, consensus-based datastores can provide a variety of consistency semantics for read operations, which make a huge difference to how the datastore scales. These trade-offs are discussed in "Distributed Consensus Performance" on page 296.

Other (nondistributed-consensus–based) systems often simply rely on timestamps to provide bounds on the age of data being returned. Timestamps are highly problematic in distributed systems because it's impossible to guarantee that clocks are synchronized across multiple machines. Spanner [Cor12] addresses this problem by modeling the worst-case uncertainty involved and slowing down processing where necessary to resolve that uncertainty.

Highly Available Processing Using Leader Election

Leader election in distributed systems is an equivalent problem to distributed consensus. Replicated services that use a single leader to perform some specific type of work in the system are very common; the single leader mechanism is a way of ensuring mutual exclusion at a coarse level.

This type of design is appropriate where the work of the service leader can be performed by one process or is sharded. System designers can construct a highly available service by writing it as though it was a simple program, replicating that process and using leader election to ensure that only one leader is working at any point in time (as shown in Figure 23-3). Often the work of the leader is that of coordinating some pool of workers in the system. This pattern was used in GFS [Ghe03] (which has been replaced by Colossus) and the Bigtable key-value store [Cha06].

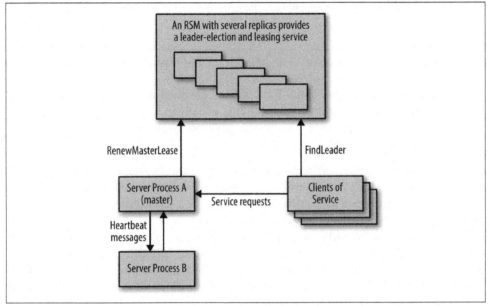

Figure 23-3. Highly available system using a replicated service for master election

In this type of component, unlike the replicated datastore, the consensus algorithm is not in the critical path of the main work the system is doing, so throughput is usually not a major concern.

Distributed Coordination and Locking Services

A *barrier* in a distributed computation is a primitive that blocks a group of processes from proceeding until some condition is met (for example, until all parts of one phase of a computation are completed). Use of a barrier effectively splits a distributed computation into logical phases. For instance, as shown in Figure 23-4, a barrier could be used in implementing the MapReduce [Dea04] model to ensure that the entire Map phase is completed before the Reduce part of the computation proceeds.

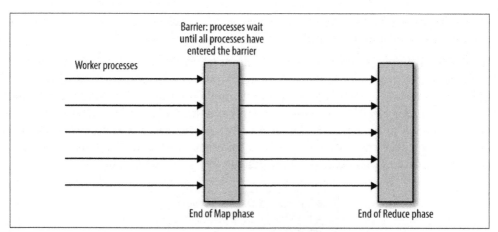

Figure 23-4. Barriers for process coordination in the MapReduce computation

The barrier could be implemented by a single coordinator process, but this implementation adds a single point of failure that is usually unacceptable. The barrier can also be implemented as an RSM. The Zookeeper consensus service can implement the barrier pattern: see [Hun10] and [Zoo14].

Locks are another useful coordination primitive that can be implemented as an RSM. Consider a distributed system in which worker processes atomically consume some input files and write results. Distributed locks can be used to prevent multiple workers from processing the same input file. In practice, it is essential to use renewable leases with timeouts instead of indefinite locks, because doing so prevents locks from being held indefinitely by processes that crash. Distributed locking is beyond the scope of this chapter, but bear in mind that distributed locks are a low-level systems primitive that should be used with care. Most applications should use a higher-level system that provides distributed transactions.

Reliable Distributed Queuing and Messaging

Queues are a common data structure, often used as a way to distribute tasks between a number of worker processes.

Queuing-based systems can tolerate failure and loss of worker nodes relatively easily. However, the system must ensure that claimed tasks are successfully processed. For that purpose, a *lease system* (discussed earlier in regard to locks) is recommended instead of an outright removal from the queue. The downside of queuing-based systems is that loss of the queue prevents the entire system from operating. Implementing the queue as an RSM can minimize the risk, and make the entire system far more robust.

Atomic broadcast is a distributed systems primitive in which messages are received reliably and in the same order by all participants. This is an incredibly powerful distributed systems concept and very useful in designing practical systems. A huge number of publish-subscribe messaging infrastructures exist for the use of system designers, although not all of them provide atomic guarantees. Chandra and Toueg [Cha96] demonstrate the equivalence of atomic broadcast and consensus.

The *queuing-as-work-distribution* pattern, which uses the queue as a load balancing device, as shown in Figure 23-5, can be considered to be point-to-point messaging. Messaging systems usually also implement a publish-subscribe queue, where messages may be consumed by many clients that subscribe to a channel or topic. In this one-to-many case, the messages on the queue are stored as a persistent ordered list. Publish-subscribe systems can be used for many types of applications that require clients to subscribe to receive notifications of some type of event. Publish-subscribe systems can also be used to implement coherent distributed caches.

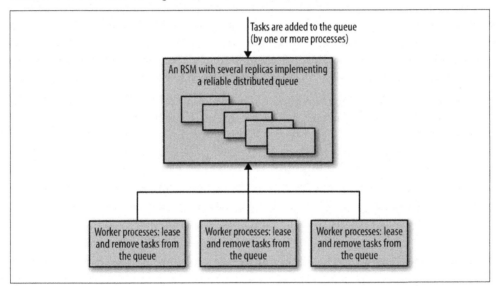

Figure 23-5. A queue-oriented work distribution system using a reliable consensus-based queuing component

Queuing and messaging systems often need excellent throughput, but don't need extremely low latency (due to seldom being directly user-facing). However, very high latencies in a system like the one just described, which has multiple workers claiming tasks from a queue, could become a problem if the percentage of processing time for each task grew significantly.

Distributed Consensus Performance

Conventional wisdom has generally held that consensus algorithms are too slow and costly to use for many systems that require high throughput *and* low latency [Bol11]. This conception is simply not true—while implementations can be slow, there are a number of tricks that can improve performance. Distributed consensus algorithms are at the core of many of Google's critical systems, described in [Ana13], [Bur06], [Cor12], and [Shu13], and they have proven extremely effective in practice. Google's scale is not an advantage here: in fact, our scale is more of a disadvantage because it introduces two main challenges: our datasets tend to be large and our systems run over a wide geographical distance. Larger datasets multiplied by several replicas represent significant computing costs, and larger geographical distances increase latency between replicas, which in turn reduces performance.

There is no one "best" distributed consensus and state machine replication algorithm for performance, because performance is dependent on a number of factors relating to workload, the system's performance objectives, and how the system is to be deployed.[2] While some of the following sections present research, with the aim of increasing understanding of what is possible to achieve with distributed consensus, many of the systems described are available and are in use now.

Workloads can vary in many ways and understanding how they can vary is critical to discussing performance. In the case of a consensus system, workload may vary in terms of:

- Throughput: the number of proposals being made per unit of time at peak load
- The type of requests: proportion of operations that change state
- The consistency semantics required for read operations
- Request sizes, if size of data payload can vary

Deployment strategies vary, too. For example:

- Is the deployment local area or wide area?
- What kinds of quorum are used, and where are the majority of processes?
- Does the system use sharding, pipelining, and batching?

Many consensus systems use a distinguished leader process and require all requests to go to this special node. As shown in Figure 23-6, as a result, the performance of the system as perceived by clients in different geographic locations may vary considera-

---

2 In particular, the performance of the original Paxos algorithm is not ideal, but has been greatly improved over the years.

---

bly, simply because more distant nodes have longer round-trip times to the leader process.

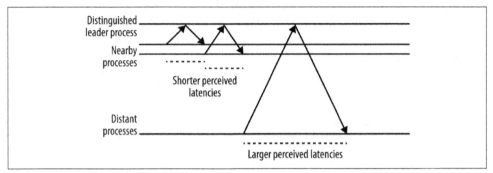

Figure 23-6. The effect of distance from a server process on perceived latency at the client

Multi-Paxos: Detailed Message Flow

The Multi-Paxos protocol uses a *strong leader process*: unless a leader has not yet been elected or some failure occurs, it requires only one round trip from the proposer to a quorum of acceptors to reach consensus. Using a strong leader process is optimal in terms of the number of messages to be passed, and is typical of many consensus protocols.

Figure 23-7 shows an initial state with a new proposer executing the first `Prepare`/`Promise` phase of the protocol. Executing this phase establishes a new numbered view, or leader term. On subsequent executions of the protocol, while the view remains the same, the first phase is unnecessary because the proposer that established the view can simply send `Accept` messages, and consensus is reached once a quorum of responses is received (including the proposer itself).

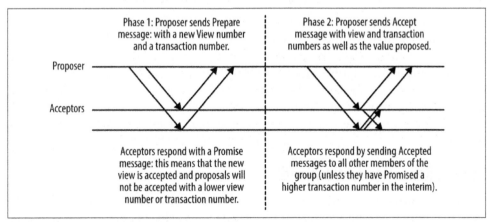

Figure 23-7. Basic Multi-Paxos message flow

Another process in the group can assume the proposer role to propose messages at any time, but changing the proposer has a performance cost. It necessitates the extra round trip to execute Phase 1 of the protocol, but more importantly, it may cause a *dueling proposers* situation in which proposals repeatedly interrupt each other and no proposals can be accepted, as shown in Figure 23-8. Because this scenario is a form of a livelock, it can continue indefinitely.

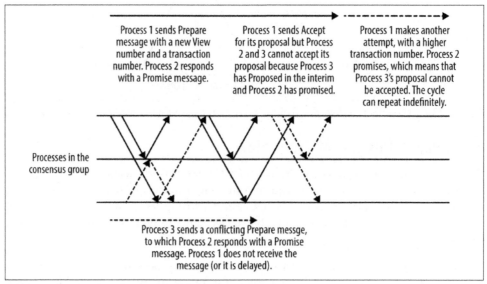

Figure 23-8. Dueling proposers in Multi-Paxos

All practical consensus systems address this issue of collisions, usually either by electing a proposer process, which makes all proposals in the system, or by using a rotating proposer that allocates each process particular slots for their proposals.

For systems that use a leader process, the leader election process must be tuned carefully to balance the system unavailability that occurs when no leader is present with the risk of dueling proposers. It's important to implement the right timeouts and backoff strategies. If multiple processes detect that there is no leader and all attempt to become leader at the same time, then none of the processes is likely to succeed (again, dueling proposers). Introducing randomness is the best approach. Raft [Ong14], for example, has a well-thought-out method of approaching the leader election process.

Scaling Read-Heavy Workloads

Scaling read workload is often critical because many workloads are read-heavy. Replicated datastores have the advantage that the data is available in multiple places, meaning that if strong consistency is not required for all reads, data could be read from *any* replica. This technique of reading from replicas works well for certain applications, such as Google's Photon system [Ana13], which uses distributed consensus to coordinate the work of multiple pipelines. Photon uses an atomic compare-and-set operation for state modification (inspired by atomic registers), which must be absolutely consistent; but read operations may be served from any replica, because stale data results in extra work being performed but not incorrect results [Gup15]. The trade-off is worthwhile.

In order to guarantee that data being read is up-to-date and consistent with any changes made before the read is performed, it is necessary to do one of the following:

- Perform a read-only consensus operation.
- Read the data from a replica that is guaranteed to be the most up-to-date. In a system that uses a stable leader process (as many distributed consensus implementations do), the leader can provide this guarantee.
- Use quorum leases, in which some replicas are granted a lease on all or part of the data in the system, allowing strongly consistent local reads at the cost of some write performance. This technique is discussed in detail in the following section.

Quorum Leases

Quorum leases [Mor14] are a recently developed distributed consensus performance optimization aimed at reducing latency and increasing throughput for read operations. As previously mentioned, in the case of classic Paxos and most other distributed consensus protocols, performing a strongly consistent read (i.e., one that is guaranteed to have the most up-to-date view of state) requires either a distributed consensus operation that reads from a quorum of replicas, or a stable leader replica that is guaranteed to have seen all recent state changing operations. In many systems, read operations vastly outnumber writes, so this reliance on either a distributed operation or a single replica harms latency and system throughput.

The quorum leasing technique simply grants a read lease on some subset of the replicated datastore's state to a quorum of replicas. The lease is for a specific (usually brief) period of time. Any operation that changes the state of that data must be acknowledged by all replicas in the read quorum. If any of these replicas becomes unavailable, the data cannot be modified until the lease expires.

Quorum leases are particularly useful for read-heavy workloads in which reads for particular subsets of the data are concentrated in a single geographic region.

Distributed Consensus Performance and Network Latency

Consensus systems face two major physical constraints on performance when committing state changes. One is network round-trip time and the other is time it takes to write data to persistent storage, which will be examined later.

Network round-trip times vary enormously depending on source and destination location, which are impacted both by the physical distance between the source and the destination, and by the amount of congestion on the network. Within a single datacenter, round-trip times between machines should be on the order of a millisecond. A typical round-trip-time (RTT) within the United States is 45 milliseconds, and from New York to London is 70 milliseconds.

Consensus system performance over a local area network can be comparable to that of an asynchronous leader-follower replication system [Bol11], such as many traditional databases use for replication. However, much of the availability benefits of distributed consensus systems require replicas to be "distant" from each other, in order to be in different failure domains.

Many consensus systems use TCP/IP as their communication protocol. TCP/IP is connection-oriented and provides some strong reliability guarantees regarding FIFO sequencing of messages. However, setting up a new TCP/IP connection requires a network round trip to perform the three-way handshake that sets up a connection before any data can be sent or received. TCP/IP slow start initially limits the bandwidth of the connection until its limits have been established. Initial TCP/IP window sizes range from 4 to 15 KB.

TCP/IP slow start is probably not an issue for the processes that form a consensus group: they will establish connections to each other and keep these connections open for reuse because they'll be in frequent communication. However, for systems with a very high number of clients, it may not be practical for all clients to keep a persistent connection to the consensus clusters open, because open TCP/IP connections do consume some resources, e.g., file descriptors, in addition to generating keepalive traffic. This overhead may be an important issue for applications that use very highly sharded consensus-based datastores containing thousands of replicas and an even larger numbers of clients. A solution is to use a pool of regional proxies, as shown in Figure 23-9, which hold persistent TCP/IP connections to the consensus group in order to avoid the setup overhead over long distances. Proxies may also be a good way to encapsulate sharding and load balancing strategies, as well as discovery of cluster members and leaders.

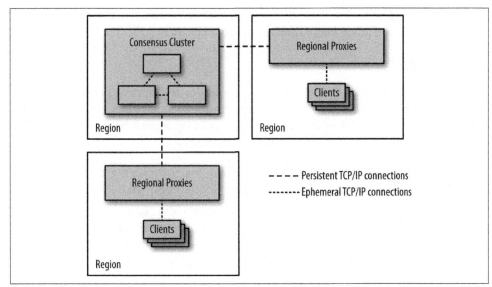

Figure 23-9. Using proxies to reduce the need for clients to open TCP/IP connections across regions

Reasoning About Performance: Fast Paxos

Fast Paxos [Lam06] is a version of the Paxos algorithm designed to improve its performance over wide area networks. Using Fast Paxos, each client can send Propose messages directly to each member of a group of acceptors, instead of through a leader, as in Classic Paxos or Multi-Paxos. The idea is to substitute one parallel message send from the client to all acceptors in Fast Paxos for two message send operations in Classic Paxos:

- One message from the client to a single proposer
- A parallel message send operation from the proposer to the other replicas

Intuitively, it seems as though Fast Paxos should always be faster than Classic Paxos. However, that's not true: if the client in the Fast Paxos system has a high RTT (round-trip time) to the acceptors, and the acceptors have fast connections to each other, we have substituted N parallel messages across the slower network links (in Fast Paxos) for one message across the slower link plus N parallel messages across the faster links (Classic Paxos). Due to the latency tail effect, the majority of the time, a single round trip across a slow link with a distribution of latencies is faster than a quorum (as shown in [Jun07]), and therefore, Fast Paxos is slower than Classic Paxos in this case.

Many systems batch multiple operations into a single transaction at the acceptor to increase throughput. Having clients act as proposers also makes it much more difficult to batch proposals. The reason for this is that proposals arrive independently at acceptors so you can't then batch them in a consistent way.

Stable Leaders

We have seen how Multi-Paxos elects a stable leader to improve performance. Zab [Jun11] and Raft [Ong14] are also examples of protocols that elect a stable leader for performance reasons. This approach can allow read optimizations, as the leader has the most up-to-date state, but also has several problems:

- All operations that change state must be sent via the leader, a requirement that adds network latency for clients that are not located near the leader.
- The leader process's outgoing network bandwidth is a system bottleneck [Mao08], because the leader's Accept message contains all of the data related to any proposal, whereas other messages contain only acknowledgments of a numbered transaction with no data payload.
- If the leader happens to be on a machine with performance problems, then the throughput of the entire system will be reduced.

Almost all distributed consensus systems that have been designed with performance in mind use either the single stable leader pattern or a system of rotating leadership in which each numbered distributed consensus algorithm is preassigned to a replica (usually by a simple modulus of the transaction ID). Algorithms that use this approach include Mencius [Mao08] and Egalitarian Paxos [Mor12a].

Over a wide area network with clients spread out geographically and replicas from the consensus group located reasonably near to the clients, such leader election leads to lower perceived latency for clients because their network RTT to the nearest replica will, on average, be smaller than that to an arbitrary leader.

Batching

Batching, as described in "Reasoning About Performance: Fast Paxos" on page 301, increases system throughput, but it still leaves replicas idle while they await replies to messages they have sent. The inefficiencies presented by idle replicas can be solved by *pipelining*, which allows multiple proposals to be in-flight at once. This optimization is very similar to the TCP/IP case, in which the protocol attempts to "keep the pipe full" using a sliding-window approach. Pipelining is normally used in combination with batching.

The batches of requests in the pipeline are still globally ordered with a view number and a transaction number, so this method does not violate the global ordering properties required to run a replicated state machine. This optimization method is discussed in [Bol11] and [San11].

Disk Access

Logging to persistent storage is required so that a node, having crashed and returned to the cluster, honors whatever previous commitments it made regarding ongoing consensus transactions. In the Paxos protocol, for instance, acceptors cannot agree to a proposal when they have already agreed to a proposal with a higher sequence number. If details of agreed and committed proposals are not logged to persistent storage, then an acceptor might violate the protocol if it crashes and is restarted, leading to inconsistent state.

The time required to write an entry to a log on disk varies greatly depending on what hardware or virtualized environment is used, but is likely to take between one and several milliseconds.

The message flow for Multi-Paxos was discussed in "Multi-Paxos: Detailed Message Flow" on page 297, but this section did not show where the protocol must log state changes to disk. A disk write must happen whenever a process makes a commitment that it must honor. In the performance-critical second phase of Multi-Paxos, these points occur before an acceptor sends an Accepted message in response to a proposal, and before the proposer sends the Accept message, because this Accept message is also an implicit Accepted message [Lam98].

This means that the latency for a single consensus operation involves the following:

- One disk write on the proposer
- Parallel messages to the acceptors
- Parallel disk writes at the acceptors
- The return messages

There is a version of the Multi-Paxos protocol that's useful for cases in which disk write time dominates: this variant doesn't consider the proposer's Accept message to be an implicit Accepted message. Instead, the proposer writes to disk in parallel with the other processes and sends an explicit Accept message. Latency then becomes proportional to the time taken to send two messages and for a quorum of processes to execute a synchronous write to disk in parallel.

If latency for performing a small random write to disk is on the order of 10 milliseconds, the rate of consensus operations will be limited to approximately 100 per minute. These times assume that network round-trip times are negligible and the proposer performs its logging in parallel with the acceptors.

As we have seen already, distributed consensus algorithms are often used as the basis for building a replicated state machine. RSMs also need to keep transaction logs for recovery purposes (for the same reasons as any datastore). The consensus algorithm's log and the RSM's transaction log can be combined into a single log. Combining these logs avoids the need to constantly alternate between writing to two different physical locations on disk [Bol11], reducing the time spent on seek operations. The disks can sustain more operations per second and therefore, the system as a whole can perform more transactions.

In a datastore, disks have purposes other than maintaining logs: system state is generally maintained on disk. Log writes must be flushed directly to disk, but writes for state changes can be written to a memory cache and flushed to disk later, reordered to use the most efficient schedule [Bol11].

Another possible optimization is batching multiple client operations together into one operation at the proposer ([Ana13], [Bol11], [Cha07], [Jun11], [Mao08], [Mor12a]). This amortizes the fixed costs of the disk logging and network latency over the larger number of operations, increasing throughput.

Deploying Distributed Consensus-Based Systems

The most critical decisions system designers must make when deploying a consensus-based system concern the number of replicas to be deployed and the location of those replicas.

Number of Replicas

In general, consensus-based systems operate using *majority quorums*, i.e., a group of $2f + 1$ replicas may tolerate f failures (if Byzantine fault tolerance, in which the system is resistant to replicas returning incorrect results, is required, then $3f + 1$ replicas may tolerate f failures [Cas99]). For non-Byzantine failures, the minimum number of replicas that can be deployed is three—if two are deployed, then there is no tolerance for failure of any process. Three replicas may tolerate one failure. Most system downtime is a result of planned maintenance [Ken12]: three replicas allow a system to operate normally when one replica is down for maintenance (assuming that the remaining two replicas can handle system load at an acceptable performance).

If an unplanned failure occurs during a maintenance window, then the consensus system becomes unavailable. Unavailability of the consensus system is usually unacceptable, and so five replicas should be run, allowing the system to operate with up to two failures. No intervention is necessarily required if four out of five replicas in a consensus system remain, but if three are left, an additional replica or two should be added.

If a consensus system loses so many of its replicas that it cannot form a quorum, then that system is, in theory, in an unrecoverable state because the durable logs of at least one of the missing replicas cannot be accessed. If no quorum remains, it's possible that a decision that was seen only by the missing replicas was made. Administrators may be able to force a change in the group membership and add new replicas that catch up from the existing one in order to proceed, but the possibility of data loss always remains—a situation that should be avoided if at all possible.

In a disaster, administrators have to decide whether to perform such a forceful reconfiguration or to wait for some period of time for machines with system state to become available. When such decisions are being made, treatment of the system's log (in addition to monitoring) becomes critical. Theoretical papers often point out that consensus can be used to construct a replicated log, but fail to discuss how to deal with replicas that may fail and recover (and thus miss some sequence of consensus decisions) or lag due to slowness. In order to maintain robustness of the system, it is important that these replicas do catch up.

The *replicated log* is not always a first-class citizen in distributed consensus theory, but it is a very important aspect of production systems. Raft describes a method for managing the consistency of replicated logs [Ong14] explicitly defining how any gaps in a replica's log are filled. If a five-instance Raft system loses all of its members except for its leader, the leader is still guaranteed to have full knowledge of all committed decisions. On the other hand, if the missing majority of members included the leader, no strong guarantees can be made regarding how up-to-date the remaining replicas are.

There is a relationship between performance and the number of replicas in a system that do not need to form part of a quorum: a minority of slower replicas may lag behind, allowing the quorum of better-performing replicas to run faster (as long as the leader performs well). If replica performance varies significantly, then every failure may reduce the performance of the system overall because slow outliers will be required to form a quorum. The more failures or lagging replicas a system can tolerate, the better the system's performance overall is likely to be.

The issue of cost should also be considered in managing replicas: each replica uses costly computing resources. If the system in question is a single cluster of processes, the cost of running replicas is probably not a large consideration. However, the cost of replicas can be a serious consideration for systems such as Photon [Ana13], which uses a sharded configuration in which each shard is a full group of processes running a consensus algorithm. As the number of shards grows, so does the cost of each additional replica, because a number of processes equal to the number of shards must be added to the system.

The decision about the number of replicas for any system is thus a trade-off between the following factors:

- The need for reliability
- Frequency of planned maintenance affecting the system

- Risk

- Performance

- Cost

This calculation will be different for each system: systems have different service level objectives for availability; some organizations perform maintenance more regularly than others; and organizations use hardware of varying cost, quality, and reliability.

Location of Replicas

Decisions about where to deploy the processes that comprise a consensus cluster are made based upon two factors: a trade-off between the failure domains that the system should handle, and the latency requirements for the system. Multiple complex issues are at play in deciding where to locate replicas.

A *failure domain* is the set of components of a system that can become unavailable as a result of a single failure. Example failure domains include the following:

- A physical machine

- A rack in a datacenter served by a single power supply

- Several racks in a datacenter that are served by one piece of networking equipment

- A datacenter that could be rendered unavailable by a fiber optic cable cut

- A set of datacenters in a single geographic area that could all be affected by a single natural disaster such as a hurricane

In general, as the distance between replicas increases, so does the round-trip time between replicas, as well as the size of the failure the system will be able to tolerate. For most consensus systems, increasing the round-trip time between replicas will also increase the latency of operations.

The extent to which latency matters, as well as the ability to survive a failure in a particular domain, is very system-dependent. Some consensus system architectures don't require particularly high throughput or low latency: for example, a consensus system that exists in order to provide group membership and leader election services for a highly available service probably isn't heavily loaded, and if the consensus transaction time is only a fraction of the leader lease time, then its performance isn't critical. Batch-oriented systems are also less affected by latency: operation batch sizes can be increased to increase throughput.

It doesn't always make sense to continually increase the size of the failure domain whose loss the system can withstand. For instance, if all of the clients using a consensus system are running within a particular failure domain (say, the New York area) and deploying a distributed consensus–based system across a wider geographical area would allow it to remain serving during outages in that failure domain (say, Hurricane Sandy), is it worth it? Probably not, because the system's clients will be down as well so the system will see no traffic. The extra cost in terms of latency, throughput, and computing resources would give no benefit.

You should take disaster recovery into account when deciding where to locate your replicas: in a system that stores critical data, the consensus replicas are also essentially online copies of the system data. However, when critical data is at stake, it's important to back up regular snapshots elsewhere, even in the case of solid consensus–based systems that are deployed in several diverse failure domains. There are two failure domains that you can never escape: the software itself, and human error on the part of the system's administrators. Bugs in software can emerge under unusual circumstances and cause data loss, while system misconfiguration can have similar effects. Human operators can also err, or perform sabotage causing data loss.

When making decisions about location of replicas, remember that the most important measure of performance is client perception: ideally, the network round-trip time from the clients to the consensus system's replicas should be minimized. Over a wide area network, leaderless protocols like Mencius or Egalitarian Paxos may have a performance edge, particularly if the consistency constraints of the application mean that it is possible to execute read-only operations on any system replica without performing a consensus operation.

Capacity and Load Balancing

When designing a deployment, you must make sure there is sufficient capacity to deal with load. In the case of *sharded deployments*, you can adjust capacity by adjusting the number of shards. However, for systems that can read from consensus group members that are not the leader, you can increase read capacity by adding more replicas. Adding more replicas has a cost: in an algorithm that uses a strong leader, adding replicas imposes more load on the leader process, while in a peer-to-peer protocol, adding replicas imposes more load on all processes. However, if there is ample capacity for write operations, but a read-heavy workload is stressing the system, adding replicas may be the best approach.

It should be noted that adding a replica in a majority quorum system can potentially decrease system availability somewhat (as shown in Figure 23-10). A typical deployment for Zookeeper or Chubby uses five replicas, so a majority quorum requires three replicas. The system will still make progress if two replicas, or 40%, are unavailable. With six replicas, a quorum requires four replicas: only 33% of the replicas can be unavailable if the system is to remain live.

Considerations regarding failure domains therefore apply even more strongly when a sixth replica is added: if an organization has five datacenters, and generally runs consensus groups with five processes, one in each datacenter, then loss of one datacenter still leaves one spare replica in each group. If a sixth replica is deployed in one of the five datacenters, then an outage in that datacenter removes both of the spare replicas in the group, thereby reducing capacity by 33%.

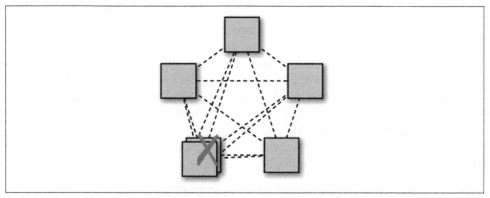

Figure 23-10. Adding an extra replica in one region may reduce system availability. Colocating multiple replicas in a single datacenter may reduce system availability: here, there is a quorum without any redundancy remaining.

If clients are dense in a particular geographic region, it is best to locate replicas close to clients. However, deciding where exactly to locate replicas may require some careful thought around load balancing and how a system deals with overload. As shown in Figure 23-11, if a system simply routes client read requests to the nearest replica, then a large spike in load concentrated in one region may overwhelm the nearest replica, and then the next-closest replica, and so on—this is *cascading failure* (see Chapter 22). This type of overload can often happen as a result of batch jobs beginning, especially if several begin at the same time.

We've already seen the reason that many distributed consensus systems use a leader process to improve performance. However, it's important to understand that the leader replicas will use more computational resources, particularly outgoing network capacity. This is because the leader sends proposal messages that include the proposed data, but replicas send smaller messages, usually just containing agreement with a particular consensus transaction ID. Organizations that run highly sharded consensus systems with a very large number of processes may find it necessary to ensure that leader processes for the different shards are balanced relatively evenly across different datacenters. Doing so prevents the system as a whole from being bottlenecked on outgoing network capacity for just one datacenter, and makes for much greater overall system capacity.

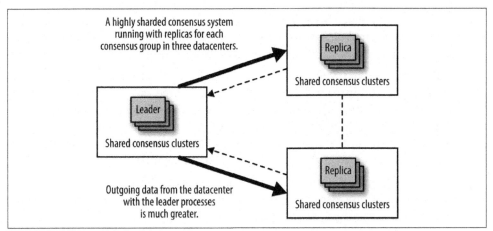

Figure 23-11. Colocating leader processes leads to uneven bandwidth utilization

Another downside of deploying consensus groups in multiple datacenters (shown by Figure 23-11) is the very extreme change in the system that can occur if the datacenter hosting the leaders suffers a widespread failure (power, networking equipment failure, or fiber cut, for instance). As shown in Figure 23-12, in this failure scenario, all of the leaders should fail over to another datacenter, either split evenly or en masse into one datacenter. In either case, the link between the other two datacenters will suddenly receive a lot more network traffic from this system. This would be an inopportune moment to discover that the capacity on that link is insufficient.

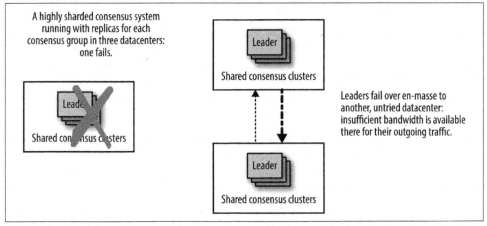

Figure 23-12. When colocated leaders fail over en masse, patterns of network utilization change dramatically

However, this type of deployment could easily be an unintended result of automatic processes in the system that have bearing on how leaders are chosen. For instance:

- Clients will experience better latency for any operations handled via the leader if the leader is located closest to them. An algorithm that attempts to site leaders near the bulk of clients could take advantage of this insight.

- An algorithm might try to locate leaders on machines with the best performance. A pitfall of this approach is that if one of the three datacenters houses faster machines, then a disproportionate amount of traffic will be sent to that datacenter, resulting in extreme traffic changes should that datacenter go offline. To avoid this problem, the algorithm must also take into account distribution balance against machine capabilities when selecting machines.

- A leader election algorithm might favor processes that have been running longer. Longer-running processes are quite likely to be correlated with location if software releases are performed on a per-datacenter basis.

Quorum composition

When determining where to locate replicas in a consensus group, it is important to consider the effect of the geographical distribution (or, more precisely, the network latencies between replicas) on the performance of the group.

One approach is to spread the replicas as evenly as possible, with similar RTTs between all replicas. All other factors being equal (such as workload, hardware, and network performance), this arrangement should lead to fairly consistent performance across all regions, regardless of where the group leader is located (or for each member of the consensus group, if a leaderless protocol is in use).

Geography can greatly complicate this approach. This is particularly true for intracontinental versus transpacific and transatlantic traffic. Consider a system that spans North America and Europe: it is impossible to locate replicas equidistant from each other because there will always be a longer lag for transatlantic traffic than for intracontinental traffic. No matter what, transactions from one region will need to make a transatlantic round trip in order to reach consensus.

However, as shown in Figure 23-13, in order to try to distribute traffic as evenly as possible, systems designers might choose to site five replicas, with two replicas roughly centrally in the US, one on the east coast, and two in Europe. Such a distribution would mean that in the average case, consensus could be achieved in North America without waiting for replies from Europe, or that from Europe, consensus can be achieved by exchanging messages only with the east coast replica. The east coast replica acts as a linchpin of sorts, where two possible quorums overlap.

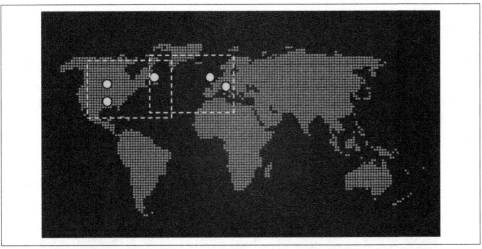

Figure 23-13. Overlapping quorums with one replica acting as a link

As shown in Figure 23-14, loss of this replica means that system latency is likely to change drastically: instead of being largely influenced by either central US to east coast RTT or EU to east coast RTT, latency will be based on EU to central RTT, which is around 50% higher than EU to east coast RTT. The geographic distance and network RTT between the nearest possible quorum increases enormously.

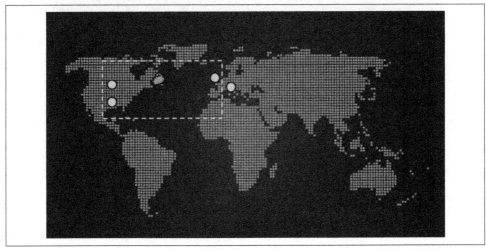

Figure 23-14. Loss of the link replica immediately leads to a longer RTT for any quorum

This scenario is a key weakness of the simple majority quorum when applied to groups composed of replicas with very different RTTs between members. In such cases, a hierarchical quorum approach may be useful. As diagrammed in Figure 23-15, nine replicas may be deployed in three groups of three. A quorum may be formed by a majority of groups, and a group may be included in the quorum if a majority of the group's members are available. This means that a replica may be lost in the central group without incurring a large impact on overall system performance because the central group may still vote on transactions with two of its three replicas.

There is, however, a resource cost associated with running a higher number of replicas. In a highly sharded system with a read-heavy workload that is largely fulfillable by replicas, we might mitigate this cost by using fewer consensus groups. Such a strategy means that the overall number of processes in the system may not change.

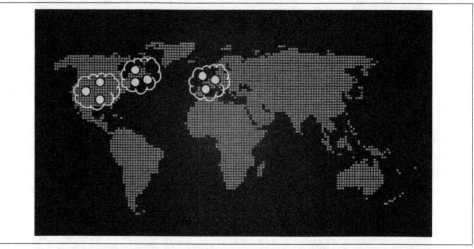

Figure 23-15. Hierarchical quorums can be used to reduce reliance on the central replica

Monitoring Distributed Consensus Systems

As we've already seen, distributed consensus algorithms are at the core of many of Google's critical systems ([Ana13], [Bur06], [Cor12], [Shu13]). All important production systems need monitoring, in order to detect outages or problems and for troubleshooting. Experience has shown us that there are certain specific aspects of distributed consensus systems that warrant special attention. These are:

The number of members running in each consensus group, and the status of each process (healthy or not healthy)
> A process may be running but unable to make progress for some (e.g., hardware-related) reason.

Persistently lagging replicas
> Healthy members of a consensus group can still potentially be in multiple different states. A group member may be recovering state from peers after startup, or lagging behind the quorum in the group, or it may be up-to-date and participating fully, and it may be the leader.

Whether or not a leader exists

A system based on an algorithm such as Multi-Paxos that uses a leader role must be monitored to ensure that a leader exists, because if the system has no leader, it is totally unavailable.

Number of leader changes

Rapid changes of leadership impair performance of consensus systems that use a stable leader, so the number of leader changes should be monitored. Consensus algorithms usually mark a leadership change with a new term or view number, so this number provides a useful metric to monitor. Too rapid of an increase in leader changes signals that the leader is flapping, perhaps due to network connectivity issues. A decrease in the view number could signal a serious bug.

Consensus transaction number

Operators need to know whether or not the consensus system is making progress. Most consensus algorithms use an increasing consensus transaction number to indicate progress. This number should be seen to be increasing over time if a system is healthy.

Number of proposals seen; number of proposals agreed upon

These numbers indicate whether or not the system is operating correctly.

Throughput and latency

Although not specific to distributed consensus systems, these characteristics of their consensus system should be monitored and understood by administrators.

In order to understand system performance and to help troubleshoot performance issues, you might also monitor the following:

- Latency distributions for proposal acceptance
- Distributions of network latencies observed between parts of the system in different locations
- The amount of time acceptors spend on durable logging
- Overall bytes accepted per second in the system

Conclusion

We explored the definition of the distributed consensus problem, and presented some system architecture patterns for distributed-consensus based systems, as well as examining the performance characteristics and some of the operational concerns around distributed consensus–based systems.

We deliberately avoided an in-depth discussion about specific algorithms, protocols, or implementations in this chapter. Distributed coordination systems and the technologies underlying them are evolving quickly, and this information would rapidly become out of date, unlike the fundamentals that are discussed here. However, these fundamentals, along with the articles referenced throughout this chapter, will enable you to use the distributed coordination tools available today, as well as future software.

If you remember nothing else from this chapter, keep in mind the sorts of problems that distributed consensus can be used to solve, and the types of problems that can arise when ad hoc methods such as heartbeats are used instead of distributed consensus. Whenever you see leader election, critical shared state, or distributed locking, think about distributed consensus: any lesser approach is a ticking bomb waiting to explode in your systems.

CHAPTER 24

Distributed Periodic Scheduling with Cron

Written by Štěpán Davidovič[1]
Edited by Kavita Guliani

This chapter describes Google's implementation of a distributed cron service that serves the vast majority of internal teams that need periodic scheduling of compute jobs. Throughout cron's existence, we have learned many lessons about how to design and implement what might seem like a basic service. Here, we discuss the problems that distributed crons face and outline some potential solutions.

Cron is a common Unix utility designed to periodically launch arbitrary jobs at user-defined times or intervals. We first analyze the base principles of cron and its most common implementations, and then review how an application such as cron can work in a large, distributed environment in order to increase the reliability of the system against single-machine failures. We describe a distributed cron system that is deployed on a small number of machines, but can launch cron jobs across an entire datacenter in conjunction with a datacenter scheduling system like Borg [Ver15].

Cron

Let's discuss how cron is typically used, in the single machine case, before diving into running it as a cross-datacenter service.

Introduction

Cron is designed so that the system administrators and common users of the system can specify commands to run, and when these commands run. Cron executes various

---

1 This chapter was previously published in part in *ACM Queue* (March 2015, vol. 13, issue 3).

types of jobs, including garbage collection and periodic data analysis. The most common time specification format is called "crontab." This format supports simple intervals (e.g., "once a day at noon" or "every hour on the hour"). Complex intervals, such as "every Saturday, which is also the 30th day of the month," can also be configured.

Cron is usually implemented using a single component, which is commonly referred to as crond. crond is a daemon that loads the list of scheduled cron jobs. Jobs are launched according to their specified execution times.

Reliability Perspective

Several aspects of the cron service are notable from a reliability perspective:

- Cron's failure domain is essentially just one machine. If the machine is not running, neither the cron scheduler nor the jobs it launches can run.[2] Consider a very simple distributed case with two machines, in which your cron scheduler launches jobs on a different worker machine (for example, using SSH). This scenario presents two distinct failure domains that could impact our ability to launch jobs: either the scheduler machine or the destination machine could fail.

- The only state that needs to persist across crond restarts (including machine reboots) is the crontab configuration itself. The cron launches are fire-and-forget, and crond makes no attempt to track these launches.

- anacron is a notable exception to this. anacron attempts to launch jobs that would have been launched when the system was down. Relaunch attempts are limited to jobs that run daily or less frequently. This functionality is very useful for running maintenance jobs on workstations and notebooks, and is facilitated by a file that retains the timestamp of the last launch for all registered cron jobs.

Cron Jobs and Idempotency

Cron jobs are designed to perform periodic work, but beyond that, it is hard to know in advance what function they have. The variety of requirements that the diverse set of cron jobs entails obviously impacts reliability requirements.

Some cron jobs, such as garbage collection processes, are idempotent. In case of system malfunction, it is safe to launch such jobs multiple times. Other cron jobs, such as a process that sends out an email newsletter to a wide distribution, should not be launched more than once.

---

2 Failure of individual jobs is beyond the scope of this analysis.

To make matters more complicated, failure to launch is acceptable for some cron jobs but not for others. For example, a garbage collection cron job scheduled to run every five minutes may be able to skip one launch, but a payroll cron job scheduled to run once a month should not be be skipped.

This large variety of cron jobs makes reasoning about failure modes difficult: in a system like the cron service, there is no single answer that fits every situation. In general, we favor skipping launches rather than risking double launches, as much as the infrastructure allows. This is because recovering from a skipped launch is more tenable than recovering from a double launch. Cron job owners can (and should!) monitor their cron jobs; for example, an owner might have the cron service expose state for its managed cron jobs, or set up independent monitoring of the effect of cron jobs. In case of a skipped launch, cron job owners can take action that appropriately matches the nature of the cron job. However, undoing a double launch, such as the previously mentioned newsletter example, may be difficult or even entirely impossible. Therefore, we prefer to "fail closed" to avoid systemically creating bad state.

Cron at Large Scale

Moving away from single machines toward large-scale deployments requires some fundamental rethinking of how to make cron work well in such an environment. Before presenting the details of the Google cron solution, we'll discuss those differences between small-scale and large-scale deployment, and describe what design changes large-scale deployments necessitated.

Extended Infrastructure

In its "regular" implementations, cron is limited to a single machine. Large-scale system deployments extend our cron solution to multiple machines.

Hosting your cron service on a single machine could be catastrophic in terms of reliability. Say this machine is located in a datacenter with exactly 1,000 machines. A failure of just 1/1000th of your available machines could knock out the entire cron service. For obvious reasons, this implementation is not acceptable.

To increase cron's reliability, we decouple processes from machines. If you want to run a service, simply specify the service requirements and which datacenter it should run in. The datacenter scheduling system (which itself should be reliable) determines the machine or machines on which to deploy your service, in addition to handling machine deaths. Launching a job in a datacenter then effectively turns into sending one or more RPCs to the datacenter scheduler.

This process is, however, not instantaneous. Discovering a dead machine entails health check timeouts, while rescheduling your service onto a different machine requires time to install software and start up the new process.

Because moving a process to a different machine can mean loss of any local state stored on the old machine (unless live migration is employed), and the rescheduling time may exceed the smallest scheduling interval of one minute, we need procedures in place to mitigate both data loss and excessive time requirements. To retain local state of the old machine, you might simply persist the state on a distributed filesystem such as GFS, and use this filesystem during startup to identify jobs that failed to launch due to rescheduling. However, this solution falls short in terms of timeliness expectations: if you run a cron job every five minutes, a one- to two-minute delay caused by the total overhead of cron system rescheduling is potentially unacceptably substantial. In this case, hot spares, which would be able to quickly jump in and resume operation, can significantly shorten this time window.

Extended Requirements

Single-machine systems typically just colocate all running processes with limited isolation. While containers are now commonplace, it's not necessary or common to use containers to isolate every single component of a service that's deployed on a single machine. Therefore, if cron were deployed on a single machine, crond and all the cron jobs it runs would likely not be isolated.

Deployment at datacenter scale commonly means deployment into containers that enforce isolation. Isolation is necessary because the base expectation is that independent processes running in the same datacenter should not negatively impact each other. In order to enforce that expectation, you should know the quantity of resources you need to acquire up front for any given process you want to run—both for the cron system and the jobs it launches. A cron job may be delayed if the datacenter does not have resources available to match the demands of the cron job. Resource requirements, in addition to user demand for monitoring of cron job launches, means that we need to track the full state of our cron job launches, from the scheduled launch to termination.

Decoupling process launches from specific machines exposes the cron system to partial launch failure. The versatility of cron job configurations also means that launching a new cron job in a datacenter may need multiple RPCs, such that sometimes we encounter a scenario in which some RPCs succeeded but others did not (for example, because the process sending the RPCs died in the middle of executing these tasks). The cron recovery procedure must also account for this scenario.

In terms of the failure mode, a datacenter is a substantially more complex ecosystem than a single machine. The cron service that began as a relatively simple binary on a single machine now has many obvious and nonobvious dependencies when deployed at a larger scale. For a service as basic as cron, we want to ensure that even if the datacenter suffers a partial failure (for example, partial power outage or problems with storage services), the service is still able to function. By requiring that the datacenter scheduler locates replicas of cron in diverse locations within the datacenter, we avoid the scenario in which failure of a single power distribution unit takes out all the processes of the cron service.

It may be possible to deploy a single cron service across the globe, but deploying cron within a single datacenter has benefits: the service enjoys low latency and shares fate with the datacenter scheduler, cron's core dependency.

Building Cron at Google

This section address the problems that must be resolved in order to provide a large-scale distributed deployment of cron reliably. It also highlights some important decisions made in regards to distributed cron at Google.

Tracking the State of Cron Jobs

As discussed in previous sections, we need to hold some amount of state about cron jobs, and be able to restore that information quickly in case of failure. Moreover, the consistency of that state is paramount. Recall that many cron jobs, like a payroll run or sending an email newsletter, are not idempotent.

We have two options to track the state of cron jobs:

- Store data externally in generally available distributed storage
- Use a system that stores a small volume of state as part of the cron service itself

When designing the distributed cron, we chose the second option. We made this choice for several reasons:

- Distributed filesystems such as GFS or HDFS often cater to the use case of very large files (for example, the output of web crawling programs), whereas the information we need to store about cron jobs is very small. Small writes on a distributed filesystem are very expensive and come with high latency, because the filesystem is not optimized for these types of writes.

- Base services for which outages have wide impact (such as cron) should have very few dependencies. Even if parts of the datacenter go away, the cron service should be able to function for at least some amount of time. But this requirement does not mean that the storage has to be part of the cron process directly (how storage is handled is essentially an implementation detail). However, cron should be able to operate independently of downstream systems that cater to a large number of internal users.

The Use of Paxos

We deploy multiple replicas of the cron service and use the Paxos distributed consensus algorithm (see Chapter 23) to ensure they have consistent state. As long as the majority of group members are available, the distributed system as a whole can successfully process new state changes despite the failure of bounded subsets of the infrastructure.

As shown in Figure 24-1, the distributed cron uses a single leader job, which is the only replica that can modify the shared state, as well as the only replica that can launch cron jobs. We take advantage of the fact that the variant of Paxos we use, Fast Paxos [Lam06], uses a leader replica internally as an optimization—the Fast Paxos leader replica also acts as the cron service leader.

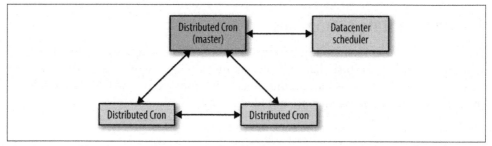

Figure 24-1. The interactions between distributed cron replicas

If the leader replica dies, the health-checking mechanism of the Paxos group discovers this event quickly (within seconds). As another cron process is already started up and available, we can elect a new leader. As soon as the new leader is elected, we follow a leader election protocol specific to the cron service, which is responsible for taking over all the work left unfinished by the previous leader. The leader specific to the cron service is the same as the Paxos leader, but the cron service needs to take additional action upon promotion. The fast reaction time for the leader re-election allows us to stay well within a generally tolerable one-minute failover time.

The most important state we keep in Paxos is information regarding which cron jobs are launched. We synchronously inform a quorum of replicas of the beginning and end of each scheduled launch for each cron job.

The Roles of the Leader and the Follower

As just described, our use of Paxos and its deployment in the cron service has two assigned roles: the leader and the follower. The following sections describe each role.

The leader

The leader replica is the only replica that actively launches cron jobs. The leader has an internal scheduler that, much like the simple crond described at the beginning of this chapter, maintains the list of cron jobs ordered by their scheduled launch time. The leader replica waits until the scheduled launch time of the first job.

Upon reaching the scheduled launch time, the leader replica announces that it is about to start this particular cron job's launch, and calculates the new scheduled launch time, just like a regular crond implementation would. Of course, as with regular crond, a cron job launch specification may have changed since the last execution, and this launch specification must be kept in sync with the followers as well. Simply identifying the cron job is not enough: we should also uniquely identify the particular launch using the start time; otherwise, ambiguity in cron job launch tracking may occur. (Such ambiguity is especially likely in the case of high-frequency cron jobs, such as those running every minute.) As seen in Figure 24-2, this communication is performed over Paxos.

It is important that Paxos communication remain synchronous, and that the actual cron job launch does not proceed until it receives confirmation that the Paxos quorum has received the launch notification. The cron service needs to understand whether each cron job has launched in order to decide the next course of action in case of leader failover. Not performing this task synchronously could mean that the entire cron job launch happens on the leader without informing the follower replicas. In case of failover, the follower replicas might attempt to perform the very same launch again because they aren't aware that the launch already occurred.

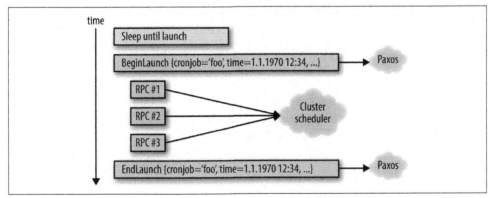

Figure 24-2. Illustration of progress of a cron job launch, from the leader's perspective

The completion of the cron job launch is announced via Paxos to the other replicas synchronously. Note that it does not matter whether the launch succeeded or failed for external reasons (for example, if the datacenter scheduler was unavailable). Here, we are simply keeping track of the fact that the cron service attempted the launch at the given scheduled time. We also need to be able to resolve failures of the cron system in the middle of this operation, as discussed in the following section.

Another extremely important feature of the leader is that as soon as it loses its leadership for any reason, it must immediately stop interacting with the datacenter scheduler. Holding the leadership should guarantee mutual exclusion of access to the datacenter scheduler. In the absence of this condition of mutual exclusion, the old and new leaders might perform conflicting actions on the datacenter scheduler.

The follower

The follower replicas keep track of the state of the world, as provided by the leader, in order to take over at a moment's notice if needed. All the state changes tracked by follower replicas are communicated via Paxos, from the leader replica. Much like the leader, followers also maintain a list of all cron jobs in the system, and this list must be kept consistent among the replicas (through the use of Paxos).

Upon receiving notification about a commenced launch, the follower replica updates its local next scheduled launch time for the given cron job. This very important state change (which is performed synchronously) ensures that all cron job schedules within the system are consistent. We keep track of all open launches (launches that have begun but not completed).

If a leader replica dies or otherwise malfunctions (e.g., is partitioned away from the other replicas on the network), a follower should be elected as a new leader. The election must converge faster than one minute, in order to avoid the risk of missing or unreasonably delaying a cron job launch. Once a leader is elected, all open launches (i.e., partial failures) must be concluded. This process can be quite complicated, imposing additional requirements on both the cron system and the datacenter infrastructure. The following section discusses how to resolve partial failures of this type.

Resolving partial failures

As mentioned, the interaction between the leader replica and the datacenter scheduler can fail in between sending multiple RPCs that describe a single logical cron job launch. Our systems should be able to handle this condition.

Recall that every cron job launch has two synchronization points:

- When we are about to perform the launch
- When we have finished the launch

These two points allow us to delimit the launch. Even if the launch consists of a single RPC, how do we know if the RPC was actually sent? Consider the case in which we know that the scheduled launch started, but we were not notified of its completion before the leader replica died.

In order to determine if the RPC was actually sent, one of the following conditions must be met:

- All operations on external systems, which we may need to continue upon re-election, must be idempotent (i.e., we can safely perform the operations again)
- We must be able to look up the state of all operations on external systems in order to unambiguously determine whether they completed or not

Each of these conditions imposes significant constraints, and may be difficult to implement, but being able to meet at least one of these conditions is fundamental to the accurate operation of a cron service in a distributed environment that could suffer a single or several partial failures. Not handling this appropriately can lead to missed launches or double launch of the same cron job.

Most infrastructure that launches logical jobs in datacenters (Mesos, for example) provides naming for those datacenter jobs, making it possible to look up the state of jobs, stop the jobs, or perform other maintenance. A reasonable solution to the idempotency problem is to construct job names ahead of time (thereby avoiding causing any mutating operations on the datacenter scheduler), and then distribute the names to all replicas of your cron service. If the cron service leader dies during launch, the new leader simply looks up the state of all the precomputed names and launches the missing names.

Note that, similar to our method of identifying individual cron job launches by their name and launch time, it is important that the constructed job names on the datacenter scheduler include the particular scheduled launch time (or have this information otherwise retrievable). In regular operation, the cron service should fail over quickly in case of leader failure, but a quick failover doesn't always happen.

Recall that we track the scheduled launch time when keeping the internal state between the replicas. Similarly, we need to disambiguate our interaction with the datacenter scheduler, also by using the scheduled launch time. For example, consider a short-lived but frequently run cron job. The cron job launches, but before the launch is communicated to all replicas, the leader crashes and an unusually long failover—long enough that the cron job finishes successfully—takes place. The new leader looks up the state of the cron job, observes its completion, and attempts to launch the job again. Had the launch time been included, the new leader would know that the job on the datacenter scheduler is the result of this particular cron job launch, and this double launch would not have happened.

The actual implementation has a more complicated system for state lookup, driven by the implementation details of the underlying infrastructure. However, the preceding description covers the implementation-independent requirements of any such system. Depending on the available infrastructure, you may also need to consider the trade-off between risking a double launch and risking skipping a launch.

Storing the State

Using Paxos to achieve consensus is only one part of the problem of how to handle the state. Paxos is essentially a continuous log of state changes, appended to synchronously as state changes occur. This characteristic of Paxos has two implications:

- The log needs to be compacted, to prevent it from growing infinitely
- The log itself must be stored somewhere

In order to prevent the infinite growth of the Paxos log, we can simply take a snapshot of the current state, which means that we can reconstruct the state without needing to replay all state change log entries leading to the current state. To provide an example: if our state changes stored in logs are "Increment a counter by 1," then after a thousand iterations, we have a thousand log entries that can be easily changed to a snapshot of "Set counter to 1,000."

In case of lost logs, we only lose the state since the last snapshot. Snapshots are in fact our most critical state—if we lose our snapshots, we essentially have to start from zero again because we've lost our internal state. Losing logs, on the other hand, just causes a bounded loss of state and sends the cron system back in time to the point when the latest snapshot was taken.

We have two main options for storing our data:

- Externally in a generally available distributed storage
- In a system that stores the small volume of state as part of the cron service itself

When designing the system, we combined elements of both options.

We store Paxos logs on local disk of the machine where cron service replicas are scheduled. Having three replicas in default operation implies that we have three copies of the logs. We store the snapshots on local disk as well. However, because they are critical, we also back them up onto a distributed filesystem, thus protecting against failures affecting all three machines.

We do not store logs on our distributed filesystem. We consciously decided that losing logs, which represent a small amount of the most recent state changes, is an acceptable risk. Storing logs on a distributed filesystem can entail a substantial performance penalty caused by frequent small writes. The simultaneous loss of all three machines is unlikely, and if simultaneous loss does occur, we automatically restore from the snapshot. We thereby lose only a small amount of logs: those taken since the last snapshot, which we perform on configurable intervals. Of course, these trade-offs may be different depending on the details of the infrastructure, as well as the requirements placed on the cron system.

In addition to the logs and snapshots stored on the local disk and snapshot backups on the distributed filesystem, a freshly started replica can fetch the state snapshot and all logs from an already running replica over the network. This ability makes replica startup independent of any state on the local machine. Therefore, rescheduling a replica to a different machine upon restart (or machine death) is essentially a nonissue for the reliability of the service.

Running Large Cron

There are other smaller but equally interesting implications of running a large cron deployment. A traditional cron is small: at most, it probably contains on the order of tens of cron jobs. However, if you run a cron service for thousands of machines in a datacenter, your usage will grow, and you may run into problems.

Beware the large and well-known problem of distributed systems: the thundering herd. Based on user configuration, the cron service can cause substantial spikes in datacenter usage. When people think of a "daily cron job," they commonly configure this job to run at midnight. This setup works just fine if the cron job launches on the same machine, but what if your cron job can spawn a MapReduce with thousands of workers? And what if 30 different teams decide to run a daily cron job like this, in the same datacenter? To solve this problem, we introduced an extension to the crontab format.

In the ordinary crontab, users specify the minute, hour, day of the month (or week), and month when the cron job should launch, or asterisk to specify any value. Running at midnight, daily, would then have crontab specification of "0 0 * * *" (i.e., zero-th minute, zero-th hour, every day of the week, every month, and every day of the week). We also introduced the use of the question mark, which means that any value is acceptable, and the cron system is given the freedom to choose the value. Users choose this value by hashing the cron job configuration over the given time range (e.g., 0..23 for hour), therefore distributing those launches more evenly.

Despite this change, the load caused by the cron jobs is still very spiky. The graph in Figure 24-3 illustrates the aggregate global number of launches of cron jobs at Google. This graph highlights the frequent spikes in cron job launches, which is often caused by cron jobs that need to be launched at a specific time—for example, due to temporal dependency on external events.

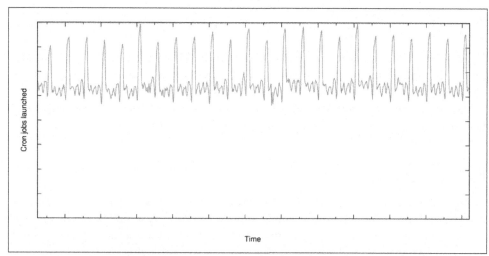

Figure 24-3. The number of cron jobs launched globally

Summary

A cron service has been a fundamental feature in UNIX systems for many decades. The industry move toward large distributed systems, in which a datacenter may be the smallest effective unit of hardware, requires changes in large portions of the stack. Cron is no exception to this trend. A careful look at the required properties of a cron service and the requirements of cron jobs drives Google's new design.

We have discussed the new constraints demanded by a distributed-system environment, and a possible design of the cron service based on Google's solution. This solution requires strong consistency guarantees in the distributed environment. The core of the distributed cron implementation is therefore Paxos, a commonplace algorithm to reach consensus in an unreliable environment. The use of Paxos and correct analysis of new failure modes of cron jobs in a large-scale, distributed environment allowed us to build a robust cron service that is heavily used in Google.

CHAPTER 25

Data Processing Pipelines

Written by Dan Dennison
Edited by Tim Harvey

This chapter focuses on the real-life challenges of managing data processing pipelines of depth and complexity. It considers the frequency continuum between periodic pipelines that run very infrequently through to continuous pipelines that never stop running, and discusses the discontinuities that can produce significant operational problems. A fresh take on the leader-follower model is presented as a more reliable and better-scaling alternative to the periodic pipeline for processing Big Data.

Origin of the Pipeline Design Pattern

The classic approach to data processing is to write a program that reads in data, transforms it in some desired way, and outputs new data. Typically, the program is scheduled to run under the control of a periodic scheduling program such as cron. This design pattern is called a *data pipeline*. Data pipelines go as far back as co-routines [Con63], the DTSS communication files [Bul80], the UNIX pipe [McI86], and later, ETL pipelines,[1] but such pipelines have gained increased attention with the rise of "Big Data," or "datasets that are so large and so complex that traditional data processing applications are inadequate."[2]

---

[1] Wikipedia: Extract, transform, load, *http://en.wikipedia.org/wiki/Extract,_transform,_load*

[2] Wikipedia: Big data, *http://en.wikipedia.org/wiki/Big_data*

Initial Effect of Big Data on the Simple Pipeline Pattern

Programs that perform periodic or continuous transformations on Big Data are usually referred to as "simple, one-phase pipelines."

Given the scale and processing complexity inherent to Big Data, programs are typically organized into a chained series, with the output of one program becoming the input to the next. There may be varied rationales for this arrangement, but it is typically designed for ease of reasoning about the system and not usually geared toward operational efficiency. Programs organized this way are called *multiphase pipelines*, because each program in the chain acts as a discrete data processing phase.

The number of programs chained together in series is a measurement known as the *depth* of a pipeline. Thus, a shallow pipeline may only have one program with a corresponding pipeline depth measurement of one, whereas a deep pipeline may have a pipeline depth in the tens or hundreds of programs.

Challenges with the Periodic Pipeline Pattern

Periodic pipelines are generally stable when there are sufficient workers for the volume of data and execution demand is within computational capacity. In addition, instabilities such as processing bottlenecks are avoided when the number of chained jobs and the relative throughput between jobs remain uniform.

Periodic pipelines are useful and practical, and we run them on a regular basis at Google. They are written with frameworks like MapReduce [Dea04] and Flume [Cha10], among others.

However, the collective SRE experience has been that the periodic pipeline model is fragile. We discovered that when a periodic pipeline is first installed with worker sizing, periodicity, chunking technique, and other parameters carefully tuned, performance is initially reliable. However, organic growth and change inevitably begin to stress the system, and problems arise. Examples of such problems include jobs that exceed their run deadline, resource exhaustion, and hanging processing chunks that entail corresponding operational load.

Trouble Caused By Uneven Work Distribution

The key breakthrough of Big Data is the widespread application of "embarrassingly parallel" [Mol86] algorithms to cut a large workload into chunks small enough to fit onto individual machines. Sometimes chunks require an uneven amount of resources relative to one another, and it is seldom initially obvious why particular chunks require different amounts of resources. For example, in a workload that is partitioned by customer, data chunks for some customers may be much larger than others.

Because the customer is the point of indivisibility, end-to-end runtime is thus capped to the runtime of the largest customer.

The "hanging chunk" problem can result when resources are assigned due to differences between machines in a cluster or overallocation to a job. This problem arises due to the difficulty of some real-time operations on streams such as sorting "steaming" data. The pattern of typical user code is to wait for the total computation to complete before progressing to the next pipeline stage, commonly because sorting may be involved, which requires all data to proceed. That can significantly delay pipeline completion time, because completion is blocked on the worst-case performance as dictated by the chunking methodology in use.

If this problem is detected by engineers or cluster monitoring infrastructure, the response can make matters worse. For example, the "sensible" or "default" response to a hanging chunk is to immediately kill the job and then allow the job to restart, because the blockage may well be the result of nondeterministic factors. However, because pipeline implementations by design usually don't include checkpointing, work on all chunks is restarted from the beginning, thereby wasting the time, CPU cycles, and human effort invested in the previous cycle.

Drawbacks of Periodic Pipelines in Distributed Environments

Big Data periodic pipelines are widely used at Google, and so Google's cluster management solution includes an alternative scheduling mechanism for such pipelines. This mechanism is necessary because, unlike continuously running pipelines, periodic pipelines typically run as lower-priority batch jobs. A lower-priority designation works well in this case because batch work is not sensitive to latency in the same way that Internet-facing web services are. In addition, in order to control cost by maximizing machine workload, Borg (Google's cluster management system, [Ver15]) assigns batch work to available machines. This priority can result in degraded startup latency, so pipeline jobs can potentially experience open-ended startup delays.

Jobs invoked through this mechanism have a number of natural limitations, resulting in various distinct behaviors. For example, jobs scheduled in the gaps left by user-facing web service jobs might be impacted in terms of availability of low-latency resources, pricing, and stability of access to resources. Execution cost is inversely proportional to requested startup delay, and directly proportional to resources consumed. Although batch scheduling may work smoothly in practice, excessive use of the batch scheduler (Chapter 24) places jobs at risk of preemptions (see section 2.5 of [Ver15]) when cluster load is high because other users are starved of batch resources. In light of the risk trade-offs, running a well-tuned periodic pipeline successfully is a delicate balance between high resource cost and risk of preemptions.

Delays of up to a few hours might well be acceptable for pipelines that run daily. However, as the scheduled execution frequency increases, the minimum time between executions can quickly reach the minimum average delay point, placing a lower bound on the latency that a periodic pipeline can expect to attain. Reducing the job execution interval below this effective lower bound simply results in undesirable behavior rather than increased progress. The specific failure mode depends on the batch scheduling policy in use. For example, each new run might stack up on the cluster scheduler because the previous run is not complete. Even worse, the currently executing and nearly finished run could be killed when the next execution is scheduled to begin, completely halting all progress in the name of increasing executions.

Note where the downward-sloping idle interval line intersects the scheduling delay in Figure 25-1. In this scenario, lowering the execution interval much below 40 minutes for this ~20-minute job results in potentially overlapping executions with undesired consequences.

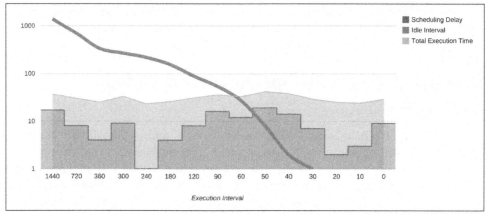

Figure 25-1. Periodic pipeline execution interval versus idle time (log scale)

The solution to this problem is to secure sufficient server capacity for proper operation. However, resource acquisition in a shared, distributed environment is subject to supply and demand. As expected, development teams tend to be reluctant to go through the processes of acquiring resources when the resources must be contributed to a common pool and shared. To resolve this, a distinction between batch scheduling resources versus production priority resources has to be made to rationalize resource acquisition costs.

Monitoring Problems in Periodic Pipelines

For pipelines of sufficient execution duration, having real-time information on run-time performance metrics can be as important, if not even more important, than knowing overall metrics. This is because real-time data is important to providing operational support, including emergency response. In practice, the standard monitoring model involves collecting metrics during job execution, and reporting metrics only upon completion. If the job fails during execution, no statistics are provided.

Continuous pipelines do not share these problems because their tasks are constantly running and their telemetry is routinely designed so that real-time metrics are available. Periodic pipelines shouldn't have inherent monitoring problems, but we have observed a strong association.

"Thundering Herd" Problems

Adding to execution and monitoring challenges is the "thundering herd" problem endemic to distributed systems, also discussed in Chapter 24. Given a large enough periodic pipeline, for each cycle, potentially thousands of workers immediately start work. If there are too many workers or if the workers are misconfigured or invoked by faulty retry logic, the servers on which they run will be overwhelmed, as will the underlying shared cluster services, and any networking infrastructure that was being used will also be overwhelmed.

Further worsening this situation, if retry logic is not implemented, correctness problems can result when work is dropped upon failure, and the job won't be retried. If retry logic is present but it is naive or poorly implemented, retry upon failure can compound the problem.

Human intervention can also contribute to this scenario. Engineers with limited experience managing pipelines tend to amplify this problem by adding more workers to their pipeline when the job fails to complete within a desired period of time.

Regardless of the source of the "thundering herd" problem, nothing is harder on cluster infrastructure and the SREs responsible for a cluster's various services than a buggy 10,000 worker pipeline job.

Moiré Load Pattern

Sometimes the thundering herd problem may not be obvious to spot in isolation. A related problem we call "Moiré load pattern" occurs when two or more pipelines run simultaneously and their execution sequences occasionally overlap, causing them to simultaneously consume a common shared resource. This problem can occur even in continuous pipelines, although it is less common when load arrives more evenly.

Moiré load patterns are most apparent in plots of pipeline usage of shared resources. For example, Figure 25-2 identifies the resource usage of three periodic pipelines. In Figure 25-3, which is a stacked version of the data of the previous graph, the peak impact causing on-call pain occurs when the aggregate load nears 1.2M.

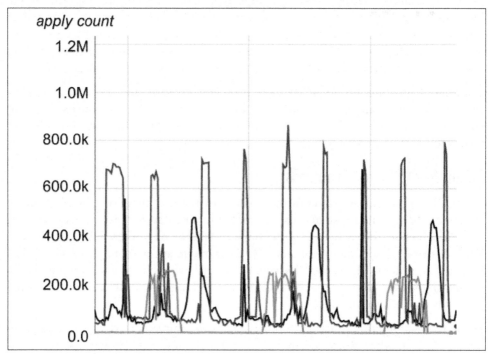

Figure 25-2. Moiré load pattern in separate infrastructure

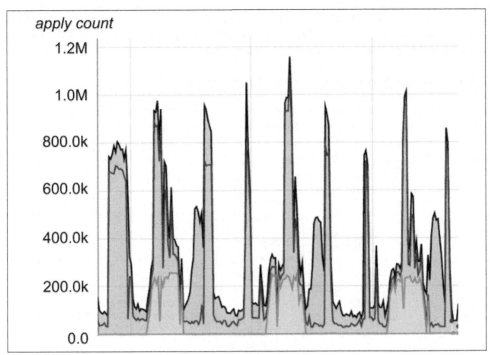

apply count

Figure 25-3. Moiré load pattern in shared infrastructure

Introduction to Google Workflow

When an inherently one-shot batch pipeline is overwhelmed by business demands for continuously updated results, the pipeline development team usually considers either refactoring the original design to satisfy current demands, or moving to a continuous pipeline model. Unfortunately, business demands usually occur at the least convenient time to refactor the pipeline system into an online continuous processing system. Newer and larger customers who are faced with forcing scaling issues typically also want to include new features, and expect that these requirements adhere to immovable deadlines. In anticipating this challenge, it's important to ascertain several details at the outset of designing a system involving a proposed data pipeline. Be sure to scope expected growth trajectory,[3] demand for design modifications, expected additional resources, and expected latency requirements from the business.

Faced with these needs, Google developed a system in 2003 called "Workflow" that makes continuous processing available at scale. Workflow uses the leader-follower

---

3 Jeff Dean's lecture on "Software Engineering Advice from Building Large-Scale Distributed Systems" is an excellent resource: [Dea07].

(workers) distributed systems design pattern [Sha00] and the system prevalence design pattern.[4] This combination enables very large-scale transactional data pipelines, ensuring correctness with exactly-once semantics.

Workflow as Model-View-Controller Pattern

Because of how system prevalence works, it can be useful to think of Workflow as the distributed systems equivalent of the model-view-controller pattern known from user interface development.[5] As shown in Figure 25-4, this design pattern divides a given software application into three interconnected parts to separate internal representations of information from the ways that information is presented to or accepted from the user.[6]

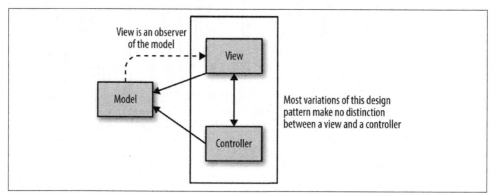

Figure 25-4. The model-view-controller pattern used in user interface design

Adapting this pattern for Workflow, the *model* is held in a server called "Task Master." The Task Master uses the system prevalence pattern to hold all job states in memory for fast availability while synchronously journaling mutations to persistent disk. The *view* is the workers that continually update the system state transactionally with the master according to their perspective as a subcomponent of the pipeline. Although all pipeline data may be stored in the Task Master, the best performance is usually achieved when only pointers to work are stored in the Task Master, and the actual input and output data is stored in a common filesystem or other storage. Supporting this analogy, the workers are completely stateless and can be discarded at any time. A *controller* can optionally be added as a third system component to efficiently support

---

4 Wikipedia: System Prevalence, *http://en.wikipedia.org/wiki/System_Prevalence*

5 The "model-view-controller" pattern is an analogy for distributed systems that was very loosely borrowed from Smalltalk, which was originally used to describe the design structure of graphical user interfaces [Fow08].

6 Wikipedia: Model-view-controller, *http://en.wikipedia.org/wiki/Model%E2%80%93view%E2%80%93controller*

---

a number of auxiliary system activities that affect the pipeline, such as runtime scaling of the pipeline, snapshotting, workcycle state control, rolling back pipeline state, or even performing global interdiction for business continuity. Figure 25-5 illustrates the design pattern.

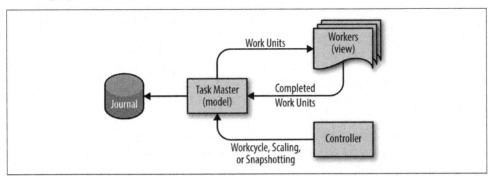

Figure 25-5. The model-view-controller design pattern as adapted for Google Workflow

Stages of Execution in Workflow

We can increase pipeline depth to any level inside Workflow by subdividing processing into task groups held in the Task Master. Each task group holds the work corresponding to a pipeline stage that can perform arbitrary operations on some piece of data. It's relatively straightforward to perform mapping, shuffling, sorting, splitting, merging, or any other operation in any stage.

A stage usually has some worker type associated with it. There can be multiple concurrent instances of a given worker type, and workers can be self-scheduled in the sense that they can look for different types of work and choose which type to perform.

The worker consumes work units from a previous stage and produces output units. The output can be an end point or input for some other processing stage. Within the system, it's easy to guarantee that all work is executed, or at least reflected in permanent state, exactly once.

Workflow Correctness Guarantees

It's not practical to store *every* detail of the pipeline's state inside the Task Master, because the Task Master is limited by RAM size. However, a double correctness guarantee persists because the master holds a collection of pointers to uniquely named data, and each work unit has a uniquely held lease. Workers acquire work with a lease and may only commit work from tasks for which they currently possess a valid lease.

To avoid the situation in which an orphaned worker may continue working on a work unit, thus destroying the work of the current worker, each output file opened by a worker has a unique name. In this way, even orphaned workers can continue writing independently of the master until they attempt to commit. Upon attempting a commit, they will be unable to do so because another worker holds the lease for that work unit. Furthermore, orphaned workers cannot destroy the work produced by a valid worker, because the unique filename scheme ensures that every worker is writing to a distinct file. In this way, the double correctness guarantee holds: the output files are always unique, and the pipeline state is always correct by virtue of tasks with leases.

As if a double correctness guarantee isn't enough, Workflow also versions all tasks. If the task updates or the task lease changes, each operation yields a new unique task replacing the previous one, with a new ID assigned to the task. Because all pipeline configuration in Workflow is stored inside the Task Master in the same form as the work units themselves, in order to commit work, a worker must own an active lease *and* reference the task ID number of the configuration it used to produce its result. If the configuration changed while the work unit was in flight, all workers of that type will be unable to commit despite owning current leases. Thus, all work performed after a configuration change is consistent with the new configuration, at the cost of work being thrown away by workers unfortunate enough to hold the old leases.

These measures provide a triple correctness guarantee: configuration, lease ownership, and filename uniqueness. However, even this isn't sufficient for all cases.

For example, what if the Task Master's network address changed, and a different Task Master replaced it at the same address? What if a memory corruption altered the IP address or port number, resulting in another Task Master on the other end? Even more commonly, what if someone (mis)configured their Task Master setup by inserting a load balancer in front of a set of independent Task Masters?

Workflow embeds a server token, a unique identifier for this particular Task Master, in each task's metadata to prevent a rogue or incorrectly configured Task Master from corrupting the pipeline. Both client and server check the token on each operation, avoiding a very subtle misconfiguration in which all operations run smoothly until a task identifier collision occurs.

To summarize, the four Workflow correctness guarantees are:

- Worker output through configuration tasks creates barriers on which to predicate work.

- All work committed requires a currently valid lease held by the worker.

- Output files are uniquely named by the workers.

- The client and server validate the Task Master itself by checking a server token on every operation.

At this point, it may occur to you that it would be simpler to forgo the specialized Task Master and use Spanner [Cor12] or another database. However, Workflow is special because each task is unique and immutable. These twin properties prevent many potentially subtle issues with wide-scale work distribution from occurring.

For example, the lease obtained by the worker is part of the task itself, requiring a brand new task even for lease changes. If a database is used directly and its transaction logs act like a "journal," each and every read must be part of a long-running transaction. This configuration is most certainly possible, but terribly inefficient.

Ensuring Business Continuity

Big Data pipelines need to continue processing despite failures of all types, including fiber cuts, weather events, and cascading power grid failures. These types of failures can disable entire datacenters. In addition, pipelines that do not employ system prevalence to obtain strong guarantees about job completion are often disabled and enter an undefined state. This architecture gap makes for a brittle business continuity strategy, and entails costly mass duplication of effort to restore pipelines and data.

Workflow resolves this problem conclusively for continuous processing pipelines. To obtain global consistency, the Task Master stores journals on Spanner, using it as a globally available, globally consistent, but low-throughput filesystem. To determine which Task Master can write, each Task Master uses the distributed lock service called Chubby [Bur06] to elect the writer, and the result is persisted in Spanner. Finally, clients look up the current Task Master using internal naming services.

Because Spanner does not make for a high-throughput filesystem, globally distributed Workflows employ two or more local Workflows running in distinct clusters, in addition to a notion of reference tasks stored in the global Workflow. As units of work (tasks) are consumed through a pipeline, equivalent reference tasks are inserted into the global Workflow by the binary labeled "stage 1" in Figure 25-6. As tasks finish, the reference tasks are transactionally removed from the global Workflow as depicted in "stage n" of Figure 25-6. If the tasks cannot be removed from the global Workflow, the local Workflow will block until the global Workflow becomes available again, ensuring transactional correctness.

To automate failover, a helper binary labeled "stage 1" in Figure 25-6 runs inside each local Workflow. The local Workflow is otherwise unaltered, as described by the "do work" box in the diagram. This helper binary acts as a "controller" in the MVC sense, and is responsible for creating reference tasks, as well as updating a special heartbeat task inside of the global Workflow. If the heartbeat task is not updated within the timeout period, the remote Workflow's helper binary seizes the work in progress as documented by the reference tasks and the pipeline continues, unhindered by whatever the environment may do to the work.

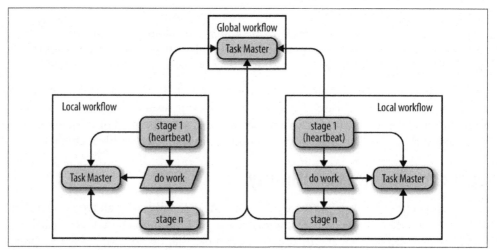

Figure 25-6. An example of distributed data and process flow using Workflow pipelines

Summary and Concluding Remarks

Periodic pipelines are valuable. However, if a data processing problem is continuous or will organically grow to become continuous, don't use a periodic pipeline. Instead, use a technology with characteristics similar to Workflow.

We have found that continuous data processing with strong guarantees, as provided by Workflow, performs and scales well on distributed cluster infrastructure, routinely produces results that users can rely upon, and is a stable and reliable system for the Site Reliability Engineering team to manage and maintain.

CHAPTER 26

Data Integrity: What You Read Is What You Wrote

Written by Raymond Blum and Rhandeev Singh
Edited by Betsy Beyer

What is "data integrity"? When users come first, data integrity is whatever users think it is.

We might say *data integrity is a measure of the accessibility and accuracy of the datastores needed to provide users with an adequate level of service*. But this definition is insufficient.

For instance, if a user interface bug in Gmail displays an empty mailbox for too long, users might believe data has been lost. Thus, even if no data was *actually* lost, the world would question Google's ability to act as a responsible steward of data, and the viability of cloud computing would be threatened. Were Gmail to display an error or maintenance message for too long while "only a bit of metadata" is repaired, the trust of Google's users would similarly erode.

How long is "too long" for data to be unavailable? As demonstrated by an actual Gmail incident in 2011 [Hic11], four days is a long time—perhaps "too long." Subsequently, we believe 24 hours is a good starting point for establishing the threshold of "too long" for Google Apps.

Similar reasoning applies to applications like Google Photos, Drive, Cloud Storage, and Cloud Datastore, because users don't necessarily draw a distinction between these discrete products (reasoning, "this product is still Google" or "Google, Amazon, whatever; this product is still part of the cloud"). Data loss, data corruption, and extended unavailability are typically indistinguishable to users. Therefore, data integrity applies to all types of data across all services. When considering data integrity, what matters is that *services in the cloud remain accessible to users. User access to data is especially important.*

Data Integrity's Strict Requirements

When considering the reliability needs of a given system, it may seem that uptime (service availability) needs are stricter than those of data integrity. For example, users may find an hour of email downtime unacceptable, whereas they may live grumpily with a four-day time window to recover a mailbox. However, there's a more appropriate way to consider the demands of uptime versus data integrity.

An SLO of 99.99% uptime leaves room for only an hour of downtime in a whole year. This SLO sets a rather high bar, which likely exceeds the expectations of most Internet and Enterprise users.

In contrast, an SLO of 99.99% good bytes in a 2 GB artifact would render documents, executables, and databases corrupt (up to 200 KB garbled). This amount of corruption is *catastrophic* in the majority of cases—resulting in executables with random opcodes and completely unloadable databases.

From the user perspective, then, every service has independent uptime and data integrity requirements, even if these requirements are implicit. The worst time to disagree with users about these requirements is after the demise of their data!

To revise our earlier definition of data integrity, we might say that *data integrity means that services in the cloud remain accessible to users. User access to data is especially important, so this access should remain in perfect shape.*

Now, suppose an artifact were corrupted or lost exactly once a year. If the loss were unrecoverable, uptime of the affected artifact is *lost* for that year. The most likely means to avoid any such loss is through proactive detection, coupled with rapid repair.

In an alternate universe, suppose the corruption were immediately detected before users were affected and that the artifact was removed, fixed, and returned to service within half an hour. Ignoring any other downtime during that 30 minutes, such an object would be 99.99% available that year.

Astonishingly, at least from the user perspective, in this scenario, data integrity is still 100% (or close to 100%) during the accessible lifetime of the object. As demonstrated by this example, *the secret to superior data integrity is proactive detection and rapid repair and recovery.*

Choosing a Strategy for Superior Data Integrity

There are many possible strategies for rapid detection, repair, and recovery of lost data. All of these strategies trade uptime against data integrity with respect to affected users. Some strategies work better than others, and some strategies require more complex engineering investment than others. With so many options available, which strategies should you utilize? The answer depends on your computing paradigm.

Most cloud computing applications seek to optimize for some combination of uptime, latency, scale, velocity, and privacy. To provide a working definition for each of these terms:

Uptime
  Also referred to as *availability*, the proportion of time a service is usable by its users.

Latency
  How responsive a service appears to its users.

Scale
  A service's volume of users and the mixture of workloads the service can handle before latency suffers or the service falls apart.

Velocity
  How fast a service can innovate to provide users with superior value at reasonable cost.

Privacy
  This concept imposes complex requirements. As a simplification, this chapter limits its scope in discussing privacy to data deletion: data must be destroyed within a reasonable time after users delete it.

Many cloud applications continually evolve atop a mixture of ACID[1] and BASE[2] APIs to meet the demands of these five components.[3] BASE allows for higher availability

---

1 Atomicity, Consistency, Isolation, Durability; see *https://en.wikipedia.org/wiki/ACID*. SQL databases such as MySQL and PostgreSQL strive to achieve these properties.

2 Basically Available, Soft state, Eventual consistency; see *https://en.wikipedia.org/wiki/Eventual_consistency*. BASE systems, like Bigtable and Megastore, are often also described as "NoSQL."

3 For further reading on ACID and BASE APIs, see [Gol14] and [Bai13].

than ACID, in exchange for a softer distributed consistency guarantee. Specifically, BASE only guarantees that once a piece of data is no longer updated, its value will *eventually* become consistent across (potentially distributed) storage locations.

The following scenario provides an example of how trade-offs between uptime, latency, scale, velocity, and privacy might play out.

When velocity trumps other requirements, the resulting applications rely on an arbitrary collection of APIs that are most familiar to the particular developers working on the application.

For example, an application may take advantage of an efficient BLOB[4] storage API, such as Blobstore, that neglects distributed consistency in favor of scaling to heavy workloads with high uptime, low latency, and at low cost. To compensate:

- The same application may entrust small amounts of authoritative metadata pertaining to its blobs to a higher latency, less available, more costly Paxos-based service such as Megastore [Bak11], [Lam98].
- Certain clients of the application may cache some of that metadata locally and access blobs directly, shaving latency still further from the vantage point of users.
- Another application may keep metadata in Bigtable, sacrificing strong distributed consistency because its developers happened to be familiar with Bigtable.

Such cloud applications face a variety of data integrity challenges at runtime, such as referential integrity between datastores (in the preceding example, Blobstore, Megastore, and client-side caches). The vagaries of high velocity dictate that schema changes, data migrations, the piling of new features atop old features, rewrites, and evolving integration points with other applications collude to produce an environment riddled with complex relationships between various pieces of data that no single engineer fully groks.

To prevent such an application's data from degrading before its users' eyes, a system of out-of-band checks and balances is needed within and between its datastores. "Third Layer: Early Detection" on page 356 discusses such a system.

In addition, if such an application relies on independent, uncoordinated backups of several datastores (in the preceding example, Blobstore and Megastore), then its ability to make effective use of restored data during a data recovery effort is complicated by the variety of relationships between restored and live data. Our example application would have to sort through and distinguish between restored blobs versus live Megastore, restored Megastore versus live blobs, restored blobs versus restored Megastore, and interactions with client-side caches.

---

4 Binary Large Object; see *https://en.wikipedia.org/wiki/Binary_large_object*.

In consideration of these dependencies and complications, how many resources should be invested in data integrity efforts, and where?

Backups Versus Archives

Traditionally, companies "protect" data against loss by investing in backup strategies. However, the real focus of such backup efforts should be data recovery, which distinguishes *real* backups from archives. As is sometimes observed: No one really *wants* to make backups; what people *really* want are *restores*.

Is your "backup" really an archive, rather than appropriate for use in disaster recovery?

The most important difference between backups and archives is that backups *can* be loaded back into an application, while archives *cannot*. Therefore, backups and archives have quite differing use cases.

Archives safekeep data for long periods of time to meet auditing, discovery, and compliance needs. Data recovery for such purposes generally doesn't need to complete within uptime requirements of a service. For example, you might need to retain financial transaction data for seven years. To achieve this goal, you could move accumulated audit logs to long-term archival storage at an offsite location once a month. Retrieving and recovering the logs during a month-long financial audit may take a week, and this weeklong time window for recovery may be acceptable for an archive.

On the other hand, when disaster strikes, data must be recovered from *real backups* quickly, preferably well within the uptime needs of a service. Otherwise, affected users are left without useful access to the application from the onset of the data integrity issue until the completion of the recovery effort.

It's also important to consider that because the most recent data is at risk until safely backed up, it may be optimal to schedule real backups (as opposed to archives) to occur daily, hourly, or more frequently, using full and incremental or continuous (streaming) approaches.

Therefore, when formulating a backup strategy, consider how quickly you need to be able to recover from a problem, and how much recent data you can afford to lose.

Requirements of the Cloud Environment in Perspective

Cloud environments introduce a unique combination of technical challenges:

- If the environment uses a mixture of transactional and nontransactional backup and restore solutions, recovered data won't necessarily be correct.

- If services must evolve without going down for maintenance, different versions of business logic may act on data in parallel.

- If interacting services are versioned independently, incompatible versions of different services may interact momentarily, further increasing the chance of accidental data corruption or data loss.

In addition, in order to maintain economy of scale, service providers must provide only a limited number of APIs. These APIs must be simple and easy to use for the vast majority of applications, or few customers will use them. At the same time, the APIs must be robust enough to understand the following:

- Data locality and caching
- Local and global data distribution
- Strong and/or eventual consistency
- Data durability, backup, and recovery

Otherwise, sophisticated customers can't migrate applications to the cloud, and simple applications that grow complex and large will need complete rewrites in order to use different, more complex APIs.

Problems arise when the preceding API features are used in certain combinations. If the service provider doesn't solve these problems, then the applications that run into these challenges must identify and solve them independently.

Google SRE Objectives in Maintaining Data Integrity and Availability

While SRE's goal of "maintaining integrity of persistent data" is a good vision, we thrive on concrete objectives with measurable indicators. SRE defines key metrics that we use to set expectations for the capabilities of our systems and processes through tests and to track their performance during an actual event.

Data Integrity Is the Means; Data Availability Is the Goal

Data integrity refers to the accuracy and consistency of data throughout its lifetime. Users need to know that information will be correct and won't change in some unexpected way from the time it's first recorded to the last time it's observed. But is such assurance enough?

Consider the case of an email provider who suffered a weeklong data outage [Kinc09]. Over the space of 10 days, users had to find other, temporary methods of conducting their business with the expectation that they'd soon return to their established email accounts, identities, and accumulated histories.

Then, the worst possible news arrived: the provider announced that despite earlier expectations, the trove of past email and contacts was in fact gone—evaporated and never to be seen again. It seemed that a series of mishaps in managing data integrity had conspired to leave the service provider with no usable backups. Furious users either stuck with their interim identities or established new identities, abandoning their troubled former email provider.

But wait! Several days after the declaration of absolute loss, the provider announced that the users' personal information *could* be recovered. There was no data loss; this was only an outage. All was well!

Except, *all was not well*. User data had been preserved, but the data was not accessible by the people who needed it for too long.

The moral of this example: From the user's point of view, data integrity without expected and regular data availability is effectively the same as having no data at all.

Delivering a Recovery System, Rather Than a Backup System

Making backups is a classically neglected, delegated, and deferred task of system administration. Backups aren't a high priority for anyone—they're an ongoing drain on time and resources, and yield no immediate visible benefit. For this reason, a lack of diligence in implementing a backup strategy is typically met with a sympathetic eye roll. One might argue that, like most measures of protection against low-risk dangers, such an attitude is pragmatic. The fundamental problem with this lackadaisical strategy is that the dangers it entails may be low risk, but they are also high impact. When your service's data is unavailable, your response can make or break your service, product, and even your company.

Instead of focusing on the thankless job of taking a backup, it's much more useful, not to mention easier, to motivate participation in taking backups by concentrating on a task with a visible payoff: the *restore*! *Backups are a tax*, one paid on an ongoing basis for the municipal service of guaranteed data availability. Instead of emphasizing the tax, draw attention to the service the tax funds: data availability. We don't make teams "practice" their backups, instead:

- Teams define service level objectives (SLOs) for data availability in a variety of failure modes.

- A team practices and demonstrates their ability to meet those SLOs.

Types of Failures That Lead to Data Loss

As illustrated by Figure 26-1, at a very high level, there are 24 distinct types of failures when the 3 factors can occur in any combination. You should consider each of these potential failures when designing a data integrity program. The factors of data integrity failure modes are as follows:

Root cause
    An unrecoverable loss of data may be caused by a number of factors: user action, operator error, application bugs, defects in infrastructure, faulty hardware, or site catastrophes.

Scope
    Some losses are widespread, affecting many entities. Some losses are narrow and directed, deleting or corrupting data specific to a small subset of users.

Rate
    Some data losses are a big bang event (for example, 1 million rows are replaced by only 10 rows in a single minute), whereas some data losses are creeping (for example, 10 rows of data are deleted every minute over the course of weeks).

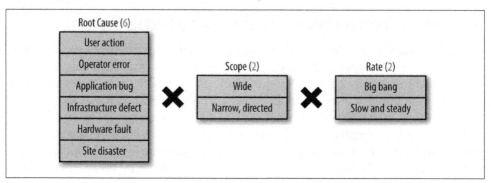

Figure 26-1. The factors of data integrity failure modes

An effective restore plan must account for any of these failure modes occurring in any conceivable combination. What may be a perfectly effective strategy for guarding against a data loss caused by a creeping application bug may be of no help whatsoever when your colocation datacenter catches fire.

A study of 19 data recovery efforts at Google found that the most common user-visible data loss scenarios involved data deletion or loss of referential integrity caused by software bugs. The most challenging variants involved low-grade corruption or deletion that was discovered weeks to months after the bugs were first released into the production environment. Therefore, the safeguards Google employs should be well suited to prevent or recover from these types of loss.

To recover from such scenarios, a large and successful application needs to retrieve data for perhaps millions of users spread across days, weeks, or months. The application may also need to recover each affected artifact to a unique point in time. This data recovery scenario is called "point-in-time recovery" outside Google, and "time-travel" inside Google.

A backup and recovery solution that provides point-in-time recovery for an application across its ACID and BASE datastores while meeting strict uptime, latency, scalability, velocity, and cost goals is a chimera today!

Solving this problem with your own engineers entails sacrificing velocity. Many projects compromise by adopting a tiered backup strategy without point-in-time recovery. For instance, the APIs beneath your application may support a variety of data recovery mechanisms. Expensive local "snapshots" may provide limited protection from application bugs and offer quick restoration functionality, so you might retain a few days of such local "snapshots," taken several hours apart. Cost-effective full and incremental copies every two days may be retained longer. Point-in-time recovery is a very nice feature to have if one or more of these strategies support it.

Consider the data recovery options provided by the cloud APIs you are about to use. Trade point-in-time recovery against a tiered strategy if necessary, but don't resort to not using either! If you can have both features, use both features. Each of these features (or both) will be valuable at some point.

Challenges of Maintaining Data Integrity Deep and Wide

In designing a data integrity program, it's important to recognize that *replication and redundancy are not recoverability*.

Scaling issues: Fulls, incrementals, and the competing forces of backups and restores

A classic but flawed response to the question "Do you have a backup?" is "We have something even better than a backup—replication!" Replication provides many benefits, including locality of data and protection from a site-specific disaster, but it can't protect you from many sources of data loss. Datastores that automatically sync multiple replicas guarantee that a corrupt database row or errant delete are pushed to all of your copies, likely before you can isolate the problem.

To address this concern, you might make nonserving copies of your data in some other format, such as frequent database exports to a native file. This additional measure adds protection from the types of errors replication doesn't protect against—user errors and application-layer bugs—but does nothing to guard against losses introduced at a lower layer. This measure also introduces a risk of bugs during data conversion (in both directions) and during storage of the native file, in addition to possible mismatches in semantics between the two formats. Imagine a zero-day attack[5] at some low level of your stack, such as the filesystem or device driver. Any copies that rely on the compromised software component, including the database exports that were written to the same filesystem that backs your database, are vulnerable.

Thus, we see that diversity is key: protecting against a failure at layer X requires storing data on diverse components at that layer. Media isolation protects against media flaws: a bug or attack in a disk device driver is unlikely to affect tape drives. If we could, we'd make backup copies of our valuable data on clay tablets.[6]

The forces of data freshness and restore completion compete against comprehensive protection. The further down the stack you push a snapshot of your data, the longer it takes to make a copy, which means that the frequency of copies decreases. At the database level, a transaction may take on the order of seconds to replicate. Exporting a database snapshot to the filesystem underneath may take 40 minutes. A full backup of the underlying filesystem may take hours.

In this scenario, you may lose up to 40 minutes of the most recent data when you restore the latest snapshot. A restore from the filesystem backup might incur hours of missing transactions. Additionally, restoring probably takes as long as backing up, so actually loading the data might take hours. You'd obviously like to have the freshest data back as quickly as possible, but depending on the type of failure, that freshest and most immediately available copy might not be an option.

Retention

Retention—how long you keep copies of your data around—is yet another factor to consider in your data recovery plans.

While it's likely that you or your customers will quickly notice the sudden emptying of an entire database, it might take days for a more gradual loss of data to attract the

---

5 See *https://en.wikipedia.org/wiki/Zero-day_(computing)*.

6 Clay tablets are the oldest known examples of writing. For a broader discussion of preserving data for the long haul, see [Con96].

---

right person's attention. Restoring the lost data in the latter scenario requires snapshots taken further back in time. When reaching back this far, you'll likely want to merge the restored data with the current state. Doing so significantly complicates the restore process.

How Google SRE Faces the Challenges of Data Integrity

Similar to our assumption that Google's underlying systems are prone to failure, we assume that any of our protection mechanisms are also subject to the same forces and can fail in the same ways and at the most inconvenient of times. Maintaining a guarantee of data integrity at large scale, a challenge that is further complicated by the high rate of change of the involved software systems, requires a number of complementary but uncoupled practices, each chosen to offer a high degree of protection on its own.

The 24 Combinations of Data Integrity Failure Modes

Given the many ways data can be lost (as described previously), there is no silver bullet that guards against the many combinations of failure modes. Instead, you need defense in depth. Defense in depth comprises multiple layers, with each successive layer of defense conferring protection from progressively less common data loss scenarios. Figure 26-2 illustrates an object's journey from soft deletion to destruction, and the data recovery strategies that should be employed along this journey to ensure defense in depth.

The first layer is *soft deletion* (or "lazy deletion" in the case of developer API offerings), which has proven to be an effective defense against inadvertent data deletion scenarios. The second line of defense is *backups and their related recovery methods*. The third and final layer is *regular data validation*, covered in "Third Layer: Early Detection" on page 356. Across all these layers, the presence of *replication* is occasionally useful for data recovery in specific scenarios (although data recovery plans should not rely upon replication).

User deletes data	Application deletes data		Application purges data	Data gone
User-visible trash	Not user-visible. Soft-deleted by application and/or within storage service.		Data being destroyed by application and storage service.	
Eligible for undeletion by users	Eligible for undeletion by user support and/or application administrators		Can't be undeleted. Restoration requires backups	
Protects against mistakes by users	Protects against bugs in applications and mistakes by application service providers		Backups protect against this and all other scenarios	

Figure 26-2. An object's journey from soft deletion to destruction

First Layer: Soft Deletion

When velocity is high and privacy matters, bugs in applications account for the vast majority of data loss and corruption events. In fact, data deletion bugs may become so common that the ability to undelete data for a limited time becomes the primary line of defense against the majority of otherwise permanent, inadvertent data loss.

Any product that upholds the privacy of its users must allow the users to delete selected subsets and/or all of their data. Such products incur a support burden due to accidental deletion. Giving users the ability to undelete their data (for example, via a trash folder) reduces but cannot completely eliminate this support burden, particularly if your service also supports third-party add-ons that can also delete data.

Soft deletion can dramatically reduce or even completely eliminate this support burden. Soft deletion means that deleted data is immediately marked as such, rendering it unusable by all but the application's administrative code paths. Administrative code paths may include legal discovery, hijacked account recovery, enterprise administration, user support, and problem troubleshooting and its related features. Conduct soft deletion when a user empties his or her trash, and provide a user support tool that enables authorized administrators to undelete any items accidentally deleted by users. Google implements this strategy for our most popular productivity applications; otherwise, the user support engineering burden would be untenable.

You can extend the soft deletion strategy even further by offering users the option to recover deleted data. For example, the Gmail trash bin allows users to access messages that were deleted fewer than 30 days ago.

Another common source of unwanted data deletion occurs as a result of account hijacking. In account hijacking scenarios, a hijacker commonly deletes the original user's data before using the account for spamming and other unlawful purposes. When you combine the commonality of accidental user deletion with the risk of data deletion by hijackers, the case for a programmatic soft deletion and undeletion interface within and/or beneath your application becomes clear.

Soft deletion implies that once data is marked as such, it is destroyed after a reasonable delay. The length of the delay depends upon an organization's policies and applicable laws, available storage resources and cost, and product pricing and market positioning, especially in cases involving much short-lived data. Common choices of soft deletion delays are 15, 30, 45, or 60 days. In Google's experience, the majority of account hijacking and data integrity issues are reported or detected within 60 days. Therefore, the case for soft deleting data for longer than 60 days may not be strong.

Google has also found that the most devastating acute data deletion cases are caused by application developers unfamiliar with existing code but working on deletion-related code, especially batch processing pipelines (e.g., an offline MapReduce or Hadoop pipeline). It's advantageous to design your interfaces to hinder developers unfamiliar with your code from circumventing soft deletion features with new code. One effective way of achieving this is to implement cloud computing offerings that include built-in soft deletion and undeletion APIs, making sure to *enable said feature*.[7] Even the best armor is useless if you don't put it on.

Soft deletion strategies cover data deletion features in consumer products like Gmail or Google Drive, but what if you support a cloud computing offering instead? Assuming your cloud computing offering already supports a programmatic soft deletion and undeletion feature with reasonable defaults, the remaining accidental data deletion scenarios will originate in mistakes made by your own internal developers or your developer customers.

In such cases, it can be useful to introduce an additional layer of soft deletion, which we will refer to as "lazy deletion." You can think of lazy deletion as behind the scenes purging, controlled by the storage system (whereas soft deletion is controlled by and expressed to the client application or service). In a lazy deletion scenario, data that is deleted by a cloud application becomes immediately inaccessible to the application, but is preserved by the cloud service provider for up to a few weeks before destruction. Lazy deletion isn't advisable in all defense in depth strategies: a long lazy deletion period is costly in systems with much short-lived data, and impractical in systems that must guarantee destruction of deleted data within a reasonable time frame (i.e., those that offer privacy guarantees).

To sum up the first layer of defense in depth:

- A trash folder that allows users to undelete data is the primary defense against user error.
- Soft deletion is the primary defense against developer error and the secondary defense against user error.
- In developer offerings, lazy deletion is the primary defense against internal developer error and the secondary defense against external developer error.

What about *revision history*? Some products provide the ability to revert items to previous states. When such a feature is available to users, it is a form of trash. When

---

7 Upon reading this advice, one might ask: since you have to offer an API on top of the datastore to implement soft deletion, why stop at soft deletion, when you could offer many other features that protect against accidental data deletion by users? To take a specific example from Google's experience, consider Blobstore: rather than allow customers to delete Blob data and metadata directly, the Blob APIs implement many safety features, including default backup policies (offline replicas), end-to-end checksums, and default tombstone lifetimes (soft deletion). It turns out that on multiple occasions, soft deletion saved Blobstore's clients from data loss that could have been much, much worse. There are certainly many deletion protection features worth calling out, but for companies with required data deletion deadlines, soft deletion was the most pertinent protection against bugs and accidental deletion in the case of Blobstore's clients.

available to developers, it may or may not substitute for soft deletion, depending on its implementation.

At Google, revision history has proven useful in recovering from certain data corruption scenarios, but not in recovering from most data loss scenarios involving accidental deletion, programmatic or otherwise. This is because some revision history implementations treat deletion as a special case in which previous states must be removed, as opposed to mutating an item whose history may be retained for a certain time period. To provide adequate protection against unwanted deletion, apply the lazy and/or soft deletion principles to revision history also.

Second Layer: Backups and Their Related Recovery Methods

Backups and data recovery are the second line of defense after soft deletion. The most important principle in this layer is that backups don't matter; what matters is recovery. The factors supporting successful recovery should drive your backup decisions, not the other way around.

In other words, the scenarios in which you want your backups to help you recover should dictate the following:

- Which backup and recovery methods to use
- How frequently you establish restore points by taking full or incremental backups of your data
- Where you store backups
- How long you retain backups

How much recent data can you afford to lose during a recovery effort? The less data you can afford to lose, the more serious you should be about an incremental backup strategy. In one of Google's most extreme cases, we used a near-real-time streaming backup strategy for an older version of Gmail.

Even if money isn't a limitation, frequent full backups are expensive in other ways. Most notably, they impose a compute burden on the live datastores of your service while it's serving users, driving your service closer to its scalability and performance limits. To ease this burden, you can take full backups during off-peak hours, and then a series of incremental backups when your service is busier.

How quickly do you need to recover? The faster your users need to be rescued, the more local your backups should be. Often Google retains costly but quick-to-restore snapshots[8] for very short periods of time within the storage instance, and stores less recent backups on random access distributed storage within the same (or nearby) datacenter for a slightly longer time. Such a strategy alone would not protect from site-level failures, so those backups are often transferred to nearline or offline locations for a longer time period before they're expired in favor of newer backups.

How far back should your backups reach? Your backup strategy becomes more costly the further back you reach, while the scenarios from which you can hope to recover increase (although this increase is subject to diminishing returns).

In Google's experience, low-grade data mutation or deletion bugs within application code demand the furthest reaches back in time, as some of those bugs were noticed months after the first data loss began. Such cases suggest that you'd like the ability to reach back in time as far as possible.

On the flip side, in a high-velocity development environment, changes to code and schema may render older backups expensive or impossible to use. Furthermore, it is challenging to recover different subsets of data to different restore points, because doing so would involve multiple backups. Yet, that is exactly the sort of recovery effort demanded by low-grade data corruption or deletion scenarios.

The strategies described in "Third Layer: Early Detection" on page 356 are meant to speed detection of low-grade data mutation or deletion bugs within application code, at least partly warding off the need for this type of complex recovery effort. Still, how do you confer reasonable protection before you know what kinds of issues to detect? Google chose to draw the line between 30 and 90 days of backups for many services. Where a service falls within this window depends on its tolerance for data loss and its relative investments in early detection.

To sum up our advice for guarding against the 24 combinations of data integrity failure modes: addressing a broad range of scenarios at reasonable cost demands a tiered backup strategy. The first tier comprises many frequent and quickly restored backups stored closest to the live datastores, perhaps using the same or similar storage technologies as the data sources. Doing so confers protection from the majority of scenarios involving software bugs and developer error. Due to relative expense, backups are retained in this tier for anywhere from hours to single-digit days, and may take minutes to restore.

The second tier comprises fewer backups retained for single-digit or low double-digit days on random access distributed filesystems local to the site. These backups may

---

8 "Snapshot" here refers to a read-only, static view of a storage instance, such as snapshots of SQL databases. Snapshots are often implemented using copy-on-write semantics for storage efficiency. They can be expensive for two reasons: first, they contend for the same storage capacity as the live datastores, and second, the faster your data mutates, the less efficiency is gained from copying-on-write.

take hours to restore and confer additional protection from mishaps affecting particular storage technologies in your serving stack, but not the technologies used to contain the backups. This tier also protects against bugs in your application that are detected too late to rely upon the first tier of your backup strategy. If you are introducing new versions of your code to production twice a week, it may make sense to retain these backups for at least a week or two before deleting them.

Subsequent tiers take advantage of nearline storage such as dedicated tape libraries and offsite storage of the backup media (e.g., tapes or disk drives). Backups in these tiers confer protection against site-level issues, such as a datacenter power outage or distributed filesystem corruption due to a bug.

It is expensive to move large amounts of data to and from tiers. On the other hand, storage capacity at the later tiers does not contend with growth of the live production storage instances of your service. As a result, backups in these tiers tend to be taken less frequently but retained longer.

Overarching Layer: Replication

In an ideal world, every storage instance, including the instances containing your backups, would be replicated. During a data recovery effort, the last thing you want is to discover is that your backups themselves lost the needed data or that the datacenter containing the most useful backup is under maintenance.

As the volume of data increases, replication of every storage instance isn't always feasible. In such cases, it makes sense to stagger successive backups across different sites, each of which may fail independently, and to write your backups using a redundancy method such as RAID, Reed-Solomon erasure codes, or GFS-style replication.[9]

When choosing a system of redundancy, don't rely upon an infrequently used scheme whose only "tests" of efficacy are your own infrequent data recovery attempts. Instead, choose a popular scheme that's in common and continual use by many of its users.

1T Versus 1E: Not "Just" a Bigger Backup

Processes and practices applied to volumes of data measured in T (terabytes) don't scale well to data measured in E (exabytes). Validating, copying, and performing round-trip tests on a few gigabytes of structured data is an interesting problem. However, assuming that you have sufficient knowledge of your schema and transaction model, this exercise doesn't present any special challenges. You typically just need to

---

9 For more information on GFS-style replication, see [Ghe03]. For more information on Reed-Solomon erasure codes, see *https://en.wikipedia.org/wiki/Reed–Solomon_error_correction*.

procure the machine resources to iterate over your data, perform some validation logic, and delegate enough storage to hold a few copies of your data.

Now let's up the ante: instead of a few gigabytes, let's try securing and validating 700 petabytes of structured data. Assuming ideal SATA 2.0 performance of 300 MB/s, a single task that iterates over all of your data and performs even the most basic of validation checks will take 8 decades. Making a few full backups, assuming you have the media, is going to take at least as long. Restore time, with some post-processing, will take even longer. We're now looking at almost a full century to restore a backup that was up to 80 years old when you started the restore. Obviously, such a strategy needs to be rethought.

The most common and largely effective technique used to back up massive amounts of data is to establish "trust points" in your data—portions of your stored data that are verified after being rendered immutable, usually by the passage of time. Once we know that a given user profile or transaction is fixed and won't be subject to further change, we can verify its internal state and make suitable copies for recovery purposes. You can then make incremental backups that only include data that has been modified or added since your last backup. This technique brings your backup time in line with your "mainline" processing time, meaning that frequent incremental backups can save you from the 80-year monolithic verify and copy job.

However, remember that we care about *restores*, not backups. Let's say that we took a full backup three years ago and have been making daily incremental backups since. A full restore of our data will serially process a chain of over 1,000 highly interdependent backups. Each independent backup incurs additional risk of failure, not to mention the logistical burden of scheduling and the runtime cost of those jobs.

Another way we can reduce the wall time of our copying and verification jobs is to distribute the load. If we shard our data well, it's possible to run N tasks in parallel, with each task responsible for copying and verifying $1/N$th of our data. Doing so requires some forethought and planning in the schema design and the physical deployment of our data in order to:

- Balance the data correctly
- Ensure the independence of each shard
- Avoid contention among the concurrent sibling tasks

Between distributing the load horizontally and restricting the work to vertical slices of the data demarcated by time, we can reduce those eight decades of wall time by several orders of magnitude, rendering our restores relevant.

Third Layer: Early Detection

"Bad" data doesn't sit idly by, it propagates. References to missing or corrupt data are copied, links fan out, and with every update the overall quality of your datastore goes down. Subsequent dependent transactions and potential data format changes make restoring from a given backup more difficult as the clock ticks. The sooner you know about a data loss, the easier and more complete your recovery can be.

Challenges faced by cloud developers

In high-velocity environments, cloud application and infrastructure services face many data integrity challenges at runtime, such as:

- Referential integrity between datastores
- Schema changes
- Aging code
- Zero-downtime data migrations
- Evolving integration points with other services

Without conscious engineering effort to track emerging relationships in its data, the data quality of a successful and growing service degrades over time.

Often, the novice cloud developer who chooses a distributed consistent storage API (such as Megastore) delegates the integrity of the application's data to the distributed consistent algorithm implemented beneath the API (such as Paxos; see Chapter 23). The developer reasons that the selected API alone will keep the application's data in good shape. As a result, they unify all application data into a single storage solution that guarantees distributed consistency, avoiding referential integrity problems in exchange for reduced performance and/or scale.

While such algorithms are infallible in theory, their implementations are often riddled with hacks, optimizations, bugs, and educated guesses. For example: in theory, Paxos ignores failed compute nodes and can make progress as long as a quorum of functioning nodes is maintained. In practice, however, ignoring a failed node may correspond to timeouts, retries, and other failure-handling approaches beneath the particular Paxos implementation [Cha07]. How long should Paxos try to contact an unresponsive node before timing it out? When a particular machine fails (perhaps intermittently) in a certain way, with a certain timing, and at a particular datacenter, unpredictable behavior results. The larger the scale of an application, the more frequently the application is affected, unbeknownst, by such inconsistencies. If this logic holds true even when applied to Paxos implementations (as has been true for Google), then it must be more true for eventually consistent implementations such as Bigtable (which has also shown to be true). Affected applications have no way to know that 100% of their data is good until they check: trust storage systems, but verify!

To complicate this problem, in order to recover from low-grade data corruption or deletion scenarios, we must recover different subsets of data to different restore points using different backups, while changes to code and schema may render older backups ineffective in high-velocity environments.

Out-of-band data validation

To prevent data quality from degrading before users' eyes, and to detect low-grade data corruption or data loss scenarios before they become unrecoverable, a system of out-of-band checks and balances is needed both within and between an application's datastores.

Most often, these data validation pipelines are implemented as collections of map-reductions or Hadoop jobs. Frequently, such pipelines are added as an afterthought to services that are already popular and successful. Sometimes, such pipelines are first attempted when services reach scalability limits and are rebuilt from the ground up. Google has built validators in response to each of these situations.

Shunting some developers to work on a data validation pipeline can slow engineering velocity in the short term. However, devoting engineering resources to data validation endows other developers with the courage to move faster in the long run, because the engineers know that data corruption bugs are less likely to sneak into production unnoticed. Similar to the effects enjoyed when units test are introduced early in the project lifecycle, a data validation pipeline results in an overall acceleration of software development projects.

To cite a specific example: Gmail sports a number of data validators, each of which has detected actual data integrity problems in production. Gmail developers derive comfort from the knowledge that bugs introducing inconsistencies in production data are detected within 24 hours, and shudder at the thought of running their data validators less often than daily. These validators, along with a culture of unit and regression testing and other best practices, have given Gmail developers the courage to introduce code changes to Gmail's production storage implementation more frequently than once a week.

Out-of-band data validation is tricky to implement correctly. When too strict, even simple, appropriate changes cause validation to fail. As a result, engineers abandon data validation altogether. If the data validation isn't strict enough, user experience–affecting data corruption can slip through undetected. To find the right balance, only validate invariants that cause devastation to users.

For example, Google Drive periodically validates that file contents align with listings in Drive folders. If these two elements don't align, some files would be missing data—

a disastrous outcome. Drive infrastructure developers were so invested in data integrity that they also enhanced their validators to automatically fix such inconsistencies. This safeguard turned a potential emergency "all-hands-on-deck-omigosh-files-are-disappearing!" data loss situation in 2013 into a business as usual, "let's go home and fix the root cause on Monday," situation. By transforming emergencies into business as usual, validators improve engineering morale, quality of life, and predictability.

Out-of-band validators can be expensive at scale. A significant portion of Gmail's compute resource footprint supports a collection of daily validators. To compound this expense, these validators also lower server-side cache hit rates, reducing server-side responsiveness experienced by users. To mitigate this hit to responsiveness, Gmail provides a variety of knobs for rate-limiting its validators and periodically refactors the validators to reduce disk contention. In one such refactoring effort, we cut the contention for disk spindles by 60% without significantly reducing the scope of the invariants they covered. While the majority of Gmail's validators run daily, the workload of the largest validator is divided into 10–14 shards, with one shard validated per day for reasons of scale.

Google Compute Storage is another example of the challenges scale entails to data validation. When its out-of-band validators could no longer finish within a day, Compute Storage engineers had to devise a more efficient way to verify its metadata than use of brute force alone. Similar to its application in data recovery, a tiered strategy can also be useful in out-of-band data validation. As a service scales, sacrifice rigor in daily validators. Make sure that daily validators continue to catch the most disastrous scenarios within 24 hours, but continue with more rigorous validation at reduced frequency to contain costs and latency.

Troubleshooting failed validations can take significant effort. Causes of an intermittent failed validation could vanish within minutes, hours, or days. Therefore, the ability to rapidly drill down into validation audit logs is essential. Mature Google services provide on-call engineers with comprehensive documentation and tools to troubleshoot. For example, on-call engineers for Gmail are provided with:

- A suite of playbook entries describing how to respond to a validation failure alert
- A BigQuery-like investigation tool
- A data validation dashboard

Effective out-of-band data validation demands all of the following:

- Validation job management
- Monitoring, alerts, and dashboards
- Rate-limiting features
- Troubleshooting tools

- Production playbooks
- Data validation APIs that make validators easy to add and refactor

The majority of small engineering teams operating at high velocity can't afford to design, build, and maintain all of these systems. If they are pressured to do so, the result is often fragile, limited, and wasteful one-offs that fall quickly into disrepair. Therefore, structure your engineering teams such that a central infrastructure team provides a data validation framework for multiple product engineering teams. The central infrastructure team maintains the out-of-band data validation framework, while the product engineering teams maintain the custom business logic at the heart of the validator to keep pace with their evolving products.

Knowing That Data Recovery Will Work

When does a light bulb break? When flicking the switch fails to turn on the light? Not always—often the bulb had already failed, and you simply notice the failure at the unresponsive flick of the switch. By then, the room is dark and you've stubbed your toe.

Likewise, your recovery dependencies (meaning mostly, but not only, your backup), may be in a latent broken state, which you aren't aware of until you attempt to recover data.

If you discover that your restore process is broken before you need to rely upon it, you can address the vulnerability before you fall victim to it: you can take another backup, provision additional resources, and change your SLO. But to take these actions proactively, you first have to know they're needed. To detect these vulnerabilities:

- Continuously test the recovery process as part of your normal operations
- Set up alerts that fire when a recovery process fails to provide a heartbeat indication of its success

What can go wrong with your recovery process? Anything and everything—which is why the only test that should let you sleep at night is a full end-to-end test. Let the proof be in the pudding. Even if you recently ran a successful recovery, parts of your recovery process can still break. If you take away just one lesson from this chapter, remember that *you only know that you can recover your recent state if you actually do so.*

If recovery tests are a manual, staged event, testing becomes an unwelcome bit of drudgery that isn't performed either deeply or frequently enough to deserve your confidence. Therefore, automate these tests whenever possible and then run them continuously.

The aspects of your recovery plan you should confirm are myriad:

- Are your backups valid and complete, or are they empty?
- Do you have sufficient machine resources to run all of the setup, restore, and post-processing tasks that comprise your recovery?
- Does the recovery process complete in reasonable wall time?
- Are you able to monitor the state of your recovery process as it progresses?
- Are you free of critical dependencies on resources outside of your control, such as access to an offsite media storage vault that isn't available 24/7?

Our testing has discovered the aforementioned failures, as well as failures of many other components of a successful data recovery. If we hadn't discovered these failures in regular tests—that is, if we came across the failures only when we needed to recover user data in real emergencies—it's quite possible that some of Google's most successful products today may not have stood the test of time.

Failures are inevitable. If you wait to discover them when you're under the gun, facing a real data loss, you're playing with fire. If testing forces the failures to happen before actual catastrophe strikes, you can fix problems before any harm comes to fruition.

Case Studies

Life imitates art (or in this case, science), and as we predicted, real life has given us unfortunate and inevitable opportunities to put our data recovery systems and processes to the test, under real-world pressure. Two of the more notable and interesting of these opportunities are discussed here.

Gmail—February, 2011: Restore from GTape

The first recovery case study we'll examine was unique in a couple of ways: the number of failures that coincided to bring about the data loss, and the fact that it was the largest use of our last line of defense, the GTape offline backup system.

Sunday, February 27, 2011, late in the evening

The Gmail backup system pager is triggered, displaying a phone number to join a conference call. The event we had long feared—indeed, the reason for the backup system's existence—has come to pass: Gmail lost a significant amount of user data. Despite the system's many safeguards and internal checks and redundancies, the data disappeared from Gmail.

This was the first large-scale use of GTape, a global backup system for Gmail, to restore live customer data. Fortunately, it was not the first such restore, as similar situations had been previously simulated many times. Therefore, we were able to:

- Deliver an estimate of how long it would take to restore the majority of the affected user accounts
- Restore all of the accounts within several hours of our initial estimate
- Recover 99%+ of the data before the estimated completion time

Was the ability to formulate such an estimate luck? No—our success was the fruit of planning, adherence to best practices, hard work, and cooperation, and we were glad to see our investment in each of these elements pay off as well as it did. Google was able to restore the lost data in a timely manner by executing a plan designed according to the best practices of *Defense in Depth* and *Emergency Preparedness*.

When Google publicly revealed that we recovered this data from our previously undisclosed tape backup system [Slo11], public reaction was a mix of surprise and amusement. Tape? Doesn't Google have lots of disks and a fast network to replicate data this important? Of course Google has such resources, but the principle of Defense in Depth dictates providing multiple layers of protection to guard against the breakdown or compromise of any single protection mechanism. Backing up online systems such as Gmail provides defense in depth at two layers:

- A failure of the internal Gmail redundancy and backup subsystems
- A wide failure or zero-day vulnerability in a device driver or filesystem affecting the underlying storage medium (disk)

This particular failure resulted from the first scenario—while Gmail had internal means of recovering lost data, this loss went beyond what internal means could recover.

One of the most internally celebrated aspects of the Gmail data recovery was the degree of cooperation and smooth coordination that comprised the recovery. Many teams, some completely unrelated to Gmail or data recovery, pitched in to help. The recovery couldn't have succeeded so smoothly without a central plan to choreograph such a widely distributed Herculean effort; this plan was the product of regular dress rehearsals and dry runs. Google's devotion to emergency preparedness leads us to view such failures as inevitable. Accepting this inevitability, we don't hope or bet to avoid such disasters, but anticipate that they will occur. Thus, we need a plan for dealing not only with the foreseeable failures, but for some amount of random undifferentiated breakage, as well.

In short, we always *knew* that adherence to best practices is important, and it was good to see that maxim proven true.

Google Music—March 2012: Runaway Deletion Detection

The second failure we'll examine entails challenges in logistics that are unique to the scale of the datastore being recovered: where do you store over 5,000 tapes, and how do you efficiently (or even feasibly) read that much data from offline media in a reasonable amount of time?

Tuesday, March 6th, 2012, mid-afternoon

Discovering the problem

A Google Music user reports that previously unproblematic tracks are being skipped. The team responsible for interfacing with Google Music's users notifies Google Music engineers. The problem is investigated as a possible media streaming issue.

On March 7th, the investigating engineer discovers that the unplayable track's metadata is missing a reference that should point to the actual audio data. He is surprised. The obvious fix is to locate the audio data and reinstate the reference to the data. However, Google engineering prides itself for a culture of fixing issues at the root, so the engineer digs deeper.

When he finds the cause of the data integrity lapse, he almost has a heart attack: the audio reference was removed by a privacy-protecting data deletion pipeline. This part of Google Music was designed to delete very large numbers of audio tracks in record time.

Assessing the damage

Google's privacy policy protects a user's personal data. As applied to Google Music specifically, our privacy policy means that music files and relevant metadata are removed within reasonable time after users delete them. As the popularity of Google Music soared, the amount of data grew rapidly, so the original deletion implementation needed to be redesigned in 2012 to be more efficient. On February 6th, the updated data deletion pipeline enjoyed its maiden run, to remove relevant metadata. Nothing seemed amiss at the time, so a second stage of the pipeline was allowed to remove the associated audio data too.

Could the engineer's worst nightmare be true? He immediately sounded the alarm, raising the priority of the support case to Google's most urgent classification and reporting the issue to engineering management and Site Reliability Engineering. A small team of Google Music developers and SREs assembled to tackle the issue, and the offending pipeline was temporarily disabled to stem the tide of external user casualties.

Next, manually checking the metadata for millions to billions of files organized across multiple datacenters would be unthinkable. So the team whipped up a hasty

MapReduce job to assess the damage and waited desperately for the job to complete. They froze as its results came in on March 8th: the refactored data deletion pipeline had removed approximately 600,000 audio references that shouldn't have been removed, affecting audio files for 21,000 users. Since the hasty diagnosis pipeline made a few simplifications, the true extent of the damage could be worse.

It had been over a month since the buggy data deletion pipeline first ran, and that maiden run itself removed hundreds of thousands of audio tracks that should not have been removed. Was there any hope of getting the data back? If the tracks weren't recovered, or weren't recovered fast enough, Google would have to face the music from its users. How could we not have noticed this glitch?

Resolving the issue

Parallel bug identification and recovery efforts. The first step in resolving the issue was to identify the actual bug, and determine how and why the bug happened. As long as the root cause wasn't identified and fixed, any recovery efforts would be in vain. We would be under pressure to re-enable the pipeline to respect the requests of users who deleted audio tracks, but doing so would hurt innocent users who would continue to lose store-bought music, or worse, their own painstakingly recorded audio files. The only way to escape the Catch-22[10] was to fix the issue at its root, and fix it quickly.

Yet there was no time to waste before mounting the recovery effort. The audio tracks themselves were backed up to tape, but unlike our Gmail case study, the encrypted backup tapes for Google Music were trucked to offsite storage locations, because that option offered more space for voluminous backups of users' audio data. To restore the experience of affected users quickly, the team decided to troubleshoot the root cause while retrieving the offsite backup tapes (a rather time-intensive restore option) in parallel.

The engineers split into two groups. The most experienced SREs worked on the recovery effort, while the developers analyzed the data deletion code and attempted to fix the data loss bug at its root. Due to incomplete knowledge of the root problem, the recovery would have to be staged in multiple passes. The first batch of nearly half a million audio tracks was identified, and the team that maintained the tape backup system was notified of the emergency recovery effort at 4:34 p.m. Pacific Time on March 8th.

The recovery team had one factor working in their favor: this recovery effort occurred just weeks after the company's annual disaster recovery testing exercise (see [Kri12]). The tape backup team already knew the capabilities and limitations of their subsystems that had been the subjects of DiRT tests and began dusting off a new tool

---

10 See *http://en.wikipedia.org/wiki/Catch-22_(logic)*.

they'd tested during a DiRT exercise. Using the new tool, the combined recovery team began the painstaking effort of mapping hundreds of thousands of audio files to backups registered in the tape backup system, and then mapping the files from backups to actual tapes.

In this way, the team determined that the initial recovery effort would involve the recall of over 5,000 backup tapes by truck. Afterwards, datacenter technicians would have to clear out space for the tapes at tape libraries. A long, complex process of registering the tapes and extracting the data from the tapes would follow, involving workarounds and mitigations in the event of bad tapes, bad drives, and unexpected system interactions.

Unfortunately, only 436,223 of the approximately 600,000 lost audio tracks were found on tape backups, which meant that about 161,000 other audio tracks were eaten before they could be backed up. The recovery team decided to figure out how to recover the 161,000 missing tracks after they initiated the recovery process for the tracks with tape backups.

Meanwhile, the root cause team had pursued and abandoned a red herring: they initially thought that a storage service on which Google Music depended had provided buggy data that misled the data deletion pipelines to remove the wrong audio data. Upon closer investigation, that theory was proven false. The root cause team scratched their heads and continued their search for the elusive bug.

First wave of recovery. Once the recovery team had identified the backup tapes, the first recovery wave kicked off on March 8th. Requesting 1.5 petabytes of data distributed among thousands of tapes from offsite storage was one matter, but extracting the data from the tapes was quite another. The custom-built tape backup software stack wasn't designed to handle a single restore operation of such a large size, so the initial recovery was split into 5,475 restore jobs. It would take a human operator typing in one restore command a minute more than three days to request that many restores, and any human operator would no doubt make many mistakes. Just requesting the restore from the tape backup system needed SRE to develop a programmatic solution.[11]

By midnight on March 9th, Music SRE finished requesting all 5,475 restores. The tape backup system began working its magic. Four hours later, it spat out a list of 5,337 backup tapes to be recalled from offsite locations. In another eight hours, the tapes arrived at a datacenter in a series of truck deliveries.

---

11 In practice, coming up with a programmatic solution was not a hurdle because the majority of SREs are experienced software engineers, as was the case here. The expectation of such experience makes SREs notoriously hard to find and hire, and from this case study and other data points, you can begin to appreciate why SRE hires practicing software engineers; see [Jon15].

While the trucks were en route, datacenter technicians took several tape libraries down for maintenance and removed thousands of tapes to make way for the massive data recovery operation. Then the technicians began painstakingly loading the tapes by hand as thousands of tapes arrived in the wee hours of the morning. In past DiRT exercises, this manual process proved hundreds of times faster for massive restores than the robot-based methods provided by the tape library vendors. Within three hours, the libraries were back up scanning the tapes and performing thousands of restore jobs onto distributed compute storage.

Despite the team's DiRT experience, the massive 1.5 petabyte recovery took longer than the two days estimated. By the morning of March 10th, only 74% of the 436,223 audio files had been successfully transferred from 3,475 recalled backup tapes to distributed filesystem storage at a nearby compute cluster. The other 1,862 backup tapes had been omitted from the tape recall process by a vendor. In addition, the recovery process had been held up by 17 bad tapes. In anticipation of a failure due to bad tapes, a redundant encoding had been used to write the backup files. Additional truck deliveries were set off to recall the redundancy tapes, along with the other 1,862 tapes that had been omitted by the first offsite recall.

By the morning of March 11th, over 99.95% of the restore operation had completed, and the recall of additional redundancy tapes for the remaining files was in progress. Although the data was safely on distributed filesystems, additional data recovery steps were necessary in order to make them accessible to users. The Google Music Team began exercising these final steps of the data recovery process in parallel on a small sample of recovered audio files to make sure the process still worked as expected.

At that moment, Google Music production pagers sounded due to an unrelated but critical user-affecting production failure—a failure that fully engaged the Google Music team for two days. The data recovery effort resumed on March 13th, when all 436,223 audio tracks were once again made accessible to their users. In just short of 7 days, 1.5 petabytes of audio data had been reinstated to users with the help of offsite tape backups; 5 of the 7 days comprised the actual data recovery effort.

Second wave of recovery. With the first wave of the recovery process behind them, the team shifted its focus to the other 161,000 missing audio files that had been deleted by the bug before they were backed up. The majority of these files were store-bought and promotional tracks, and the original store copies were unaffected by the bug. Such tracks were quickly reinstated so that the affected users could enjoy their music again.

However, a small portion of the 161,000 audio files had been uploaded by the users themselves. The Google Music Team prompted their servers to request that the Google Music clients of affected users re-upload files dating from March 14th onward.

This process lasted more than a week. Thus concluded the complete recovery effort for the incident.

Addressing the root cause

Eventually, the Google Music Team identified the flaw in their refactored data deletion pipeline. To understand this flaw, you first need context about how offline data processing systems evolve on a large scale.

For a large and complex service comprising several subsystems and storage services, even a task as simple as removing deleted data needs to be performed in stages, each involving different datastores.

For data processing to finish quickly, the processing is parallelized to run across tens of thousands of machines that exert a large load on various subsystems. This distribution can slow the service for users, or cause the service to crash under the heavy load.

To avoid these undesirable scenarios, cloud computing engineers often make a short-lived copy of data on secondary storage, where the data processing is then performed. Unless the relative age of the secondary copies of data is carefully coordinated, this practice introduces race conditions.

For instance, two stages of a pipeline may be designed to run in strict succession, three hours apart, so that the second stage can make a simplifying assumption about the correctness of its inputs. Without this simplifying assumption, the logic of the second stage may be hard to parallelize. But the stages may take longer to complete as the volume of data grows. Eventually, the original design assumptions may no longer hold for certain pieces of data needed by the second stage.

At first, this race condition may occur for a tiny fraction of data. But as the volume of data increases, a larger and larger fraction of the data is at risk for triggering a race condition. Such a scenario is probabilistic—the pipeline works correctly for the vast majority of data and for most of the time. When such race conditions occur in a data deletion pipeline, the wrong data can be deleted nondeterministically.

Google Music's data deletion pipeline was designed with coordination and large margins for error in place. But when upstream stages of the pipeline began to require increased time as the service grew, performance optimizations were put in place so Google Music could continue to meet privacy requirements. As a result, the probability of an inadvertent data-deleting race condition in this pipeline began to increase. When the pipeline was refactored, this probability again significantly increased, up to a point at which the race conditions occurred more regularly.

In the wake of the recovery effort, Google Music redesigned its data deletion pipeline to eliminate this type of race condition. In addition, we enhanced production monitoring and alerting systems to detect similar large-scale runaway deletion bugs with the aim of detecting and fixing such issues before users notice any problems.[12]

General Principles of SRE as Applied to Data Integrity

General principles of SRE can be applied to the specifics of data integrity and cloud computing as described in this section.

Beginner's Mind

Large-scale, complex services have inherent bugs that can't be fully grokked. Never think you understand enough of a complex system to say it won't fail in a certain way. Trust but verify, and apply defense in depth. (Note: "Beginner's mind" does *not* suggest putting a new hire in charge of that data deletion pipeline!)

Trust but Verify

Any API upon which you depend won't work perfectly *all* of the time. It's a given that regardless of your engineering quality or rigor of testing, the API will have defects. Check the correctness of the most critical elements of your data using out-of-band data validators, even if API semantics suggest that you need not do so. Perfect algorithms may not have perfect implementations.

Hope Is Not a Strategy

System components that aren't continually exercised fail when you need them most. Prove that data recovery works with regular exercise, or data recovery won't work. Humans lack discipline to continually exercise system components, so automation is your friend. However, when you staff such automation efforts with engineers who have competing priorities, you may end up with temporary stopgaps.

Defense in Depth

Even the most bulletproof system is susceptible to bugs and operator error. In order for data integrity issues to be fixable, services must detect such issues quickly. Every strategy eventually fails in changing environments. The best data integrity strategies

---

12 In our experience, cloud computing engineers are often reluctant to set up production alerts on data deletion rates due to natural variation of per-user data deletion rates with time. However, since the intent of such an alert is to detect global rather than local deletion rate anomalies, it would be more useful to alert when the global data deletion rate, aggregated across all users, crosses an extreme threshold (such as 10x the observed 95th percentile), as opposed to less useful per-user deletion rate alerts.

are multitiered—multiple strategies that fall back to one another and address a broad swath of scenarios together at reasonable cost.

Revisit and Reexamine

The fact that your data "was safe yesterday" isn't going to help you tomorrow, or even today. Systems and infrastructure change, and you've got to prove that your assumptions and processes remain relevant in the face of progress. Consider the following.

The Shakespeare service has received quite a bit of positive press, and its user base is steadily increasing. No real attention was paid to data integrity as the service was being built. Of course, we don't want to serve *bad* bits, but if the index Bigtable is lost, we can easily re-create it from the original Shakespeare texts and a MapReduce. Doing so would take very little time, so we never made backups of the index.

Now a new feature allows users to make text annotations. Suddenly, our dataset can no longer be easily re-created, while the user data is increasingly valuable to our users. Therefore, we need to revisit our replication options—we're not just replicating for latency and bandwidth, but for data integrity, as well. Therefore, we need to create and test a backup and restore procedure. This procedure is also periodically tested by a DiRT exercise to ensure that we can restore users' annotations from backups within the time set by the SLO.

Conclusion

Data availability must be a foremost concern of any data-centric system. Rather than focusing on the means to the end, Google SRE finds it useful to borrow a page from test-driven development by proving that our systems can maintain data availability with a predicted maximum down time. The means and mechanisms that we use to achieve this end goal are necessary evils. By keeping our eyes on the goal, we avoid falling into the trap in which "The operation was a success, but the system died."

Recognizing that not just *anything* can go wrong, but that *everything* will go wrong is a significant step toward preparation for any real emergency. A matrix of all possible combinations of disasters with plans to address each of these disasters permits you to sleep soundly for at least one night; keeping your recovery plans current and exercised permits you to sleep the other 364 nights of the year.

As you get better at recovering from any breakage in reasonable time N, find ways to whittle down that time through more rapid and finer-grained loss detection, with the goal of approaching $N = 0$. You can then switch from planning recovery to planning prevention, with the aim of achieving the holy grail of *all the data, all the time*. Achieve this goal, and you can sleep on the beach on that well-deserved vacation.

CHAPTER 27

Reliable Product Launches at Scale

Written by Rhandeev Singh and Sebastian Kirsch with Vivek Rau
Edited by Betsy Beyer

Internet companies like Google are able to launch new products and features in far more rapid iterations than traditional companies. Site Reliability's role in this process is to enable a rapid pace of change without compromising stability of the site. We created a dedicated team of "Launch Coordination Engineers" to consult with engineering teams on the technical aspects of a successful launch.

The team also curated a "launch checklist" of common questions to ask about a launch, and recipes to solve common issues. The checklist proved to be a useful tool for ensuring reproducibly reliable launches.

Consider an ordinary Google service—for example, Keyhole, which serves satellite imagery for Google Maps and Google Earth. On a normal day, Keyhole serves up to several thousand satellite images per second. But on Christmas Eve in 2011, it received 25 times its normal peak traffic—upward of one million requests per second. What caused this massive surge in traffic?

Santa was coming.

A few years ago, Google collaborated with NORAD (the North American Aerospace Defense Command) to host a Christmas-themed website that tracked Santa's progress around the world, allowing users to watch him deliver presents in real time. Part of the experience was a "virtual fly-over," which used satellite imagery to track Santa's progress over a simulated world.

While a project like NORAD Tracks Santa may seem whimsical, it had all the characteristics that define a difficult and risky launch: a hard deadline (Google couldn't ask

Santa to come a week later if the site wasn't ready), a lot of publicity, an audience of millions, and a very steep traffic ramp-up (everybody was going to be watching the site on Christmas Eve). Never underestimate the power of millions of kids anxious for presents—this project had a very real possibility of bringing Google's servers to their knees.

Google's Site Reliability Engineering team worked hard to prepare our infrastructure for this launch, making sure that Santa could deliver all his presents on time under the watchful eyes of an expectant audience. The last thing we wanted was to make children cry because they couldn't watch Santa deliver presents. In fact, we dubbed the various kill switches built into the experience to protect our services "Make-children-cry switches." Anticipating the many different ways this launch could go wrong and coordinating between the different engineering groups involved in the launch fell to a special team within Site Reliability Engineering: the Launch Coordination Engineers (LCE).

Launching a new product or feature is the moment of truth for every company—the point at which months or years of effort are presented to the world. Traditional companies launch new products at a fairly low rate. The launch cycle at Internet companies is markedly different. Launches and rapid iterations are far easier because new features can be rolled out on the server side, rather than requiring software rollout on individual customer workstations.

Google defines a launch as any new code that introduces an externally visible change to an application. Depending on a launch's characteristics—the combination of attributes, the timing, the number of steps involved, and the complexity—the launch process can vary greatly. According to this definition, Google sometimes performs up to 70 launches per week.

This rapid rate of change provides both the rationale and the opportunity for creating a streamlined launch process. A company that only launches a product every three years doesn't need a detailed launch process. By the time a new launch occurs, most components of the previously developed launch process will be outdated. Nor do traditional companies have the opportunity to design a detailed launch process, because they don't accumulate enough experience performing launches to generate a robust and mature process.

Launch Coordination Engineering

Good software engineers have a great deal of expertise in coding and design, and understand the technology of their own products very well. However, the same engineers may be unfamiliar with the challenges and pitfalls of launching a product to millions of users while simultaneously minimizing outages and maximizing performance.

Google approached the challenges inherent to launches by creating a dedicated consulting team within SRE tasked with the technical side of launching a new product or feature. Staffed by software engineers and systems engineers—some with experience in other SRE teams—this team specializes in guiding developers toward building reliable and fast products that meet Google's standards for robustness, scalability, and reliability. This consulting team, Launch Coordination Engineering (LCE), facilitates a smooth launch process in a few ways:

- Auditing products and services for compliance with Google's reliability standards and best practices, and providing specific actions to improve reliability

- Acting as a liaison between the multiple teams involved in a launch

- Driving the technical aspects of a launch by making sure that tasks maintain momentum

- Acting as gatekeepers and signing off on launches determined to be "safe"

- Educating developers on best practices and on how to integrate with Google's services, equipping them with internal documentation and training resources to speed up their learning

Members of the LCE team audit services at various times during the service lifecycle. Most audits are conducted before a new product or service launches. If a product development team performs a launch without SRE support, LCE provides the appropriate domain knowledge to ensure a smooth launch. But even products that already have strong SRE support often engage with the LCE team during critical launches. The challenges teams face when launching a new product are substantially different from the day-to-day operation of a reliable service (a task at which SRE teams already excel), and the LCE team can draw on the experience from hundreds of launches. The LCE team also facilitates service audits when new services first engage with SRE.

The Role of the Launch Coordination Engineer

Our Launch Coordination Engineering team is composed of Launch Coordination Engineers (LCEs), who are either hired directly into this role, or are SREs with hands-on experience running Google services. LCEs are held to the same technical requirements as any other SRE, and are also expected to have strong communication and leadership skills—an LCE brings disparate parties together to work toward a common goal, mediates occasional conflicts, and guides, coaches, and educates fellow engineers.

A team dedicated to coordinating launches offers the following advantages:

Breadth of experience
As a true cross-product team, the members are active across almost all of Google's product areas. Extensive cross-product knowledge and relationships with many teams across the company make LCEs excellent vehicles for knowledge transfer.

Cross-functional perspective
LCEs have a holistic view of the launch, which enables them to coordinate among disparate teams in SRE, development, and product management. This holistic approach is particularly important for complicated launches that can span more than half a dozen teams in multiple time zones.

Objectivity
As a nonpartisan advisor, an LCE plays a balancing and mediating role between stakeholders including SRE, product developers, product managers, and marketing.

Because Launch Coordination Engineer is an SRE role, LCEs are incentivized to prioritize reliability over other concerns. A company that does not share Google's reliability goals, but shares its rapid rate of change, may choose a different incentive structure.

Setting Up a Launch Process

Google has honed its launch process over a period of more than 10 years. Over time we have identified a number of criteria that characterize a good launch process:

Lightweight
Easy on developers

Robust
Catches obvious errors

Thorough
Addresses important details consistently and reproducibly

Scalable
Accommodates both a large number of simple launches and fewer complex launches

Adaptable
Works well for common types of launches (for example, adding a new UI language to a product) and new types of launches (for example, the initial launch of the Chrome browser or Google Fiber)

As you can see, some of these requirements are in obvious conflict. For example, it's hard to design a process that is simultaneously lightweight and thorough. Balancing these criteria against each other requires continuous work. Google has successfully employed a few tactics to help us achieve these criteria:

Simplicity
Get the basics right. Don't plan for every eventuality.

A high touch approach
Experienced engineers customize the process to suit each launch.

Fast common paths
Identify classes of launches that always follow a common pattern (such as launching a product in a new country), and provide a simplified launch process for this class.

Experience has demonstrated that engineers are likely to sidestep processes that they consider too burdensome or as adding insufficient value—especially when a team is already in crunch mode, and the launch process is seen as just another item blocking their launch. For this reason, LCE must optimize the launch experience continuously to strike the right balance between cost and benefit.

The Launch Checklist

Checklists are used to reduce failure and ensure consistency and completeness across a variety of disciplines. Common examples include aviation preflight checklists and surgical checklists [Gaw09]. Similarly, LCE employs a launch checklist for launch qualification. The checklist (Appendix E) helps an LCE assess the launch and provides the launching team with action items and pointers to more information. Here are some examples of items a checklist might include:

- **Question**: Do you need a new domain name?
  - **Action item**: Coordinate with marketing on your desired domain name, and request registration of the domain. Here is a link to the marketing form.
- **Question**: Are you storing persistent data?
  - **Action item**: Make sure you implement backups. Here are instructions for implementing backups.
- **Question**: Could a user potentially abuse your service?
  - **Action item**: Implement rate limiting and quotas. Use the following shared service.

In practice, there is a near-infinite number of questions to ask about any system, and it is easy for the checklist to grow to an unmanageable size. Maintaining a manageable burden on developers requires careful curation of the checklist. In an effort to curb its growth, at one point, adding new questions to Google's launch checklist required approval from a vice president. LCE now uses the following guidelines:

- Every question's importance must be substantiated, ideally by a previous launch disaster.
- Every instruction must be concrete, practical, and reasonable for developers to accomplish.

The checklist needs continuous attention in order to remain relevant and up-to-date: recommendations change over time, internal systems are replaced by different systems, and areas of concern from previous launches become obsolete due to new policies and processes. LCEs curate the checklist continuously and make small updates when team members notice items that need to be modified. Once or twice a year a team member reviews the entire checklist to identify obsolete items, and then works with service owners and subject matter experts to modernize sections of the checklist.

Driving Convergence and Simplification

In a large organization, engineers may not be aware of available infrastructure for common tasks (such as rate limiting). Lacking proper guidance, they're likely to reimplement existing solutions. Converging on a set of common infrastructure libraries avoids this scenario, and provides obvious benefits to the company: it cuts down on duplicate effort, makes knowledge more easily transferable between services, and results in a higher level of engineering and service quality due to the concentrated attention given to infrastructure.

Almost all groups at Google participate in a common launch process, which makes the launch checklist a vehicle for driving convergence on common infrastructure. Rather than implementing a custom solution, LCE can recommend existing infrastructure as building blocks—infrastructure that is already hardened through years of experience and that can help mitigate capacity, performance, or scalability risks. Examples include common infrastructure for rate limiting or user quotas, pushing new data to servers, or releasing new versions of a binary. This type of standardization helped to radically simplify the launch checklist: for example, long sections of the checklist dealing with requirements for rate limiting could be replaced with a single line that stated, "Implement rate limiting using system X."

Due to their breadth of experience across all of Google's products, LCEs are also in a unique position to identify opportunities for simplification. While working on a launch, they witness the stumbling blocks firsthand: which parts of a launch are causing the most struggle, which steps take a disproportionate amount of time, which problems get solved independently over and over again in similar ways, where common infrastructure is lacking, or where duplication exists in common infrastructure.

LCEs have various ways to streamline the launch experience and act as advocates for the launching teams. For example, LCEs might work with the owners of a particularly arduous approval process to simplify their criteria and implement automatic approvals for common cases. LCEs can also escalate pain points to the owners of common infrastructure and create a dialogue with the customers. By leveraging experience gained over the course of multiple previous launches, LCEs can devote more attention to individual concerns and suggestions.

Launching the Unexpected

When a project enters into a new product space or vertical, an LCE may need to create an appropriate checklist from scratch. Doing so often involves synthesizing experience from relevant domain experts. When drafting a new checklist, it can be helpful to structure the checklist around broad themes such as reliability, failure modes, and processes.

For example, before launching Android, Google had rarely dealt with mass consumer devices with client-side logic that we didn't directly control. While we can more or less easily fix a bug in Gmail within hours or days by pushing new versions of JavaScript to browsers, such fixes aren't an option with mobile devices. Therefore, LCEs working on mobile launches engaged mobile domain experts to determine which sections of existing checklists did or did not apply, and where new checklist questions were needed. In such conversations, it's important to keep the *intent* of each question in mind in order to avoid mindlessly applying a concrete question or action item that's not relevant to the design of the unique product being launched. An LCE facing an unusual launch must return to abstract first principles of how to execute a safe launch, then respecialize to make the checklist concrete and useful to developers.

Developing a Launch Checklist

A checklist is instrumental to launching new services and products with reproducible reliability. Our launch checklist grew over time and was periodically curated by members of the Launch Coordination Engineering team. The details of a launch checklist will be different for every company, because the specifics must be tailored to a company's internal services and infrastructure. In the following sections, we extract a number of themes from Google's LCE checklists and provide examples of how such themes might be fleshed out.

Architecture and Dependencies

An architecture review allows you to determine if the service is using shared infrastructure correctly and identifies the owners of shared infrastructure as additional stakeholders in the launch. Google has a large number of internal services that are used as building blocks for new products. During later stages of capacity planning (see [Hix15a]), the list of dependencies identified in this section of the checklist can be used to make sure that every dependency is correctly provisioned.

Example checklist questions

- What is your request flow from user to frontend to backend?
- Are there different types of requests with different latency requirements?

Example action items

- Isolate user-facing requests from non user–facing requests.
- Validate request volume assumptions. One page view can turn into many requests.

Integration

Many companies' services run in an internal ecosystem that entails guidelines on how to set up machines, configure new services, set up monitoring, integrate with load balancing, set up DNS addresses, and so forth. These internal ecosystems usually grow over time, and often have their own idiosyncrasies and pitfalls to navigate. Thus, this section of the checklist will vary widely from company to company.

Example action items

- Set up a new DNS name for your service.
- Set up load balancers to talk to your service.
- Set up monitoring for your new service.

Capacity Planning

New features may exhibit a temporary increase in usage at launch that subsides within days. The type of workload or traffic mix from a launch spike could be substantially different from steady state, throwing off load test results. Public interest is notoriously hard to predict, and some Google products had to accommodate launch spikes up to 15 times higher than initially estimated. Launching initially in one region or country at a time helps develop the confidence to handle larger launches.

Capacity interacts with redundancy and availability. For instance, if you need three replicated deployments to serve 100% of your traffic at peak, you need to maintain four or five deployments, one or two of which are redundant, in order to shield users from maintenance and unexpected malfunctions. Datacenter and network resources often have a long lead time and need to be requested far enough in advance for your company to obtain them.

Example checklist questions

- Is this launch tied to a press release, advertisement, blog post, or other form of promotion?
- How much traffic and rate of growth do you expect during and after the launch?
- Have you obtained all the compute resources needed to support your traffic?

Failure Modes

A systematic look at the possible failure modes of a new service ensures high reliability from the start. In this portion of the checklist, examine each component and dependency and identify the impact of its failure. Can the service deal with individual machine failures? Datacenter outages? Network failures? How do we deal with bad input data? Are we prepared for the possibility of a denial-of-service (DoS) attack? Can the service continue serving in degraded mode if one of its dependencies fails? How do we deal with unavailability of a dependency upon startup of the service? During runtime?

Example checklist questions

- Do you have any single points of failure in your design?
- How do you mitigate unavailability of your dependencies?

Example action items

- Implement request deadlines to avoid running out of resources for long-running requests.
- Implement load shedding to reject new requests early in overload situations.

Client Behavior

On a traditional website, there is rarely a need to take abusive behavior from legitimate users into account. When every request is triggered by a user action such as a click on a link, the request rates are limited by how quickly users can click. To double the load, the number of users would have to double.

This axiom no longer holds when we consider clients that initiate actions without user input—for example, a cell phone app that periodically syncs its data into the cloud, or a website that periodically refreshes. In either of these scenarios, abusive client behavior can very easily threaten the stability of a service. (There is also the topic of protecting a service from abusive traffic such as scrapers and denial-of-service attacks—which is different from designing safe behavior for first-party clients.)

Example checklist question

- Do you have auto-save/auto-complete/heartbeat functionality?

Example action items

- Make sure that your client backs off exponentially on failure.
- Make sure that you jitter automatic requests.

Processes and Automation

Google encourages engineers to use standard tools to automate common processes. However, automation is never perfect, and every service has processes that need to be executed by a human: creating a new release, moving the service to a different data center, restoring data from backups, and so on. For reliability reasons, we strive to minimize single points of failure, which include humans.

These remaining processes should be documented before launch to ensure that the information is translated from an engineer's mind onto paper while it is still fresh, and that it is available in an emergency. Processes should be documented in such a way that any team member can execute a given process in an emergency.

Example checklist question

- Are there any manual processes required to keep the service running?

Example action items

- Document all manual processes.
- Document the process for moving your service to a new datacenter.
- Automate the process for building and releasing a new version.

Development Process

Google is an extensive user of version control, and almost all development processes are deeply integrated with the version control system. Many of our best practices

---

revolve around how to use the version control system effectively. For example, we perform most development on the mainline branch, but releases are built on separate branches per release. This setup makes it easy to fix bugs in a release without pulling in unrelated changes from the mainline.

Google also uses version control for other purposes, such as storing configuration files. Many of the advantages of version control—history tracking, attributing changes to individuals, and code reviews—apply to configuration files as well. In some cases, we also propagate changes from the version control system to the live servers automatically, so that an engineer only needs to submit a change to make it go live.

Example action items

- Check all code and configuration files into the version control system.
- Cut each release on a new release branch.

External Dependencies

Sometimes a launch depends on factors beyond company control. Identifying these factors allows you to mitigate the unpredictability they entail. For instance, the dependency may be a code library maintained by third parties, or a service or data provided by another company. When a vendor outage, bug, systematic error, security issue, or unexpected scalability limit actually occurs, prior planning will enable you to avert or mitigate damage to your users. In Google's history of launches, we've used filtering and/or rewriting proxies, data transcoding pipelines, and caches to mitigate some of these risks.

Example checklist questions

- What third-party code, data, services, or events does the service or the launch depend upon?
- Do any partners depend on your service? If so, do they need to be notified of your launch?
- What happens if you or the vendor can't meet a hard launch deadline?

Rollout Planning

In large distributed systems, few events happen instantaneously. For reasons of reliability, such immediacy isn't usually ideal anyway. A complicated launch might require enabling individual features on a number of different subsystems, and each of those configuration changes might take hours to complete. Having a working configuration in a test instance doesn't guarantee that the same configuration can be rolled out to the live instance. Sometimes a complicated dance or special functionality is required to make all components launch cleanly and in the correct order.

External requirements from teams like marketing and PR might add further complications. For example, a team might need a feature to be available in time for the keynote at a conference, but need to keep the feature invisible before the keynote.

Contingency measures are another part of rollout planning. What if you don't manage to enable the feature in time for the keynote? Sometimes these contingency measures are as simple as preparing a backup slide deck that says, "We will be launching this feature over the next days" rather than "We have launched this feature."

Example action items

- Set up a launch plan that identifies actions to take to launch the service. Identify who is responsible for each item.
- Identify risk in the individual launch steps and implement contingency measures.

Selected Techniques for Reliable Launches

As described in other parts of this book, Google has developed a number of techniques for running reliable systems over the years. Some of these techniques are particularly well suited to launching products safely. They also provide advantages during regular operation of the service, but it's particularly important to get them right during the launch phase.

Gradual and Staged Rollouts

One adage of system administration is "never change a running system." Any change represents risk, and risk should be minimized in order to assure reliability of a system. What's true for any small system is doubly true for highly replicated, globally distributed systems like those run by Google.

Very few launches at Google are of the "push-button" variety, in which we launch a new product at a specific time for the entire world to use. Over time, Google has developed a number of patterns that allow us to launch products and features gradually and thereby minimize risk; see Appendix B.

Almost all updates to Google's services proceed gradually, according to a defined process, with appropriate verification steps interspersed. A new server might be installed on a few machines in one datacenter and observed for a defined period of time. If all looks well, the server is installed on all machines in one datacenter, observed again, and then installed on all machines globally. The first stages of a rollout are usually called "canaries"—an allusion to canaries carried by miners into a coal mine to detect dangerous gases. Our canary servers detect dangerous effects from the behavior of the new software under real user traffic.

Canary testing is a concept embedded into many of Google's internal tools used to make automated changes, as well as for systems that change configuration files. Tools that manage the installation of new software typically observe the newly started server for a while, making sure that the server doesn't crash or otherwise misbehave. If the change doesn't pass the validation period, it's automatically rolled back.

The concept of gradual rollouts even applies to software that does not run on Google's servers. New versions of an Android app can be rolled out in a gradual manner, in which the updated version is offered to a subset of the installs for upgrade. The percentage of upgraded instances gradually increases over time until it reaches 100%. This type of rollout is particularly helpful if the new version results in additional traffic to the backend servers in Google's datacenters. This way, we can observe the effect on our servers as we gradually roll out the new version and detect problems early.

The invite system is another type of gradual rollout. Frequently, rather than allowing free signups to a new service, only a limited number of users are allowed to sign up per day. Rate-limited signups are often coupled with an invite system, in which a user can send a limited number of invites to friends.

Feature Flag Frameworks

Google often augments prelaunch testing with strategies that mitigate the risk of an outage. A mechanism to roll out changes slowly, allowing for observation of total system behavior under real workloads, can pay for its engineering investment in reliability, engineering velocity, and time to market. These mechanisms have proven particularly useful in cases where realistic test environments are impractical, or for particularly complex launches for which the effects can be hard to predict.

Furthermore, not all changes are equal. Sometimes you simply want to check whether a small tweak to the user interface improves the experience of your users. Such small changes shouldn't involve thousands of lines of code or a heavyweight launch process. You may want to test hundreds of such changes in parallel.

Finally, sometimes you want to find out whether a small sample of users like using an early prototype of a new, hard-to-implement feature. You don't want to spend months of engineering effort to harden a new feature to serve millions of users, only to find that the feature is a flop.

To accommodate the preceding scenarios, several Google products devised feature flag frameworks. Some of those frameworks were designed to roll out new features gradually from 0% to 100% of users. Whenever a product introduced any such framework, the framework itself was hardened as much as possible so that most of its applications would not need any LCE involvement. Such frameworks usually meet the following requirements:

- Roll out many changes in parallel, each to a few servers, users, entities, or datacenters
- Gradually increase to a larger but limited group of users, usually between 1 and 10 percent
- Direct traffic through different servers depending on users, sessions, objects, and/or locations
- Automatically handle failure of the new code paths by design, without affecting users
- Independently revert each such change immediately in the event of serious bugs or side effects
- Measure the extent to which each change improves the user experience

Google's feature flag frameworks fall into two general classes:

- Those that primarily facilitate user interface improvements
- Those that support arbitrary server-side and business logic changes

The simplest feature flag framework for user interface changes in a stateless service is an HTTP payload rewriter at frontend application servers, limited to a subset of cookies or another similar HTTP request/response attribute. A configuration mechanism may specify an identifier associated with the new code paths and the scope of the change (e.g., cookie hash mod range), whitelists, and blacklists.

Stateful services tend to limit feature flags to a subset of unique logged-in user identifiers or to the actual product entities accessed, such as the ID of documents, spreadsheets, or storage objects. Rather than rewrite HTTP payloads, stateful services are more likely to proxy or reroute requests to different servers depending on the change, conferring the ability to test improved business logic and more complex new features.

Dealing with Abusive Client Behavior

The simplest example of abusive client behavior is a misjudgment of update rates. A new client that syncs every 60 seconds, as opposed to every 600 seconds, causes 10 times the load on the service. Retry behavior has a number of pitfalls that affect user-initiated requests, as well as client-initiated requests. Take the example of a service that is overloaded and is therefore failing some requests: if the clients retry the failed requests, they add load to an already overloaded service, resulting in more retries and even more requests. Instead, clients need to reduce the frequency of retries, usually by adding exponentially increasing delay between retries, in addition to carefully considering the types of errors that warrant a retry. For example, a network error usually warrants a retry, but a 4xx HTTP error (which indicates an error on the client's side) usually does not.

Intentional or inadvertent synchronization of automated requests in a thundering herd (much like those described in Chapters 24 and 25) is another common example of abusive client behavior. A phone app developer might decide that 2 a.m. is a good time to download updates, because the user is most likely asleep and won't be inconvenienced by the download. However, such a design results in a barrage of requests to the download server at 2 a.m. every night, and almost no requests at any other time. Instead, every client should choose the time for this type of request randomly.

Randomness also needs to be injected into other periodic processes. To return to the previously mentioned retries: let's take the example of a client that sends a request, and when it encounters a failure, retries after 1 second, then 2 seconds, then 4 seconds, and so on. Without randomness, a brief request spike that leads to an increased error rate could repeat itself due to retries after 1 second, then 2 seconds, then 4 seconds. In order to even out these synchronized events, each delay needs to be jittered (that is, adjusted by a random amount).

The ability to control the behavior of a client from the server side has proven an important tool in the past. For an app on a device, such control might mean instructing the client to check in periodically with the server and download a configuration file. The file might enable or disable certain features or set parameters, such as how often the client syncs or how often it retries.

The client configuration might even enable completely new user-facing functionality. By hosting the code that supports new functionality in the client application before we activate that feature, we greatly reduce the risk associated with a launch. Releasing a new version becomes much easier if we don't need to maintain parallel release tracks for a version with the new functionality versus without the functionality. This holds particularly true if we're not dealing with a single piece of new functionality, but a set of independent features that might be released on different schedules, which would necessitate maintaining a combinatorial explosion of different versions.

Having this sort of dormant functionality also makes aborting launches easier when adverse effects are discovered during a rollout. In such cases, we can simply switch the feature off, iterate, and release an updated version of the app. Without this type of client configuration, we would have to provide a new version of the app without the feature, and update the app on all users' phones.

Overload Behavior and Load Tests

Overload situations are a particularly complex failure mode, and therefore deserve additional attention. Runaway success is usually the most welcome cause of overload when a new service launches, but there are myriad other causes, including load balancing failures, machine outages, synchronized client behavior, and external attacks.

A naive model assumes that CPU usage on a machine providing a particular service scales linearly with the load (for example, number of requests or amount of data processed), and once available CPU is exhausted, processing simply becomes slower. Unfortunately, services rarely behave in this ideal fashion in the real world. Many services are much slower when they are not loaded, usually due to the effect of various kinds of caches such as CPU caches, JIT caches, and service-specific data caches. As load increases, there is usually a window in which CPU usage and load on the service correspond linearly, and response times stay mostly constant.

At some point, many services reach a point of nonlinearity as they approach overload. In the most benign cases, response times simply begin to increase, resulting in a degraded user experience but not necessarily causing an outage (although a slow dependency might cause user-visible errors up the stack, due to exceeded RPC deadlines). In the most drastic cases, a service locks up completely in response to overload.

To cite a specific example of overload behavior: a service logged debugging information in response to backend errors. It turned out that logging debugging information was more expensive than handling the backend response in a normal case. Therefore, as the service became overloaded and timed out backend responses inside its own RPC stack, the service spent even more CPU time logging these responses, timing out more requests in the meantime until the service ground to a complete halt. In services running on the Java Virtual Machine (JVM), a similar effect of grinding to a halt is sometimes called "GC (garbage collection) thrashing." In this scenario, the virtual machine's internal memory management runs in increasingly closer cycles, trying to free up memory until most of the CPU time is consumed by memory management.

Unfortunately, it is very hard to predict from first principles how a service will react to overload. Therefore, load tests are an invaluable tool, both for reliability reasons and capacity planning, and load testing is required for most launches.

Development of LCE

In Google's formative years, the size of the engineering team doubled every year for several years in a row, fragmenting the engineering department into many small teams working on many experimental new products and features. In such a climate, novice engineers run the risk of repeating the mistakes of their predecessors, especially when it comes to launching new features and products successfully.

To mitigate the repetition of such mistakes by capturing the lessons learned from past launches, a small band of experienced engineers, called the "Launch Engineers," volunteered to act as a consulting team. The Launch Engineers developed checklists for new product launches, covering topics such as:

- When to consult with the legal department
- How to select domain names
- How to register new domains without misconfiguring DNS
- Common engineering design and production deployment pitfalls

"Launch Reviews," as the Launch Engineers' consulting sessions came to be called, became a common practice days to weeks before the launch of many new products.

Within two years, the product deployment requirements in the launch checklist grew long and complex. Combined with the increasing complexity of Google's deployment environment, it became more and more challenging for product engineers to stay up-to-date on how to make changes safely. At the same time, the SRE organization was growing quickly, and inexperienced SREs were sometimes overly cautious and averse to change. Google ran a risk that the resulting negotiations between these two parties would reduce the velocity of product/feature launches.

To mitigate this scenario from the engineering perspective, SRE staffed a small, full-time team of LCEs in 2004. They were responsible for accelerating the launches of new products and features, while at the same time applying SRE expertise to ensure that Google shipped reliable products with high availability and low latency.

LCEs were responsible for making sure launches were executing quickly without the services falling over, and that if a launch did fail, it didn't take down other products. LCEs were also responsible for keeping stakeholders informed of the nature and likelihood of such failures whenever corners were cut in order to accelerate time to market. Their consulting sessions were formalized as Production Reviews.

Evolution of the LCE Checklist

As Google's environment grew more complex, so did both the Launch Coordination Engineering checklist (see Appendix E) and the volume of launches. In 3.5 years, one LCE ran 350 launches through the LCE Checklist. As the team averaged five engineers during this time period, this translates into a Google launch throughput of over 1,500 launches in 3.5 years!

While each question on the LCE Checklist is simple, much complexity is built in to what prompted the question and the implications of its answer. In order to fully understand this degree of complexity, a new LCE hire requires about six months of training.

As the volume of launches grew, keeping pace with the annual doubling of Google's engineering team, LCEs sought ways to streamline their reviews. LCEs identified categories of low-risk launches that were highly unlikely to face or cause mishaps. For example, a feature launch involving no new server executables and a traffic increase under 10% would be deemed low risk. Such launches were faced with an almost trivial checklist, while higher-risk launches underwent the full gamut of checks and balances. By 2008, 30% of reviews were considered low-risk.

Simultaneously, Google's environment was scaling up, removing constraints on many launches. For instance, the acquisition of YouTube forced Google to build out its network and utilize bandwidth more efficiently. This meant that many smaller products would "fit within the cracks," avoiding complex network capacity planning and provisioning processes, thus accelerating their launches. Google also began building very large datacenters capable of hosting several dependent services under one roof. This development simplified the launch of new products that needed large amounts of capacity at multiple preexisting services upon which they depended.

Problems LCE Didn't Solve

Although LCEs tried to keep the bureaucracy of reviews to a minimum, such efforts were insufficient. By 2009, the difficulties of launching a small new service at Google had become a legend. Services that grew to a larger scale faced their own set of problems that Launch Coordination could not solve.

Scalability changes

When products are successful far beyond any early estimates, and their usage increases by more than two orders of magnitude, keeping pace with their load necessitates many design changes. Such scalability changes, combined with ongoing feature additions, often make the product more complex, fragile, and difficult to operate. At some point, the original product architecture becomes unmanageable and the product needs to be completely rearchitected. Rearchitecting the product and then migrating all users from the old to the new architecture requires a large investment of time and resources from developers and SREs alike, slowing down the rate of new feature development during that period.

Growing operational load

When running a service after it launches, operational load, the amount of manual and repetitive engineering needed to keep a system functioning, tends to grow over time unless efforts are made to control such load. Noisiness of automated notifications, complexity of deployment procedures, and the overhead of manual maintenance work tend to increase over time and consume increasing amounts of the service owner's bandwidth, leaving the team less time for feature development. SRE has an internally advertised goal of keeping operational work below a maximum of

50%; see Chapter 5. Staying below this maximum requires constant tracking of sources of operational work, as well as directed effort to remove these sources.

Infrastructure churn

If the underlying infrastructure (such as systems for cluster management, storage, monitoring, load balancing, and data transfer) is changing due to active development by infrastructure teams, the owners of services running on the infrastructure must invest large amounts of work to simply keep up with the infrastructure changes. As infrastructure features upon which services rely are deprecated and replaced by new features, service owners must continually modify their configurations and rebuild their executables, consequently "running fast just to stay in the same place." The solution to this scenario is to enact some type of churn reduction policy that prohibits infrastructure engineers from releasing backward-incompatible features until they also automate the migration of their clients to the new feature. Creating automated migration tools to accompany new features minimizes the work imposed on service owners to keep up with infrastructure churn.

Solving these problems requires company-wide efforts that are far beyond the scope of LCE: a combination of better platform APIs and frameworks (see Chapter 32), continuous build and test automation, and better standardization and automation across Google's production services.

Conclusion

Companies undergoing rapid growth with a high rate of change to products and services may benefit from the equivalent of a Launch Coordination Engineering role. Such a team is especially valuable if a company plans to double its product developers every one or two years, if it must scale its services to hundreds of millions of users, and if reliability despite a high rate of change is important to its users.

The LCE team was Google's solution to the problem of achieving safety without impeding change. This chapter introduced some of the experiences accumulated by our unique LCE role over a 10-year period under exactly such circumstances. We hope that our approach will help inspire others facing similar challenges in their respective organizations.

PART IV

Management

Our final selection of topics covers working together in a team, and working as teams. No SRE is an island, and there are some distinctive ways in which we work.

Any organization that aspires to be serious about running an effective SRE arm needs to consider training. Teaching SREs how to think in a complicated and fast-changing environment with a well-thought-out and well-executed training program has the promise of instilling best practices within a new hire's first few weeks or months that otherwise would take months or years to accumulate. We discuss strategies for doing just that in Chapter 28, *Accelerating SREs to On-Call and Beyond*.

As anyone in the operations world knows, responsibility for any significant service comes with a lot of interruptions: production getting in a bad state, people requesting updates to their favorite binary, a long queue of consultation requests…managing interrupts under turbulent conditions is a necessary skill, as we'll discuss in Chapter 29, *Dealing with Interrupts*.

If the turbulent conditions have persisted for long enough, an SRE team needs to start recovering from operational overload. We have just the flight plan for you in Chapter 30, *Embedding an SRE to Recover from Operational Overload*.

We write in Chapter 31, *Communication and Collaboration in SRE*, about the different roles within SRE; cross-team, cross-site, and cross-continent communication; running production meetings; and case studies of how SRE has collaborated well.

Finally, Chapter 32, *The Evolving SRE Engagement Model*, examines a cornerstone of the operation of SRE: the production readiness review (PRR), a crucial step in onboarding a new service. We discuss how to conduct PRRs, and how to move beyond this successful, but also limited, model.

Further Reading from Google SRE

Building reliable systems requires a carefully calibrated mix of skills, ranging from software development to the arguably less-well-known systems analysis and engineering disciplines. We write about the latter disciplines in "The Systems Engineering Side of Site Reliability Engineering" [Hix15b].

Hiring SREs well is critical to having a high-functioning reliability organization, as explored in "Hiring Site Reliability Engineers" [Jon15]. Google's hiring practices have been detailed in texts like *Work Rules!* [Boc15],[1] but hiring SREs has its own set of particularities. Even by Google's overall standards, SRE candidates are difficult to find and even harder to interview effectively.

---

1 Written by Laszlo Bock, Google's Senior VP of People Operations.

CHAPTER 28

Accelerating SREs to On-Call and Beyond

How Can I Strap a Jetpack to My Newbies
While Keeping Senior SREs Up to Speed?

Written by Andrew Widdowson
Edited by Shylaja Nukala

You've Hired Your Next SRE(s), Now What?

You've hired new employees into your organization, and they're starting as Site Reliability Engineers. Now you have to train them on the job. Investing up front in the education and technical orientation of new SREs will shape them into better engineers. Such training will accelerate them to a state of proficiency faster, while making their skill set more robust and balanced.

Successful SRE teams are built on trust—in order to maintain a service consistently and globally, you need to trust that your fellow on-callers know how your system works,[1] can diagnose atypical system behaviors, are comfortable with reaching out for help, and can react under pressure to save the day. It is essential, then, but not sufficient, to think of SRE education through the lens of, "What does a newbie need to learn to go on-call?" Given the requirements regarding trust, you also need to ask questions like:

- How can my existing on-callers assess the readiness of the newbie for on-call?
- How can we harness the enthusiasm and curiosity in our new hires to make sure that existing SREs benefit from it?

---

1 And doesn't work!

- What activities can I commit our team to that benefit everyone's education, but that everyone will like?

Students have a wide range of learning preferences. Recognizing that you will hire people who have a mix of these preferences, it would be shortsighted to only cater to one style at the expense of the others. Thus, there is no style of education that works best to train new SREs, and there is certainly no one magic formula that will work for all SRE teams. Table 28-1 lists recommended training practices (and their corresponding anti-patterns) that are well known to SRE at Google. These practices represent a wide range of options available for making your team well educated in SRE concepts, both now and on an ongoing basis.

Table 28-1. SRE education practices

Recommended patterns	Anti-patterns
Designing concrete, sequential learning experiences for students to follow	Deluging students with menial work (e.g., alert/ticket triage) to train them; "trial by fire"
Encouraging reverse engineering, statistical thinking, and working from fundamental principles	Training strictly through operator procedures, checklists, and playbooks
Celebrating the analysis of failure by suggesting postmortems for students to read	Treating outages as secrets to be buried in order to avoid blame
Creating contained but realistic breakages for students to fix using real monitoring and tooling	Having the first chance to fix something only occur after a student is already on-call
Role-playing theoretical disasters as a group, to intermingle a team's problem-solving approaches	Creating experts on the team whose techniques and knowledge are compartmentalized
Enabling students to shadow their on-call rotation early, comparing notes with the on-caller	Pushing students into being primary on-call before they achieve a holistic understanding of their service
Pairing students with expert SREs to revise targeted sections of the on-call training plan	Treating on-call training plans as static and untouchable except by subject matter experts
Carving out nontrivial project work for students to undertake, allowing them to gain partial ownership in the stack	Awarding all new project work to the most senior SREs, leaving junior SREs to pick up the scraps

The rest of this chapter presents major themes that we have found to be effective in accelerating SREs to on-call and beyond. These concepts can be visualized in a blueprint for bootstrapping SREs (Figure 28-1).

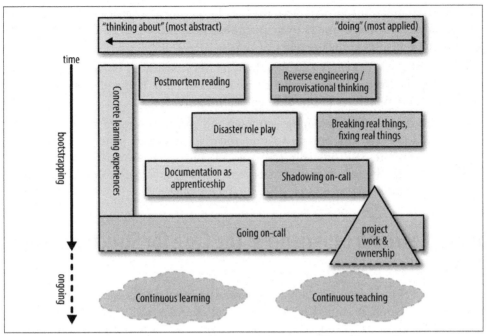

Figure 28-1. A blueprint for bootstrapping an SRE to on-call and beyond

This illustration captures best practices that SRE teams can pick from to help bootstrap new members, while keeping senior talent fresh. From the many tools here, you can pick and choose the activities that best suit your team.

The illustration has two axes:

- The x-axis represents the *spectrum between different types of work*, ranging from abstract to applied activities.
- The y-axis represents *time*. Read from the top down, new SREs have very little knowledge about the systems and services they'll be responsible for, so postmortems detailing how these systems have failed in the past are a good starting point. New SREs can also try to reverse engineer systems from fundamentals, since they're starting from zero. Once they understand more about their systems and have done some hands-on work, SREs are ready to shadow on-call and to start mending incomplete or out-of-date documentation.

Tips for interpreting this illustration:

- *Going on-call* is a milestone in a new SRE's career, after which point learning becomes a lot more nebulous, undefined, and self-directed—hence the dashed lines around activities that happen at or after the SRE goes on-call.

- The triangular shape of *project work & ownership* indicates that project work starts out small and builds over time, becoming more complex and likely continuing well after going on-call.

- Some of these activities and practices are very abstract/passive, and some are very applied/active. A few activities are mixes of both. It's good to have a variety of learning modalities to suit different learning styles.

- For maximum effect, training activities and practices should be appropriately paced: some are appropriate to undertake straightaway, some should happen right before an SRE officially goes on-call, and some should be continual and ongoing even by seasoned SREs. *Concrete learning experiences* should happen for the entire time leading up to the SRE going on-call.

Initial Learning Experiences: The Case for Structure Over Chaos

As discussed elsewhere in this book, SRE teams undertake a natural mix of proactive[2] and reactive[3] work. It should be a strong goal of every SRE team to contain and reduce reactive work through ample proactivity, and the approach you take to onboarding your newbie(s) should be no exception. Consider the following all-too-common, but sadly suboptimal, onboarding process:

> John is the newest member of the FooServer SRE team. Senior SREs on this team are tasked with a lot of grunt work, such as responding to tickets, dealing with alerts, and performing tedious binary rollouts. On John's first day on the job, he is assigned all new incoming tickets. He is told that he can ask any member of the SRE team to help him obtain the background necessary to decipher a ticket. "Sure, there will be a lot of upfront learning that you'll have to do," says John's manager, "but eventually you'll get much faster at these tickets. One day, it will just *click* and you'll know a lot about all of the tools we use, the procedures we follow, and the systems we maintain." A senior team member comments, "We're throwing you in the deep end of the pool here."

This "trial by fire" method of orienting one's newbies is often born out of a team's current environment; ops-driven, reactive SRE teams "train" their newest members by making them...well, react! Over and over again. If you're lucky, the engineers who are already good at navigating ambiguity will crawl out of the hole you've put them in. But chances are, this strategy has alienated several capable engineers. While such an approach may eventually produce great operations employees, its results will fall short of the mark. The trial-by-fire approach also presumes that many or most aspects of a team can be taught strictly by doing, rather than by reasoning. If the set

---

2 Examples of proactive SRE work include software automation, design consulting, and launch coordination.

3 Examples of reactive SRE work include debugging, troubleshooting, and handling on-call escalations.

of work one encounters in a tickets queue will adequately provide training for said job, then this is not an SRE position.

SRE students will have questions like the following:

- What am I working on?
- How much progress have I made?
- When will these activities accumulate enough experience for me to go on-call?

Making the jump from a previous company or university, while changing job roles (from traditional software engineer or traditional systems administrator) to this nebulous *Site Reliability Engineer* role is often enough to knock students' confidence down several times. For more introspective personalities (especially regarding questions #2 and #3), the uncertainties incurred by nebulous or less-than-clear answers can lead to slower development or retention problems. Instead, consider the approaches outlined in the following sections. These suggestions are as concrete as any ticket or alert, but they are also sequential, and thus far more rewarding.

Learning Paths That Are Cumulative and Orderly

Put some amount of learning order into your system(s) so that your new SREs see a path before them. Any type of training is better than random tickets and interrupts, but do make a conscious effort to combine the right mix of theory and application: abstract concepts that will recur multiple times in a newbie's journey should be frontloaded in their education, while the student should also receive hands-on experience as soon as practically possible.

Learning about your stack(s) and subsystem(s) requires a starting point. Consider whether it makes more sense to group trainings together by similarity of purpose, or by normal-case order of execution. For example, if your team is responsible for a real-time, user-facing serving stack, consider a curriculum order like the following:

1) How a query enters the system
Networking and datacenter fundamentals, frontend load balancing, proxies, etc.

2) Frontend serving
Application frontend(s), query logging, user experience SLO(s), etc.

3) Mid-tier services
Caches, backend load balancing

4) Infrastructure
Backends, infrastructure, and compute resources

5) Tying it all together
Debugging techniques, escalation procedures, and emergency scenarios

How you choose to present the learning opportunities (informal whiteboard chats, formal lectures, or hands-on discovery exercises) is up to you and the SREs helping you structure, design, and deliver training. The Google Search SRE team structures this learning through a document called the "on-call learning checklist." A simplified section of an on-call learning checklist might look like the following:

The Results Mixing Server ("Mixer")	
Frontended by: Frontend server **Backends called**: Results Retrieval Server, Geolocation Server, Personalization Database **SRE experts**: Sally W, Dave K, Jen P **Developer contacts**: Jim T, *results-team@*	**Know before moving on**: • Which clusters have Mixer deployed • How to roll back a Mixer release • Which backends of Mixer are considered "critical path" and why
Read and understand the following docs: • Results Mixing Overview: "Query execution" section • Results Mixing Overview: "Production" section • Playbook: How to Roll Out a New Results Mixing Server • A Performance Analysis of Mixer	**Comprehension questions**: • Q: How does the release schedule change if a company holiday occurs on the normal release build day? • Q: How can you fix a bad push of the geolocation dataset?

Note that the preceding section does not directly encode procedures, diagnostic steps, or playbooks; instead, it's a relatively future-proof write-up focusing strictly on enumerating expert contacts, highlighting the most useful documentation resources, establishing basic knowledge you must gather and internalize, and asking probing questions that can only be answered once that basic knowledge has been absorbed. It also provides concrete outcomes, so that the student knows what kinds of knowledge and skills they will have gained from completing this section of the learning checklist.

It's a good idea for all interested parties to get a sense of how much information the trainee is retaining. While this feedback mechanism perhaps doesn't need to be as formal as a quiz, it is a good practice to have complete bits of homework that pose questions about how your service(s) work. Satisfactory answers, checked by a student's mentor, are a sign that learning should continue to the next phase. Questions about the inner workings of your service might look similar to the following:

• Which backends of this server are considered "in the critical path," and why?

• What aspects of this server could be simplified or automated?

• Where do you think the first bottleneck is in this architecture? If that bottleneck were to be saturated, what steps could you take to alleviate it?

Depending on how the access permissions are configured for your service, you can also consider implementing a tiered access model. The first tier of access would allow your student read-only access to the inner workings of the components, and a later tier would permit them to mutate the production state. Completing sections of the on-call learning checklist satisfactorily would earn the student progressively deeper access to the system. The Search SRE team calls these attained levels "powerups"[4] on the route to on-call, as trainees are eventually added into the highest level of systems access.

Targeted Project Work, Not Menial Work

SREs are problem solvers, so give them a hearty problem to solve! When starting out, having even a minor sense of ownership in the team's service can do wonders for learning. In the reverse, such ownership can also make great inroads for trust building among senior colleagues, because they will approach their junior colleague to learn about the new component(s) or processes. Early opportunities for ownership are standard across Google in general: all engineers are given a starter project that's meant to provide a tour through the infrastructure sufficient to enable them to make a small but useful contribution early. Having the new SRE split time between learning *and* project work will also give them a sense of purpose and productivity, which would not happen if they spent time only on learning *or* project work. Several starter project patterns that seem to work well include:

- Making a trivial user-visible feature change in a serving stack, and subsequently shepherding the feature release all the way through to production. Understanding both the development toolchain and the binary release process encourages empathy for the developers.

- Adding monitoring to your service where there are currently blind spots. The newbie will have to reason with the monitoring logic, while reconciling their understanding of a system with how it actually (mis)behaves.

- Automating a pain point that isn't quite painful enough to have been automated already, providing the new SRE with an appreciation for the value SREs place on removing toil from our day-to-day operations.

Creating Stellar Reverse Engineers and Improvisational Thinkers

We can propose a set of guidelines for *how* to train new SREs, but *what* should we train them on? Training material will depend on the technologies being used on the job, but the more important question is: what kind of engineers are we trying to create? At the scale and complexity at which SREs operate, they cannot afford to merely

---

4 A nod to video games of yesteryear.

be operations-focused, traditional system administrators. In addition to having a large-scale engineering mindset, SREs should exhibit the following characteristics:

- In the course of their jobs, they will come across systems they've never seen before, so they need to have *strong reverse engineering skills*.
- At scale, there will be anomalies that are hard to detect, so they'll need the ability to *think statistically*, rather than procedurally, to uncloak problems.
- When standard operating procedures break down, they'll need to be able to *improvise fully*.

Let's examine these attributes further, so that we can understand how to equip our SREs for these skills and behaviors.

Reverse Engineers: Figuring Out How Things Work

Engineers are curious about how systems they've never seen before work—or, more likely, how the current versions of systems they used to know quite well work. By having a baseline understanding of how systems work at your company, along with a willingness to dig deep into the debugging tools, RPC boundaries, and logs of your binaries to unearth their flows, SREs will become more efficient at homing in on unexpected problems in unexpected system architectures. Teach your SREs about the diagnostic and debugging surfaces of your applications and have them practice drawing inferences from the information these surfaces reveal, so that such behavior becomes reflexive when dealing with future outages.

Statistical and Comparative Thinkers: Stewards of the Scientific Method Under Pressure

You can think of an SRE's approach to incident response for large-scale systems as navigating through a massive decision tree unfolding in front of them. In the limited time window afforded by the demands of incident response, the SRE can take a few actions out of hundreds with the goal of mitigating the outage, either in the short term or the long term. Because time is often of the utmost importance, the SRE has to effectively and efficiently prune this decision tree. The ability to do so is partially gained through experience, which only comes with time and exposure to a breadth of production systems. This experience must be paired with careful construction of hypotheses that, when proven or disproven, even further narrow down that decision space. Put another way, tracking down system breakages is often akin to playing a game of "which of these things is not like the other?" where "things" might entail kernel version, CPU architecture, binary version(s) in your stack, regional traffic mix, or a hundred other factors. Architecturally, it's the team's responsibility to ensure all of these factors can be controlled for and individually analyzed and compared. However, we should also train our newest SREs to become good analysts and comparators from their earliest moments on the job.

Improv Artists: When the Unexpected Happens

You try out a fix for the breakage, but it doesn't work. The developer(s) behind the failing system are nowhere to be found. What do you do now? You improvise! Learning multiple tools that can solve parts of your problem allows you to practice defense in depth in your own problem-solving behaviors. Being too procedural in the face of an outage, thus forgetting your analytical skills, can be the difference between getting stuck and finding the root cause. A case of bogged-down troubleshooting can be further compounded when an SRE brings too many untested assumptions about the cause of an outage into their decision making. Demonstrating that there are many analytical traps that SREs can fall into, which require "zooming out" and taking a different approach to resolution, is a valuable lesson for SREs to learn early on.

Given these three aspirational attributes of high-performing SREs, what courses and experiences can we provide new SREs in order to send them along a path in the right direction? You need to come up with your own course content that embodies these attributes, in addition to the other attributes specific to your SRE culture. Let's consider one class that we believe hits all of the aforementioned points.

Tying This Together: Reverse Engineering a Production Service

> "When it came time to learn [part of the Google Maps stack], [a new SRE] asked if, rather than passively having someone explain the service, she could do this herself—learning everything via Reverse Engineering class techniques, and having the rest of us correct her/fill in the blanks for whatever she missed or got wrong. The result? Well, it was probably more correct and useful than it would have been if I'd given the talk, and I've been on-call for this for over 5 years!"
>
> —Paul Cowan, *Google Site Reliability Engineer*

One popular class we offer at Google is called "Reverse Engineering a Production Service (without help from its owners)." The problem scenario presented appears simple at first. The entire Google News Team—SRE, Software Engineers, Product Management, and so forth—has gone on a company trip: a cruise of the Bermuda Triangle. We haven't heard from the team for 30 days, so our students are the newly appointed Google News SRE Team. They need to figure out how the serving stack works from end-to-end in order to commandeer it and keep it running.

After being given this scenario, the students are led through interactive, purpose-driven exercises in which they trace the inbound path of their web browser's query through Google's infrastructure. At each stage in the process, we emphasize that it is important to learn multiple ways to discover the connectivity between production servers, so that connections are not missed. In the middle of the class, we challenge the students to find another endpoint for the incoming traffic, demonstrating that our initial assumption was too narrowly scoped. We then challenge our students to find other ways into the stack. We exploit the highly instrumented nature of our production binaries, which self-report their RPC connectivity, as well as our available white-box and black-box monitoring, to determine which path(s) users' queries take.[5] Along the way, we build a system diagram and also discuss components that are shared infrastructure that our students are likely to see again in the future.

At the end of the class, the students are charged with a task. Each student returns to their home team and asks a senior SRE to help them select a stack or slice of a stack for which they'll be on-call. Using the skills learned in classes, the student then diagrams that stack on their own and presents their findings to the senior SRE. Undoubtedly the student will miss a few subtle details, which will make for a good discussion. It's also likely that the senior SRE will learn something from the exercise as well, exposing drifts in their prior understanding of the ever-changing system. Because of the rapid change of production systems, it is important that your team welcome any chance to refamiliarize themselves with a system, including by learning from the newest, rather than oldest, members of the team.

Five Practices for Aspiring On-Callers

Being on-call is not the single most important purpose of any SRE, but production engineering responsibilities usually do involve some kind of urgent notification coverage. Someone who is capable of responsibly taking on-call is someone who understands the system that they work on to a reasonable depth and breadth. So we'll use "able to take on-call" as a useful proxy for "knows enough and can figure out the rest."

A Hunger for Failure: Reading and Sharing Postmortems

> "Those who cannot remember the past are condemned to repeat it."
> —George Santayana, *philosopher and essayist*

Postmortems (see Chapter 15) are an important part of continuous improvement. They are a blame-free way of getting at the many root causes of a significant or visible outage. When writing a postmortem, keep in mind that its most appreciative audience might be an engineer who hasn't yet been hired. Without radical editing, subtle changes can be made to our best postmortems to make them "teachable" postmortems.

---

5 This "follow the RPC" approach also works well for batch/pipeline systems; start with the operation that kicks off the system. For batch systems, this operation could be data arriving that needs to be processed, a transaction that needs to be validated, or many other events.

Even the best postmortems aren't helpful if they languish in the bottom of a virtual filing cabinet. It then follows that your team should collect and curate valuable post-mortems to serve as educational resources for future newbies. Some postmortems are rote, but "teachable postmortems" that provide insights into structural or novel fail-ures of large-scale systems are as good as gold for new students.

Ownership of postmortems isn't limited just to authorship. It's a point of pride for many teams to have survived and documented their largest outages. Collect your best postmortems and make them prominently available for your newbies—in addition to interested parties from related and/or integrating teams—to read. Ask related teams to publish their best postmortems where you can access them.

Some SRE teams at Google run "postmortem reading clubs" where fascinating and insightful postmortems are circulated, pre-read, and then discussed. The original author(s) of the postmortem can be the guest(s) of honor at the meeting. Other teams organize "tales of fail" gatherings where the postmortem author(s) semiformally present, recounting the outage and effectively driving the discussion themselves.

Regular readings or presentations on outages, including trigger conditions and miti-gation steps, do wonders for building a new SRE's mental map and understanding of production and on-call response. Postmortems are also excellent fuel for future abstract disaster scenarios.

Disaster Role Playing

> "Once a week we have a meeting where a victim is chosen to be on the spot in front of the group, and a scenario—often a real one taken from the annals of Google history—is thrown at him or her. The victim, whom I think of as a game show contestant, tells the game show host what s/he would do or query to understand or solve the problem, and the host tells the victim what happens with each action or observation. It's like *SRE Zork*. You are in a maze of twisty monitoring consoles, all alike. You must save inno-cent users from slipping into the Chasm of Excessive Query Latency, save datacenters from Near-Certain Meltdown, and spare us all the embarrassment of Erroneous Goo-gle Doodle Display."
>
> —Robert Kennedy, former Site Reliability Engineer for Google Search and healthcare.gov[6]

When you have a group of SREs of wildly different experience levels, what can you do to bring them all together, and enable them to learn from each other? How do you impress the SRE culture and problem-solving nature of your team upon a newbie, while also keeping grizzled veterans apprised of new changes and features in your stack? Google SRE teams address these challenges through a time-honored tradition

---

6 See "Life in the Trenches of healthcare.gov" (*http://www.thedotpost.com/2014/05/robert-kennedy-life-in-the-trenches-of-healthcare-gov*).

of regular disaster role playing. Among other names, this exercise is commonly referred to as "Wheel of Misfortune" or "Walk the Plank." The sense of humorous danger such titles lend the exercise makes it less intimidating to freshly hired SREs.

At its best, these exercises become a weekly ritual in which every member of the group learns something. The formula is straightforward and bears some resemblance to a tabletop RPG (Role Playing Game): the "game master" (GM) picks two team members to be primary and secondary on-call; these two SREs join the GM at the front of the room. An incoming page is announced, and the on-call team responds with what they would do to mitigate and investigate the outage.

The GM has carefully prepared a scenario that is about to unfold. This scenario might be based upon a previous outage for which the newer team members weren't around or that older team members have forgotten. Or perhaps the scenario is a foray into a hypothetical breakage of a new or soon-to-be-launched feature in the stack, rendering all members of the room equally unprepared to grapple with the situation. Better still, a coworker might find a new and novel breakage in production, and today's scenario expands on this new threat.

Over the next 30–60 minutes, the primary and secondary on-callers attempt to root-cause the issue. The GM happily provides additional context as the problem unfolds, perhaps informing the on-callers (and their audience) of what the graphs on their monitoring dashboard might look like during the outage. If the incident requires escalation outside of the home team, the GM pretends to be a member of that other team for the purposes of the scenario. No virtual scenario will be perfect, so at times the GM may have to steer participants back on track by redirecting the on-callers away from red herrings, introducing urgency and clarity by adding other stimuli,[7] or asking urgent and pointed questions.[8]

When your disaster RPG is successful, everyone will have learned something: perhaps a new tool or trick, a different perspective on how to solve a problem, or (especially gratifying to new team members) a validation that you could have solved this week's problem if you had been picked. With some luck, this exercise will inspire teammates to eagerly look forward to next week's adventure or to ask to become the game master for an upcoming week.

Break Real Things, Fix Real Things

A newbie can learn much about SRE by reading documentation, postmortems, and taking trainings. Disaster role playing can help get a newbie's mind into the game.

---

7 For example: "You're getting paged by another team that brings you more information. Here's what they say…"

8 For example: "We're losing money quickly! How could you stop the bleeding in the short term?"

However, the experience derived from hands-on experience breaking and/or fixing *real* production systems is even better. There will be plenty of time for hands-on experience once a newbie has gone on-call, but such learning should happen *before* a new SRE reaches that point. Therefore, provide for such hands-on experiences much earlier in order to develop the student's reflexive responses for using your company's tooling and monitoring to approach a developing outage.

Realism is paramount in these interactions. Ideally, your team has a stack that is multihomed and provisioned in such a way that you have at least one instance you can divert from live traffic and temporarily loan to a learning exercise. Alternatively, you might have a smaller, but still fully featured, staging or QA instance of your stack that can be borrowed for a short time. If possible, subject the stack to synthetic load that approximates real user/client traffic, in addition to resource consumption, if possible.

The opportunities for learning from a real production system under synthetic load are abundant. Senior SREs will have experienced all sorts of troubles: misconfigurations, memory leaks, performance regressions, crashing queries, storage bottlenecks, and so forth. In this realistic but relatively risk-free environment, proctors can manipulate the job set in ways that alter the behavior of the stack, forcing new SREs to find differences, determine contributing factors, and ultimately repair systems to restore appropriate behavior.

As an alternative to the overhead of asking a senior SRE to carefully plan a specific type of breakage that the new SRE(s) must repair, you can also work in the opposite direction with an exercise that may also increase participation from the entire team: work from a known good configuration and slowly impair the stack at selected bottlenecks, observing upstream and downstream efforts through your monitoring. This exercise is valued by the Google Search SRE team, whose version of this exercise is called "Let's burn a search cluster to the ground!" The exercise proceeds as follows:

1. As a group, we discuss what observable performance characteristics might change as we cripple the stack.
2. Before inflicting the planned damage, we poll the participants for their guesses and reasoning about their predictions about how the system will react.
3. We validate assumptions and justify the reasoning behind the behaviors we see.

This exercise, which we perform on a quarterly basis, shakes out new bugs that we eagerly fix, because our systems do not always degrade as gracefully as we would expect.

Documentation as Apprenticeship

Many SRE teams maintain an "on-call learning checklist," which is an organized reading and comprehension list of the technologies and concepts relevant to the system(s) they maintain. This list must be internalized by a student before they're eligible to serve as a shadow on-caller. Take a moment to revisit the example on-call learning checklist in Table 28-1. The learning checklist serves different purposes for different people:

- **To the student**:
  - This doc helps establish the boundaries of the system their team supports.
  - By studying this list, the student gains a sense of what systems are most important and why. When they understand the information therein, they can move on to other topics they need to learn, rather than dwelling on learning esoteric details that can be learned over time.
- **To mentors and managers**: Student progress through the learning checklist can be observed. The checklist answers questions such as:
  - What sections are you working on today?
  - What sections are the most confusing?
- **To all team members**: The doc becomes a social contract by which (upon mastery) the student joins the ranks of on-call. The learning checklist sets the standard that all team members should aspire to and uphold.

In a rapidly changing environment, documentation can fall out of date quickly. Outdated documentation is less of a problem for senior SREs who are already up to speed, because they keep state on the world and its changes in their own heads. Newbie SREs are much more in need of up-to-date documentation, but may not feel empowered or knowledgeable enough to make changes. When designed with just the right amount of structure, on-call documentation can become an adaptable body of work that harnesses newbie enthusiasm and senior knowledge to keep everyone fresh.

In Search SRE, we anticipate the arrival of new team member(s) by reviewing our on-call learning checklist, and sorting its sections by how up-to-date they are. As the new team member arrives, we point them to the overall learning checklist, but also task them with overhauling one or two of the most outdated sections. As you can see in Table 28-1, we label the senior SRE and developer contacts for each technology. We encourage the student to make an early connection with those subject matter experts, so that they might learn the inner workings of the selected technology directly. Later, as they become more familiar with the scope and tone of the learning checklist, they are expected to contribute a revised learning checklist section, which must be peer-reviewed by one or more senior SREs that are listed as experts.

Shadow On-Call Early and Often

Ultimately, no amount of hypothetical disaster exercises or other training mechanisms will fully prepare an SRE for going on-call. At the end of the day, tackling real outages will always be more beneficial from a learning standpoint than engaging with hypotheticals. Yet it's unfair to make newbies wait until their first real page to have a chance to learn and retain knowledge.

After the student has made their way through all system fundamentals (by completing, for example, an on-call learning checklist), consider configuring your alerting system to copy incoming pages to your newbie, at first only during business hours. Rely on their curiosity to lead the way. These "shadow" on-call shifts are a great way for a mentor to gain visibility into a student's progress, and for a student to gain visibility into the responsibilities of being on-call. By arranging for the newbie to shadow multiple members of their team, the team will become increasingly comfortable with the thought of this person entering the on-call rotation. Instilling confidence in this manner is an effective method of building trust, allowing more senior members to detach when they aren't on-call, thus helping to avoid team burnout.

When a page comes in, the new SRE is not the appointed on-caller, a condition which removes any time pressure for the student. They now have a front-row seat to the outage while it unfolds, rather than after the issue is resolved. It may be that the student and the primary on-caller share a terminal session, or sit near each other to readily compare notes. At a time of mutual convenience after the outage is complete, the on-caller can review the reasoning and processes followed for the student's benefit. This exercise will increase the shadow on-caller's retention of what actually occurred.

 Should an outage occur for which writing a postmortem is beneficial, the on-caller should include the newbie as a coauthor. *Do not dump the writeup solely on the student, because it could be mislearned that postmortems are somehow grunt work to be passed off on those most junior. It would be a mistake to create such an impression.*

Some teams will also include a final step: having the experienced on-caller "reverse shadow" the student. The newbie will become primary on-call and own all incoming escalations, but the experienced on-caller will lurk in the shadows, independently diagnosing the situation without modifying any state. The experienced SRE will be available to provide active support, help, validation, and hints as necessary.

On-Call and Beyond: Rites of Passage, and Practicing Continuing Education

As comprehension increases, the student will reach a point in their career at which they are capable of reasoning through most of the stack comfortably, and can improvise their way through the rest. At this point, they should go on-call for their service. Some teams create a final exam of sorts that tests their students one last time before bestowing them with on-call powers and responsibilities. Other new SREs will submit their completion of the on-call learning checklist as evidence that they are ready. Regardless of how you gate this milestone, going on-call is a rite of passage and it should be celebrated as a team.

Does learning stop when a student joins the ranks of on-call? Of course not! To remain vigilant as SREs, your team will always need to be active and aware of changes to come. While your attention is elsewhere, portions of your stack may be rearchitected and extended, leaving your team's operational knowledge as historic at best.

Set up a regular learning series for your whole team, where overviews of new and upcoming changes to your stack are given as presentations by the SREs who are shepherding the changes, who can co-present with developers as needed. If you can, record the presentations so that you can build a training library for future students.

With some practice, you'll gain much timely involvement from both SREs within your team and developers who work closely with your team, all while keeping everyone's minds fresh about the future. There are other venues for educational engagement, too: consider having SREs give talks to your developer counterparts. The better your development peers understand your work and the challenges your team faces, the easier it will be to reach fully informed decisions on later projects.

Closing Thoughts

An upfront investment in SRE training is absolutely worthwhile, both for the students eager to grasp their production environment and for the teams grateful to welcome students into the ranks of on-call. Through the use of applicable practices outlined in this chapter, you will create well-rounded SREs faster, while sharpening team skills in perpetuity. How you apply these practices is up to you, but the charge is clear: as SRE, you have to scale your humans faster than you scale your machines. Good luck to you and your teams in creating a culture of learning and teaching!

CHAPTER 29

Dealing with Interrupts

Written by Dave O'Connor
Edited by Diane Bates

"Operational load," when applied to complex systems, is the work that must be done to maintain the system in a functional state. For example, if you own a car, you (or someone you pay) always end up servicing it, putting gas in it, or doing other regular maintenance to keep it performing its function.

Any complex system is as imperfect as its creators. In managing the operational load created by these systems, remember that its creators are also imperfect machines.

Operational load, when applied to managing complex systems, takes many forms, some more obvious than others. The terminology may change, but operational load falls into three general categories: pages, tickets, and ongoing operational activities.

Pages concern production alerts and their fallout, and are triggered in response to production emergencies. They can sometimes be monotonous and recurring, requiring little thought. They can also be engaging and involve tactical in-depth thought. Pages always have an expected response time (SLO), which is sometimes measured in minutes.

Tickets concern customer requests that require you to take an action. Like pages, tickets can be either simple and boring, or require real thought. A simple ticket might request a code review for a config the team owns. A more complex ticket might entail a special or unusual request for help with a design or capacity plan. Tickets may also have an SLO, but response time is more likely measured in hours, days, or weeks.

Ongoing operational responsibilities (also known as "Kicking the can down the road" and "toil"; see Chapter 5) include activities like team-owned code or flag rollouts, or responses to ad hoc, time-sensitive questions from customers. While they may not have a defined SLO, these tasks can interrupt you.

Some types of operational load are easily anticipated or planned for, but much of the load is unplanned, or can interrupt someone at a nonspecific time, requiring that person to determine if the issue can wait.

Managing Operational Load

Google has several methods of managing each type of operational load at the team level.

Pages are most commonly managed by a dedicated primary on-call engineer. This is a single person who responds to pages and manages the resulting incidents or outages. The primary on-call engineer might also manage user support communications, escalation to product developers, and so on. In order to both minimize the interruption a page causes to a team and avoid the bystander effect, Google on-call shifts are manned by a single engineer. The on-call engineer might escalate pages to another team member if a problem isn't well understood.

Typically, a secondary on-call engineer acts as a backup for the primary. The secondary engineer's duties vary. In some rotations, the secondary's only duty is to contact the primary if pages fall through. In this case, the secondary might be on another team. The secondary engineer may or may not consider themselves *on interrupts*, depending on duties.

Tickets are managed in a few different ways, depending on the SRE team: a primary on-call engineer might work on tickets while on-call, a secondary engineer might work on tickets while on-call, or a team can have a dedicated ticket person who is *not* on-call. Tickets might be randomly autodistributed among team members, or team members might be expected to service tickets ad hoc.

Ongoing operational responsibilities are also managed in varying ways. Sometimes, the on-call engineer does the work (pushes, flag flips, etc.). Alternately, each responsibility can be assigned to team members ad hoc, or an on-call engineer might pick up a lasting responsibility (i.e., a multiweek rollout or ticket) that lasts beyond their shift week.

Factors in Determining How Interrupts Are Handled

To take a step back from the mechanics of how operational load is managed, there are a number of metrics that factor into how each of these interrupts are handled. Some SRE teams at Google have found the following metrics to be useful in deciding how to manage interrupts:

- Interrupt SLO or expected response time
- The number of interrupts that are usually backlogged

- The severity of the interrupts
- The frequency of the interrupts
- The number of people available to handle a certain kind of interrupt (e.g., some teams require a certain amount of ticket work before going on-call)

You might notice that all of these metrics are suited to meeting the lowest possible response time, without factoring in more human costs. Trying to take stock of the human and productivity cost is difficult.

Imperfect Machines

Humans are imperfect machines. They get bored, they have processors (and sometimes UIs) that aren't very well understood, and they aren't very efficient. Recognizing the human element as "Working as Intended" and trying to work around or ameliorate how humans work could fill a much larger space than provided here; for the moment, some basic ideas might be useful in determining how interrupts should work.

Cognitive Flow State

The concept of *flow state*[1] is widely accepted and can be empirically acknowledged by pretty much everyone who works in Software Engineering, Sysadmin, SRE, or most other disciplines that require focused periods of concentration. Being in "the zone" can increase productivity, but can also increase artistic and scientific creativity. Achieving this state encourages people to actually master and improve the task or project they're working on. Being interrupted can kick you right out of this state, if the interrupt is disruptive enough. You want to maximize the amount of time spent in this state.

Cognitive flow can also apply to less creative pursuits where the skill level required is lower, and the essential elements of flow are still fulfilled (clear goals, immediate feedback, a sense of control, and the associated time distortion); examples include housework or driving.

You can get in the zone by working on low-skill, low-difficulty problems, such as playing a repetitive video game. You can just as easily get there by doing high-skill, high-difficulty problems, such as those an engineer might face. The methods of arriving at a cognitive flow state differ, but the outcome is essentially the same.

---

1 See Wikipedia: Flow (psychology), *http://en.wikipedia.org/wiki/Flow_(psychology)*.

Cognitive flow state: Creative and engaged

This is the zone: someone works on a problem for a while, is aware of and comfortable with the parameters of the problem, and feels like they can fix it or solve it. The person works intently on the problem, losing track of time and ignoring interrupts as much as possible. Maximizing the amount of time a person can spend in this state is very desirable—they're going to produce creative results and do good work by volume. They'll be happier at the job they're doing.

Unfortunately, many people in SRE-type roles spend much of their time either trying and failing to get into this mode and getting frustrated when they cannot, or never even attempting to reach this mode, instead languishing in the interrupted state.

Cognitive flow state: Angry Birds

People enjoy performing tasks they know how to do. In fact, executing such tasks is one of the clearest paths to cognitive flow. Some SREs are on-call when they reach a state of cognitive flow. It can be very fulfilling to chase down the causes of problems, work with others, and improve the overall health of the system in such a tangible way. Conversely, for most stressed-out on-call engineers, stress is caused either by pager volume, or because they're treating on-call as an interrupt. They're trying to code or work on projects while simultaneously being on-call or on full-time interrupts. These engineers exist in a state of constant interruption, or *interruptability*. This working environment is extremely stressful.

On the other hand, when a person is concentrating full-time on interrupts, *interrupts stop being interrupts*. At a very visceral level, making incremental improvements to the system, whacking tickets, and fixing problems and outages becomes a clear set of goals, boundaries, and clear feedback: you close X bugs, or you stop getting paged. All that's left is distractions. *When you're doing interrupts, your projects are a distraction.* Even though interrupts may be a satisfying use of time in the short term, in a mixed project/on-call environment, people are ultimately happier with a balance between these two types of work. The ideal balance varies from engineer to engineer. It's important to be aware that some engineers may not actually know what balance best motivates them (or might think they know, but you may disagree).

Do One Thing Well

You might be wondering about the practical implications of what you've read thus far.

The following suggestions, based on what's worked for various SRE teams that I've managed at Google, are mainly for the benefit of team managers or influencers. This document is agnostic to personal habits—people are free to manage their own time as they see fit. The concentration here is on directing the structure of how the team itself manages interrupts, so that people aren't set up for failure because of team function or structure.

Distractibility

The ways in which an engineer may be distracted and therefore prevented from achieving a state of cognitive flow are numerous. For example: consider a random SRE named Fred. Fred comes into work on Monday morning. Fred isn't on-call or on interrupts today, so Fred would clearly like to work on his projects. He grabs a coffee, sticks on his "do not disturb" headphones, and sits at his desk. Zone time, right?

Except, at any time, any of the following things might happen:

- Fred's team uses an automated ticket system to randomly assign tickets to the team. A ticket gets assigned to him, due today.
- Fred's colleague is on-call and receives a page about a component that Fred is expert in, and interrupts him to ask about it.
- A user of Fred's service raises the priority of a ticket that's been assigned to him since last week, when he was on-call.
- A flag rollout that's rolling out over 3–4 weeks and is assigned to Fred goes wrong, forcing Fred to drop everything to examine the rollout, roll back the change, and so forth.
- A user of Fred's service contacts Fred to ask a question, because Fred is such a helpful chap.
- And so on.

The end result is that even though Fred has the entire calendar day free to work on projects, he remains extremely distractible. Some of these distractions he can manage himself by closing email, turning off IM, or taking other similar measures. Some distractions are caused by policy, or by assumptions around interrupts and ongoing responsibilities.

You can claim that some level of distraction is inevitable and by design. This assumption is correct: people do hang onto bugs for which they're the primary contact, and people also build up other responsibilities and obligations. However, there are ways that a team can manage interrupt response so that more people (on average) can come into work in the morning and *feel undistractible*.

Polarizing time

In order to limit your distractibility, you should try to minimize context switches. Some interrupts are inevitable. However, viewing an engineer as an interruptible unit of work, whose context switches are free, is suboptimal if you want people to be happy and productive. Assign a cost to context switches. A 20-minute interruption while working on a project entails two context switches; realistically, this interruption results in a loss of a couple hours of truly productive work. To avoid constant occurrences of productivity loss, aim for polarized time between work styles, with each work period lasting as long as possible. Ideally, this time period is a week, but a day or even a half-day may be more practical. This strategy also fits in with the complementary concept of *make time* [Gra09].

Polarizing time means that when a person comes into work each day, they should know if they're doing *just* project work or *just* interrupts. Polarizing their time in this way means they get to concentrate for longer periods of time on the task at hand. They don't get stressed out because they're being roped into tasks that drag them away from the work they're supposed to be doing.

Seriously, Tell Me What to Do

If the general model presented in this chapter doesn't work for you, here are some specific suggestions of components you can implement piecemeal.

General suggestions

For any given class of interrupt, if the volume of interrupts is too high for one person, *add another person*. This concept most obviously applies to tickets, but can potentially apply to pages, too—the on-call can start bumping things to their secondary, or downgrading pages to tickets.

On-call

The primary on-call engineer should focus solely on on-call work. If the pager is quiet for your service, tickets or other interrupt-based work that can be abandoned fairly quickly should be part of on-call duties. When an engineer is on-call for a week, that week should be written off as far as project work is concerned. If a project is too important to let slip by a week, that person shouldn't be on-call. Escalate in order to assign someone else to the on-call shift. *A person should never be expected to be on-call and also make progress on projects (or anything else with a high context switching cost).*

Secondary duties depend on how onerous those duties are. If the function of the secondary is to back up the primary in the case of a fallthrough, then maybe you can safely assume that the secondary can also accomplish project work. If someone other than the secondary is assigned to handling tickets, consider merging the roles. If the secondary is expected to actually help the primary in the case of high pager volume, they should do interrupt work, too.

(Aside: *You never run out of cleanup work.* Your ticket count might be at zero, but there is always documentation that needs updating, configs that need cleanup, etc. Your future on-call engineers will thank you, and it means they're less likely to interrupt you during your precious make time).

Tickets

If you currently assign tickets randomly to victims on your team, *stop*. Doing so is extremely disrespectful of your team's time, and works completely counter to the principle of not being interruptible as much as possible.

Tickets should be a full-time role, for an amount of time that's manageable for a person. If you happen to be in the unenviable position of having more tickets than can be closed by the primary and secondary on-call engineers combined, then structure your ticket rotation to have two people handling tickets at any given time. Don't spread the load across the entire team. People are not machines, and you're just causing context switches that impact valuable flow time.

Ongoing responsibilities

As much as possible, define roles that let anyone on the team take up the mantle. If there's a well-defined procedure for performing and verifying pushes or flag flips, then there's no reason a person has to shepherd that change for its entire lifetime, even after they stop being on-call or on interrupts. Define a *push manager* role who can juggle pushes for the duration of their time on-call or on interrupts. Formalize the handover process—it's a small price to pay for uninterrupted make time for the people not on-call.

Be on interrupts, or don't be

Sometimes when a person isn't on interrupts, the team receives an interrupt that the person is uniquely qualified to handle. While ideally this scenario should never happen, it sometimes does. You should work to make such occurrences rare.

Sometimes people work on tickets when they're not assigned to handle tickets because it's an easy way to look busy. Such behavior isn't helpful. It means the person is less effective than they should be. They skew the numbers in terms of how manageable the ticket load is. If one person is assigned to tickets, but two or three other people also take a stab at the ticket queue, you might still have an unmanageable ticket queue even though you don't realize it.

Reducing Interrupts

Your team's interrupt load may be unmanageable if it requires too many team members to simultaneously staff interrupts at any given time. There are a number of techniques you can use to reduce your ticket load overall.

Actually analyze tickets

Lots of ticket rotations or on-call rotations function like a gauntlet. This is especially true of rotations on larger teams. If you're only on interrupts every couple of months, it's easy to run the gauntlet,[2] heave a sigh of relief, and then return to your regular duties. Your successor then does the same, and the root causes of tickets are never investigated. Rather than achieving forward movement, your team is bogged down by a succession of people getting annoyed by the same issues.

There should be a handoff for tickets, as well as for on-call work. A handoff process maintains shared state between ticket handlers as responsibility switches over. Even some basic introspection into the root causes of interrupts can provide good solutions for reducing the overall rate. *Lots* of teams conduct on-call handoffs and page reviews. *Very few* teams do the same for tickets.

Your team should conduct a regular scrub for tickets and pages, in which you examine classes of interrupts to see if you can identify a root cause. If you think the root cause is fixable in a reasonable amount of time, then *silence the interrupts until the root cause is expected to be fixed*. Doing so provides relief for the person handling interrupts and creates a handy deadline enforcement for the person fixing the root cause.

Respect yourself, as well as your customers

This maxim applies more to user interrupts than automated interrupts, although the principles stand for both scenarios. If tickets are particularly annoying or onerous to resolve, you can effectively use policy to mitigate the burden.

Remember:

- Your team sets the level of service provided by your service.
- It's OK to push back some of the effort onto your customers.

If your team is responsible for handling tickets or interrupts for customers, you can often use policy to make your work load more manageable. A policy fix can be temporary or permanent, depending on what makes sense. Such a fix should strike a good balance between respect for the customer and respect for yourself. Policy can be as powerful a tool as code.

For example, if you support a particularly flaky tool that doesn't have many developer resources, and a small number of needy customers use it, consider other options. Think about the value of the time you spend doing interrupts for this system, and if you're spending this time wisely. At some point, if you can't get the attention you need to fix the root cause of the problems causing interrupts, perhaps the component you're supporting isn't that important. You should consider giving the pager back, deprecating it, replacing it, or another strategy in this vein that might make sense.

---

2 See *http://en.wikipedia.org/wiki/Running_the_gauntlet*.

If there are particular steps for an interrupt that are time-consuming or tricky, but don't require your privileges to accomplish, consider using policy to push the request back to the requestor. For example, if people need to donate compute resources, prepare a code or config change or some similar step, and then instruct the customer to execute that step and send it for your review. Remember that if the customer wants a certain task to be accomplished, they should be prepared to spend some effort getting what they want.

A caveat to the preceding solutions is that you need to find a balance between respect for the customer and for yourself. Your guiding principle in constructing a strategy for dealing with customer requests is that the request should be meaningful, be rational, and provide all the information and legwork you need in order to fulfill the request. In return, your response should be helpful and timely.

CHAPTER 30

Embedding an SRE to Recover from Operational Overload

Written by Randall Bosetti
Edited by Diane Bates

It's standard policy for Google's SRE teams to evenly split their time between projects and reactive ops work. In practice, this balance can be upset for months at a time by an increase in the daily ticket volume. A burdensome amount of ops work is especially dangerous because the SRE team might burn out or be unable to make progress on project work. When a team must allocate a disproportionate amount of time to resolving tickets at the cost of spending time improving the service, scalability and reliability suffer.

One way to relieve this burden is to temporarily transfer an SRE into the overloaded team. Once embedded in a team, the SRE focuses on improving the team's practices instead of simply helping the team empty the ticket queue. The SRE observes the team's daily routine and makes recommendations to improve their practices. This consultation gives the team a fresh perspective on its routines that team members can't provide for themselves.

When you are using this approach, it isn't necessary to transfer more than one engineer. Two SREs don't necessarily produce better results and may actually cause problems if the team reacts defensively.

If you are starting your first SRE team, the approach outlined in this chapter will help you to avoid turning into an operation team solely focused on a ticket rotation. If you decide to embed yourself or one of your reports in a team, take time to review SRE practices and philosophy in Ben Treynor Sloss's introduction and the material on monitoring in Chapter 6.

The following sections provide guidance to the SRE who will be embedded on a team.

Phase 1: Learn the Service and Get Context

Your job while embedded with the team is to articulate why processes and habits contribute to, or detract from, the service's scalability. Remind the team that more tickets should not require more SREs: the goal of the SRE model is to only introduce more humans as more complexity is added to the system. Instead, try to draw attention to how healthy work habits reduce the time spent on tickets. Doing so is as important as pointing out missed opportunities for automation or simplification of the service.

Ops Mode Versus Nonlinear Scaling

The term *ops mode* refers to a certain method of keeping a service running. Various work items increase with the size of the service. For example, a service needs a way to increase the number of configured virtual machines (VMs) as it grows. A team in ops mode responds by having a greater number of administrators managing those VMs. SRE instead focuses on writing software or eliminating scalability concerns so that the number of people required to run a service doesn't increase as a function of load on the service.

Teams sliding into ops mode might be convinced that scale doesn't matter for them ("my service is tiny"). Shadow an on-call session to determine whether the assessment is true, because the element of scale affects your strategy.

If the primary service is important to the business but actually is tiny (entailing few resources or low complexity), put more focus on ways in which the team's current approach prevents them from improving the service's reliability. Remember that your job is to make the service work, not to shield the development team from alerts.

On the other hand, if the service is just getting started, focus on ways to prepare the team for explosive growth. A 100 request/second service can turn into a 10k request/second service in a year.

Identify the Largest Sources of Stress

SRE teams sometimes fall into ops mode because they focus on how to quickly address emergencies instead of how to reduce the number of emergencies. A default to ops mode usually happens in response to an overwhelming pressure, real *or imagined*. After you've learned enough about the service to ask hard questions about its design and deployment, spend some time prioritizing various service outages according to their impact on the team's stress levels. Keep in mind that, due to the team's perspective and history, some very small problems or outages may produce an inordinate amount of stress.

Identify Kindling

Once you identify a team's largest existing problems, move on to emergencies waiting to happen. Sometimes impending emergencies come in the form of a new subsystem that isn't designed to be self-managing. Other sources include:

Knowledge gaps
> In large teams, people can overspecialize without immediate consequence. When a person specializes, they run the risk of either not having the broad knowledge they need to perform on-call support or allowing team members to ignore the critical pieces of the system that they own.

Services developed by SRE that are quietly increasing in importance
> These services often don't get the same careful attention as new feature launches because they're smaller in scale and implicitly endorsed by at least one SRE.

Strong dependence on "the next big thing"
> People might ignore problems for months at a time because they believe the new solution that's on the horizon obviates temporary fixes.

Common alerts that aren't diagnosed by either the dev team or SREs
> Such alerts are frequently triaged as *transient*, but still distract your teammates from fixing real problems. Either investigate such alerts fully, or fix the alerting rules.

Any service that is both the subject of complaints from your clients and lacks a formal SLI/SLO/SLA
> See Chapter 4 for a discussion of SLIs, SLOs, and SLAs.

Any service with a capacity plan that is effectively "Add more servers: our servers were running out of memory last night"
> Capacity plans should be sufficiently forward-looking. If your system model predicts that servers need 2 GB, a loadtest that passes in the short term (revealing 1.99 GB in its last run) doesn't necessarily mean that your system capacity is in adequate shape.

Postmortems that only have action items for rolling back the specific changes that caused an outage
> For example, "Change the streaming timeout back to 60 seconds," instead of "Figure out why it sometimes takes 60 seconds to fetch the first megabyte of our promo videos."

Any serving-critical component for which the existing SREs respond to questions by saying, "We don't know anything about that; the devs own it"
> To give acceptable on-call support for a component, you should at least know the consequences when it breaks and the urgency needed to fix problems.

Phase 2: Sharing Context

After scoping the dynamics and pain points of the team, lay the groundwork for improvement through best practices like postmortems and by identifying sources of toil and how to best address them.

Write a Good Postmortem for the Team

Postmortems offer much insight into a team's collective reasoning. Postmortems conducted by unhealthy teams are often ineffectual. Some team members might consider postmortems punitive, or even useless. While you might be tempted to review the postmortem archives and leave comments for improvement, doing so doesn't help the team. Instead, the exercise might put the team on the defensive.

Instead of trying to correct previous mistakes, take ownership of the next postmortem. There *will* be an outage while you're embedded. If you aren't the person on-call, team up with the on-call SRE to write a great, blameless postmortem. This document is an opportunity to demonstrate how a shift toward the SRE model benefits the team by making bug fixes more permanent. More permanent bug fixes reduce the impact of outages on team members' time.

As mentioned, you might encounter responses such as "Why me?" This response is especially likely when a team believes that the postmortem process is retaliatory. This attitude comes from subscribing to the Bad Apple Theory: the system is working fine, and if we get rid of all the bad apples and their mistakes, the system will continue to be fine. The Bad Apple Theory is demonstrably false, as shown by evidence [Dek14] from several disciplines, including airline safety. You should point out this falsity. The most effective phrasing for a postmortem is to say, "Mistakes are inevitable in any system with multiple subtle interactions. You were on-call, and I trust you to make the right decisions with the right information. I'd like you to write down what you were thinking at each point in time, so that we can find out where the system misled you, and where the cognitive demands were too high."

Sort Fires According to Type

There are two types of fires in this simplified-for-convenience model:

- Some fires shouldn't exist. They cause what is commonly called ops work or toil (see Chapter 5).
- Other fires that cause stress and/or furious typing are actually part of the job. In either case, the team needs to build tools to control the burn.

Sort the team fires into toil and not-toil. When you're finished, present the list to the team and clearly explain why each fire is either work that should be automated or acceptable overhead for running the service.

Phase 3: Driving Change

Team health is a process. As such, it's not something that you can solve with heroic effort. To ensure that the team can self-regulate, you can help them build a good mental model for an ideal SRE engagement.

 Humans are pretty good at homeostasis, so *focus on creating (or restoring) the right initial conditions and teaching the small set of principles needed to make healthy choices.*

Start with the Basics

Teams struggling with the distinction between the SRE and traditional ops model are generally unable to articulate *why* certain aspects of the team's code, processes, or culture bother them. Rather than trying to address each of these issues point-by-point, work forward from the principles outlined in Chapters 1 and 6.

Your first goal for the team should be writing a service level objective (SLO), if one doesn't already exist. The SLO is important because it provides a quantitative measure of the impact of outages, in addition to how important a process change could be. An SLO is probably the single most important lever for moving a team from reactive ops work to a healthy, long-term SRE focus. If this agreement is missing, no other advice in this chapter will be helpful. *If you find yourself on a team without SLOs, first read Chapter 4, then get the tech leads and management in a room and start arbitrating.*

Get Help Clearing Kindling

You may have a strong urge to simply fix the issues you identify. Please resist the urge to fix these issues yourself, because doing so bolsters the idea that "making changes is for other people." Instead, take the following steps:

1. Find useful work that can be accomplished by one team member.
2. Clearly explain how this work addresses an issue from the postmortem *in a permanent way*. Even otherwise healthy teams can produce shortsighted action items.
3. Serve as the reviewer for the code changes and document revisions.
4. Repeat for two or three issues.

When you identify an additional issue, put it in a bug report or a doc for the team to consult. Doing so serves the dual purposes of distributing information and encouraging team members to write docs (which are often the first victim of deadline pressure). Always explain your reasoning, and emphasize that good documentation ensures that the team doesn't repeat old mistakes in a slightly new context.

Explain Your Reasoning

As the team recovers its momentum and grasps the basics of your suggested changes, move on to tackle the quotidian decisions that originally led to ops overload. Prepare for this undertaking to be challenged. If you're lucky, the challenge will be along the lines of, "Explain why. Right now. In the middle of the weekly production meeting."

If you're unlucky, no one demands an explanation. Sidestep this problem entirely by simply explaining all of your decisions, whether or not someone requests an explanation. Refer to the basics that underscore your suggestions. Doing so helps build the team's mental model. *After you leave, the team should be able to predict what your comment on a design or changelist would be.* If you don't explain your reasoning, or do so poorly, there is a risk that the team will simply emulate that lackadaisical behavior, so be explicit.

Examples of a thorough explanation of your decision:

- "I'm not pushing back on the latest release because the tests are bad. I'm pushing back because the error budget we set for releases is exhausted."

- "Releases need to be rollback-safe because our SLO is tight. Meeting that SLO requires that the mean time to recovery is small, so in-depth diagnosis before a rollback is not realistic."

Examples of an insufficient explanation of your decision:

- "I don't think having every server generate its routing config is safe, because we can't see it."

This decision is probably correct, but the reasoning is poor (or poorly explained). The team can't read your mind, so they very likely might emulate the observed poor reasoning. Instead, try "[...] isn't safe because a bug in that code can cause a correlated failure across the service and the additional code is a source of bugs that might slow down a rollback."

- "The automation should give up if it encounters a conflicting deployment."

Like the previous example, this explanation is probably correct, but insufficient. Instead, try "[...] because we're making the simplifying assumption that all changes pass through the automation, and something has clearly violated that rule. If this happens often, we should identify and remove sources of unorganized change."

Ask Leading Questions

Leading questions are not loaded questions. When talking with the SRE team, try to ask questions in a way that encourages people to think about the basic principles. It's particularly valuable for *you* to model this behavior because, by definition, a team in ops mode rejects this sort of reasoning from its own constituents. Once you've spent some time explaining your reasoning for various policy questions, this practice reinforces the team's understanding of SRE philosophy.

Examples of leading questions:

- "I see that the TaskFailures alert fires frequently, but the on-call engineers usually don't do anything to respond to the alert. How does this impact the SLO?"
- "This turnup procedure looks pretty complicated. Do you know why there are so many config files to update when creating a new instance of the service?"

Counterexamples of leading questions:

- "What's up with all of these old, stalled releases?"
- "Why does the Frobnitzer do so many things?"

Conclusion

Following the tenets outlined in this chapter provides an SRE team with the following:

- A technical, possibly quantitative, perspective on why they should change.
- A strong example of what change looks like.
- A logical explanation for much of the "folk wisdom" used by SRE.
- The core principles needed to address novel situations in a scalable manner.

Your final task is to write an after-action report. This report should reiterate your perspective, examples, and explanation. It should also provide some action items for the team to ensure they exercise what you've taught them. You can organize the report as a postvitam,[1] explaining the critical decisions at each step that led to success.

---

1 In contrast to a postmortem.

The bulk of the engagement is now complete. Once your embedded assignment concludes, you should remain available for design and code reviews. Keep an eye on the team for the next few months to confirm that they're slowly improving their capacity planning, emergency response, and rollout processes.

CHAPTER 31

Communication and Collaboration in SRE

Written by Niall Murphy with Alex Rodriguez, Carl Crous, Dario
Freni, Dylan Curley, Lorenzo Blanco, and Todd Underwood
Edited by Betsy Beyer

The organizational position of SRE in Google is interesting, and has effects on how we communicate and collaborate.

To begin with, there is a tremendous diversity in what SRE does, and how we do it. We have infrastructural teams, service teams, and horizontal product teams. We have relationships with product development teams ranging from teams that are many times our size, to teams roughly the same size as their counterparts, and situations in which we *are* the product development team. SRE teams are made up of people with systems engineering or architectural skills (see [Hix15b]), software engineering skills, project management skills, leadership instincts, backgrounds in all kinds of industries (see Chapter 33), and so on. We don't have just one model, and we have found a variety of configurations that work; this flexibility suits our ultimately pragmatic nature.

It's also true that SRE is not a command-and-control organization. Generally, we owe allegiance to at least two masters: for service or infrastructure SRE teams, we work closely with the corresponding product development teams that work on those services or that infrastructure; we also obviously work in the context of SRE generally. The service relationship is very strong, since we are held accountable for the performance of those systems, but despite that relationship, our actual reporting lines are through SRE as a whole. Today, we spend more time supporting our individual services than on cross-production work, but our culture and our shared values produce strongly homogeneous approaches to problems. This is by design.[1]

---

1 And, as we all know, culture beats strategy every time: [Mer11].

The two preceding facts have steered the SRE organization in certain directions when it comes to two crucial dimensions of how our teams operate—communications and collaboration. Data flow would be an apt computing metaphor for our communications: just like data must flow around production, data also has to flow around an SRE team—data about projects, the state of the services, production, and the state of the individuals. For maximum effectiveness of a team, the data has to flow in reliable ways from one interested party to another. One way to think of this flow is to think of the interface that an SRE team must present to other teams, such as an API. Just like an API, a good design is crucial for effective operation, and if the API is wrong, it can be painful to correct later on.

The API-as-contract metaphor is also relevant for collaboration, both among SRE teams, and between SRE and product development teams—all have to make progress in an environment of unrelenting change. To that extent, our collaboration looks quite like collaboration in any other fast-moving company. The difference is the mix of software engineering skills, systems engineering expertise, and the wisdom of production experience that SRE brings to bear on that collaboration. The best designs and the best implementations result from the joint concerns of production and the product being met in an atmosphere of mutual respect. This is the promise of SRE: an organization charged with reliability, with the same skills as the product development teams, will improve things measurably. Our experience suggests that simply having someone in charge of reliability, without also having the complete skill set, is not enough.

Communications: Production Meetings

Although literature about running effective meetings abounds [Kra08], it's difficult to find someone who's lucky enough to *only* have useful, effective meetings. This is equally true for SRE.

However, there's one kind of meeting that we have that is more useful than the average, called a *production meeting*. Production meetings are a special kind of meeting where an SRE team carefully articulates to itself—and to its invitees—the state of the service(s) in their charge, so as to increase general awareness among everyone who cares, and to improve the operation of the service(s). In general, these meetings are *service-oriented*; they are not directly about the status updates of individuals. The goal is for everyone to leave the meeting with an idea of what's going on—the *same* idea. The other major goal of production meetings is to improve our services by bringing the wisdom of production to bear on our services. That means we talk in detail about the operational performance of the service, and relate that operational performance to design, configuration, or implementation, and make recommendations for how to fix the problems. Connecting the performance of the service with design decisions in a regular meeting is an immensely powerful feedback loop.

Our production meetings usually happen weekly; given SRE's antipathy to pointless meetings, this frequency seems to be just about right: time to allow enough relevant material to accumulate to make the meeting worthwhile, while not so frequent that people find excuses to not attend. They usually last somewhere between 30 and 60 minutes. Any less and you're probably cutting something unnecessarily short, or you should probably be growing your service portfolio. Any more and you're probably getting mired in the detail, or you've got too much to talk about and you should shard the team or service set.

Just like any other meeting, the production meeting should have a chair. Many SRE teams rotate the chair through various team members, which has the advantage of making everyone feel they have a stake in the service and some notional ownership of the issues. It's true that not everyone has equal levels of chairing skill, but the value of group ownership is so large that the trade-off of temporary suboptimality is worthwhile. Furthermore, this is a chance to instill chairing skills, which are very useful in the kind of incident coordination situations commonly faced by SRE.

In cases where two SRE teams are meeting by video, and one of the teams is much larger than the other, we have noticed an interesting dynamic at play. We recommend placing your chair on the *smaller* side of the call by default. The larger side naturally tends to quiet down and some of the bad effects of imbalanced team sizes (made worse by the delays inherent in video conferencing) will improve.[2] We have no idea if this technique has any scientific basis, but it does tend to work.

Agenda

There are many ways to run a production meeting, attesting to the diversity of what SRE looks after and how we do it. To that extent, it's not appropriate to be prescriptive on how to run one of these meetings. However, a default agenda (see Appendix F for an example) might look something like the following:

Upcoming production changes
    Change-tracking meetings are well known throughout the industry, and indeed whole meetings have often been devoted to stopping change. However, in our production environment, we usually default to enabling change, which requires tracking the useful set of properties of that change: start time, duration, expected effect, and so on. This is near-term horizon visibility.

---

2 The larger team generally tends to unintentionally talk over the smaller team, it's more difficult to control distracting side conversations, etc.

Metrics

One of the major ways we conduct a service-oriented discussion is by talking about the core metrics of the systems in question; see Chapter 4. Even if the systems didn't dramatically fail that week, it's very common to be in a position where you're looking at gradually (or sharply!) increasing load throughout the year. Keeping track of how your latency figures, CPU utilization figures, etc., change over time is incredibly valuable for developing a feeling for the performance envelope of a system.

Some teams track resource usage and efficiency, which is also a useful indicator of slower, perhaps more insidious system changes.

Outages

This item addresses problems of approximately postmortem size, and is an indispensable opportunity for learning. A good postmortem analysis, as discussed in Chapter 15, should always set the juices flowing.

Paging events

These are pages from your monitoring system, relating to problems that *can* be postmortem worthy, but often aren't. In any event, while the Outages portion looks at the larger picture of an outage, this section looks at the tactical view: the list of pages, who was paged, what happened then, and so on. There are two implicit questions for this section: should that alert have paged in the way it did, and should it have paged at all? If the answer to the last question is no, remove those unactionable pages.

Nonpaging events

This bucket contains three items:

- *An issue that probably should have paged, but didn't.* In these cases, you should probably fix the monitoring so that such events do trigger a page. Often you encounter the issue while you're trying to fix something else, or it's related to a metric you're tracking but for which you haven't got an alert.

- *An issue that is not pageable but requires attention,* such as low-impact data corruption or slowness in some non-user-facing dimension of the system. Tracking reactive operational work is also appropriate here.

- *An issue that is not pageable and does not require attention.* These alerts should be removed, because they create extra noise that distracts engineers from issues that do merit attention.

Prior action items

The preceding detailed discussions often lead to actions that SRE needs to take—fix this, monitor that, develop a subsystem to do the other. Track these improvements just as they would be tracked in any other meeting: assign action items to people and track their progress. It's a good idea to have an explicit agenda item that acts as a catchall, if nothing else. Consistent delivery is also a wonderful credibility and trust builder. It doesn't matter how such delivery is done, just that it *is* done.

Attendance

Attendance is compulsory for all the members of the SRE team in question. This is particularly true if your team is spread across multiple countries and/or time zones, because this is your major opportunity to interact as a group.

The major stakeholders should also attend this meeting. Any partner product development teams you may have should also attend. Some SRE teams shard their meeting so SRE-only matters are kept to the first half; that practice is fine, as long as everyone, as stated previously, leaves with the same idea of what's going on. From time to time representatives from other SRE teams might turn up, particularly if there's some larger cross-team issue to discuss, but in general, the SRE team in question plus major other teams should attend. If your relationship is such that you cannot invite your product development partners, you need to fix that relationship: perhaps the first step is to invite a representative from that team, or to find a trusted intermediary to proxy communication or model healthy interactions. There are many reasons why teams don't get along, and a wealth of writing on how to solve that problem: this information is also applicable to SRE teams, but it is important that the end goal of having a feedback loop from operations is fulfilled, or a large part of the value of having an SRE team is lost.

Occasionally you'll have too many teams or busy-yet-crucial attendees to invite. There are a number of techniques you can use to handle those situations:

- Less active services might be attended by a single representative from the product development team, or only have commitment from the product development team to read and comment on the agenda minutes.
- If the production development team is quite large, nominate a subset of representatives.
- Busy-yet-crucial attendees can provide feedback and/or steering in advance to individuals, or using the prefilled agenda technique (described next).

Most of the meeting strategies we've discussed are common sense, with a service-oriented twist. One unique spin on making meetings more efficient *and* more inclusive is to use the real-time collaborative features of Google Docs. Many SRE teams have such a doc, with a well-known address that anyone in engineering can access. Having such a doc enables two great practices:

- Pre-populating the agenda with "bottom up" ideas, comments, and information.
- Preparing the agenda in parallel *and* in advance is really efficient.

Fully use the multiple-person collaboration features enabled by the product. There's nothing quite like seeing a meeting chair type in a sentence, then seeing someone else supply a link to the source material in brackets after they have finished typing, and then seeing yet another person tidy up the spelling and grammar in the original sentence. Such collaboration gets stuff done faster, and makes more people feel like they own a slice of what the team does.

Collaboration within SRE

Obviously, Google is a multinational organization. Because of the emergency response and pager rotation component of our role, we have very good business reasons to be a distributed organization, separated by at least a few time zones. The practical impact of this distribution is that we have very fluid definitions for "team" compared to, for example, the average product development team. We have local teams, the team on the site, the cross-continental team, virtual teams of various sizes and coherence, and everything in between. This creates a cheerfully chaotic mix of responsibilities, skills, and opportunities. Much of the same dynamics could be expected to pertain to any sufficiently large company (although they might be particularly intense for tech companies). Given that most local collaboration faces no particular obstacle, the interesting case collaboration-wise is cross-team, cross-site, across a virtual team, and similar.

This pattern of distribution also informs how SRE teams tend to be organized. Because our *raison d'être* is bringing value through technical mastery, and technical mastery tends to be hard, we therefore try to find a way to have mastery over some related subset of systems or infrastructures, in order to decrease cognitive load. Specialization is one way of accomplishing this objective; i.e., team X works only on product Y. Specialization is good, because it leads to higher chances of improved technical mastery, but it's also bad, because it leads to siloization and ignorance of the broader picture. We try to have a crisp team charter to define what a team will—and more importantly, won't—support, but we don't always succeed.

Team Composition

We have a wide array of skill sets in SRE, ranging from systems engineering through software engineering, and into organization and management. The one thing we can say about collaboration is that your chances of successful collaboration—and indeed just about anything else—are improved by having more diversity in your team. There's a lot of evidence suggesting that diverse teams are simply better teams [Nel14]. Running a diverse team implies particular attention to communication, cognitive biases, and so on, which we can't cover in detail here.

Formally, SRE teams have the roles of "tech lead" (TL), "manager" (SRM), and "project manager" (also known as PM, TPM, PgM). Some people operate best when those roles have well-defined responsibilities: the major benefit of this being they can make in-scope decisions quickly and safely. Others operate best in a more fluid environment, with shifting responsibilities depending on dynamic negotiation. In general, the more fluid the team is, the more developed it is in terms of the capabilities of the individuals, and the more able the team is to adapt to new situations—but at the cost of having to communicate more and more often, because less background can be assumed.

Regardless of how well these roles are defined, at a base level the tech lead is responsible for technical direction in the team, and can lead in a variety of ways—everything from carefully commenting on everyone's code, to holding quarterly direction presentations, to building consensus in the team. In Google, TLs can do almost all of a manager's job, because our managers are highly technical, but the manager has two special responsibilities that a TL doesn't have: the performance management function, and being a general catchall for everything that isn't handled by someone else. Great TLs, SRMs, and TPMs have a complete set of skills and can cheerfully turn their hand to organizing a project, commenting on a design doc, or writing code as necessary.

Techniques for Working Effectively

There are a number of ways to engineer effectively in SRE.

In general, singleton projects fail unless the person is particularly gifted or the problem is straightforward. To accomplish anything significant, you pretty much need multiple people. Therefore, you also need good collaboration skills. Again, lots of material has been written on this topic, and much of this literature is applicable to SRE.

In general, good SRE work calls for excellent communication skills when you're working outside the boundary of your purely local team. For collaborations outside the building, effectively working across time zones implies either great written communication, or lots of travel to supply the in-person experience that is deferrable but ultimately necessary for a high-quality relationship. Even if you're a great writer, over time you decay into just being an email address until you turn up in the flesh again.

Case Study of Collaboration in SRE: Viceroy

One example of a successful cross-SRE collaboration is a project called Viceroy, which is a monitoring dashboard framework and service. The current organizational architecture of SRE can end up with teams producing multiple, slightly different copies of the same piece of work; for various reasons, monitoring dashboard frameworks were a particularly fertile ground for duplication of work.[3]

The incentives that led to the serious litter problem of many smoldering, abandoned hulks of monitoring frameworks lying around were pretty simple: each team was rewarded for developing its own solution, working outside of the team boundary was hard, and the infrastructure that tended to be provided SRE-wide was typically closer to a toolkit than a product. This environment encouraged individual engineers to use the toolkit to make another burning wreck rather than fix the problem for the largest number of people possible (an effort that would therefore take much longer).

The Coming of the Viceroy

Viceroy was different. It began in 2012 when a number of teams were considering how to move to Monarch, the new monitoring system at Google. SRE is deeply conservative with respect to monitoring systems, so Monarch somewhat ironically took a longer while to get traction within SRE than within non-SRE teams. But no one could argue that our legacy monitoring system, Borgmon (see Chapter 10), had no room for improvement. For example, our consoles were cumbersome because they used a custom HTML templating system that was special-cased, full of funky edge cases, and difficult to test. At that time, Monarch had matured enough to be accepted in principle as the replacement for the legacy system and was therefore being adopted by more and more teams across Google, but it turned out we still had a problem with consoles.

Those of us who tried using Monarch for our services soon found that it fell short in its console support for two main reasons:

- Consoles were easy to set up for a small service, but didn't scale well to services with complex consoles.
- They also didn't support the legacy monitoring system, making the transition to Monarch very difficult.

---

3 In this particular case, the road to hell was indeed paved with JavaScript.

Because no viable alternative to deploying Monarch in this way existed at the time, a number of team-specific projects launched. Since there was little enough in the way of coordinated development solutions or even cross-group tracking at the time (a problem that has since been fixed), we ended up duplicating efforts yet again. Multiple teams from Spanner, Ads Frontend, and a variety of other services spun up their own efforts (one notable example was called Consoles++) over the course of 12–18 months, and eventually sanity prevailed when engineers from all those teams woke up and discovered each other's respective efforts. They decided to do the sensible thing and join forces in order to create a general solution for all of SRE. Thus, the Viceroy project was born in mid 2012.

By the beginning of 2013, Viceroy had started to gather interest from teams who had yet to move off the legacy system, but who were looking to put a toe in the water. Obviously, teams with larger existing monitoring projects had fewer incentives to move to the new system: it was hard for these teams to rationalize jettisoning the low maintenance cost for their existing solution that basically worked fine, for something relatively new and unproven that would require lots of effort to make work. The sheer diversity of requirements added to the reluctance of these teams, even though all monitoring console projects shared two main requirements, notably:

- Support complex curated dashboards
- Support both Monarch and the legacy monitoring system

Each project *also* had its own set of technical requirements, which depended on the author's preference or experience. For example:

- Multiple data sources outside the core monitoring systems
- Definition of consoles using configuration versus explicit HTML layout
- No JavaScript versus full embrace of JavaScript with AJAX
- Sole use of static content, so the consoles can be cached in the browser

Although some of these requirements were stickier than others, overall they made merging efforts difficult. Indeed, although the Consoles++ team was interested in seeing how their project compared to Viceroy, their initial examination in the first half of 2013 determined that the fundamental differences between the two projects were significant enough to prevent integration. The largest difficulty was that Viceroy by design did not use much JavaScript, while Consoles++ was mostly written in Java-Script. There was a glimmer of hope, however, in that the two systems did have a number of underlying similarities:

- They used similar syntaxes for HTML template rendering.

- They shared a number of long-term goals, which neither team had yet begun to address. For example, both systems wanted to cache monitoring data and support an offline pipeline to periodically produce data that the console can use, but was too computationally expensive to produce on demand.

We ended up parking the unified console discussion for a while. However, by the end of 2013, both Consoles++ and Viceroy had developed significantly. Their technical differences had narrowed, because Viceroy had started using JavaScript to render its monitoring graphs. The two teams met and figured out that integration was a lot easier, now that integration boiled down to serving the Consoles++ data out of the Viceroy server. The first integrated prototypes were completed in early 2014, and proved that the systems could work well together. Both teams felt comfortable committing to a joint effort at that point, and because Viceroy had already established its brand as a common monitoring solution, the combined project retained the Viceroy name. Developing full functionality took a few quarters, but by the end of 2014, the combined system was complete.

Joining forces reaped huge benefits:

- Viceroy received a host of data sources and the JavaScript clients to access them.

- JavaScript compilation was rewritten to support separate modules that can be selectively included. This is essential to scale the system to any number of teams with their own JavaScript code.

- Consoles++ benefited from the many improvements actively being made to Viceroy, such as the addition of its cache and background data pipeline.

- Overall, the development velocity on *one* solution was much larger than the sum of all the development velocity of the duplicative projects.

Ultimately, the common future vision was the key factor in combining the projects. Both teams found value in expanding their development team and benefited from each other's contributions. The momentum was such that, by the end of 2014, Viceroy was officially declared the general monitoring solution for all of SRE. Perhaps characteristically for Google, this declaration didn't require that teams adopt Viceroy: rather, it recommended that teams should use Viceroy instead of writing another monitoring console.

Challenges

While ultimately a success, Viceroy was not without difficulties, and many of those arose due to the cross-site nature of the project.

Once the extended Viceroy team was established, initial coordination among remote team members proved difficult. When meeting people for the first time, subtle cues in writing and speaking can be misinterpreted, because communication styles vary substantially from person to person. At the start of the project, team members who weren't located in Mountain View also missed out on the impromptu water cooler discussions that often happened shortly before and after meetings (although communication has since improved considerably).

While the core Viceroy team remained fairly consistent, the extended team of contributors was fairly dynamic. Contributors had other responsibilities that changed over time, and therefore many were able to dedicate between one and three months to the project. Thus, the developer contributor pool, which was inherently larger than the core Viceroy team, was characterized by a significant amount of churn.

Adding new people to the project required training each contributor on the overall design and structure of the system, which took some time. On the other hand, when an SRE contributed to the core functionality of Viceroy and later returned to their own team, they were a local expert on the system. That unanticipated dissemination of local Viceroy experts drove more usage and adoption.

As people joined and left the team, we found that casual contributions were both useful and costly. The primary cost was the dilution of ownership: once features were delivered and the person left, the features became unsupported over time, and were generally dropped.

Furthermore, the scope of the Viceroy project grew over time. It had ambitious goals at launch but the initial *scope* was limited. As the scope grew, however, we struggled to deliver core features on time, and had to improve project management and set clearer direction to ensure the project stayed on track.

Finally, the Viceroy team found it difficult to completely own a component that had significant (determining) contributions from distributed sites. Even with the best will in the world, people generally default to the path of least resistance and discuss issues or make decisions locally without involving the remote owners, which can lead to conflict.

Recommendations

You should only develop projects cross-site when you have to, but often there are good reasons to have to. The cost of working across sites is higher latency for actions and more communication being required; the benefit is—if you get the mechanics right—much higher throughput. The single site project can also fall foul of no one outside of that site knowing what you're doing, so there are costs to both approaches.

Motivated contributors are valuable, but not all contributions are equally valuable. Make sure project contributors are actually committed, and aren't just joining with some nebulous self-actualization goal (wanting to earn a notch on their belt attaching their name to a shiny project; wanting to code on a new exciting project without committing to maintaining that project). Contributors with a specific goal to achieve will generally be better motivated and will better maintain their contributions.

As projects develop, they usually grow, and you're not always in the lucky position of having people in your local team to contribute to the project. Therefore, think carefully about the project structure. The project leaders are important: they provide long-term vision for the project and make sure all work aligns with that vision and is prioritized correctly. You also need to have an agreed way of making decisions, and should specifically optimize for making more decisions locally if there is a high level of agreement and trust.

The standard "divide and conquer" strategy applies to cross-site projects; you reduce communication costs primarily by splitting the project into as many reasonably sized components as possible, and trying to make sure that each component can be assigned to a small group, preferably within one site. Divide these components among the project subteams, and establish clear deliverables and deadlines. (Try not to let Conway's law distort the natural shape of the software too deeply.)[4]

A goal for a project team works best when it's oriented toward providing some functionality or solving some problem. This approach ensures that the individuals working on a component know what is expected of them, and that their work is only complete once that component is fully integrated and used within the main project.

Obviously, the usual engineering best practices apply to collaborative projects: each component should have design documents and reviews with the team. In this way, everyone in the team is given the opportunity to stay abreast of changes, in addition to the chance to influence and improve designs. Writing things down is one of the major techniques you have to offset physical and/or logical distance—use it.

Standards are important. Coding style guidelines are a good start, but they're usually quite tactical and therefore only a starting point for establishing team norms. Every time there is a debate around which choice to make on an issue, argue it out fully with the team but with a strict time limit. Then pick a solution, document it, and move on. If you can't agree, you need to pick some arbitrator that everyone respects, and again just move forward. Over time you'll build up a collection of these best practices, which will help new people come up to speed.

Ultimately, there's no substitute for in-person interaction, although some portion of face-to-face interaction can be deferred by good use of VC and good written communication. If you can, have the leaders of the project meet the rest of the team in per-

---

4 That is, software has the same structure as the communications structure of the organization that produces the software—see *https://en.wikipedia.org/wiki/Conway%27s_law*.

son. If time and budget allows, organize a team summit so that all members of the team can interact in person. A summit also provides a great opportunity to hash out designs and goals. For situations where neutrality is important, it's advantageous to hold team summits at a neutral location so that no individual site has the "home advantage."

Finally, use the project management style that suits the project in its current state. Even projects with ambitious goals will start out small, so the overhead should be correspondingly low. As the project grows, it's appropriate to adapt and change how the project is managed. Given sufficient growth, full project management will be necessary.

Collaboration Outside SRE

As we suggested, and Chapter 32 discusses, collaboration between the product development organization and SRE is really at its best when it occurs early on in the design phase, ideally before any line of code has been committed. SREs are best placed to make recommendations about architecture and software behavior that can be quite difficult (if not impossible) to retrofit. Having that voice present in the room when a new system is being designed goes better for everyone. Broadly speaking, we use the Objectives & Key Results (OKR) process [Kla12] to track such work. For some service teams, such collaboration is the mainstay of what they do—tracking new designs, making recommendations, helping to implement them, and seeing those through to production.

Case Study: Migrating DFP to F1

Large migration projects of existing services are quite common at Google. Typical examples include porting service components to a new technology or updating components to support a new data format. With the recent introduction of database technologies that can scale to a global level such as Spanner [Cor12] and F1 [Shu13], Google has undertaken a number of large-scale migration projects involving databases. One such project was the migration of the main database of DoubleClick for Publishers (DFP)[5] from MySQL to F1. In particular, some of this chapter's authors were in charge of a portion of the serving system (shown in Figure 31-1) that continually extracts and processes data from the database, in order to generate a set of indexed files that are then loaded and served around the world. This system was distributed over several datacenters and used about 1,000 CPUs and 8 TB of RAM to index 100 TB of data every day.

---

5 DoubleClick for Publishers is a tool for publishers to manage ads served on their websites and in their apps.

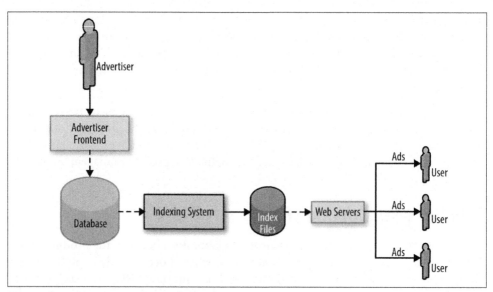

Figure 31-1. A generic ads serving system

The migration was nontrivial: in addition to migrating to a new technology, the database schema was significantly refactored and simplified thanks to the ability of F1 to store and index protocol buffer data in table columns. The goal was to migrate the processing system so that it could produce an output perfectly identical to the existing system. This allowed us to leave the serving system untouched and to perform, from the user's perspective, a seamless migration. As an added restriction, the product required that we complete a live migration without any disruption of the service to our users at any time. In order to achieve this, the product development team and the SRE team started working closely, from the very beginning, to develop the new indexing service.

As its main developers, product development teams are typically more familiar with the Business Logic (BL) of the software, and are also in closer contact with the Product Managers and the actual "business need" component of products. On the other hand, SRE teams usually have more expertise pertaining to the infrastructure components of the software (e.g., libraries to talk to distributed storage systems or databases), because SREs often reuse the same building blocks across different services, learning the many caveats and nuances that allow the software to run scalably and reliably over time.

From the start of the migration project, product development and SRE knew they would have to collaborate even more closely, conducting weekly meetings to sync on the project's progress. In this particular case the BL changes were partially dependent upon infrastructure changes. For this reason the project started with the design of the new infrastructure; the SREs, who had extensive knowledge about the domain of extracting and processing data at scale, drove the design of the infrastructure changes. This involved designing how to extract the various tables from F1, how to filter and join the data, how to extract only the data that changed (as opposed to the entire database), how to sustain the loss of some of the machines without impacting the service, how to ensure that the resource usage grows linearly with the amount of extracted data, the capacity planning, and many other similar aspects. The new proposed infrastructure was similar to other services that were already extracting and processing data from F1. Therefore, we could be sure of the soundness of the solution and reuse parts of the monitoring and tooling.

Before proceeding with the development of this new infrastructure, two SREs produced a detailed design document. Then, both the product development and SRE teams thoroughly reviewed the document, tweaking the solution to handle some edge cases, and eventually agreed on a design plan. Such a plan clearly identified what kind of changes the new infrastructure would bring to the BL. For example, we designed the new infrastructure to extract only changed data, instead of repeatedly extracting the entire database; the BL had to take into account this new approach. Early on, we defined the new interfaces between infrastructure and BL, and doing so allowed the product development team to work independently on the BL changes. Similarly, the product development team kept SRE informed of BL changes. Where they interacted (e.g., BL changes dependent on infrastructure), this coordination structure allowed us to know changes were happening, and to handle them quickly and correctly.

In later phases of the project, SREs began deploying the new service in a testing environment that resembled the project's eventual finished production environment. This step was essential to measure the expected behavior of the service—in particular, performance and resource utilization—while the development of BL was still underway. The product development team used this testing environment to perform validation of the new service: the index of the ads produced by the old service (running in production) had to match perfectly the index produced by the new service (running in the testing environment). As suspected, the validation process highlighted discrepancies between the old and new services (due to some edge cases in the new data format), which the product development team was able to resolve iteratively: for each ad they debugged the cause of the difference and fixed the BL that produced the bad output. In the meantime, the SRE team began preparing the production environment: allocating the necessary resources in a different datacenter, setting up processes and monitoring rules, and training the engineers designated to be on-call for the service. The SRE team also set up a basic release process that included validation, a task usually completed by the product development team or by Release Engineers but in this specific case was completed by SREs to speed up the migration.

When the service was ready the SREs prepared a rollout plan in collaboration with the product development team and launched the new service. The launch was very successful and proceeded smoothly, without any visible user impact.

Conclusion

Given the globally distributed nature of SRE teams, effective communication has always been a high priority in SRE. This chapter has discussed the tools and techniques that SRE teams use to maintain effective relationships among their team and with their various partner teams.

Collaboration between SRE teams has its challenges, but potentially great rewards, including common approaches to platforms for solving problems, letting us focus on solving more difficult problems.

CHAPTER 32

The Evolving SRE Engagement Model

Written by Acacio Cruz and Ashish Bhambhani
Edited by Betsy Beyer and Tim Harvey

SRE Engagement: What, How, and Why

We've discussed in most of the rest of this book what happens when SRE is *already* in charge of a service. Few services begin their lifecycle enjoying SRE support, so there needs to be a process for evaluating a service, making sure that it merits SRE support, negotiating how to improve any deficits that bar SRE support, and actually instituting SRE support. We call this process *onboarding*. If you are in an environment where you are surrounded by a lot of existing services in varying states of perfection, your SRE team will probably be running through a prioritized queue of onboardings for quite a while until the team has finished taking on the highest-value targets.

Although this is very common, and a completely reasonable way of dealing with a *fait accompli* environment, there are actually at least two better ways of bringing the wisdom of production, and SRE support, to services old and new alike.

In the first case, just as in software engineering—where the earlier the bug is found, the cheaper it is to fix—the earlier an SRE team consultation happens, the better the service will be and the quicker it will feel the benefit. When SRE is engaged during the earliest stages of *design*, the time to onboard is lowered and the service is more reliable "out of the gate," usually because we don't have to spend the time unwinding suboptimal design or implementation.

Another way, perhaps the best, is to short-circuit the process by which specially created systems with lots of individual variations end up "arriving" at SRE's door. Provide product development with a *platform* of SRE-validated infrastructure, upon which they can build their systems. This platform will have the double benefit of being both reliable and scalable. This avoids certain classes of cognitive load problems entirely, and by addressing common infrastructure practices, allows product development teams to focus on innovation at the application layer, where it mostly belongs.

In the following sections, we'll spend some time looking at each of these models in turn, beginning with the "classic" one, the PRR-driven model.

The PRR Model

The most typical initial step of SRE engagement is the Production Readiness Review (PRR), a process that identifies the reliability needs of a service based on its specific details. Through a PRR, SREs seek to apply what they've learned and experienced to ensure the reliability of a service operating in production. A PRR is considered a prerequisite for an SRE team to accept responsibility for managing the production aspects of a service.

Figure 32-1 illustrates the lifecycle of a typical service. The Production Readiness Review can be started at any point of the service lifecycle, but the stages at which SRE engagement is applied have expanded over time. This chapter describes the Simple PRR Model, then discusses how its modification into the Extended Engagement Model and the Frameworks and SRE Platform structure allowed SRE to scale their engagement process and impact.

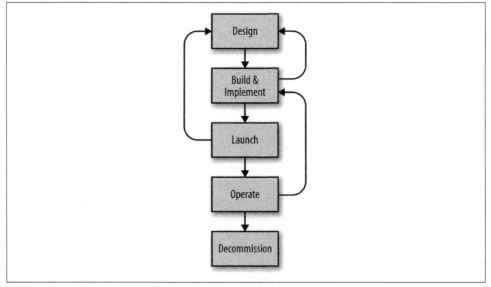

Figure 32-1. A typical service lifecycle

The SRE Engagement Model

SRE seeks production responsibility for important services for which it can make concrete contributions to reliability. SRE is concerned with several aspects of a service, which are collectively referred to as *production*. These aspects include the following:

- System architecture and interservice dependencies
- Instrumentation, metrics, and monitoring
- Emergency response
- Capacity planning
- Change management
- Performance: availability, latency, and efficiency

When SREs engage with a service, we aim to improve it along all of these axes, which makes managing production for the service easier.

Alternative Support

Not all Google services receive close SRE engagement. A couple of factors are at play here:

- Many services don't need high reliability and availability, so support can be provided by other means.
- By design, the number of development teams that request SRE support exceeds the available bandwidth of SRE teams (see Chapter 1).

When SRE can't provide full-fledged support, it provides other options for making improvements to production, such as documentation and consultation.

Documentation

Development guides are available for internal technologies and clients of widely used systems. Google's Production Guide documents production best practices for services, as determined by the experiences of SRE and development teams alike. Developers can implement the solutions and recommendations in such documentation to improve their services.

Consultation

Developers may also seek SRE consulting to discuss specific services or problem areas. The Launch Coordination Engineering (LCE) team (see Chapter 27) spends a majority of its time consulting with development teams. SRE teams that aren't specifically dedicated to launch consultations also engage in consultation with development teams.

When a new service or a new feature has been implemented, developers usually consult with SRE for advice about preparing for the Launch phase. Launch consultation usually involves one or two SREs spending a few hours studying the design and implementation at a high level. The SRE consultants then meet with the development team to provide advice on risky areas that need attention and to discuss well-known patterns or solutions that can be incorporated to improve the service in production. Some of this advice may come from the Production Guide mentioned earlier.

Consultation sessions are necessarily broad in scope because it's not possible to gain a deep understanding of a given system in the limited time available. For some development teams, consultation is not sufficient:

- Services that have grown by orders of magnitude since they launched, which now require more time to understand than is feasible through documentation and consultation.

- Services upon which many other services have subsequently come to rely upon, which now host significantly more traffic from many different clients.

These types of services may have grown to the point at which they begin to encounter significant difficulties in production while simultaneously becoming important to users. In such cases, long-term SRE engagement becomes necessary to ensure that they are properly maintained in production as they grow.

Production Readiness Reviews: Simple PRR Model

When a development team requests that SRE take over production management of a service, SRE gauges both the importance of the service and the availability of SRE teams. If the service merits SRE support, and the SRE team and development organization agree on staffing levels to facilitate this support, SRE initiates a Production Readiness Review with the development team.

The objectives of the Production Readiness Review are as follows:

- Verify that a service meets accepted standards of production setup and operational readiness, and that service owners are prepared to work with SRE and take advantage of SRE expertise.

- Improve the reliability of the service in production, and minimize the number and severity of incidents that might be expected. A PRR targets all aspects of production that SRE cares about.

After sufficient improvements are made and the service is deemed ready for SRE support, an SRE team assumes its production responsibilities.

This brings us to the Production Readiness Review process itself. There are three different but related engagement models (Simple PRR Model, Early Engagement Model, and Frameworks and SRE Platform), which will be discussed in turn.

We will first describe the Simple PRR Model, which is usually targeted at a service that is already launched and will be taken over by an SRE team. A PRR follows several phases, much like a development lifecycle, although it may proceed independently in parallel with the development lifecycle.

Engagement

SRE leadership first decides which SRE team is a good fit for taking over the service. Usually one to three SREs are selected or self-nominated to conduct the PRR process. This small group then initiates discussion with the development team. The discussion covers matters such as:

- Establishing an SLO/SLA for the service
- Planning for potentially disruptive design changes required to improve reliability
- Planning and training schedules

The goal is to arrive at a common agreement about the process, end goals, and outcomes that are necessary for the SRE team to engage with the development team and their service.

Analysis

Analysis is the first large segment of work. During this phase, the SRE reviewers learn about the service and begin analyzing it for production shortcomings. They aim to gauge the maturity of the service along the various axes of concern to SRE. They also examine the service's design and implementation to check if it follows production best practices. Usually, the SRE team establishes and maintains a PRR checklist explicitly for the Analysis phase. The checklist is specific to the service and is generally based on domain expertise, experience with related or similar systems, and best practices from the Production Guide. The SRE team may also consult other teams that have more experience with certain components or dependencies of the service.

A few examples of checklist items include:

- Do updates to the service impact an unreasonably large percentage of the system at once?
- Does the service connect to the appropriate serving instance of its dependencies? For example, end-user requests to a service should not depend on a system that is designed for a batch-processing use case.
- Does the service request a sufficiently high network quality-of-service when talking to a critical remote service?
- Does the service report errors to central logging systems for analysis? Does it report all exceptional conditions that result in degraded responses or failures to the end users?
- Are all user-visible request failures well instrumented and monitored, with suitable alerting configured?

The checklist may also include operational standards and best practices followed by a specific SRE team. For example, a perfectly functional service configuration that doesn't follow an SRE team's "gold standard" might be refactored to work better with SRE tools for scalably managing configurations. SREs also look at recent incidents and postmortems for the service, as well as follow-up tasks for the incidents. This evaluation gauges the demands of emergency response for the service and the availability of well-established operational controls.

Improvements and Refactoring

The Analysis phase leads to the identification of recommended improvements for the service. This next phase proceeds as follows:

1. Improvements are prioritized based upon importance for service reliability.
2. The priorities are discussed and negotiated with the development team, and a plan of execution is agreed upon.
3. Both SRE and product development teams participate and assist each other in refactoring parts of the service or implementing additional features.

This phase typically varies the most in duration and amount of effort. How much time and effort this phase will involve depends upon the availability of engineering time for refactoring, the maturity and complexity of the service at the start of the review, and myriad other factors.

Training

Responsibility for managing a service in production is generally assumed by an entire SRE team. To ensure that the team is prepared, the SRE reviewers who led the PRR take ownership of training the team, which includes the documentation necessary to support the service. Typically with the help and participation of the development team, these engineers organize a series of training sessions and exercises. Instruction can include:

- Design overviews
- Deep dives on various request flows in the system
- A description of the production setup
- Hands-on exercises for various aspects of system operations

When the training is concluded, the SRE team should be prepared to manage the service.

Onboarding

The Training phase unblocks onboarding of the service by the SRE team. It involves a progressive transfer of responsibilities and ownership of various production aspects of the service, including parts of operations, the change management process, access rights, and so forth. The SRE team continues to focus on the various areas of production mentioned earlier. To complete the transition, the development team must be available to back up and advise the SRE team for a period of time as it settles in managing production for the service. This relationship becomes the basis for the ongoing work between the teams.

Continuous Improvement

Active services continuously change in response to new demands and conditions, including user requests for new features, evolving system dependencies, and technology upgrades, in addition to other factors. The SRE team must maintain service reliability standards in the face of these changes by driving continuous improvement. The responsible SRE team naturally learns more about the service in the course of operating the service, reviewing new changes, responding to incidents, and especially when conducting postmortems/root cause analyses. This expertise is shared with the development team as suggestions and proposals for changes to the service whenever new features, components, and dependencies may be added to the service. Lessons from managing the service are also contributed to best practices, which are documented in the Production Guide and elsewhere.

Engaging with Shakespeare

Initially, the developers of the Shakespeare service were responsible for the product, including carrying the pager for emergency response. However, with growing use of the service and the growth of the revenue coming from the service, SRE support became desirable. The product has already been launched, so SRE conducted a Production Readiness Review. One of the things they found was that the dashboards were not completely covering some of the metrics defined in the SLO, so that needed to be fixed. After all the issues that had been filed had been fixed, SRE took over the pager for the service, though two developers were in the on-call rotation as well. The developers are participating in the weekly on-call meeting discussing last week's problems and how to handle upcoming large-scale maintenance or cluster turndowns. Also future plans for the service are now discussed with the SREs to make sure that new launches will go flawlessly (though Murphy's law is always looking for opportunities to spoil that).

Evolving the Simple PRR Model: Early Engagement

Thus far, we've discussed the Production Readiness Review as it's used in the Simple PRR Model, which is limited to services that have already entered the Launch phase. There are several limitations and costs associated with this model. For example:

- Additional communication between teams can increase some process overhead for the development team, and cognitive burden for the SRE reviewers.

- The right SRE reviewers must be available, and capable of managing their time and priorities with regards to their existing engagements.

- Work done by SREs must be highly visible and sufficiently reviewed by the development team to ensure effective knowledge sharing. SREs should essentially work as a part of the development team, rather than an external unit.

However, the main limitations of the PRR Model stem from the fact that the service is launched and serving at scale, and the SRE engagement starts very late in the development lifecycle. If the PRR occurred earlier in the service lifecycle, SRE's opportunity to remedy potential issues in the service would be markedly increased. As a result, the success of the SRE engagement and the future success of the service itself would likely improve. The resulting drawbacks can pose a significant challenge to the success of the SRE engagement and the future success of the service itself.

Candidates for Early Engagement

The Early Engagement Model introduces SRE earlier in the development lifecycle in order to achieve significant additional advantages. Applying the Early Engagement Model requires identifying the importance and/or business value of a service early in the development lifecycle, and determining if the service will have sufficient scale or complexity to benefit from SRE expertise. Applicable services often have the following characteristics:

- The service implements significant new functionality and will be part of an existing system already managed by SRE.
- The service is a significant rewrite or alternative to an existing system, targeting the same use cases.
- The development team sought SRE advice or approached SRE for takeover upon launch.

The Early Engagement Model essentially immerses SREs in the development process. SRE's focus remains the same, though the means to achieve a better production service are different. SRE participates in Design and later phases, eventually taking over the service any time during or after the Build phase. This model is based on active collaboration between the development and SRE teams.

Benefits of the Early Engagement Model

While the Early Engagement Model does entail certain risks and challenges discussed previously, additional SRE expertise and collaboration during the entire lifecycle of the product creates significant benefits compared to an engagement initiated later in the service lifecycle.

Design phase

SRE collaboration during the Design phase can prevent a variety of problems or incidents from occurring later in production. While design decisions can be reversed or rectified later in the development lifecycle, such changes come at a high cost in terms of effort and complexity. The best production incidents are those that never happen!

Occasionally, difficult trade-offs lead to the selection of a less-than-ideal design. Participation in the Design phase means that SREs are aware up front of the trade-offs and are part of the decision to pick a less-than-ideal option. Early SRE involvement aims to minimize future disputes over design choices once the service is in production.

Build and implementation

The Build phase addresses production aspects such as instrumentation and metrics, operational and emergency controls, resource usage, and efficiency. During this phase, SRE can influence and improve the implementation by recommending specific existing libraries and components, or helping build certain controls into the system. SRE participation at this stage helps enable ease of operations in the future and allows SRE to gain operational experience in advance of the launch.

Launch

SRE can also help implement widely used launch patterns and controls. For example, SRE might help implement a "dark launch" setup, in which part of the traffic from existing users is sent to the new service in addition to being sent to the live production service. The responses from the new service are "dark" since they are thrown away and not actually shown to users. Practices such as dark launches allow the team to gain operational insight, resolve issues without impacting existing users, and reduce the risk of encountering issues after launch. A smooth launch is immensely helpful in keeping the operational burden low and maintaining the development momentum after the launch. Disruptions around launch can easily result in emergency changes to source code and production, and disrupt the development team's work on future features.

Post-launch

Having a stable system at launch time generally leads to fewer conflicting priorities for the development team in terms of choosing between improving service reliability versus adding new features. In later phases of the service, the lessons from earlier phases can better inform refactoring or redesign.

With extended involvement, the SRE team can be ready to take over the new service much sooner than is possible with the Simple PRR Model. The longer and closer engagement between the SRE and development teams also creates a collaborative relationship that can be sustained long term. A positive cross-team relationship fosters a mutual feeling of solidarity, and helps SRE establish ownership of the production responsibility.

Disengaging from a service

Sometimes a service doesn't warrant full-fledged SRE team management—this determination might be made post-launch, or SRE might engage with a service but never officially take it over. This is a positive outcome, because the service has been engineered to be reliable and low maintenance, and can therefore remain with the development team.

It is also possible that SRE engages early with a service that fails to meet the levels of usage projected. In such cases, the SRE effort spent is simply part of the overall business risk that comes with new projects, and a small cost relative to the success of projects that meet expected scale. The SRE team can be reassigned, and lessons learned can be incorporated into the engagement process.

Evolving Services Development: Frameworks and SRE Platform

The Early Engagement Model made strides in evolving SRE engagement beyond the Simple PRR Model, which applied only to services that had already launched. However, there was still progress to be made in scaling SRE engagement to the next level by designing for reliability.

Lessons Learned

Over time, the SRE engagement model described thus far produced several distinct patterns:

- Onboarding each service required two or three SREs and typically lasted two or three quarters. The lead times for a PRR were relatively high (quarters away). The effort level required was proportional to the number of services under review, and was constrained by the insufficient number of SREs available to conduct PRRs. These conditions led to serialization of service takeovers and strict service prioritization.

- Due to differing software practices across services, each production feature was implemented differently. To meet PRR-driven standards, features usually had to be reimplemented specifically for each service or, at best, once for each small subset of services sharing code. These reimplementations were a waste of engineering effort. One canonical example is the implementation of functionally similar logging frameworks repeatedly in the same language because different services didn't implement the same coding structure.

- A review of common service issues and outages revealed certain patterns, but there was no way to easily replicate fixes and improvements across services. Typical examples included service overload situations and data hot-spotting.

- SRE software engineering contributions were often local to the service. Thus, building generic solutions to be reused was difficult. As a consequence, there was no easy way to implement new lessons individual SRE teams learned and best practices across services that had already been onboarded.

External Factors Affecting SRE

External factors have traditionally pressured the SRE organization and its resources in several ways.

Google is increasingly following the industry trend of moving toward microservices.[1] As a result, both the number of requests for SRE support and the cardinality of services to support have increased. Because each service has a base fixed operational cost, even simple services demand more staffing. Microservices also imply an expectation of lower lead time for deployment, which was not possible with the previous PRR model (which had a lead time of months).

Hiring experienced, qualified SREs is difficult and costly. Despite enormous effort from the recruiting organization, there are never enough SREs to support all the services that need their expertise. Once SREs are hired, their training is also a lengthier process than is typical for development engineers.

Finally, the SRE organization is responsible for serving the needs of the large and growing number of development teams that do not already enjoy direct SRE support. This mandate calls for extending the SRE support model far beyond the original concept and engagement model.

Toward a Structural Solution: Frameworks

To effectively respond to these conditions, it became necessary to develop a model that allowed for the following principles:

Codified best practices
> The ability to commit what works well in production to code, so services can simply use this code and become "production ready" by design.

Reusable solutions
> Common and easily shareable implementations of techniques used to mitigate scalability and reliability issues.

A common production platform with a common control surface
> Uniform sets of interfaces to production facilities, uniform sets of operational controls, and uniform monitoring, logging, and configuration for all services.

Easier automation and smarter systems
> A common control surface that enables automation and smart systems at a level not possible before. For example, SREs can readily receive a single view of

---

1 See the Wikipedia page on microservices at *http://en.wikipedia.org/wiki/Microservices*.

relevant information for an outage, rather than hand collecting and analyzing mostly raw data from disparate sources (logs, monitoring data, and so on).

Based upon these principles, a set of SRE-supported platform and service frameworks were created, one for each environment we support (Java, C++, Go). Services built using these frameworks share implementations that are designed to work with the SRE-supported platform, and are maintained by both SRE and development teams. The main shift brought about by frameworks was to enable product development teams to design applications using the framework solution that was built and blessed by SRE, as opposed to either retrofitting the application to SRE specifications after the fact, or retrofitting more SREs to support a service that was markedly different than other Google services.

An application typically comprises some business logic, which in turn depends on various infrastructure components. SRE production concerns are largely focused on the infrastructure-related parts of a service. The service frameworks implement infrastructure code in a standardized fashion and address various production concerns. Each concern is encapsulated in one or more framework modules, each of which provides a cohesive solution for a problem domain or infrastructure dependency. Framework modules address the various SRE concerns enumerated earlier, such as:

- Instrumentation and metrics
- Request logging
- Control systems involving traffic and load management

SRE builds framework modules to implement canonical solutions for the concerned production area. As a result, development teams can focus on the business logic, because the framework already takes care of correct infrastructure use.

A framework essentially is a prescriptive implementation for using a set of software components and a canonical way of combining these components. The framework can also expose features that control various components in a cohesive manner. For example, a framework might provide the following:

- Business logic organized as well-defined semantic components that can be referenced using standard terms
- Standard dimensions for monitoring instrumentation
- A standard format for request debugging logs
- A standard configuration format for managing load shedding
- Capacity of a single server and determination of "overload" that can both use a semantically consistent measure for feedback to various control systems

Frameworks provide multiple upfront gains in consistency and efficiency. They free developers from having to glue together and configure individual components in an ad hoc service-specific manner, in ever-so-slightly incompatible ways, that then have to be manually reviewed by SREs. They drive a single reusable solution for production concerns across services, which means that framework users end up with the same common implementation and minimal configuration differences.

Google supports several major languages for application development, and frameworks are implemented across all of these languages. While different implementations of the framework (say in C++ versus Java) can't share code, the goal is to expose the same API, behavior, configuration, and controls for identical functionality. Therefore, development teams can choose the language platform that fits their needs and experience, while SREs can still expect the same familiar behavior in production and standard tools to manage the service.

New Service and Management Benefits

The structural approach, founded on service frameworks and a common production platform and control surface, provided a host of new benefits.

Significantly lower operational overhead

A production platform built on top of frameworks with stronger conventions significantly reduced operational overhead, for the following reasons:

- It supports strong conformance tests for coding structure, dependencies, tests, coding style guides, and so on. This functionality also improves user data privacy, testing, and security conformance.
- It features built-in service deployment, monitoring, and automation for all services.
- It facilitates easier management of large numbers of services, especially microservices, which are growing in number.
- It enables much faster deployment: an idea can graduate to fully deployed SRE-level production quality in a matter of days!

Universal support by design

The constant growth in the number of services at Google means that most of these services can neither warrant SRE engagement nor be maintained by SREs. Regardless, services that don't receive full SRE support can be built to use production features that are developed and maintained by SREs. This practice effectively breaks the SRE staffing barrier. Enabling SRE-supported production standards and tools for all teams improves the overall service quality across Google. Furthermore, all services that are implemented with frameworks automatically benefit from improvements made over time to frameworks modules.

Faster, lower overhead engagements

The frameworks approach results in faster PRR execution because we can rely upon:

- Built-in service features as part of the framework implementation
- Faster service onboarding (usually accomplished by a single SRE during one quarter)
- Less cognitive burden for the SRE teams managing services built using frameworks

These properties allow SRE teams to lower the assessment and qualification effort for service onboarding, while maintaining a high bar on service production quality.

A new engagement model based on shared responsibility

The original SRE engagement model presented only two options: either full SRE support, or approximately no SRE engagement.[2]

A production platform with a common service structure, conventions, and software infrastructure made it possible for an SRE team to provide support for the "platform" infrastructure, while the development teams provide on-call support for functional issues with the service—that is, for bugs in the application code. Under this model, SREs assume responsibility for the development and maintenance of large parts of service software infrastructure, particularly control systems such as load shedding, overload, automation, traffic management, logging, and monitoring.

This model represents a significant departure from the way service management was originally conceived in two major ways: it entails a new relationship model for the interaction between SRE and development teams, and a new staffing model for SRE-supported service management.[3]

---

2 Occasionally, there were consulting engagements by SRE teams with some non-onboarded services, but consultations were a best-effort approach and limited in number and scope.

3 The new model of service management changes the SRE staffing model in two ways: (1) because a lot of service technology is common, it reduces the number of required SREs per service; (2) it enables the creation of production platforms with separation of concerns between production platform support (done by SREs) and service-specific business-logic support, which remains with the development team. These platforms teams are staffed based upon the need to maintain the platform rather than upon service count, and can be shared across products.

Conclusion

Service reliability can be improved through SRE engagement, in a process that includes systematic review and improvement of its production aspects. Google SRE's initial such systematic approach, the Simple Production Readiness Review, made strides in standardizing the SRE engagement model, but was only applicable to services that had already entered the Launch phase.

Over time, SRE extended and improved this model. The Early Engagement Model involved SRE earlier in the development lifecycle in order to "design for reliability." As demand for SRE expertise continued to grow, the need for a more scalable engagement model became increasingly apparent. Frameworks for production services were developed to meet this demand: code patterns based on production best practices were standardized and encapsulated in frameworks, so that use of frameworks became a recommended, consistent, and relatively simple way of building production-ready services.

All three of the engagement models described are still practiced within Google. However, the adoption of frameworks is becoming a prominent influence on building production-ready services at Google as well as profoundly expanding the SRE contribution, lowering service management overhead, and improving baseline service quality across the organization.

PART V

Conclusions

Having covered much ground in terms of how SRE works at Google, and how the principles and practices we've developed might be applied to other organizations in our field, it now seems appropriate to turn our view to Chapter 33, *Lessons Learned from Other Industries*, to examine how SRE's practices compare to other industries where reliability is critically important.

Finally, Google's VP for Site Reliability Engineering, Benjamin Lutch, writes about SRE's evolution over the course of his career in his conclusion, examining SRE through the lens of some observations on the aviation industry.

Lessons Learned from Other Industries

Written by Jennifer Petoff
Edited by Betsy Beyer

A deep dive into SRE culture and practices at Google naturally leads to the question of how other industries manage their businesses for reliability. Compiling this book on Google SRE created an opportunity to speak to a number of Google's engineers about their previous work experiences in a variety of other high-reliability fields in order to address the following comparative questions:

- Are the principles used in Site Reliability Engineering also important outside of Google, or do other industries tackle the requirements of high reliability in markedly different ways?

- If other industries also adhere to SRE principles, how are the principles manifested?

- What are the similarities and differences in the implementation of these principles across industries?

- What factors drive similarities and differences in implementation?

- What can Google and the tech industry learn from these comparisons?

A number of principles fundamental to Site Reliability Engineering at Google are discussed throughout this text. To simplify our comparison of best practices in other industries, we distilled these concepts into four key themes:

- Preparedness and Disaster Testing
- Postmortem Culture

- Automation and Reduced Operational Overhead
- Structured and Rational Decision Making

This chapter introduces the industries that we profiled and the industry veterans we interviewed. We define key SRE themes, discuss how these themes are implemented at Google, and give examples of how these principles reveal themselves in other industries for comparative purposes. We conclude with some insights and discussion on the patterns and anti-patterns we discovered.

Meet Our Industry Veterans

Peter Dahl is a Principal Engineer at Google. Previously, he worked as a defense contractor on several high-reliability systems including many airborne and wheeled vehicle GPS and inertial guidance systems. Consequences of a lapse in reliability in such systems include vehicle malfunction or loss, and the financial consequences associated with that failure.

Mike Doherty is a Site Reliability Engineer at Google. He worked as a lifeguard and lifeguard trainer for a decade in Canada. Reliability is absolutely essential by nature in this field, because lives are on the line every day.

Erik Gross is currently a software engineer at Google. Before joining the company, he spent seven years designing algorithms and code for the lasers and systems used to perform refractive eye surgery (e.g., LASIK). This is a high-stakes, high-reliability field, in which many lessons relevant to reliability in the face of government regulations and human risk were learned as the technology received FDA approval, gradually improved, and finally became ubiquitous.

Gus Hartmann and **Kevin Greer** have experience in the telecommunications industry, including maintaining the E911 emergency response system.[1] Kevin is currently a software engineer on the Google Chrome team and Gus is a systems engineer for Google's Corporate Engineering team. User expectations of the telecom industry demand high reliability. Implications of a lapse of service range from user inconvenience due to a system outage to fatalities if E911 goes down.

Ron Heiby is a Technical Program Manager for Site Reliability Engineering at Google. Ron has experience in development for cell phones, medical devices, and the automotive industry. In some cases he worked on interface components of these industries (for example, on a device to allow EKG readings[2] in ambulances to be transmitted over the digital wireless phone network). In these industries, the impact

---

1 E911 (Enhanced 911): Emergency response line in the US that leverages location data.

2 Electrocardiogram readings: *https://en.wikipedia.org/wiki/Electrocardiography*.

of a reliability issue can range from harm to the business incurred by equipment recalls to indirectly impacting life and health (e.g., people not getting the medical attention they need if the EKG cannot communicate with the hospital).

Adrian Hilton is a Launch Coordination Engineer at Google. Previously, he worked on UK and USA military aircraft, naval avionics and aircraft stores management systems, and UK railway signaling systems. Reliability is critical in this space because impact of incidents ranges from multimillion-dollar loss of equipment to injuries and fatalities.

Eddie Kennedy is a project manager for the Global Customer Experience team at Google and a mechanical engineer by training. Eddie spent six years working as a Six Sigma Black Belt process engineer in a manufacturing facility that makes synthetic diamonds. This industry is characterized by a relentless focus on safety, because the extremes of temperature and pressure demands of the process pose a high level of danger to workers on a daily basis.

John Li is currently a Site Reliability Engineer at Google. John previously worked as a systems administrator and software developer at a proprietary trading company in the finance industry. Reliability issues in the financial sector are taken quite seriously because they can lead to serious fiscal consequences.

Dan Sheridan is a Site Reliability Engineer at Google. Before joining the company, he worked as a safety consultant in the civil nuclear industry in the UK. Reliability is important in the nuclear industry because an incident can have serious repercussions: outages can incur millions a day in lost revenue, while risks to workers and those in the community are even more dire, dictating zero tolerance for failure. Nuclear infrastructure is designed with a series of failsafes that halt operations before an incident of any such magnitude is reached.

Jeff Stevenson is currently a hardware operations manager at Google. He has past experience as a nuclear engineer in the US Navy on a submarine. Reliability stakes in the nuclear Navy are high—problems that arise in the case of incidents range from damaged equipment, to long-standing environmental impact, to potential loss of life.

Matthew Toia is a Site Reliability Manager focused on storage systems. Prior to Google, he worked on software development and deployment of air traffic control software systems. Effects from incidents in this industry range from inconveniences to passengers and airlines (e.g., delayed flights, diverted planes) to potential loss of life in the event of a crash. Defense in depth is a key strategy to avoiding catastrophic failures.

Now that you've met our experts and gained a high-level understanding of why reliability is important in their respective former fields, we'll delve into the four key themes of reliability.

Preparedness and Disaster Testing

"Hope is not a strategy." This rallying cry of the SRE team at Google sums up what we mean by preparedness and disaster testing. The SRE culture is forever vigilant and constantly questioning: What could go wrong? What action can we take to address those issues before they lead to an outage or data loss? Our annual Disaster and Recovery Testing (DiRT) drills seek to address these questions head-on [Kri12]. In DiRT exercises, SREs push production systems to the limit and inflict actual outages in order to:

- Ensure that systems react the way we think they will
- Determine unexpected weaknesses
- Figure out ways to make the systems more robust in order to prevent uncontrolled outages

Several strategies for testing disaster readiness and ensuring preparedness in other industries emerged from our conversations. Strategies included the following:

- Relentless organizational focus on safety
- Attention to detail
- Swing capacity
- Simulations and live drills
- Training and certification
- Obsessive focus on detailed requirements gathering and design
- Defense in depth

Relentless Organizational Focus on Safety

This principle is particularly important in an industrial engineering context. According to Eddie Kennedy, who worked on a manufacturing floor where workers faced safety hazards, "every management meeting started with a discussion of safety." The manufacturing industry prepares itself for the unexpected by establishing highly defined processes that are strictly followed at every level of the organization. It is critical that all employees take safety seriously, and that workers feel empowered to speak up if and when anything seems amiss. In the case of nuclear power, military aircraft, and railway signaling industries, safety standards for software are well detailed (e.g., UK Defence Standard 00-56, IEC 61508, IEC513, US DO-178B/C, and DO-254) and levels of reliability for such systems are clearly identified (e.g., Safety Integrity Level (SIL) 1–4),[3] with the aim of specifying acceptable approaches to delivering a product.

Attention to Detail

From his time spent in the US Navy, Jeff Stevenson recalls an acute awareness of how a lack of diligence in executing small tasks (for example, lube oil maintenance) could lead to major submarine failure. A very small oversight or mistake can have big effects. Systems are highly interconnected, so an accident in one area can impact multiple related components. The nuclear Navy focuses on routine maintenance to ensure that small issues don't snowball.

Swing Capacity

System utilization in the telecom industry can be highly unpredictable. Absolute capacity can be strained by unforeseeable events such as natural disasters, as well as large, predictable events like the Olympics. According to Gus Hartmann, the industry deals with these incidents by deploying swing capacity in the form of a SOW (switch on wheels), a mobile telco office. This excess capacity can be rolled out in an emergency or in anticipation of a known event that is likely to overload the system. Capacity issues veer into the unexpected in matters unrelated to absolute capacity, as well. For example, when a celebrity's private phone number was leaked in 2005 and thousands of fans simultaneously attempted to call her, the telecom system exhibited symptoms similar to a DDoS or massive routing error.

Simulations and Live Drills

Google's Disaster Recovery tests have a lot in common with the simulations and live drills that are a key focus of many of the established industries we researched. The potential consequences of a system outage determine whether using a simulation or a live drill is appropriate. For example, Matthew Toia points out that the aviation industry can't perform a live test "in production" without putting equipment and passengers at risk. Instead, they employ extremely realistic simulators with live data feeds, in which the control rooms and equipment are modeled down to the tiniest details to ensure a realistic experience without putting real people at risk. Gus Hartmann reports that the telecom industry typically focuses on live drills centered on surviving hurricanes and other weather emergencies. Such modeling led to the creation of weatherproof facilities with generators inside the building capable of outlasting a storm.

---

3 *https://en.wikipedia.org/wiki/Safety_integrity_level*

The US nuclear Navy uses a mixture of "what if" thought exercises and live drills. According to Jeff Stevenson, the live drills involve "actually breaking real stuff but with control parameters. Live drills are carried out religiously, every week, two to three days per week." For the nuclear Navy, thought exercises are useful, but not sufficient to prepare for actual incidents. Responses must be practiced so they are not forgotten.

According to Mike Doherty, lifeguards face disaster testing exercises more akin to a "mystery shopper" experience. Typically, a facility manager works with a child or an incognito lifeguard in training to stage a mock drowning. These scenarios are conducted to be as realistic as possible so that lifeguards aren't able to differentiate between real and staged emergencies.

Training and Certification

Our interviews suggest that training and certification are particularly important when lives are at stake. For example, Mike Doherty described how lifeguards complete a rigorous training certification, in addition to a periodic recertification process. Courses include fitness components (e.g., a lifeguard must be able to hold someone heavier than themselves with shoulders out of the water), technical components like first aid and CPR, and operational elements (e.g., if a lifeguard enters the water, how do other team members respond?). Every facility also has site-specific training, because lifeguarding in a pool is markedly different from lifeguarding on a lakeside beach or on the ocean.

Focus on Detailed Requirements Gathering and Design

Some of the engineers we interviewed discussed the importance of detailed requirements gathering and design docs. This practice was particularly important when working with medical devices. In many of these cases, actual use or maintenance of the equipment doesn't fall within the purview of product designers. Thus, usage and maintenance requirements must be gathered from other sources.

For example, according to Erik Gross, laser eye surgery machines are designed to be as foolproof as possible. Thus, soliciting requirements from the surgeons who actually use these machines and the technicians responsible for maintaining them is particularly important. In another example, former defense contractor Peter Dahl described a very detailed design culture in which creating a new defense system commonly entailed an entire year of design, followed by just three weeks of writing the code to actualize the design. Both of these examples are markedly different from Google's launch and iterate culture, which promotes a much faster rate of change at a calculated risk. Other industries (e.g., the medical industry and the military, as previously discussed) have very different pressures, risk appetites, and requirements, and their processes are very much informed by these circumstances.

Defense in Depth and Breadth

In the nuclear power industry, defense in depth is a key element to preparedness [IAEA12]. Nuclear reactors feature redundancy on all systems and implement a design methodology that mandates fallback systems behind primary systems in case of failure. The system is designed with multiple layers of protection, including a final physical barrier to radioactive release around the plant itself. Defense in depth is particularly important in the nuclear industry due to the zero tolerance for failures and incidents.

Postmortem Culture

Corrective and preventative action (CAPA)[4] is a well-known concept for improving reliability that focuses on the systematic investigation of root causes of identified issues or risks in order to prevent recurrence. This principle is embodied by SRE's strong culture of blameless postmortems. When something goes wrong (and given the scale, complexity, and rapid rate of change at Google, something inevitably *will* go wrong), it's important to evaluate all of the following:

- What happened
- The effectiveness of the response
- What we would do differently next time
- What actions will be taken to make sure a particular incident doesn't happen again

This exercise is undertaken without pointing fingers at any individual. Instead of assigning blame, it is far more important to figure out *what* went wrong, and how, as an organization, we will rally to ensure it doesn't happen again. Dwelling on *who* might have caused the outage is counterproductive. Postmortems are conducted after incidents and published across SRE teams so that all can benefit from the lessons learned.

Our interviews uncovered that many industries perform a version of the postmortem (although many do not use this specific moniker, for obvious reasons). The *motivation* behind these exercises appears to be the main differentiator among industry practices.

Many industries are heavily regulated and are held accountable by specific government authorities when something goes wrong. Such regulation is especially ingrained when the stakes of failure are high (e.g., lives are at stake). Relevant government agen-

---

4 *https://en.wikipedia.org/wiki/Corrective_and_preventive_action*

cies include the FCC (telecommunications), FAA (aviation), OSHA (the manufacturing and chemical industries), FDA (medical devices), and the various National Competent Authorities in the EU.[5] The nuclear power and transportation industries are also heavily regulated.

Safety considerations are another motivating factor behind postmortems. In the manufacturing and chemical industries, the risk of injury or death is ever-present due to the nature of the conditions required to produce the final product (high temperature, pressure, toxicity, and corrosivity, to name a few). For example, Alcoa features a noteworthy safety culture. Former CEO Paul O'Neill required staff to notify him within 24 hours of any injury that lost a worker day. He even distributed his home phone number to workers on the factory floor so that they could personally alert him to safety concerns.[6]

The stakes are so high in the manufacturing and chemical industries that even "near misses"—when a given event could have caused serious harm, but did not—are carefully scrutinized. These scenarios function as a type of preemptive postmortem. According to VM Brasseur in a talk given at YAPC NA 2015, "There are multiple near misses in just about every disaster and business crisis, and typically they're ignored at the time they occur. Latent error, plus an enabling condition, equals things not working quite the way you planned" [Bra15]. Near misses are effectively disasters waiting to happen. For example, scenarios in which a worker doesn't follow the standard operating procedure, an employee jumps out of the way at the last second to avoid a splash, or a spill on the staircase isn't cleaned up, all represent near misses and opportunities to learn and improve. Next time, the employee and the company might not be so lucky. The United Kingdom's CHIRP (Confidential Reporting Programme for Aviation and Maritime) seeks to raise awareness about such incidents across the industry by providing a central reporting point where aviation and maritime personnel can report near misses confidentially. Reports and analyses of these near misses are then published in periodic newsletters.

Lifeguarding has a deeply embedded culture of post-incident analysis and action planning. Mike Doherty quips, "If a lifeguard's feet go in the water, there will be paperwork!" A detailed write-up is required after any incident at the pool or on the beach. In the case of serious incidents, the team collectively examines the incident end to end, discussing what went right and what went wrong. Operational changes are then made based on these findings, and training is often scheduled to help people build confidence around their ability to handle a similar incident in the future. In cases of particularly shocking or traumatic incidents, a counselor is brought on site to help staff cope with the psychological aftermath. The lifeguards may have been well

---

5 *https://en.wikipedia.org/wiki/Competent_authority*

6 *http://ehstoday.com/safety/nsc-2013-oneill-exemplifies-safety-leadership.*

---

prepared for what happened in practice, but might *feel* like they haven't done an adequate job. Similar to Google, lifeguarding embraces a culture of blameless incident analysis. Incidents are chaotic, and many factors contribute to any given incident. In this field, it's not helpful to place blame on a single individual.

Automating Away Repetitive Work and Operational Overhead

At their core, Google's Site Reliability Engineers are software engineers with a low tolerance for repetitive reactive work. It is strongly ingrained in our culture to avoid repeating an operation that doesn't add value to a service. If a task can be automated away, why would you run a system on repetitive work that is of low value? Automation lowers operational overhead and frees up time for our engineers to proactively assess and improve the services they support.

The industries that we surveyed were mixed in terms of if, how, and why they embraced automation. Certain industries trusted humans more than machines. During the tenure of our industry veteran, the US nuclear Navy eschewed automation in favor of a series of interlocks and administrative procedures. For example, according to Jeff Stevenson, operating a valve required an operator, a supervisor, and a crew member on the phone with the engineering watch officer tasked with monitoring the response to the action taken. These operations were very manual due to concern that an automated system might not spot a problem that a human would definitely notice. Operations on a submarine are ruled by a trusted human decision chain—a *series* of people, rather than one individual. The nuclear Navy was also concerned that automation and computers move so rapidly that they are all too capable of committing a large, irreparable mistake. When you are dealing with nuclear reactors, a slow and steady methodical approach is more important than accomplishing a task quickly.

According to John Li, the proprietary trading industry has become increasingly cautious in its application of automation in recent years. Experience has shown that incorrectly configured automation can inflict significant damage and incur a great deal of financial loss in a very short period of time. For example, in 2012 Knight Capital Group encountered a "software glitch" that led to a loss of $440M in just a few hours.[7] Similarly, in 2010 the US stock market experienced a Flash Crash that was ultimately blamed on a rogue trader attempting to manipulate the market with automated means. While the market was quick to recover, the Flash Crash resulted in a

---

7 See "FACTS, Section B" for the discussion of Knight and Power Peg software in [Sec13].

loss on the magnitude of trillions of dollars in just *30 minutes*.[8] Computers can execute tasks very quickly, and speed can be a negative if these tasks are configured incorrectly.

In contrast, some companies embrace automation precisely *because* computers act more quickly than people. According to Eddie Kennedy, efficiency and monetary savings are key in the manufacturing industry, and automation provides a means to accomplish tasks more efficiently and cost-effectively. Furthermore, automation is generally more reliable and repeatable than work conducted manually by humans, which means that it produces higher-quality standards and tighter tolerances. Dan Sheridan discussed automation as deployed in the UK nuclear industry. Here, a rule of thumb dictates that if a plant is required to respond to a given situation in less than 30 minutes, that response must be automated.

In Matt Toia's experience, the aviation industry applies automation selectively. For example, operational failover is performed automatically, but when it comes to certain other tasks, the industry trusts automation only when it's verified by a human. While the industry employs a good deal of automatic monitoring, actual air-traffic-control-system implementations must be manually inspected by humans.

According to Erik Gross, automation has been quite effective in reducing user error in laser eye surgery. Before LASIK surgery is performed, the doctor measures the patient using a refractive eye test. Originally, the doctor would type in the numbers and press a button, and the laser would go to work correcting the patient's vision. However, data entry errors could be a big issue. This process also entailed the possibility of mixing up patient data or jumbling numbers for the left and right eye.

Automation now greatly lessens the chance that humans make a mistake that impacts someone's vision. A computerized sanity check of manually entered data was the first major automated improvement: if a human operator inputs measurements outside an expected range, automation promptly and prominently flags this case as unusual. Other automated improvements followed this development: now the iris is photographed during the preliminary refractive eye test. When it's time to perform the surgery, the iris of the patient is automatically matched to the iris in the photo, thus eliminating the possibility of mixing up patient data. When this automated solution was implemented, an entire class of medical errors disappeared.

---

8 "Regulators blame computer algorithm for stock market 'flash crash,'" Computerworld, *http://www.computer world.com/article/2516076/financial-it/regulators-blame-computer-algorithm-for-stock-market—flash-crash-.html.*

Structured and Rational Decision Making

At Google in general, and in Site Reliability Engineering in particular, data is critical. The team aspires to make decisions in a structured and rational way by ensuring that:

- The basis for the decision is agreed upon advance, rather than justified ex post facto
- The inputs to the decision are clear
- Any assumptions are explicitly stated
- Data-driven decisions win over decisions based on feelings, hunches, or the opinion of the most senior employee in the room

Google SRE operates under the baseline assumption that everyone on the team:

- Has the best interests of a service's users at heart
- Can figure out how to proceed based on the data available

Decisions should be informed rather than prescriptive, and are made without deference to personal opinions—even that of the most-senior person in the room, who Eric Schmidt and Jonathan Rosenberg dub the "HiPPO," for "Highest-Paid Person's Opinion" [Sch14].

Decision making in different industries varies widely. We learned that some industries use an approach of *if it ain't broke, don't fix it…ever*. Industries featuring systems whose design entailed much thought and effort are often characterized by a reluctance to change the underlying technology. For example, the telecom industry still uses long-distance switches that were implemented in the 1980s. Why do they rely on technology developed a few decades ago? These switches "are pretty much bulletproof and massively redundant," according to Gus Hartmann. As reported by Dan Sheridan, the nuclear industry is similarly slow to change. All decisions are underpinned by the thought: *if it works now, don't change it*.

Many industries heavily focus on playbooks and procedures rather than open-ended problem solving. Every humanly conceivable scenario is captured in a checklist or in "the binder." When something goes wrong, this resource is the authoritative source for how to react. This prescriptive approach works for industries that evolve and develop relatively slowly, because the scenarios of what could go wrong are not constantly evolving due to system updates or changes. This approach is also common in industries in which the skill level of the workers may be limited, and the best way to make sure that people will respond appropriately in an emergency is to provide a simple, clear set of instructions.

Other industries also take a clear, data-driven approach to decision making. In Eddie Kennedy's experience, research and manufacturing environments are characterized by a rigorous experimentation culture that relies heavily on formulating and testing hypotheses. These industries regularly conduct controlled experiments to make sure that a given change yields the expected result at a statistically significant level and that nothing unexpected occurs. Changes are only implemented when data yielded by the experiment supports the decision.

Finally, some industries, like proprietary trading, divide decision making to better manage risk. According to John Li, this industry features an enforcement team separate from the traders to ensure that undue risks aren't taken in pursuit of achieving a profit. The enforcement team is responsible for monitoring events on the floor and halting trading if events spin out of hand. If a system abnormality occurs, the enforcement team's first response is to shut down the system. As put by John Li, "If we aren't trading, we aren't losing money. We aren't making money either, but at least we aren't losing money." Only the enforcement team can bring the system back up, despite how excruciating a delay might seem to traders who are missing a potentially profitable opportunity.

Conclusions

Many of the principles that are core to Site Reliability Engineering at Google are evident across a wide range of industries. The lessons already learned by well-established industries likely inspired some of the practices in use at Google today.

A main takeaway of our cross-industry survey was that in many parts of its software business, Google has a higher appetite for velocity than players in most other industries. The ability to move or change quickly must be weighed against the differing implications of a failure. In the nuclear, aviation, or medical industries, for example, people could be injured or even die in the event of an outage or failure. When the stakes are high, a conservative approach to achieving high reliability is warranted.

At Google, we constantly walk a tightrope between user expectations for high reliability versus a laser-sharp focus on rapid change and innovation. While Google is incredibly serious about reliability, we must adapt our approaches to our high rate of change. As discussed in earlier chapters, many of our software businesses such as Search make conscious decisions as to how reliable "reliable enough" really is.

Google has that flexibility in most of our software products and services, which operate in an environment in which lives are not directly at risk if something goes wrong. Therefore, we're able to use tools such as error budgets ("Motivation for Error Budgets" on page 33) as a means to "fund" a culture of innovation and calculated risk taking. In essence, Google has adapted known reliability principles that were in many cases developed and honed in other industries to create its own unique reliability culture, one that addresses a complicated equation that balances scale, complexity, and velocity with high reliability.

CHAPTER 34

Conclusion

Written by Benjamin Lutch[1]
Edited by Betsy Beyer

I read through this book with enormous pride. From the time I began working at Excite in the early '90s, where my group was a sort of neanderthal SRE group dubbed "Software Operations," I've spent my career fumbling through the process of building systems. In light of my experiences over the years in the tech industry, it's amazing to see how the idea of SRE took root at Google and evolved so quickly. SRE has grown from a few hundred engineers when I joined Google in 2006 to over 1,000 people today, spread over a dozen sites and running what I think is the most interesting computing infrastructure on the planet.

So what has enabled the SRE organization at Google to evolve over the past decade to maintain this massive infrastructure in an intelligent, efficient, and scalable way? I think that the key to the overwhelming success of SRE is the nature of the principles by which it operates.

SRE teams are constructed so that our engineers divide their time between two equally important types of work. SREs staff on-call shifts, which entail putting our hands around the systems, observing where and how these systems break, and understanding challenges such as how to best scale them. But we also have time to then reflect and decide what to build in order to make those systems easier to manage. In essence, we have the pleasure of playing both the roles of the pilot *and* the engineer/ designer. Our experiences running massive computing infrastructure are codified in actual code and then packaged as a discrete product.

---

1 Vice President, Site Reliability Engineering, for Google, Inc.

These solutions are then easily usable by other SRE teams and ultimately by anyone at Google (or even outside of Google...think Google Cloud!) who wants to use or improve upon the experience we've accumulated and the systems we've built.

When you approach building a team or a system, ideally its foundation should be a set of rules or axioms that are general enough to be immediately useful, but that will remain relevant in the future. Much of what Ben Treynor Sloss outlined in this book's introduction represents just that: a flexible, mostly future-proof set of responsibilities that remain spot-on 10 years after they were conceived, despite the changes and growth Google's infrastructure and the SRE team have undergone.

As SRE has grown, we've noticed a couple different dynamics at play. The first is the consistent nature of SRE's primary responsibilities and concerns over time: our systems might be 1,000 times larger or faster, but ultimately, they still need to remain reliable, flexible, easy to manage in an emergency, well monitored, and capacity planned. At the same time, the typical activities undertaken by SRE evolve by necessity as Google's services and SRE's competencies mature. For example, what was once a goal to "build a dashboard for 20 machines" might now instead be "automate discovery, dashboard building, and alerting over a fleet of tens of thousands of machines."

For those who haven't been in the trenches of SRE for the past decade, an analogy between how SRE thinks about complex systems and how the aircraft industry has approached plane flight is useful in conceptualizing how SRE has evolved and matured over time. While the stakes of failure between the two industries are very different, certain core similarities hold true.

Imagine that you wanted to fly between two cities a hundred years ago. Your airplane probably had a single engine (two, if you were lucky), a few bags of cargo, and a pilot. The pilot also filled the role of mechanic, and possibly additionally acted as cargo loader and unloader. The cockpit had room for the pilot, and if you were lucky, a co-pilot/navigator. Your little plane would bounce off a runway in good weather, and if everything went well, you'd slowly climb your way through the skies and eventually touch down in another city, maybe a few hundred miles away. Failure of any of the plane's systems was catastrophic, and it wasn't unheard of for a pilot to have to climb out of the cockpit to perform repairs in-flight! The systems that fed into the cockpit were essential, simple, and fragile, and most likely were not redundant.

Fast-forward a hundred years to a huge 747 sitting on the tarmac. Hundreds of passengers are loading up on both floors, while tons of cargo are simultaneously being loaded into the hold below. The plane is chock-full of reliable, redundant systems. It's a model of safety and reliability; in fact, you're actually safer in the air than on the ground in a car. Your plane will take off from a dotted line on a runway on one continent, and land easily on a dotted line on another runway 6,000 miles away, right on schedule—within minutes of its forecasted landing time. But take a look into the cockpit and what do you find? Just two pilots again!

How has every other element of the flight experience—safety, capacity, speed, and reliability—scaled up so beautifully, while there are still only two pilots? The answer to this question is a great parallel to how Google approaches the enormous, fantastically complex systems that SRE runs. The interfaces to the plane's operating systems are well thought out and approachable enough that learning how to pilot them in normal conditions is not an insurmountable task. Yet these interfaces also provide enough flexibility, and the people operating them are sufficiently trained, that responses to emergencies are robust and quick. The cockpit was designed by people who understand complex systems and how to present them to humans in a way that's both consumable and scalable. The systems underlying the cockpit have all the same properties discussed in this book: availability, performance optimization, change management, monitoring and alerting, capacity planning, and emergency response.

Ultimately, SRE's goal is to follow a similar course. An SRE team should be as compact as possible and operate at a high level of abstraction, relying upon lots of backup systems as failsafes and thoughtful APIs to communicate with the systems. At the same time, the SRE team should also have comprehensive knowledge of the systems —how they operate, how they fail, and how to respond to failures—that comes from operating them day-to-day.

Availability Table

Availability is generally calculated based on how long a service was unavailable over some period. Assuming no planned downtime, Table A-1 indicates how much downtime is permitted to reach a given availability level.

Table A-1. Availability table

Availability level	Allowed unavailability window					
	per year	**per quarter**	**per month**	**per week**	**per day**	**per hour**
90%	36.5 days	9 days	3 days	16.8 hours	2.4 hours	6 minutes
95%	18.25 days	4.5 days	1.5 days	8.4 hours	1.2 hours	3 minutes
99%	3.65 days	21.6 hours	7.2 hours	1.68 hours	14.4 minutes	36 seconds
99.5%	1.83 days	10.8 hours	3.6 hours	50.4 minutes	7.20 minutes	18 seconds
99.9%	8.76 hours	2.16 hours	43.2 minutes	10.1 minutes	1.44 minutes	3.6 seconds
99.95%	4.38 hours	1.08 hours	21.6 minutes	5.04 minutes	43.2 seconds	1.8 seconds
99.99%	52.6 minutes	12.96 minutes	4.32 minutes	60.5 seconds	8.64 seconds	0.36 seconds
99.999%	5.26 minutes	1.30 minutes	25.9 seconds	6.05 seconds	0.87 seconds	0.04 seconds

Using an aggregate unavailability metric (i.e., "*X*% of all operations failed") is more useful than focusing on outage lengths for services that may be partially available—for instance, due to having multiple replicas, only some of which are unavailable—and for services whose load varies over the course of a day or week rather than remaining constant.

See Equations 3-1 and 3-2 in Chapter 3 for calculations.

A Collection of Best Practices for Production Services

Written by Ben Treynor Sloss
Edited by Betsy Beyer

Fail Sanely

Sanitize and validate configuration inputs, and respond to implausible inputs by *both* continuing to operate in the previous state *and* alerting to the receipt of bad input. Bad input often falls into one of these categories:

Incorrect data
> Validate both syntax and, if possible, semantics. Watch for empty data and partial or truncated data (e.g., alert if the configuration is *N*% smaller than the previous version).

Delayed data
> This may invalidate current data due to timeouts. Alert well before the data is expected to expire.

Fail in a way that preserves function, possibly at the expense of being overly permissive or overly simplistic. We've found that it's generally safer for systems to continue functioning with their previous configuration and await a human's approval before using the new, perhaps invalid, data.

In 2005, Google's global DNS load- and latency-balancing system received an empty DNS entry file as a result of file permissions. It accepted this empty file and served NXDOMAIN for six minutes for all Google properties. In response, the system now performs a number of sanity checks on new configurations, including confirming the presence of virtual IPs for *google.com*, and will continue serving the previous DNS entries until it receives a new file that passes its input checks.

In 2009, incorrect (but valid) data led to Google marking the entire Web as containing malware [May09]. A configuration file containing the list of suspect URLs was replaced by a single forward slash character (/), which matched all URLs. Checks for dramatic changes in file size and checks to see whether the configuration is matching sites that are believed unlikely to contain malware would have prevented this from reaching production.

Progressive Rollouts

Nonemergency rollouts *must* proceed in stages. Both configuration and binary changes introduce risk, and you mitigate this risk by applying the change to small fractions of traffic and capacity at one time. The size of your service or rollout, as well as your risk profile, will inform the percentages of production capacity to which the rollout is pushed, and the appropriate time frame between stages. It's also a good idea to perform different stages in different geographies, in order to detect problems related to diurnal traffic cycles and geographical traffic mix differences.

Rollouts should be supervised. To ensure that nothing unexpected is occurring during the rollout, it must be monitored either by the engineer performing the rollout stage or—preferably—a demonstrably reliable monitoring system. If unexpected behavior is detected, roll back first and diagnose afterward in order to minimize Mean Time to Recovery.

Define SLOs Like a User

Measure availability and performance in terms that matter to an end user. See Chapter 4 for more discussion.

Error Budgets

Balance reliability and the pace of innovation with error budgets (see "Motivation for Error Budgets" on page 33), which define the acceptable level of failure for a service, over some period; we often use a month. A budget is simply 1 minus a service's SLO; for instance, a service with a 99.99% availability target has a 0.01% "budget" for unavailability. As long as the service hasn't spent its error budget for the month through the background rate of errors plus any downtime, the development team is free (within reason) to launch new features, updates, and so on.

If the error budget is spent, the service freezes changes (except urgent security and bug fixes addressing any cause of the increased errors) until either the service has earned back room in the budget, or the month resets. For mature services with an SLO greater than 99.99%, a quarterly rather than monthly budget reset is appropriate, because the amount of allowable downtime is small.

Error budgets eliminate the structural tension that might otherwise develop between SRE and product development teams by giving them a common, data-driven mechanism for assessing launch risk. They also give both SRE and product development teams a common goal of developing practices and technology that allow faster innovation and more launches without "blowing the budget."

Monitoring

Monitoring may have only three output types:

Pages
A human must do something *now*

Tickets
A human must do something within a few days

Logging
No one need look at this output immediately, but it's available for later analysis if needed

If it's important enough to bother a human, it should either *require* immediate action (i.e., page) or be treated as a bug and entered into your bug-tracking system. Putting alerts into email and hoping that someone will read all of them and notice the important ones is the moral equivalent of piping them to */dev/null*: they will eventually be ignored. History demonstrates this strategy is an attractive nuisance because it can work for a while, but it relies on eternal human vigilance, and the inevitable outage is thus more severe when it happens.

Postmortems

Postmortems (see Chapter 15) should be blameless and focus on process and technology, not people. Assume the people involved in an incident are intelligent, are well intentioned, and were making the best choices they could given the information they had available at the time. It follows that we can't "fix" the people, but must instead fix their environment: e.g., improving system design to avoid entire classes of problems, making the appropriate information easily available, and automatically validating operational decisions to make it difficult to put systems in dangerous states.

Capacity Planning

Provision to handle a simultaneous planned and unplanned outage, without making the user experience unacceptable; this results in an "$N + 2$" configuration, where peak traffic can be handled by N instances (possibly in degraded mode) while the largest 2 instances are unavailable:

- Validate prior demand forecasts against reality until they consistently match. Divergence implies unstable forecasting, inefficient provisioning, and risk of a capacity shortfall.

- Use load testing rather than tradition to establish the resource-to-capacity ratio: a cluster of X machines could handle Y queries per second three months ago, but can it still do so given changes to the system?

- Don't mistake day-one load for steady-state load. Launches often attract more traffic, while they're also the time you especially want to put the product's best foot forward. See Chapter 27 and Appendix E.

Overloads and Failure

Services should produce reasonable but suboptimal results if overloaded. For example, Google Search will search a smaller fraction of the index, and stop serving features like Instant to continue to provide good quality web search results when overloaded. Search SRE tests web search clusters beyond their rated capacity to ensure they perform acceptably when overloaded with traffic.

For times when load is high enough that even degraded responses are too expensive for all queries, practice graceful load shedding, using well-behaved queuing and dynamic timeouts; see Chapter 21. Other techniques include answering requests after a significant delay ("tarpitting") and choosing a consistent subset of clients to receive errors, preserving a good user experience for the remainder.

Retries can amplify low error rates into higher levels of traffic, leading to cascading failures (see Chapter 22). Respond to cascading failures by dropping a fraction of traffic (including retries!) upstream of the system once total load exceeds total capacity.

Every client that makes an RPC must implement exponential backoff (with jitter) for retries, to dampen error amplification. Mobile clients are especially troublesome because there may be millions of them and updating their code to fix behavior takes a significant amount of time—possibly weeks—and requires that users install updates.

SRE Teams

SRE teams should spend no more than 50% of their time on operational work (see Chapter 5); operational overflow should be directed to the product development team. Many services also include the product developers in the on-call rotation and ticket handling, even if there is currently no overflow. This provides incentives to design systems that minimize or eliminate operational toil, along with ensuring that the product developers are in touch with the operational side of the service. A regular production meeting between SREs and the development team (see Chapter 31) is also helpful.

We've found that at least eight people need to be part of the on-call team, in order to avoid fatigue and allow sustainable staffing and low turnover. Preferably, those on-call should be in two well-separated geographic locations (e.g., California and Ireland) to provide a better quality of life by avoiding nighttime pages; in this case, six people at each site is the minimum team size.

Expect to handle no more than two events per on-call shift (e.g., per 12 hours): it takes time to respond to and fix outages, start the postmortem, and file the resulting bugs. More frequent events may degrade the quality of response, and suggest that something is wrong with (at least one of) the system's design, monitoring sensitivity, and response to postmortem bugs.

Ironically, if you implement these best practices, the SRE team may eventually end up out of practice in responding to incidents due to their infrequency, making a long outage out of a short one. Practice handling hypothetical outages (see "Disaster Role Playing" on page 401) routinely and improve your incident-handling documentation in the process.

Example Incident State Document

Shakespeare Sonnet++ Overload: 2015-10-21
Incident management info: *http://incident-management-cheat-sheet*

(Communications lead to keep summary updated.)
Summary: Shakespeare search service in cascading failure due to newly discovered sonnet not in search index.

Status: active, incident #465

Command Post(s): #shakespeare on IRC

Command Hierarchy *(all responders)*

- Current Incident Commander: jennifer
    - Operations lead: docbrown
    - Planning lead: jennifer
    - Communications lead: jennifer
- Next Incident Commander: *to be determined*

(Update at least every four hours and at handoff of Comms Lead role.)
Detailed Status (last updated at 2015-10-21 15:28 UTC by jennifer)

Exit Criteria:

- New sonnet added to Shakespeare search corpus **TODO**
- Within availability (99.99%) and latency (99%ile < 100 ms) SLOs for 30+ minutes **TODO**

TODO list and bugs filed:

- Run MapReduce job to reindex Shakespeare corpus **DONE**
- Borrow emergency resources to bring up extra capacity **DONE**
- Enable flux capacitor to balance load between clusters (Bug 5554823) **TODO**

Incident timeline *(most recent first: times are in UTC)*

- 2015-10-21 15:28 UTC jennifer

  — Increasing serving capacity globally by 2x
- 2015-10-21 15:21 UTC jennifer

  — Directing all traffic to USA-2 sacrificial cluster and draining traffic from other clusters so they can recover from cascading failure while spinning up more tasks

  — MapReduce index job complete, awaiting Bigtable replication to all clusters
- 2015-10-21 15:10 UTC martym

  — Adding new sonnet to Shakespeare corpus and starting index MapReduce
- 2015-10-21 15:04 UTC martym

  — Obtains text of newly discovered sonnet from *shakespeare-discuss@* mailing list
- 2015-10-21 15:01 UTC docbrown

  — Incident declared due to cascading failure
- 2015-10-21 14:55 UTC docbrown

  — Pager storm, `ManyHttp500s` in all clusters

Example Postmortem

Shakespeare Sonnet++ Postmortem (incident #465)

Date: 2015-10-21

Authors: jennifer, martym, agoogler

Status: Complete, action items in progress

Summary: Shakespeare Search down for 66 minutes during period of very high interest in Shakespeare due to discovery of a new sonnet.

Impact:[1] Estimated 1.21B queries lost, no revenue impact.

Root Causes:[2] Cascading failure due to combination of exceptionally high load and a resource leak when searches failed due to terms not being in the Shakespeare corpus. The newly discovered sonnet used a word that had never before appeared in one of Shakespeare's works, which happened to be the term users searched for. Under normal circumstances, the rate of task failures due to resource leaks is low enough to be unnoticed.

Trigger: Latent bug triggered by sudden increase in traffic.

Resolution: Directed traffic to sacrificial cluster and added 10x capacity to mitigate cascading failure. Updated index deployed, resolving interaction with latent bug. Maintaining extra capacity until surge in public interest in new sonnet passes. Resource leak identified and fix deployed.

---

1 Impact is the effect on users, revenue, etc.

2 An explanation of the circumstances in which this incident happened. It's often helpful to use a technique such as the 5 Whys [Ohn88] to understand the contributing factors.

Detection: Borgmon detected high level of HTTP 500s and paged on-call.

Action Items:[3]

Action Item	Type	Owner	Bug
Update playbook with instructions for responding to cascading failure	mitigate	jennifer	n/a **DONE**
Use flux capacitor to balance load between clusters	prevent	martym	Bug 5554823 **TODO**
Schedule cascading failure test during next DiRT	process	docbrown	n/a **TODO**
Investigate running index MR/fusion continuously	prevent	jennifer	Bug 5554824 **TODO**
Plug file descriptor leak in search ranking subsystem	prevent	agoogler	Bug 5554825 **DONE**
Add load shedding capabilities to Shakespeare search	prevent	agoogler	Bug 5554826 **TODO**
Build regression tests to ensure servers respond sanely to queries of death	prevent	clarac	Bug 5554827 **TODO**
Deploy updated search ranking subsystem to prod	prevent	jennifer	n/a **DONE**
Freeze production until 2015-11-20 due to error budget exhaustion, or seek exception due to grotesque, unbelievable, bizarre, and unprecedented circumstances	other	docbrown	n/a **TODO**

Lessons Learned

What went well

- Monitoring quickly alerted us to high rate (reaching ~100%) of HTTP 500s
- Rapidly distributed updated Shakespeare corpus to all clusters

What went wrong

- We're out of practice in responding to cascading failure
- We exceeded our availability error budget (by several orders of magnitude) due to the exceptional surge of traffic that essentially all resulted in failures

---

3 "Knee-jerk" AIs often turn out to be too extreme or costly to implement, and judgment may be needed to re-scope them in a larger context. There's a risk of over-optimizing for a particular issue, adding specific moni-toring/alerting when reliable mechanisms like unit tests can catch problems much earlier in the development process.

Where we got lucky[4]

- Mailing list of Shakespeare aficionados had a copy of new sonnet available
- Server logs had stack traces pointing to file descriptor exhaustion as cause for crash
- Query-of-death was resolved by pushing new index containing popular search term

Timeline[5]

2015-10-21 (all times UTC)

- 14:51 News reports that a new Shakespearean sonnet has been discovered in a Delorean's glove compartment
- 14:53 Traffic to Shakespeare search increases by 88x after post to */r/shakespeare* points to Shakespeare search engine as place to find new sonnet (except we don't have the sonnet yet)
- 14:54 **OUTAGE BEGINS** — Search backends start melting down under load
- 14:55 docbrown receives pager storm, ManyHttp500s from all clusters
- 14:57 All traffic to Shakespeare search is failing: see *http://monitor/shakespeare? end_time=20151021T145700*
- 14:58 docbrown starts investigating, finds backend crash rate very high
- 15:01 **INCIDENT BEGINS** docbrown declares incident #465 due to cascading failure, coordination on #shakespeare, names jennifer incident commander
- 15:02 someone coincidentally sends email to *shakespeare-discuss@* re sonnet discovery, which happens to be at top of martym's inbox
- 15:03 jennifer notifies *shakespeare-incidents@* list of the incident
- 15:04 martym tracks down text of new sonnet and looks for documentation on corpus update
- 15:06 docbrown finds that crash symptoms identical across all tasks in all clusters, investigating cause based on application logs

---

4 This section is really for near misses, e.g., "The goat teleporter was available for emergency use with other animals despite lack of certification."

5 A "screenplay" of the incident; use the incident timeline from the Incident Management document to start filling in the postmortem's timeline, then supplement with other relevant entries.

- 15:07 martym finds documentation, starts prep work for corpus update
- 15:10 martym adds sonnet to Shakespeare's known works, starts indexing job
- 15:12 docbrown contacts clarac & agoogler (from Shakespeare dev team) to help with examining codebase for possible causes
- 15:18 clarac finds smoking gun in logs pointing to file descriptor exhaustion, confirms against code that leak exists if term not in corpus is searched for
- 15:20 martym's index MapReduce job completes
- 15:21 jennifer and docbrown decide to increase instance count enough to drop load on instances that they're able to do appreciable work before dying and being restarted
- 15:23 docbrown load balances all traffic to USA-2 cluster, permitting instance count increase in other clusters without servers failing immediately
- 15:25 martym starts replicating new index to all clusters
- 15:28 docbrown starts 2x instance count increase
- 15:32 jennifer changes load balancing to increase traffic to nonsacrificial clusters
- 15:33 tasks in nonsacrificial clusters start failing, same symptoms as before
- 15:34 found order-of-magnitude error in whiteboard calculations for instance count increase
- 15:36 jennifer reverts load balancing to resacrifice USA-2 cluster in preparation for additional global 5x instance count increase (to a total of 10x initial capacity)
- 15:36 **OUTAGE MITIGATED,** updated index replicated to all clusters
- 15:39 docbrown starts second wave of instance count increase to 10x initial capacity
- 15:41 jennifer reinstates load balancing across all clusters for 1% of traffic
- 15:43 nonsacrificial clusters' HTTP 500 rates at nominal rates, task failures intermittent at low levels
- 15:45 jennifer balances 10% of traffic across nonsacrificial clusters
- 15:47 nonsacrificial clusters' HTTP 500 rates remain within SLO, no task failures observed
- 15:50 30% of traffic balanced across nonsacrificial clusters
- 15:55 50% of traffic balanced across nonsacrificial clusters
- 16:00 **OUTAGE ENDS,** all traffic balanced across all clusters
- 16:30 **INCIDENT ENDS,** reached exit criterion of 30 minutes' nominal performance

Supporting information:[6]

- Monitoring dashboard,
  http://monitor/shakespeare?end_time=20151021T160000&duration=7200

---

6 Useful information, links, logs, screenshots, graphs, IRC logs, IM logs, etc.

Launch Coordination Checklist

This is Google's original Launch Coordination Checklist, circa 2005, slightly abridged for brevity:

Architecture

- Architecture sketch, types of servers, types of requests from clients
- Programmatic client requests

Machines and datacenters

- Machines and bandwidth, datacenters, N+2 redundancy, network QoS
- New domain names, DNS load balancing

Volume estimates, capacity, and performance

- HTTP traffic and bandwidth estimates, launch "spike," traffic mix, 6 months out
- Load test, end-to-end test, capacity per datacenter at max latency
- Impact on other services we care most about
- Storage capacity

System reliability and failover

- What happens when:
  - Machine dies, rack fails, or cluster goes offline
  - Network fails between two datacenters

- For each type of server that talks to other servers (its backends):
  — How to detect when backends die, and what to do when they die
  — How to terminate or restart without affecting clients or users
  — Load balancing, rate-limiting, timeout, retry and error handling behavior
- Data backup/restore, disaster recovery

Monitoring and server management

- Monitoring internal state, monitoring end-to-end behavior, managing alerts
- Monitoring the monitoring
- Financially important alerts and logs
- Tips for running servers within cluster environment
- Don't crash mail servers by sending yourself email alerts in your own server code

Security

- Security design review, security code audit, spam risk, authentication, SSL
- Prelaunch visibility/access control, various types of blacklists

Automation and manual tasks

- Methods and change control to update servers, data, and configs
- Release process, repeatable builds, canaries under live traffic, staged rollouts

Growth issues

- Spare capacity, 10x growth, growth alerts
- Scalability bottlenecks, linear scaling, scaling with hardware, changes needed
- Caching, data sharding/resharding

External dependencies

- Third-party systems, monitoring, networking, traffic volume, launch spikes
- Graceful degradation, how to avoid accidentally overrunning third-party services
- Playing nice with syndicated partners, mail systems, services within Google

Schedule and rollout planning

- Hard deadlines, external events, Mondays or Fridays
- Standard operating procedures for this service, for other services

Example Production Meeting Minutes

Date: 2015-10-23

Attendees: agoogler, clarac, docbrown, jennifer, martym

Announcements:

- Major outage (#465), blew through error budget

Previous Action Item Review

- Certify Goat Teleporter for use with cattle (bug 1011101)
  - Nonlinearities in mass acceleration now predictable, should be able to target accurately in a few days.

Outage Review

- New Sonnet (outage 465)
  - 1.21B queries lost due to cascading failure after interaction between latent bug (leaked file descriptor on searches with no results) + not having new sonnet in corpus + unprecedented & unexpected traffic volume
  - File descriptor leak bug fixed (bug 5554825) and deployed to prod
  - Looking into using flux capacitor for load balancing (bug 5554823) and using load shedding (bug 5554826) to prevent recurrence
  - Annihilated availability error budget; pushes to prod frozen for 1 month unless docbrown can obtain exception on grounds that event was bizarre & unforeseeable (but consensus is that exception is unlikely)

Paging Events

- `AnnotationConsistencyTooEventual`: paged 5 times this week, likely due to cross-regional replication delay between Bigtables.
  — Investigation still ongoing, see bug 4821600
  — No fix expected soon, will raise acceptable consistency threshold to reduce unactionable alerts

Nonpaging Events

- None

Monitoring Changes and/or Silences

- `AnnotationConsistencyTooEventual`, acceptable delay threshold raised from 60s to 180s, see bug 4821600; TODO(martym).

Planned Production Changes

- USA-1 cluster going offline for maintenance between 2015-10-29 and 2015-11-02.
  — No response required, traffic will automatically route to other clusters in region.

Resources

- Borrowed resources to respond to sonnet++ incident, will spin down additional server instances and return resources next week
- Utilization at 60% of CPU, 75% RAM, 44% disk (up from 40%, 70%, 40% last week)

Key Service Metrics

- **OK** 99ile latency: 88 ms < 100 ms SLO target [trailing 30 days]
- **BAD** availability: 86.95% < 99.99% SLO target [trailing 30 days]

Discussion / Project Updates

- Project Molière launching in two weeks.

New Action Items

- TODO(martym): Raise `AnnotationConsistencyTooEventual` threshold.
- TODO(docbrown): Return instance count to normal and return resources.

Bibliography

[Ada15] Bram Adams, Stephany Bellomo, Christian Bird, Tamara Marshall-Keim, Foutse Khomh, and Kim Moir, "The Practice and Future of Release Engineering: A Roundtable with Three Release Engineers" (*http://resources.sei.cmu.edu/library/asset-view.cfm?assetid=434819*), *IEEE Software*, vol. 32, no. 2 (March/April 2015), pp. 42–49.

[Agu10] M. K. Aguilera, "Stumbling over Consensus Research: Misunderstandings and Issues" (*http://dl.acm.org/citation.cfm?id=2172342*), in *Replication*, Lecture Notes in Computer Science 5959, 2010.

[All10] J. Allspaw and J. Robbins, *Web Operations: Keeping the Data on Time*: O'Reilly, 2010.

[All12] J. Allspaw, "Blameless PostMortems and a Just Culture" (*https://codeas craft.com/2012/05/22/blameless-postmortems/*), blog post, 2012.

[All15] J. Allspaw, "Trade-Offs Under Pressure: Heuristics and Observations of Teams Resolving Internet Service Outages" (*http://lup.lub.lu.se/student-papers/record/8084520/file/8084521.pdf*), MSc thesis, Lund University, 2015.

[Ana07] S. Anantharaju, "Automating web application security testing" (*https://googleonlinesecurity.blogspot.com/2007/07/automating-web-application-security.html*), blog post, July 2007.

[Ana13] R. Ananatharayan et al., "Photon: Fault-tolerant and Scalable Joining of Continuous Data Streams" (*https://research.google.com/pubs/pub41318.html*), in *SIGMOD '13*, 2013.

[And05] A. Andrieux, K. Czajkowski, A. Dan, et al., "Web Services Agreement Specification (WS-Agreement)" (*http://www.ogf.org/documents/GFD.107.pdf*), September 2005.

[Bai13] P. Bailis and A. Ghodsi, "Eventual Consistency Today: Limitations, Extensions, and Beyond" (*http://dl.acm.org/citation.cfm?id=2462076*), in *ACM Queue*, vol. 11, no. 3, 2013.

[Bai83] L. Bainbridge, "Ironies of Automation" (*http://dx.doi.org/ 10.1016/0005-1098(83)90046-8*), in *Automatica*, vol. 19, no. 6, November 1983.

[Bak11] J. Baker et al., "Megastore: Providing Scalable, Highly Available Storage for Interactive Services" (*https://research.google.com/pubs/pub36971.html*), in *Proceedings of the Conference on Innovative Data System Research*, 2011.

[Bar11] L. A. Barroso, "Warehouse-Scale Computing: Entering the Teenage Decade" (*http://dl.acm.org/citation.cfm?id=2019527*), talk at 38th Annual Symposium on Computer Architecture, video available online, 2011.

[Bar13] L. A. Barroso, J. Clidaras, and U. Hölzle, *The Datacenter as a Computer: An Introduction to the Design of Warehouse-Scale Machines, Second Edition* (*https:// research.google.com/pubs/pub41606.html*), Morgan & Claypool, 2013.

[Ben12] C. Bennett and A. Tseitlin, "Chaos Monkey Released Into The Wild" (*http:// techblog.netflix.com/2012/07/chaos-monkey-released-into-wild.html*), blog post, July 2012.

[Bla14] M. Bland, "Goto Fail, Heartbleed, and Unit Testing Culture" (*http://martin fowler.com/articles/testing-culture.html*), blog post, June 2014.

[Boc15] L. Bock, *Work Rules!* (*https://www.workrules.net*), Twelve Books, 2015.

[Bol11] W. J. Bolosky, D. Bradshaw, R. B. Haagens, N. P. Kusters, and P. Li, "Paxos Replicated State Machines as the Basis of a High-Performance Data Store" (*https:// www.usenix.org/legacy/event/nsdi11/tech/full_papers/Bolosky.pdf*), in *Proc. NSDI 2011*, 2011.

[Boy13] P. G. Boysen, "Just Culture: A Foundation for Balanced Accountability and Patient Safety" (*http://www.ncbi.nlm.nih.gov/pmc/articles/PMC3776518/*), in *The Ochsner Journal*, Fall 2013.

[Bra15] VM Brasseur, "Failure: Why it happens & How to benefit from it" (*https:// youtu.be/DLn4fZsZsKM?t=29m05s*), YAPC 2015.

[Bre01] E. Brewer, "Lessons From Giant-Scale Services" (*http://ieeexplore.ieee.org/xpl/ articleDetails.jsp?arnumber=939450*), in *IEEE Internet Computing*, vol. 5, no. 4, July / August 2001.

[Bre12] E. Brewer, "CAP Twelve Years Later: How the "Rules" Have Changed" (*http:// ieeexplore.ieee.org/xpl/articleDetails.jsp?arnumber=6133253*), in *Computer*, vol. 45, no. 2, February 2012.

[Bro15] M. Brooker, "Exponential Backoff and Jitter" (*http://www.awsarchitecture blog.com/2015/03/backoff.html*), on *AWS Architecture Blog*, March 2015.

[Bro95] F. P. Brooks Jr., "No Silver Bullet—Essence and Accidents of Software Engineering", in *The Mythical Man-Month*, Boston: Addison-Wesley, 1995, pp. 180–186.

[Bru09] J. Brutlag, "Speed Matters" (*http://googleresearch.blogspot.com/2009/06/speed-matters.html*), on *Google Research Blog*, June 2009.

[Bul80] G. M. Bull, *The Dartmouth Time-sharing System*: Ellis Horwood, 1980.

[Bur99] M. Burgess, *Principles of Network and System Administration*: Wiley, 1999.

[Bur06] M. Burrows, "The Chubby Lock Service for Loosely-Coupled Distributed Systems" (*https://research.google.com/archive/chubby.html*), in *OSDI '06: Seventh Symposium on Operating System Design and Implementation*, November 2006.

[Bur16] B. Burns, B. Grant, D. Oppenheimer, E. Brewer, and J. Wilkes, "Borg, Omega, and Kubernetes" (*http://dl.acm.org/citation.cfm?id=2898444*) in *ACM Queue*, vol. 14, no. 1, 2016.

[Cas99] M. Castro and B. Liskov, "Practical Byzantine Fault Tolerance" (*http://www.pmg.lcs.mit.edu/papers/osdi99.pdf*), in *Proc. OSDI 1999*, 1999.

[Cha10] C. Chambers, A. Raniwala, F. Perry, S. Adams, R. Henry, R. Bradshaw, and N. Weizenbaum, "FlumeJava: Easy, Efficient Data-Parallel Pipelines" (*http://research.google.com/pubs/pub35650.html*), in *ACM SIGPLAN Conference on Programming Language Design and Implementation*, 2010.

[Cha96] T. D. Chandra and S. Toueg, "Unreliable Failure Detectors for Reliable Distributed Systems" (*http://dl.acm.org/citation.cfm?id=226647*), in *J. ACM*, 1996.

[Cha07] T. Chandra, R. Griesemer, and J. Redstone, "Paxos Made Live—An Engineering Perspective" (*http://research.google.com/archive/paxos_made_live.html*), in *PODC '07: 26th ACM Symposium on Principles of Distributed Computing*, 2007.

[Cha06] F. Chang et al., "Bigtable: A Distributed Storage System for Structured Data" (*https://research.google.com/archive/bigtable.html*), in *OSDI '06: Seventh Symposium on Operating System Design and Implementation*, November 2006.

[Chr09] G. P. Chrousous, "Stress and Disorders of the Stress System" (*http://www.ncbi.nlm.nih.gov/pubmed/19488073*), in *Nature Reviews Endocrinology*, vol 5., no. 7, 2009.

[Clos53] C. Clos, "A Study of Non-Blocking Switching Networks" (*http://dx.doi.org/10.1002/j.1538-7305.1953.tb01433.x*), in *Bell System Technical Journal*, vol. 32, no. 2, 1953.

[Con15] C. Contavalli, W. van der Gaast, D. Lawrence, and W. Kumari, "Client Subnet in DNS Queries" (*https://tools.ietf.org/html/draft-vandergaast-edns-client-subnet*), *IETF Internet-Draft*, 2015.

[Con63] M. E. Conway, "Design of a Separable Transition-Diagram Compiler" (*http://dl.acm.org/citation.cfm?id=366704*), in *Commun. ACM 6*, 7 (July 1963), 396–408.

[Con96] P. Conway, "Preservation in the Digital World" (*http://www.clir.org/pubs/reports/conway2/index.html*), report published by the Council on Library and Information Resources, 1996.

[Coo00] R. I. Cook, "How Complex Systems Fail" (*http://web.mit.edu/2.75/resources/ random/How%20Complex%20Systems%20Fail.pdf*), in *Web Operations*: O'Reilly, 2010.

[Cor12] J. C. Corbett et al., "Spanner: Google's Globally-Distributed Database" (*https://research.google.com/archive/spanner.html*), in *OSDI '12: Tenth Symposium on Operating System Design and Implementation*, October 2012.

[Cra10] J. Cranmer, "Visualizing code coverage" (*https://quetzalcoatal.blogspot.com/ 2010/03/visualizing-code-coverage.html*), blog post, March 2010.

[Dea13] J. Dean and L. A. Barroso, "The Tail at Scale" (*http://research.google.com/ pubs/pub40801.html*), in *Communications of the ACM*, vol. 56, 2013.

[Dea04] J. Dean and S. Ghemawat, "MapReduce: Simplified Data Processing on Large Clusters" (*https://research.google.com/archive/mapreduce.html*), in *OSDI'04: Sixth Symposium on Operating System Design and Implementation*, December 2004.

[Dea07] J. Dean, "Software Engineering Advice from Building Large-Scale Distributed Systems" (*https://static.googleusercontent.com/media/ research.google.com/en//people/jeff/stanford-295-talk.pdf*), Stanford CS297 class lecture, Spring 2007.

[Dek02] S. Dekker, "Reconstructing human contributions to accidents: the new view on error and performance" (*http://citeseerx.ist.psu.edu/viewdoc/download? doi=10.1.1.411.4985&rep=rep1&type=pdf*), in *Journal of Safety Research*, vol. 33, no. 3, 2002.

[Dek14] S. Dekker, *The Field Guide to Understanding "Human Error"*, 3rd edition: Ashgate, 2014.

[Dic14] C. Dickson, "How Embracing Continuous Release Reduced Change Complexity" (*http://usenix.org/conference/ures14west/summit-program/presentation/dick son*), presentation at USENIX Release Engineering Summit West 2014, video available online.

[Dur05] J. Durmer and D. Dinges, "Neurocognitive Consequences of Sleep Deprivation" (*http://www.ncbi.nlm.nih.gov/pubmed/15798944*), in *Seminars in Neurology*, vol. 25, no. 1, 2005.

[Eis16] D. E. Eisenbud et al., "Maglev: A Fast and Reliable Software Network Load Balancer" (*https://research.google.com/pubs/pub44824.html*), in NSDI '16: 13th USENIX Symposium on Networked Systems Design and Implementation, March 2016.

[Ere03] J. R. Erenkrantz, "Release Management Within Open Source Projects" (*http:// www.erenkrantz.com/Geeks/Research/Publications/ReleaseManagement.pdf*), in *Proceedings of the 3rd Workshop on Open Source Software Engineering*, Portland, Oregon, May 2003.

[Fis85] M. J. Fischer, N. A. Lynch, and M. S. Paterson, "Impossibility of Distributed Consensus with One Faulty Process" (*http://dl.acm.org/citation.cfm?id=214121*), J. *ACM*, 1985.

[Fit12] B. W. Fitzpatrick and B. Collins-Sussman, *Team Geek: A Software Developer's Guide to Working Well with Others*: O'Reilly, 2012.

[Flo94] S. Floyd and V. Jacobson, "The Synchronization of Periodic Routing Messages" (*http://dl.acm.org/citation.cfm?id=187045*), in IEEE/ACM Transactions on Networking, vol. 2, issue 2, April 1994, pp. 122–136.

[For10] D. Ford et al, "Availability in Globally Distributed Storage Systems" (*http://research.google.com/pubs/pub36737.html*), in *Proceedings of the 9th USENIX Symposium on Operating Systems Design and Implementation*, 2010.

[Fox99] A. Fox and E. A. Brewer, "Harvest, Yield, and Scalable Tolerant Systems" (*http://ieeexplore.ieee.org/xpls/abs_all.jsp?arnumber=798396*), in *Proceedings of the 7th Workshop on Hot Topics in Operating Systems*, Rio Rico, Arizona, March 1999.

[Fow08] M. Fowler, "GUI Architectures" (*http://martinfowler.com/eaaDev/uiArchs.html*), blog post, 2006.

[Gal78] J. Gall, *SYSTEMANTICS: How Systems Really Work and How They Fail*, 1st ed., Pocket, 1977.

[Gal03] J. Gall, *The Systems Bible: The Beginner's Guide to Systems Large and Small*, 3rd ed., General Systemantics Press/Liberty, 2003.

[Gaw09] A. Gawande, *The Checklist Manifesto: How to Get Things Right*: Henry Holt and Company, 2009.

[Ghe03] S. Ghemawat, H. Gobioff, and S-T. Leung, "The Google File System" (*https://research.google.com/archive/gfs.html*), in *19th ACM Symposium on Operating Systems Principles*, October 2003.

[Gil02] S. Gilbert and N. Lynch, "Brewer's Conjecture and the Feasibility of Consistent, Available, Partition-Tolerant Web Services" (*http://dl.acm.org/citation.cfm?id=564601*), in *ACM SIGACT News*, vol. 33, no. 2, 2002.

[Gla02] R. Glass, *Facts and Fallacies of Software Engineering*, Addison-Wesley Professional, 2002.

[Gol14] W. Golab et al., "Eventually Consistent: Not What You Were Expecting?" (*http://dl.acm.org/citation.cfm?id=2582994*), in *ACM Queue*, vol. 12, no. 1, 2014.

[Gra09] P. Graham, "Maker's Schedule, Manager's Schedule" (*http://paulgraham.com/makersschedule.html*), blog post, July 2009.

[Gup15] A. Gupta and J. Shute, "High-Availability at Massive Scale: Building Google's Data Infrastructure for Ads" (*https://research.google.com/pubs/pub44686.html*), in *Workshop on Business Intelligence for the Real Time Enterprise*, 2015.

[Ham07] J. Hamilton, "On Designing and Deploying Internet-Scale Services" (*https://www.usenix.org/legacy/event/lisa07/tech/hamilton.html*), in *Proceedings of the 21st Large Installation System Administration Conference*, November 2007.

[Han94] S. Hanks, T. Li, D. Farinacci, and P. Traina, "Generic Routing Encapsulation over IPv4 networks" (*https://tools.ietf.org/html/rfc1702*), *IETF Informational RFC*, 1994.

[Hic11] M. Hickins, "Tape Rescues Google in Lost Email Scare" (*http://blogs.wsj.com/digits/2011/03/01/tape-rescues-google-in-lost-email-scare/*), in *Digits, Wall Street Journal*, 1 March 2011.

[Hix15a] D. Hixson, "Capacity Planning" (*https://www.usenix.org/publications/login/feb15/capacity-planning*), in *;login:*, vol. 40, no. 1, February 2015.

[Hix15b] D. Hixson, "The Systems Engineering Side of Site Reliability Engineering" (*https://www.usenix.org/publications/login/june15/hixson*), in *;login:* vol. 40, no. 3, June 2015.

[Hod13] J. Hodges, "Notes on Distributed Systems for Young Bloods" (*https://www.somethingsimilar.com/2013/01/14/notes-on-distributed-systems-for-young-bloods/*), blog post, 14 January 2013.

[Hol14] L. Holmwood, "Applying Cardiac Alarm Management Techniques to Your On-Call" (*http://fractio.nl/2014/08/26/cardiac-alarms-and-ops/*), blog post, 26 August 2014.

[Hum06] J. Humble, C. Read, D. North, "The Deployment Production Line", in *Proceedings of the IEEE Agile Conference*, July 2006.

[Hum10] J. Humble and D. Farley, *Continuous Delivery: Reliable Software Releases through Build, Test, and Deployment Automation*: Addison-Wesley, 2010.

[Hun10] P. Hunt, M. Konar, F. P. Junqueira, and B. Reed, "ZooKeeper: Wait-free coordination for Internet-scale systems" (*https://www.usenix.org/legacy/events/atc10/tech/full_papers/Hunt.pdf*), in *USENIX ATC*, 2010.

[IAEA12] International Atomic Energy Agency, "Safety of Nuclear Power Plants: Design, SSR-2/1" (*http://www-pub.iaea.org/MTCD/publications/PDF/Pub1534_web.pdf*), 2012.

[Jai13] S. Jain et al., "B4: Experience with a Globally-Deployed Software Defined WAN" (*https://research.google.com/pubs/pub41761.html*), in *SIGCOMM '13*.

[Jon15] C. Jones, T. Underwood, and S. Nukala, "Hiring Site Reliability Engineers" (*https://www.usenix.org/publications/login/june15/hiring-site-reliability-engineers*), in *;login:*, vol. 40, no. 3, June 2015.

[Jun07] F. Junqueira, Y. Mao, and K. Marzullo, "Classic Paxos vs. Fast Paxos: Caveat Emptor" (*http://dl.acm.org/citation.cfm?id=1323158*), in *Proc. HotDep '07*, 2007.

[Jun11] F. P. Junqueira, B. C. Reid, and M. Serafini, "Zab: High-performance broadcast for primary-backup systems." (*http://ieeexplore.ieee.org/xpls/abs_all.jsp?arnum ber=5958223&tag=1*), in *Dependable Systems & Networks (DSN), 2011 IEEE/IFIP 41st International Conference* on 27 Jun 2011: 245–256.

[Kah11] D. Kahneman, *Thinking, Fast and Slow*: Farrar, Straus and Giroux, 2011.

[Kar97] D. Karger et al., "Consistent hashing and random trees: distributed caching protocols for relieving hot spots on the World Wide Web" (*http://dl.acm.org/cita tion.cfm?id=258660*), in *Proc. STOC '97*, 29th annual ACM symposium on theory of computing, 1997.

[Kem11] C. Kemper, "Build in the Cloud: How the Build System Works" (*https:// google-engtools.blogspot.com/2011/08/build-in-cloud-how-build-system-works.html*), *Google Engineering Tools* blog post, August 2011.

[Ken12] S. Kendrick, "What Takes Us Down?" (*http://usenix.org/publications/login/ october-2012-volume-37-number-5/what-takes-us-down*), in *;login:*, vol. 37, no. 5, October 2012.

[Kinc09] Kincaid, Jason. "T-Mobile Sidekick Disaster: Danger's Servers Crashed, And They Don't Have A Backup." *Techcrunch.* n.p., 10 Oct. 2009. Web. 20 Jan. 2015, *http://techcrunch.com/2009/10/10/t-mobile-sidekick-disaster-microsofts-servers-crashed-and-they-dont-have-a-backup.*

[Kin15] K. Kingsbury, "The trouble with timestamps" (*http://www.aphyr.com/posts/ 299-the-trouble-with-timestamps*), blog post, 2013.

[Kir08] J. Kirsch and Y. Amir, "Paxos for System Builders: An Overview" (*http:// dl.acm.org/citation.cfm?id=1529979*), in *Proc. LADIS '08*, 2008.

[Kla12] R. Klau, "How Google Sets Goals: OKRs" (*https://library.gv.com/how-google-sets-goals-okrs-a1f69b0b72c7*), blog post, October 2012.

[Kle06] D. V. Klein, "A Forensic Analysis of a Distributed Two-Stage Web-Based Spam Attack" (*https://www.usenix.org/legacy/event/lisa06/tech/klein/klein_html/ index.html*), in *Proceedings of the 20th Large Installation System Administration Conference*, December 2006.

[Kle14] D. V. Klein, D. M. Betser, and M. G. Monroe, "Making *Push On Green* a Reality" (*https://www.usenix.org/publications/login/october-2014-vol-39-no-5/making-push-green-reality*), in *;login:*, vol. 39, no. 5, October 2014.

[Kra08] T. Krattenmaker, "Make Every Meeting Matter" (*https://hbr.org/2008/02/ make-every-meeting-matter*), in *Harvard Business Review*, February 27, 2008.

[Kre12] J. Kreps, "Getting Real About Distributed System Reliability" (*http:// blog.empathybox.com/post/19574936361/getting-real-about-distributed-system-reliability*), blog post, 19 March 2012.

[Kri12] K. Krishan, "Weathering The Unexpected" (*http://dl.acm.org/citation.cfm? id=2366332*), in *Communications of the ACM*, vol. 55, no. 11, November 2012.

[Kum15] A. Kumar et al., "BwE: Flexible, Hierarchical Bandwidth Allocation for WAN Distributed Computing" (*https://research.google.com/pubs/pub43838.html*), in *SIGCOMM '15*.

[Lam98] L. Lamport, "The Part-Time Parliament" (*http://research.microsoft.com/en-us/um/people/lamport/pubs/lamport-paxos.pdf*), in *ACM Transactions on Computer Systems 16, 2*, May 1998.

[Lam01] L. Lamport, "Paxos Made Simple" (*http://research.microsoft.com/en-us/um/people/lamport/pubs/paxos-simple.pdf*), in *ACM SIGACT News 121*, December 2001.

[Lam06] L. Lamport, "Fast Paxos" (*http://research.microsoft.com/pubs/64624/tr-2005-112.pdf*), in *Distributed Computing 19.2*, October 2006.

[Lim14] T. A. Limoncelli, S. R. Chalup, and C. J. Hogan, *The Practice of Cloud System Administration: Designing and Operating Large Distributed Systems, Volume 2*: Addison-Wesley, 2014.

[Loo10] J. Loomis, "How to Make Failure Beautiful: The Art and Science of Postmortems", in *Web Operations*: O'Reilly, 2010.

[Lu15] H. Lu et al, "Existential Consistency: Measuring and Understanding Consistency at Facebook" (*http://sigops.org/sosp/sosp15/current/2015-Monterey/printable/240-lu.pdf*), in *SOSP '15*, 2015.

[Mao08] Y. Mao, F. P. Junqueira, and K. Marzullo, "Mencius: Building Efficient Replicated State Machines for WANs" (*https://www.usenix.org/legacy/events/osdi08/tech/full_papers/mao/mao.pdf*), in *OSDI '08*, 2008.

[Mas43] A. H. Maslow, "A Theory of Human Motivation", in *Psychological Review* 50(4), 1943.

[Mau15] B. Maurer, "Fail at Scale" (*http://dl.acm.org/citation.cfm?id=2839461*), in *ACM Queue*, vol. 13, no. 12, 2015.

[May09] M. Mayer, "*This site may harm your computer* on every search result?!?!" (*https://googleblog.blogspot.com/2009/01/this-site-may-harm-your-computer-on.html*), blog post, January 2009.

[McI86] M. D. McIlroy, "A Research Unix Reader: Annotated Excerpts from the Programmer's Manual, 1971–1986" (*http://www.cs.dartmouth.edu/~doug/reader.pdf*).

[McN13] D. McNutt, "Maintaining Consistency in a Massively Parallel Environment" (*https://www.usenix.org/conference/ucms13/summit-program/presentation/mcnutt*), presentation at USENIX Configuration Management Summit 2013, video available online.

[McN14a] D. McNutt, "Accelerating the Path from Dev to DevOps" (*https:// www.usenix.org/system/files/login/articles/05_mcnutt.pdf*), in *;login:*, vol. 39, no. 2, April 2014.

[McN14b] D. McNutt, "The 10 Commandments of Release Engineering" (*https:// www.youtube.com/watch?v=RNMjYV_UsQ8*), presentation at 2nd International Workshop on Release Engineering 2014, April 2014.

[McN14c] D. McNutt, "Distributing Software in a Massively Parallel Environment" (*https://www.usenix.org/conference/lisa14/conference-program/presentation/ mcnutt*), presentation at USENIX LISA 2014, video available online.

[Mic03] Microsoft TechNet, "What is SNMP?", last modified March 28, 2003, *https:// technet.microsoft.com/en-us/library/cc776379%28v=ws.10%29.aspx*.

[Mea08] D. Meadows, *Thinking in Systems*: Chelsea Green, 2008.

[Men07] P. Menage, "Adding Generic Process Containers to the Linux Kernel" (*https://www.kernel.org/doc/ols/2007/ols2007v2-pages-45-58.pdf*), in *Proc. of Ottawa Linux Symposium*, 2007.

[Mer11] N. Merchant, "Culture Trumps Strategy, Every Time" (*https://hbr.org/ 2011/03/culture-trumps-strategy-every*), in *Harvard Business Review*, March 22, 2011.

[Moc87] P. Mockapetris, "Domain Names - Implementation and Specification" (*https://tools.ietf.org/html/rfc1035*), *IETF Internet Standard*, 1987.

[Mol86] C. Moler, "Matrix Computation on Distributed Memory Multiprocessors", in *Hypercube Multiprocessors 1986*, 1987.

[Mor12a] I. Moraru, D. G. Andersen, and M. Kaminsky, "Egalitarian Paxos" (*http:// www.pdl.cmu.edu/PDL-FTP/associated/CMU-PDL-12-108.pdf*), *Carnegie Mellon University Parallel Data Lab Technical Report CMU-PDL-12-108*, 2012.

[Mor14] I. Moraru, D. G. Andersen, and M. Kaminsky, "Paxos Quorum Leases: Fast Reads Without Sacrificing Writes" (*http://dl.acm.org/citation.cfm?id=2671001*), in *Proc. SOCC '14*, 2014.

[Mor12b] J. D. Morgenthaler, M. Gridnev, R. Sauciuc, and S. Bhansali, "Searching for Build Debt: Experiences Managing Technical Debt at Google" (*https:// research.google.com/pubs/pub37755.html*), in *Proceedings of the 3rd Int'l Workshop on Managing Technical Debt*, 2012.

[Nar12] C. Narla and D. Salas, "Hermetic Servers" (*http://googletesting.blogspot.com/ 2012/10/hermetic-servers.html*), blog post, 2012.

[Nel14] B. Nelson, "The Data on Diversity" (*http://dl.acm.org/citation.cfm? id=2684442.2597886*), in *Communications of the ACM*, vol. 57, 2014.

[Nic12] K. Nichols and V. Jacobson, "Controlling Queue Delay" (*http://dl.acm.org/ citation.cfm?id=2209336*), in *ACM Queue*, vol. 10, no. 5, 2012.

[Oco12] P. O'Connor and A. Kleyner, *Practical Reliability Engineering*, 5th edition: Wiley, 2012.

[Ohn88] T. Ohno, *Toyota Production System: Beyond Large-Scale Production*: Productivity Press, 1988.

[Ong14] D. Ongaro and J. Ousterhout, "In Search of an Understandable Consensus Algorithm (Extended Version)" (*https://ramcloud.stanford.edu/raft.pdf*).

[Pen10] D. Peng and F. Dabek, "Large-scale Incremental Processing Using Distributed Transactions and Notifications" (*https://research.google.com/pubs/pub36726.html*), in *Proc. of the 9th USENIX Symposium on Operating System Design and Implementation*, November 2010.

[Per99] C. Perrow, *Normal Accidents: Living with High-Risk Technologies*, Princeton University Press, 1999.

[Per07] A. R. Perry, "Engineering Reliability into Web Sites: Google SRE" (*https://research.google.com/pubs/pub32583.html*), in *Proc. of LinuxWorld 2007*, 2007.

[Pik05] R. Pike, S. Dorward, R. Griesemer, S. Quinlan, "Interpreting the Data: Parallel Analysis with Sawzall" (*https://research.google.com/archive/sawzall.html*), in *Scientific Programming Journal* vol. 13, no. 4, 2005.

[Pot16] R. Potvin and J. Levenberg, "The Motivation for a Monolithic Codebase: Why Google stores billions of lines of code in a single repository", in *Communications of the ACM*, forthcoming July 2016. Video available on YouTube (*https://www.youtube.com/watch?v=W71BTkUbdqE*).

[Roo04] J. J. Rooney and L. N. Vanden Heuvel, "Root Cause Analysis for Beginners" (*http://asq.org/quality-progress/2004/07/quality-tools/root-cause-analysis-for-beginners.html*), in *Quality Progress*, July 2004.

[Sai39] A. de Saint Exupéry, *Terre des Hommes* (Paris: Le Livre de Poche, 1939, in translation by Lewis Galantière as *Wind, Sand and Stars*.

[Sam14] R. R. Sambasivan, R. Fonseca, I. Shafer, and G. R. Ganger, "So, You Want To Trace Your Distributed System? Key Design Insights from Years of Practical Experience" (*http://pdl.cmu.edu/PDL-FTP/SelfStar/CMU-PDL-14-102_abs.shtml*), Carnegie Mellon University Parallel Data Lab Technical Report CMU-PDL-14-102, 2014.

[San11] N. Santos and A. Schiper, "Tuning Paxos for High-Throughput with Batching and Pipelining" (*http://rd.springer.com/chapter/10.1007%2F978-3-642-25959-3_11*), in *13th Int'l Conf. on Distributed Computing and Networking*, 2012.

[Sar97] N. B. Sarter, D. D. Woods, and C. E. Billings, "Automation Surprises", in *Handbook of Human Factors & Ergonomics*, 2nd edition, G. Salvendy (ed.), Wiley, 1997.

[Sch14] E. Schmidt, J. Rosenberg, and A. Eagle, *How Google Works* (*http://www.howgoogleworks.net*): Grand Central Publishing, 2014.

[Sch15] B. Schwartz, "The Factors That Impact Availability, Visualized" (*https://www.vividcortex.com/blog/the-factors-that-impact-availability-visualized*), blog post, 21 December 2015.

[Sch90] F. B. Schneider, "Implementing Fault-Tolerant Services Using the State Machine Approach: A Tutorial" (*http://dl.acm.org/citation.cfm?id=98167*), in *ACM Computing Surveys*, vol. 22, no. 4, 1990.

[Sec13] Securities and Exchange Commission, "Order In the Matter of Knight Capital Americas LLC" (*https://www.sec.gov/litigation/admin/2013/34-70694.pdf*), file 3-15570, 2013.

[Sha00] G. Shao, F. Berman, and R. Wolski, "Master/Slave Computing on the Grid" (*http://www.cs.ucsb.edu/~rich/publications/shao-hcw.pdf*), in *Heterogeneous Computing Workshop*, 2000.

[Shu13] J. Shute et al., "F1: A Distributed SQL Database That Scales" (*https://research.google.com/pubs/pub41344.html*), in *Proc. VLDB 2013*, 2013.

[Sig10] B. H. Sigelman et al., "Dapper, a Large-Scale Distributed Systems Tracing Infrastructure" (*https://research.google.com/pubs/pub36356.html*), Google Technical Report, 2010.

[Sin15] A. Singh et al., "Jupiter Rising: A Decade of Clos Topologies and Centralized Control in Google's Datacenter Network" (*https://research.google.com/pubs/pub43837.html*), in *SIGCOMM '15*.

[Skel13] M. Skelton, "Operability can Improve if Developers Write a Draft Run Book" (*http://blog.softwareoperability.com/2013/10/16/operability-can-improve-if-developers-write-a-draft-run-book/*), blog post, 16 October 2013.

[Slo11] B. Treynor Sloss, "Gmail back soon for everyone" (*http://gmailblog.blogspot.com/2011/02/gmail-back-soon-for-everyone.html*), blog post, 28 February 2011.

[Tat99] S. Tatham, "How to Report Bugs Effectively" (*http://www.chiark.greenend.org.uk/~sgtatham/bugs.html*), 1999.

[Ver15] A. Verma, L. Pedrosa, M. R. Korupolu, D. Oppenheimer, E. Tune, and J. Wilkes, "Large-scale cluster management at Google with Borg" (*https://research.google.com/pubs/pub43438.html*), in *Proceedings of the European Conference on Computer Systems*, 2015.

[Wal89] D. R. Wallace and R. U. Fujii, "Software Verification and Validation: An Overview" (*http://www-usr.inf.ufsm.br/~ceretta/papers/fujii89_software_vv.pdf*), *IEEE Software*, vol. 6, no. 3 (May 1989), pp. 10, 17.

[War14] R. Ward and B. Beyer, "BeyondCorp: A New Approach to Enterprise Security" (*https://www.usenix.org/publications/login/dec14/ward*), in *;login:*, vol. 39, no. 6, December 2014.

[Whi12] J. A. Whittaker, J. Arbon, and J. Carollo, *How Google Tests Software*: Addison-Wesley, 2012.

[Woo96] A. Wood, "Predicting Software Reliability" (*http://ieeexplore.ieee.org/stamp/stamp.jsp?arnumber=544240*), in *Computer*, vol. 29, no. 11, 1996.

[Wri12a] H. K. Wright, "Release Engineering Processes, Their Faults and Failures" (*http://www.hyrumwright.org/papers/dissertation.pdf*), (section 7.2.2.2) PhD Thesis, University of Texas at Austin, 2012.

[Wri12b] H. K. Wright and D. E. Perry, "Release Engineering Practices and Pitfalls" (*http://www.hyrumwright.org/papers/icse2012.pdf*), in *Proceedings of the 34th International Conference on Software Engineering (ICSE '12)*. (IEEE, 2012), pp. 1281–1284.

[Wri13] H. K. Wright, D. Jasper, M. Klimek, C. Carruth, Z. Wan, "Large-Scale Automated Refactoring Using ClangMR" (*http://static.googleusercontent.com/media/research.google.com/en/us/pubs/archive/41342.pdf*), in *Proceedings of the 29th International Conference on Software Maintenance (ICSM '13)*, (IEEE, 2013), pp. 548–551.

[Zoo14] ZooKeeper Project (Apache Foundation), "ZooKeeper Recipes and Solutions" (*http://zookeeper.apache.org/doc/trunk/recipes.html*), in ZooKeeper 3.4 documentation, 2014.

Index

About the Authors

Betsy Beyer is a Technical Writer for Google in New York City specializing in Site Reliability Engineering. She has previously written documentation for Google's Data Center and Hardware Operations Teams in Mountain View and across its globally distributed datacenters. Before moving to New York, Betsy was a lecturer on technical writing at Stanford University. En route to her current career, Betsy studied International Relations and English Literature, and holds degrees from Stanford and Tulane.

Chris Jones is a Site Reliability Engineer for Google App Engine, a cloud platform-as-a-service product serving over 28 billion requests per day. Based in San Francisco, he has previously been responsible for the care and feeding of Google's advertising statistics, data warehousing, and customer support systems. In other lives, Chris has worked in academic IT, analyzed data for political campaigns, and engaged in some light BSD kernel hacking, picking up degrees in Computer Engineering, Economics, and Technology Policy along the way. He's also a licensed professional engineer.

Jennifer Petoff is a Program Manager for Google's Site Reliability Engineering team and based in Dublin, Ireland. She has managed large global projects across wide-ranging domains including scientific research, engineering, human resources, and advertising operations. Jennifer joined Google after spending eight years in the chemical industry. She holds a PhD in Chemistry from Stanford University and a BS in Chemistry and a BA in Psychology from the University of Rochester.

Niall Murphy leads the Ads Site Reliability Engineering team at Google Ireland. He has been involved in the Internet industry for about 20 years, and is currently chairperson of INEX, Ireland's peering hub. He is the author or coauthor of a number of technical papers and/or books, including *IPv6 Network Administration* for O'Reilly, and a number of RFCs. He is currently cowriting a history of the Internet in Ireland, and is the holder of degrees in Computer Science, Mathematics, and Poetry Studies, which is surely some kind of mistake. He lives in Dublin with his wife and two sons.

Colophon

The animal on the cover of *Site Reliability Engineering* is the ornate monitor lizard, a reptile native to West and Middle Africa. Until 1997, it was considered a subspecies of the Nile monitor lizard (*Varanus niloticus*), but is now classified as a polymorph of both *Varanus stellatus* and *Varanus niloticus* due to its different skin patterns. It also has a smaller range than the Nile monitor, preferring a habitat of lowland rainforest.

Ornate monitors are large lizards, able to grow up to 6–7 feet long. They are more brightly colored than Nile monitors, with darker olive skin and fewer bands of bright yellow spots running from the shoulder to the tail. Like all monitor lizards, this animal has a muscular stout body, sharp claws, and an elongated head. Their nostrils are placed high on their snout, permitting them to spend time in the water. They are excellent swimmers and climbers, which allows them to sustain a diet of fish, frogs, eggs, insects, and small mammals.

Monitor lizards are often kept as pets, though they require a lot of care and are not suitable for beginners. They can be dangerous when they feel threatened (lashing their powerful tails, scratching, or biting), but it is possible to tame them somewhat with regular handling and teaching them to associate their keeper's presence with the delivery of food.

Many of the animals on O'Reilly covers are endangered; all of them are important to the world. To learn more about how you can help, go to *animals.oreilly.com*.

The cover image is from *Brockhaus Lexicon*. The cover fonts are URW Typewriter and Guardian Sans. The text font is Adobe Minion Pro; the heading font is Adobe Myriad Condensed; and the code font is Dalton Maag's Ubuntu Mono.

Get even more for your money.

Join the O'Reilly Community, and register the O'Reilly books you own. It's free, and you'll get:

- $4.99 ebook upgrade offer
- 40% upgrade offer on O'Reilly print books
- Membership discounts on books and events
- Free lifetime updates to ebooks and videos
- Multiple ebook formats, DRM FREE
- Participation in the O'Reilly community
- Newsletters
- Account management
- 100% Satisfaction Guarantee

Signing up is easy:

1. Go to: oreilly.com/go/register
2. Create an O'Reilly login.
3. Provide your address.
4. Register your books.

Note: English-language books only

To order books online:
oreilly.com/store

For questions about products or an order:
orders@oreilly.com

To sign up to get topic-specific email announcements and/or news about upcoming books, conferences, special offers, and new technologies:
elists@oreilly.com

For technical questions about book content:
booktech@oreilly.com

To submit new book proposals to our editors:
proposals@oreilly.com

O'Reilly books are available in multiple DRM-free ebook formats. For more information:
oreilly.com/ebooks

O'REILLY®

CPSIA information can be obtained at www.ICGtesting.com
Printed in the USA
BVOW08s0835140416

444089BV00001BD/1/P